Cahokia, the Great Native American Metropolis

CAHOKIA

The Great Native American Metropolis

Biloine Whiting Young
and Melvin L. Fowler

UNIVERSITY OF ILLINOIS PRESS

URBANA AND CHICAGO

Library of Congress Cataloging-in-Publication Data

Young, Biloine W., 1926–
Cahokia, the great Native American metropolis / Biloine Whiting Young
and Melvin L. Fowler.
p.   cm.
Includes bibliographical references and index.
ISBN 0-252-02502-4 (cloth : alk. paper)
ISBN 0-252-06821-1 (pbk. : alk. paper)
1. Cahokia Mounds State Historic Site (Ill.)
2. Mississippian culture—Illinois—American Bottom.
3. Indians of North America—Urban residence—Illinois—American Bottom.
4. Excavations (Archaeology)—Illinois—American Bottom—History.
5. American Bottom (Ill.)—Antiquities.
I. Fowler, Melvin L. (Melvin Leo), 1924–
II. Title.
E99.M6815Y68   2000
977.3'89—dc21   99-6273
CIP

1 2 3 4 5 C P 5 4 3 2 1

CONTENTS

CAHOKIA was the largest and most complex expression of Precolumbian Native American civilization in North America, a veritable city on the Mississippi. Though field reports, articles, and monographs had been written by archaeologists about that western Illinois site, I knew of no book about Cahokia for the interested general reader. That, it seemed to me, was a major oversight. The present book project began in the spring of 1997 when I wrote to Melvin Fowler, an archaeologist who had worked on Cahokia for decades and a family friend of many years, asking if he would collaborate with me on a volume about the metropolis and its people.

When I would mention Cahokia to the most cosmopolitan of my friends, few of them had ever heard of it. People who could locate Petra on a map of Jordan gave me a blank look when I asked if they knew of Cahokia. Why, I wondered, were they conversant with the great ancient monuments in other countries—Xian in China, Teotihuacán in Mexico, Abu Simbel in Egypt—but had no inkling that the pre-conquest peoples of North America had also had a major urban center with temples, a priestly hierarchy, and a population in the tens of thousands?

Why were we so slow to recognize that a thousand years ago Native Americans built a great city that flourished for three hundred years in the heart of the North American continent? Could the failure to celebrate Cahokia have anything to do with the persistence of a stereotype, handed down from the days of the pioneers, which regarded the Indians as a nomadic people, Noble Savages living in simple societies of hunter-gatherers who were destined to become victims of Europeans' relentless advance across the continent?

It is hazardous when one who is not a social scientist attempts to write about a complex social science subject. The writer's attempt to clarify, to strip away extraneous detail and move past the debates on minutiae that go on among scholars, can result in oversimplification and a disregard of the complexities that lie at the heart of a subject. The archaeologist's ability to say, "On the other hand . . ." acknowledges the layers of ambiguities inherent in a site as complex as Cahokia. Where the writer longs for certainty the archaeologist looks for more data, alternative explanations, insights from ethnographers and fellow researchers, and expresses conclusions tentatively, knowing they may well be modified or overturned by the next season's analysis of laboriously collected field data.

Acknowledging the tensions inherent in the two approaches to the subject, I believe the collaboration with Melvin Fowler has been remarkably successful. He has been generous with his time, always cheerful, accepting of suggestions, tolerant of my initial lack of familiarity with the field. Mike, as he is known to his friends, treated me as a fellow researcher, shared his data, prevailed upon his colleagues to talk into my tape recorder, corrected my misinterpretations, and granted me the freedom to write about Cahokia from the perspective of the nonscientist.

Our nontechnical approach called for the use, in some cases, of general terms that lack the precision professional archaeologists prefer. Mike, though ever the scientist, suffered the use of familiar expressions and condensed interpretations because he shares with me the strong desire to make the story of Cahokia known and accessible to a wider audience.

Where conclusions are supported by a consensus in the archaeological community, they are stated in this book as fact. Where there are differences of opinion, the major positions are presented. Where we are dealing with conjecture, the sentences are salted with qualifiers.

I am indebted and most grateful to Robert Hall, Pat Munson, Al Harn, Elizabeth Benchley, Guy Gibbon, Clark Dobbs, Roland Rodell, Dan Morse, Kenneth Williams, William Woods, William Iseminger, Thomas Emerson, Timothy Pauketat, Jerome Rose, Barbara Vander Leest, James Stoltman, Nelson Reed, Robert Watson, and Margaret Brown for sharing their knowledge of Cahokia with me.

A word of appreciation is extended to Dr. Orrin Shane, of the Science Museum of Minnesota, and Mary Wilson for their reading of the manuscript and numerous corrections—and most especially to Rhoda Gilman, of the Minnesota Historical Society, whose insightful suggestions for the organization of the manuscript made all of the difference.

Research for the book was supported by grants from the Minnesota Historical Society and the Minnesota Council for the Humanities. I am most grateful to those institutions and to Dr. Susan Cole, former president of Metropolitan State University, St. Paul, for her assistance.

Cahokia remains a vast puzzle on the landscape of the American Bottom that has confounded and intrigued visitors from Henry Brackenridge's time to the present—as well as four generations of archaeologists. Some, like Fowler and

Iseminger, have invested a major portion of their careers in its investigation. The great mounds have been slow to give up their secrets. But with each passing season of work archaeologists learn more about that sacred city, North America's first metropolis, that we, not even knowing its name, have called Cahokia.

—Biloine Whiting Young

I have, for years, wanted to write a book about Cahokia. I am, however, trained as an engineer and archaeologist, disciplines not known for producing great writers. Moreover, archaeologists fill their writings with cautionary phrases and caveats, off-putting for the general reader but reasonable considering the romanticized balderdash that has been passed off as archaeology. None the less, prehistory does not belong to anyone but to everyone. Those of us who work in this field have a professional obligation to communicate with the owners of our common heritage, the past.

Biloine (Billie) Whiting Young's letter suggesting a collaboration came as a vast relief to me. I introduced her to many of my Cahokia colleagues and she immediately begin taping interviews with them. My role in this production has been to be meticulously interviewed by Billie, to edit and amend her transcriptions and interpretations, and to write sections of the text that were in turn carefully scrutinized and revised by her in her diligent and unrelenting search for clarity of thought and expression.

Our target audience for this book is not only my professional colleagues but a broader public. To reach this wider audience we have used some terms more loosely than my colleagues would have liked. The term "city" is one of these. It has come to have a special meaning in archaeology and is usually associated with societies more complex than Cahokia. However, to many readers a city connotes a place where a large number of people live together and share a variety of productive and religious activities. In order to communicate to these readers we have opted for broader interpretations of these terms.

Quotations in the book are mostly taken from taped interviews with the individuals involved. Where they are taken from a published reference, that source is cited in the footnotes. Where a broad topic is being discussed, the notes contain a series of references that deal with that topic. The references section at the back of the book contains works beyond those referred to in the text so that interested readers may pursue a particular scholar's point of view or research a topic in more detail.

I owe a debt of gratitude to the same people who are mentioned by Billie. Without their openness and willingness to communicate with us, this book would not have been possible.

—Melvin L. Fowler

Cahokia, the Great Native American Metropolis

ONE

The Making of a Cahokia Archaeologist

THE director of the Illinois State Museum in Springfield, Illinois, Dr. Thorne Deuel, called his young curator of anthropology to his office. It was a summons, not a request. A small man, Deuel was a graduate of West Point, from the same class as Dwight D. Eisenhower, and he ran the museum in a hierarchical, autocratic manner.

"Yes, sir?" The curator, Melvin Fowler, was a thin young man of medium height with a high forehead, dark hair, the beginnings of a mustache, and a perpetually rumpled appearance. He had had a brief and undistinguished stint in the marine corps officers candidate school near the end of World War II, and he knew a military situation when he saw one. Fowler stepped through the director's door and stood not quite at attention.

"I've heard rumors that the highway department may be putting a new highway through the Cahokia site," said Deuel. "Go find out what is happening." Fowler knew better than to ask questions. Deuel did not consult with his associates at the museum—he gave orders. Fowler smiled to himself. He thinks I'm his NCO, he thought. He remembered a story Deuel had told of his military service before World War I when he had served under General "Black Jack" Pershing on the West Texas–Mexican border. Deuel, a lieutenant, had one of the few cars on the base. When the temperature dropped to below 32 degrees he would order the enlisted men under him to spend the night soaking towels in a bucket of hot water and spreading them over the engine of his car to keep it from freezing. To Deuel, that was the natural order of things.

At least I'm not soaking towels, thought Fowler, as he drove out of town in the museum car for the 90-mile trip to the site of some Indian mounds, called Cahokia, located near East St. Louis. As he drove, Fowler tried to recall what he had read about Cahokia—besides the fact that it contained the largest Precolumbian earthwork in North America.

The central and southeastern United States, he knew, had once been home to organized Precolumbian societies. These Native American civilizations had large population centers and powerful rulers; they had constructed buildings on the summits of flat-topped earthen pyramids and created fine works of art. Few people, including most writers of textbooks on American history, were even aware of the remarkable cultural legacy of these indigenous American civilizations. Beginning at least as early as 1500 B.C. and continuing up to the time of the European conquest, ancient peoples had constructed massive earthworks up and down the Mississippi and Ohio River Valleys, extending them throughout the southeastern United States from the Great Lakes to the Gulf of Mexico and east to the foothills of the Appalachian Mountains.

These earthen constructions numbered in the hundreds of thousands. Many mounds were in the shapes of animals and must have taken thousands of hours to construct. Fowler thought of the serpent mound in Ohio that was more than a quarter mile long. Other mounds were shaped like cones, haystacks, terraced platforms, and flat-topped pyramids. Some mounds had been found to be tombs while others appeared to have been elevated bases for houses, temples, and other communal building such as granaries and warehouses.

The largest of the mounds, Monks Mound[1] at Cahokia,[2] had a larger base circumference than that of the Great Pyramid of Khufu in Egypt or the Pyramid of the Sun at Teotihuacán in Mexico. Cahokia had been part of the last mound-builder culture, called Mississippian, that had existed in the valley of the Mississippi River and in the southeastern states from about A.D. 600 until the arrival of Europeans.

Despite the size of the mounds at Cahokia, most early European visitors to the area appear to have missed them. The first of the European invasions came from the north as French explorers from Canada traveled down the Mississippi River as far south as Arkansas. Louis Joliet and Jacques Marquette, though fluent in six Indian languages and interested in Indian lore, floated right by the site in 1673 without recognizing it. They may have supposed that the mounds rising abruptly from the river bottoms, a mile and a half east of the main channel of the river, were natural hills as there was no sizable population of Native Americans in the vicinity. Father Louis Hennepin, traveling with the La Salle expedition in 1698, wrote in detail about Indian life and customs of that section of the Mississippi but made no mention of the mounds.

At the beginning of the eighteenth century the locus of French control

---

1. Skele 1988.
2. Benchley 1974; Iseminger 1998; Reed et al. 1968; Walthall and Benchley 1987; Williams 1975.

moved from Canada to New Orleans and instead of coming down from the north, travelers began moving up the river. One of these was a French general, Georges Collot, who made a map of the region in 1796 showing some mounds to the southeast, but he apparently never saw the constructions at Cahokia. Collot's map had several errors. He spelled the growing settlement of St. Louis "St. Lewis" and the Mississippi River "Mississipi," and he drew the north arrow on the map pointing in the wrong direction.[3]

The name "Cahokia" was taken from a tribe of the Illinois Confederacy that lived in the area until about 1820. The French named a village about 12 miles southwest of the mounds "Cahokia" and it became the county seat in 1795.

General George Rogers Clark visited the area in about 1775 and wrote a letter to the editor of *American Museum* magazine about "the works on the Mississippi near the Caw (Kaskaskia) River . . . one of the largest we know," but he did not make a clear reference to the great mound of Cahokia. However, he did describe in his diary the Pulcher site, a collection of mounds about 10 miles south of Cahokia.[4]

Nine years later Clark's brother, William, with Meriwether Lewis, arrived in the area to begin their ascent up the Missouri. They spent the winter at a camp at the mouth of the Wood River, called by the French the DuBois. On January 9, 1804, a cold, snowy evening, Clark went out to shoot ducks for their dinner. In an area east of their camp, he broke through the ice of a frozen slough and discovered a circle of nine mounds, which he thought might be an Indian fortification. He later reported seeing great quantities of earthenware and flints on the ground and a grave on an eminence about one-half mile north of his position. Though he had stumbled onto some of the mounds near Cahokia, the great mound itself eluded him.

The first visitor to Cahokia to write a detailed description of the giant mound was Henry Brackenridge,[5] a friend of Thomas Jefferson, and a scholar who was deeply interested in the mounds and ruins scattered about the countryside. In 1811 Brackenridge visited St. Louis, a town that for years had been known as Mound City because of the many mounds in the area. Brackenridge was particularly interested in the mounds that lay near the west bank of the Mississippi and when he learned that there were other, even larger, mounds on the east side of the river, he resolved to visit them.

He was told that a group of Trappist monks had established a monastery two years before, first near Florissant, Missouri, and then on the east side of the

---

3. Fowler 1997, chap. 2.
4. Tucker 1942.
5. Brackenridge 1813, 1814, 1818.

Mississippi, on the banks of a creek named Cahokia that drained a large area of the river bottomlands. The monks' settlement was reported to be near some very large earthen mounds. This information piqued Brackenridge's curiosity and one day he set off to find the monastery and the mounds.

Brackenridge crossed the Mississippi on a ferry and landed at Illinois Town, now the city of East St. Louis, near the mouth of Cahokia Creek. To reach the monks and the mounds, he had only to follow the creek bank as it meandered northeastward. Illinois Town was in a wet, swampy lowland, but a wide ridge along the southern bank of Cahokia Creek formed a clear path into the interior of the floodplain. This area had been named the American Bottom and it extended, in a wide, flat crescent, from the mouth of the Illinois River on the north to about 80 miles south, where the Kaskaskia River emptied into the Mississippi. The American Bottom is the widest portion of the central Mississippi River floodplain, measuring 10 miles at its widest, from the river to the eastern bluffs, and two and a half miles at its narrowest. Like the valley of the Nile in ancient Egypt, the American Bottom is the gift of a river and is submerged at intervals by the fertilizing waters that gave it birth.

Brackenridge had gone barely a mile from Illinois Town when he noted that the land had changed. No longer a swamp, it was now prairie, waving grasslands interspersed with oxbow lakes, the remnants of ancient river channels from the time the Mississippi had flowed closer to the eastern bluffs. Willow trees grew on the shores of the lakes. In the distance Brackenridge could see the bluffs, covered with cedar trees, rising 80 feet above the prairie. At the base of the bluffs, where the soil had eroded and created a sloping upland, he could see a forest of oak, hickory, maple, and other deciduous trees. Behind the bluff, the massive upland prairies of Illinois began.

Though Brackenridge encountered a few isolated farms, land claims that went back to the French occupation of the area, he found that for the most part the land was empty. He had been walking for about fifteen minutes when he came to his first group of mounds. There were 45 of them, arranged in a semicircle about a mile in diameter. Brackenridge climbed one of the mounds and later wrote a description of it: "One of the largest which I ascended was two hundred paces in circumference at the bottom, the form nearly square, though it had evidently undergone considerable alteration from the washing of the rains. The top was level, with an area sufficient to contain several hundred men."[6]

Brackenridge walked on. He now came upon mounds spaced at regular and frequent intervals along the ridge. It was as if his path was a formal ceremonial route leading him into the heart of a city. Brackenridge had hiked about four

---

6. Brackenridge 1814:187.

miles from Illinois Town when he came to the greatest mound of all. He stopped and looked up at it in amazement.

"What a stupendous pile of earth," he wrote to Thomas Jefferson. "When I arrived at the foot of the principal mound I was struck with a degree of astonishment, not unlike that which is experienced in contemplating the Egyptian pyramids. To heap up such a mass must have required years and the labors of thousands."[7]

Brackenridge spent his afternoon walking among the mounds. He noted "small elevations" at "regular distances from each other" and quantities of flint, animal bones, and broken pottery lying on the ground. He came to the conclusion that "a very populous town had once existed here, similar to those of Mexico" and that it could not have been "the work of thinly scattered tribes." As he stood on the mounds and gazed about him, he imagined that the entire American Bottom must have been "filled with habitations and villages" and concluded that "if the city of Philadelphia and its environs were deserted, there would not be more numerous traces of human existence."[8]

While he was at Cahokia, Brackenridge tried to call on the monks but without success. They had erected buildings on one of the mounds and cultivated the terraces of what came to be called Monks Mound, but because of their vow of silence they neither spoke to him nor invited him into their houses. Nevertheless, he peered into their doorways, watched them at work in their fields, and then left for the walk back to Illinois Town and the ferry to St. Louis. Brackenridge's excitement over discovering the colossal mound was not shared by others, as he complained in a letter to Jefferson on July 25, 1813: "When I examined it in 1811, I was astonished that this stupendous monument of antiquity should have been unnoticed by any traveler: I afterwards published an account in the newspapers of St. Louis, detailing its dimensions, describing its form, position, etc. but this, which I . . . considered a discovery, attracted no notice."[9]

The citizens of the St. Louis area were not alone in failing to recognize Cahokia. Almost 150 years later, Melvin Fowler, on his trip for Dr. Deuel of the Illinois State Museum, drove right past the giant Monks Mound on U.S. Route 40 and missed it completely. According to his map it should have been there, but instead of coming upon an archaeological site Fowler found himself on a busy highway in a commercial-industrial area with small shops and factories, a restaurant-bar called Mexico City, and a smattering of working-class houses. He

---

7. Brackenridge 1814:187.
8. Brackenridge 1814:186.
9. Brackenridge 1813:155.

could see nothing else. Continuing a mile and a half down the road he stopped at a farmhouse to ask directions. A woman warily answered his knock. He asked about the location of the Indian mounds. She had never heard of them. He explained what they were. "Oh," she said, looking relieved, "You mean those hills back there." She and her family were living next to the preeminent archaeological site in North America, the third largest prehistoric construction in the hemisphere, and did not know it.

Fowler turned his car around and drove back the way he had come. A mile down the road he found a narrow lane on the north side of the highway leading to a parking lot and, set back from the highway in a grove of trees, the headquarters of the Cahokia archaeological site. The building, constructed in 1930 after the area had become a state park, had a vaguely southwestern style, with a flat roof and stuccoed walls, as if the builders believed that a structure for an archaeological site should look like a southwestern adobe. The building housed Joe Webb, the ranger, with one room set aside as a museum for a private collection of arrowheads and stone axes. Melvin looked through the doorway of the museum and sighed. The artifacts, without labels or any explanatory materials, lay jumbled on dusty shelves about the room. "There is nothing educational or instructive about this exhibit," he thought. "These are simply piles of unidentified stuff."

The ranger, a man in his early fifties, was happy to have a visitor. He pointed out the path to the top of Monks Mound and returned to his house. Fowler still could not see the mound even though the headquarters building was adjacent to its southwest side. Everything was covered with trees. The path was overgrown with brush and the trees arched overhead creating a dark, leafy tunnel over the path. Following the path up the side of the mound, Fowler felt as if he were in a deep woods. When he reached the summit there were fewer trees and the flat top had been partially cleared. He discovered that he was standing on a mound as tall as a 10-story building. In the distance, across the river in Missouri, he could see the skyscrapers of St. Louis. The immediate area around the mounds was obscured because of the dense stand of trees and shrubs.

Fowler stayed on the summit for only a few minutes, wondering what he was supposed to do. It was impossible to distinguish any features of the mound because of the underbrush and he felt under pressure to get to the highway department. As he hurried back down the path to his car, he had no idea that the mystery of Monks Mound and Cahokia would, for the next half century, be a central focus of his professional career.

The visit to the highway department at French Village, Illinois, was no more auspicious than had been his visit to Cahokia. The interstate highway program was just getting underway and the highway engineers were wary of other interest groups possibly interfering with their plans. The engineer Fowler talked to was tight lipped. He professed to have no information on the proposed routes for Interstates 70 and 55 around St. Louis, or even, he implied, if the roadways would be built. It was late afternoon before Fowler could leave for the drive back to Springfield. He believed that it had been an unsuccessful trip and as he drove he tried to compose a report in his mind that would satisfy Dr. Deuel.

Melvin Fowler had taken an indirect route to becoming an archaeologist. He had been born in Gordon, Nebraska, a small town east of the Sand Hill region of the state, to parents who had homesteaded their land. The Fowlers were devout members of the Reorganized Church of Jesus Christ of Latter Day Saints, one of the Mormon churches that had grown out of the religious experiences of Joseph Smith. A central tenet of the faith was belief in the Book of Mormon, a treatise that held that the American Indians were descendants of ancient Hebrews. The Precolumbian ruins of Mexico and Peru and the mounds observed throughout the Midwest were believed to be the remains of these ancient Indian-Hebrew civilizations.

Because his family lived near Indian reservations, Melvin had always been interested in Native Americans. His birthplace was near the Pine Ridge Indian Reservation and his father and grandfather had hired Indians to help them with their farm work. Melvin's father had taken his sons to collect arrowheads in the rural fields of eastern Nebraska. In the evenings he would tell stories about the Lakota people and teach his family a few words of the language. Later, when the family lived near the Omaha-Winnebago reservation, they made friends there.

Throughout his childhood Melvin had heard faint rumors that his paternal grandmother was Native American. The subject was never brought up in the family due to the prevailing negative social attitudes toward having Indian forebears. One day Melvin's older brother was looking through a family photo album when he came upon an 1890s picture of his grandmother. Without thinking he blurted out, "Why, she looks like a squaw."

Melvin's mother calmly replied, "She was a good Christian." The children accepted their mother's explanation and nothing further was said in the Fowler family about the ethnic background of the children's grandmother.

When Fowler was four years old his family moved to Fremont, Nebraska, where his father took a job with the highway department and the family joined a larger church of their faith. One Sunday, when he was about eight years old, Melvin heard a sermon about the Book of Mormon and speculation that evidence for the truth of the book was waiting to be found amid the ruins of Central America. That Sunday, the young Fowler determined to become an archaeologist.

After graduating from high school in 1942, Melvin began his freshman year at Graceland College, a church-affiliated school in Lamoni, Iowa. When the dean

asked the new student what career he planned to follow, Fowler replied, "archaeology," expecting the dean's approval of a choice that was central to the church's
beliefs.

To his surprise the dean replied, "Oh, no. You can't make a living at that."
He looked at Fowler's high school transcript and, seeing that he had taken numerous courses in mathematics, told him, "You should go into engineering. If
you aren't a success at that you can always go into teaching."

So Melvin Fowler entered the engineering curriculum. That was a fortunate
decision because in 1942 military service recruiters were visiting college cam-
puses to recruit young men for service in World War II. If the youths did not
enlist, they would be drafted. Fowler chose to enter the marine corps, in which
one of his brothers was already serving. After one year at Graceland College,
Fowler, as a marine recruit, was sent to Purdue University to continue his engineering studies. Because the military's need for engineers was acute, he was to
be stationed at Purdue University to finish his degree and would then be sent
to Marine Officer's Candidate School.

At Purdue, Fowler learned two skills that were to be significant years later
at Cahokia. He learned how to make and read maps and he learned how to interpret aerial photographs. The latter came about almost by chance. The air force
had begun taking aerial photographs of Pacific islands during World War II in
its search for appropriate locations for airfields. Military officials found that
aerial photos could reveal a great deal about soil conditions. After taking the
pictures, they would send Navy Seals in rubber boats onto Japanese-held islands
at night to get soil samples to validate their reading of the photographs. Melvin
heard several lectures on aerial photography, learned the basic principles of air
photo interpretation, and filed the information away in his head.

After three years it was obvious that the war in Europe was coming to an
end, and the invasion of Japan loomed large. With one semester left to go for
his engineering degree, Fowler was taken out of Purdue and sent to Parris Island for officer's training prior to being shipped out to participate in the invasion. Though he had succeeded in his studies at Purdue, Fowler, despite his best
efforts, was not a success at Parris Island. Worse, he was never sure what he was
doing wrong. Fowler began to think he was not cut out to be a marine officer.

As it turned out, he need not have worried. While Fowler was trying to adapt
to the ways of the marines, the atomic bombs were dropped on Japan and the
war ended. He went back to Purdue, finished his last semester, got his engineering degree, and took a job in Iowa working for the Civil Aeronautics Administration. The job was a good one. Fowler had a career and (for that time) a substantial paycheck. He had worked at his job for three months, however, when
he realized he did not want an engineering career. What he wanted to be was
an archaeologist.

Outside of the elite eastern schools, the university best known at the time for its archaeology program was the University of New Mexico at Albuquerque. Fowler applied there. The admissions officer wrote back that Fowler's engineering background did not qualify him for archaeology and advised him to attend a smaller school first. If he was successful in a smaller institution, the admissions officer wrote, he could reapply at New Mexico. So Fowler looked around for a smaller school. The University of Chicago, he noted, had a smaller enrollment than the University of New Mexico and also had a faculty member, Robert Redfield, who, though not an archaeologist, taught courses in Latin American archaeology and had worked in Mexico and Yucatán. In addition, the University of Chicago was one of the few schools outside of the Ivy League that had an anthropology department. Fowler applied and, after an interview with Fay-Cooper Cole, the department chairman, was admitted.

Cole had come to the University of Chicago from fieldwork in the Philippines for the Field Museum. He founded the Department of Anthropology and soon thereafter started a program of field schools to train graduate students in archaeological research. The Chicago school was one of the few field schools in the country and students came from all over the United States to participate.

Before the Chicago field-school program, investigators had developed their own systems for recording data and laying out a grid on a site. As a result, the grids were all of different sizes. The Chicago school used a five-foot-square area as the unit of the grid, and the practice quickly spread among archaeologists throughout the country. The Chicago faculty also developed techniques for properly excavating mounds and other sites, designed forms on which to record data, and standardized the system of horizontal and vertical controls for archaeological excavations.

The GI Bill paid Fowler 50 dollars a month plus his tuition and books. To support himself he took odd jobs around campus and worked as a draftsman with the South Side Planning Board, a private city-planning agency in Chicago. The Graceland dean's discouraging comment about the difficulty of making a living in archaeology still echoed in Fowler's mind and he had decided to minor in city planning, under Rexford Tugwell. Tugwell's lectures on the principles of city planning, which focused on the human and social use of space in urban settings, would one day give Fowler insights into the plans of the prehistoric designers who had laid out Cahokia.

Though he studied hard at Chicago, Fowler found the three-year graduate curriculum a difficult one. As the administrators at the University of New Mexico had warned him, a degree in engineering had not prepared him for graduate work in the social sciences. While his fellow students had been studying the Great Books he had been learning calculus and surveying. When he received his M.A. degree in anthropology, with a specialty in archaeology, the

University of Chicago classified his degree as "terminal." "Terminal," to Fowler, carried about the same import as if he had been diagnosed with a serious disease. His career opportunities, if not ended, were sharply curtailed. As far as the University of Chicago was concerned, he had completed his work at that institution and was not welcome to come back.

Having a terminal degree, while discouraging, did not leave him completely disheartened. It was at the University of Chicago that he met his future wife, Dorothy Mills, who was a fellow student. They were married in March 1948 and their son, Michael, was born in February 1949.

As graduation time approached, Melvin wrote letters to the leaders in the field of archaeology, people he had read about who worked at Harvard and the Peabody Museum, asking for their advice on his career. To his dismay he received very few replies and those who did respond discouraged him. "You shouldn't be in archaeology at all," they wrote. "You can't make a living at it and unless you have a personal income there is no reason for you to go into it."

It was true that many of the people in archaeology prior to World War II were wealthy or had independent family incomes. Archaeology was a small field and those in it—mostly men—tended to be swashbuckling adventurers with strong egos. The 1980s film character "Indiana Jones," an archaeologist, exemplified those early individuals in the field who tended to be secretive and opinionated, and who did archaeology, as one of them said, "just for the hell of it." They were specialized detectives, figuring out the lives of prehistoric peoples from the clues they left behind them in the ground—broken tools, pottery, ornaments, weapons, traces of houses, storage pits, and trash heaps of animal bones and broken shells. Nothing was exempt from the early archaeologists' scrutiny. They opened burials to probe the bodies of the dead and examined the teeth in skulls as if they were dentists. As a group they were argumentative, hard drinking, intuitive, and often brilliant. They were also scholars, people who were consumed with curiosity about the peoples and cultures of the past and who could extract an astonishing amount of information from the ground as they painstakingly excavated it with trowels, orange sticks, and soft-bristle brushes. Focused solely on the past, as many of them were, they did not foresee that the great postwar influx of young GIs into the universities would forever change academia, including the field of archaeology.

One place where Fowler had done well in his University of Chicago studies was the summer archaeological field school and he received high recommendations from his professor. On the strength of those recommendations, when he graduated in August 1949, he was hired by the Illinois State Museum to work under Thorne Deuel, first as a research assistant and later as curator of anthropology. Deuel was also a University of Chicago graduate and had gotten his Ph.D. under Fay-Cooper Cole.

Archaeology was a small field in the 1950s. The national meeting of the Society for American Archaeology in 1952 drew 80 people, which the organizers thought was quite a crowd. In the state of Illinois there were six archaeologists, three of whom worked for the Field Museum in Chicago. At the first meeting of the Midwest Archaeological Conference, held in Springfield, Illinois, in about 1958, 18 people attended and met in an old house converted to an archaeology lab for the Illinois State Museum.

The day following his graduation, Melvin and Dorothy packed all of their possessions and their six-month-old baby into the back of a two-door 1937 Pontiac, which Melvin had purchased for 100 dollars, and drove to Springfield. His salary at the museum, after three years of graduate school, was 50 dollars a month less than he had been making as an engineer.

In 1949, Springfield, the capital of Illinois, was a city of around 80,000 inhabitants with a housing shortage. All construction had been suspended during the war, and housing starts had not yet caught up with demand. While Deuel owned a large house in an exclusive neighborhood, there were few rental properties available to young families just starting out. Dorothy's frantic househunting finally found them a basement apartment in a private residence. The entrance was at the back of the house, down some concrete steps, and the apartment was jiggered around the furnace and other mechanical systems. It was far from their dream home but it was shelter.

They had been in their basement apartment only a few days when Mrs. Deuel, a southern lady of a gracious bent who believed it was her role to pay formal visits to the new hires at the museum, came to call on them. She gave no advance warning of her visit but simply appeared one morning at the top of the Fowlers' basement entrance, peering uncertainly into the dimness below. Dorothy coped with drying diapers and Mrs. Deuel as best she could but the next day Melvin received a summons from Deuel.

"You know," began Deuel, "my wife was out there and that is not a very nice area you are living in—in that basement apartment. There is a house for sale right across the street from us, just like ours. Why don't you look into that?"

Melvin was astounded. Deuel knew what he was paying him and that on his salary he could not support a family—let alone a house in an expensive neighborhood. Deuel had assumed that since he, himself, had family money, Fowler must have a private income as well. Fowler had no idea how to respond to his boss's suggestion. A few months later he got a raise. In addition to the raise, Deuel offered him an extra 50 dollars a year to edit the *Journal of Illinois Archaeology*, a journal for amateurs and collectors. When Fowler got his first paycheck he found that the extra income had bumped him into a higher tax bracket and he now had less take-home pay than he had had before.

Though Deuel could not find money for his staff, he did find it to support digs. Melvin's departure time for a dig on the Wabash River the next summer coincided with the due date of the second Fowler child. The baby was late and Melvin kept postponing his departure. Finally Deuel told him that he would have to go. Reluctantly Melvin left and was at an isolated archaeological site on the Wabash River when the couple's second child, Erika, was born.[10]

Archaeological work was often carried out under conditions of real hardship. The following summer Melvin was in charge of a crew of nine people working at a site on the bottomlands of the Wabash River in southern Illinois. The site was 20 miles from the nearest town and the workers' sole transportation was a 1947 Chevrolet sedan. The crew members slept at the site and every morning all nine of them would pile into the car, drive to the town for breakfast, buy supplies to carry back to the site with them for lunch, and then return to the town in the evening for dinner.

Melvin was concerned about Dorothy, who, back in Springfield, was holding a job and caring for their two small children at the same time. One weekend Melvin left the car for his crew and hitchhiked the 200 miles back to Springfield to check on his family. Somehow Dr. Deuel heard that Fowler was in town. Melvin received an order.

"Stay over and report to me on Monday morning," Deuel commanded. He was incensed that Fowler had left the dig without his authorization. Melvin tried to explain that he had not seen his family for six weeks and they had two young children, one of them an infant. This made no impression on Deuel, who ordered his young assistant back to the site, where Fowler stayed the rest of the summer.

---

10. The family was completed by the birth of Kirstin in 1958 in Springfield and Arthur in 1960 in Carbondale, Illinois. The only child born when Fowler was not in the field was Michael. At most, Melvin had only a day or two to be home, away from fieldwork, when his children were born. All of the children later went with him on digs as a sort of "summer camp."

TWO

The Illinois Archaeological Survey and the Prehistory of Cahokia

Melvin Fowler had failed to learn anything of the plans of the federal highway department to build an interstate highway through the archaeological site of Cahokia, yet rumors of the highway project persisted. As a means to gather information and to coordinate their activities in Illinois archaeology, the anthropology departments of the University of Illinois at Urbana-Champaign and Southern Illinois University at Carbondale joined with the Illinois State Museum at Springfield in 1956 to form an organization called the Illinois Archaeological Survey. The head of each university's anthropology department and the director of the museum were to represent their institutions at the group's meetings. The survey was to play a major role in Cahokia archaeology for the next thirty years.

Representing the University of Illinois was the anthropology department chairman, John McGregor. Thorne Deuel was to represent the Illinois State Museum, and Harvard graduate J. Charles Kelley, head of the newly established Department of Anthropology and director of the museum at Southern Illinois University, represented that institution. Therein lay a problem. John McGregor and Thorne Deuel thoroughly disliked each other. Their colleagues suspected that even their wives did not get along.

John McGregor, who had virtually established the anthropology department at the University of Illinois, was a relative of the movie actor Clark Gable. McGregor was highly conscious of this relationship and wore his neatly clipped mustache in the same style as the actor. When he was in a group, he would turn his head so it was in profile, point to his ears, and invite comparisons to Gable's. Despite this affectation, McGregor was a good archaeologist. He had done early work in the Southwest and written a textbook on southwest archaeology that for years was the only available reference work on the area.

McGregor and Deuel had been graduate students together at the University of Chicago, part of an unusual cadre of students that included many who went on to make outstanding contributions to archaeology. Deuel, Fay-Cooper Cole's principal graduate assistant, was not well regarded by the other graduate students, perhaps because he displayed then the same West Point attitude that irked Fowler. The graduate students, led by one of their group, James B. Griffin, banded together in an effort to get rid of Deuel. Their plan was to present a request to Dr. Cole that Deuel be removed.[1] The attempted coup failed, however, and Griffin[2] moved to the University of Michigan. The hard feelings between Deuel and McGregor[3] may have dated back to this incident.

After graduation McGregor continued to work in the Southwest and Deuel went to the Illinois State Museum. When the Second World War broke out, Deuel left the museum to resume his commission in the army and was sent to China and Burma as a colonel in charge of supply. Fay-Cooper Cole, who besides chairing the Department of Anthropology at the University of Chicago was also chair of the Illinois State Museum Board of Advisors, activated his old Chicago network and called McGregor back from the Southwest to take Deuel's position at the museum, where he was to remain for what was called in the war years "the duration." McGregor even moved into Deuel's house in Springfield.

In the early years of American archaeology, professional archaeologists formed networks of uneasy alliances with collectors and pot hunters. Every archaeologist had his own private network of these relic collectors. Collecting archaeological relics was, if not illegal, at least frowned upon. Because the Midwest had so much primary archaeological material, the region was full of grave robbers—people who located Indian burial sites and looted them of artifacts, either for their own private collections or to sell to others. These collectors knew, far better than the few archaeologists in the area, where the prime archaeological sites were and jealously guarded their information.

A few of these informants were amateur archaeologists who, while not professionally trained, had an interest in the history of the past and kept careful records of where they found their artifacts. Most, however, simply had arrowheads jumbled together in a box and, in their spare time, mounted them in picture frames in exotic designs—for example, an Indian in a war bonnet composed of arrowheads. Although the archaeologists were chagrined by such activity, they would have to negotiate with the secretive pot hunters if they were to locate sites

---

1. Jennings 1997.
2. Green, 1997:125–157. James B. Griffin, commonly referred to as Jimmy by his colleagues and students, was a major influence, if not dominant figure, in the intellectual development and growth of the prehistory of North America from the mid-1920s until his death on May 31, 1998. His career has been summarized in a series of publications in his honor. The most recent is in the fall 1997 issue of the *Midcontinental Journal of Archaeology.*
3. Lathrap and Douglas 1973.

of Precolumbian occupation. Each archaeology department in the state, therefore, had what was in effect its own private network of relic informers. When McGregor took over Deuel's job at the Illinois State Museum he also gained access to the museum's extensive files of amateur diggers.

With the end of World War II, Deuel returned to his old job as director of the Illinois State Museum. McGregor was demoted to the curator position that, a few years later, Fowler was to take. This did not please McGregor and he soon left to head the Department of Anthropology at the University of Illinois.

One of the purposes in founding the Illinois Archeological Survey was to compile information on the location of all the sites known to the informal network of pot hunters. This had to be done very carefully, with the promise that the institutions and the archaeologists involved would not reveal any of the pot hunters' private information. If they did, the collectors would not cooperate. Deuel believed that McGregor had gone off with names of some of his prized collectors, and this was an additional source of conflict between the two men.

Feelings between the two ran so strong that Deuel often refused to attend meetings where McGregor was present. As a result, Fowler was sent to the meetings of the Illinois Archaeological Survey in Urbana in Deuel's place. The new department head at Southern Illinois University, J. Charles Kelley, was not greatly interested in midwestern archeology (his specialty was Mexico) so he sent Howard Winters as his representative.

The new Archaeological Survey soon found that it had more to do than map the collectors' sites in the state. McGregor had a better pipeline into the workings of the Illinois Department of Transportation than had Deuel, and he and Fowler went together to the highway department offices in Springfield. There they learned that the department *was* planning to carry out the federal program to construct a complex of interstate highways near East St. Louis and that parts of them were planned to go through the archaeological site of Cahokia. The highway engineer got out his maps and Fowler and McGregor pored over them. Interstates 55, 70, and 270 were routed through the area, one just to the north of Monks Mound, through Cahokia Creek and a nearby swamp area. Altogether, four portions of the site were scheduled to be invaded by interstate highways or their interchanges.

There was no possibility of changing the routes of the highways or of preserving monuments in the 1950s. Highways had precedence over historic sites. All the engineers could offer was some funding. In the Federal Aid Highway Act of 1956 a maximum of one-tenth of one percent of the budget of federally constructed projects was set aside for "salvage archaeology."

Salvage archaeology meant that archaeologists would be permitted to go onto a site ahead of the bulldozers, on the contractors' own strict time schedule, to salvage what they could before the area would be dug up and paved over for a highway. The Cahokia site was to become the first example of large-scale salvage archaeology in connection with highway building in the state of Illinois and the largest in the nation. The huge project would be under the direction of the fledgling Illinois Archaeological Survey.

The site the Illinois Archaeological Survey was about to investigate had a very long history. Until about 10,000 B.C., the northern portions of eastern North America were covered with glacial ice as far south as southern Wisconsin. During the Ice Age the climate of this area was obviously much colder and wetter than it is at present. The southern fringes of the glaciers were bordered with lakes, and the boreal forest was pushed far south of its present boundaries.

Human inhabitants were first documented in the central region of North America toward the end of the Ice Age. They were known as people of the Clovis culture, or the Paleoindian period. Though evidence of the Clovis culture had been found as scattered surface finds in the Midwest, it was not until the 1970s that the Clovis culture was documented to be in direct association with the long-extinct mastodon at the site of Kimmswick, about 100 miles south of St. Louis.[4] The Clovis people inhabited the midwestern landscape around 8000 B.C., a time when there were still massive ice sheets in southern Canada.

As the glaciers started to recede they left behind the Great Lakes and large gravel deposits or moraines. The vegetation zones also gradually pushed northward and the deep valleys that had been cut by the torrential outwash of the melting glaciers began to fill in with sediments. As the Laurentide ice sheet melted and retreated north, midwestern rivers became so flooded with water and sediment that the Mississippi River blocked the flow of tributaries, causing even major rivers like the Illinois to flow backwards. Icebergs calved from the glacier in central Illinois and Wisconsin floated down Mississippi tributaries and deposited exotic sediments that had been scraped from land far to the north. It was these powerful alluvial processes that created the expansive floodplain known as the American Bottom.

After 3000 B.C., the area of North America east of the Rocky Mountains looked about as it did when first seen by European explorers and pioneers. The effects of the massive glacial ice that had covered the northern latitudes of North America had waned. While some glacial remnants probably still covered Hudson's Bay, in effect, the glacial age had ended. Taiga and boreal forests had followed the northward movement of the receding ice, and the modern configuration of forests, prairies, plains, lakes, and mountains was established. The large animals, such as mastodons, were gone, rendered extinct because of the rapidly changing natural zones and, perhaps, because of human predation.

---

4. Graham et al. 1981.

The ox-bow lakes, marshes, ponds, and ridge-and-swale topography of the American Bottom are remnants of this post–Ice Age in-filling. People inhabited the area after the Clovis big-game hunters but they lived a very different way of life. This period is called the Archaic and it lasted in the American Bottom and in the surrounding region until at least 1000 B.C. Evidence of the Archaic way of life is found in the southern end of the American Bottom at the Modoc Rock Shelter and at scattered subsurface and surface sites throughout the region. Many events took place during the Archaic period that formed the foundations from which later cultures, and eventually the Cahokia development, could emerge.

The Archaic way of life utilized a variety of resources that became seasonally available in local areas. To take advantage of these, people gradually developed a round of journeys to find food. Small bands, perhaps of related families, would set up camps near a particular food resource to take advantage of it. At the appropriate time, the group would move to another station as a new food resource came into season. In this way a migratory style of living evolved, based on the seasonal availability of food, impelling the group from camp to camp and often returning them to the same locations they had occupied the previous year.

Where there were abundant food resources, larger groups of people could live and move together through the seasonal round. In certain locations, where a food resource was particularly abundant, several of the small bands would meet at the same location year after year.

What were they like, these precursors who laid the foundation for Cahokia? One clue lies in their burials. On the assumption that the way an individual is treated in death reflects how he or she was treated in life, the presence or absence of grave goods can indicate status in a society. For much of the Archaic period, the societies appear to have been egalitarian with little manifest social differentiation. Only toward the end of the period did grave goods begin to be found. Some individuals were buried with more specialized goods than others, suggesting a developing concern with burial ceremonialism and social distinctions among individuals. Evidence for this comes from an area outside the American Bottom.

At about 2000 B.C. over a thousand individuals were buried at the Indian Knoll site in Kentucky.[5] This site was probably a cemetery and a nearby living area of Archaic people. About 300 individuals had been buried with grave goods, suggesting at least two divisions in the society. The people with the grave goods must have been those who had achieved some notoriety during their lives, thus becoming "Big Men," a common social distinction among egalitarian societies.

There were two curious things about the grave goods. First, a small percent-

---

5. Webb 1946.

age of the burials included goods that had come from a long distance. There were copper artifacts, which had probably come from the Lake Superior region, and pendants made of conch shell from the Gulf Coast. Since these types of items represented a major investment by the group, the people with whom they were buried must have had very high status. The second point of curiosity was that the grave goods were buried with individuals of both sexes and with children. How had the children achieved status unless it had been inherited? Did the articles buried at Indian Knoll indicate that the social distinctions being made within the society were both ascribed and inherited?

A defining characteristic of the Archaic people is that they traded goods over great distances in what archaeologists call "exchange networks."[6] While these probably began as a way to exchange food to balance out unequal resources or to provide relief in time of scarcity, they developed into a method of procuring exotic goods such as copper, special types of flint, Gulf Coast shells, and perishable goods.

The Archaic people everywhere depended on plants for a major portion of their diet. These foods were the seeds of trees, such as acorns, walnuts, and pecans. Other abundant seed foods were "disturbed habitat" types of plants, such as amaranths, chenopods, sumpweed, and sunflowers. These plants, while prolific in nutritious seed production, can survive in the same habitat for only a few years before they will be replaced by other plants in the succession toward climax vegetation. In the midcontinent region during the Archaic period, people slowly began to encourage the growth of these plants and take steps toward their domestication.

One way they accomplished this was by burning the area to provide a less-competitive habitat for the plants. Or they may merely have taken advantage of the mud flats that were regularly disturbed by the flooding of nearby rivers. Fowler suggested that a human campsite with its associated trash is an ideal disturbed habitat. In his "dump theory" of early seed plant domestication, he noted that large late-Archaic sites would have been congenial to a mutual dependence of plant and humans. At first, volunteer seed plants would have been harvested. But gradually, selection and replanting of the most productive plants could have taken place. In this process of coevolution, some plants would have become domesticated and produced more food and the human community would have become increasingly dependent on them for a stable food supply. The same process would have taken place when bands revisited the riverine bottomland localities year after year, selecting and harvesting seeds, and trampling down the competing growths.[7]

---

6. Winters 1968.
7. Fowler 1971, 1992; Smith 1992.

Sunflowers, sumpweed, amaranths, gourds, and squash were first domesticated during the Archaic period in the area of the midcontinent and spread from there to other parts of North America. This complex of starchy seed plants remained a major source of grain foods into much later periods, when maize moving up from Mexico began partially to replace it.

The increasing social complexity in the late Archaic period is evidenced by the first earthworks or burial mounds. No Archaic earthworks have been found in the American Bottom but they have been located in the lower Illinois River Valley. It is further to the south that the late Archaic earthwork constructions took place.

One well-documented and elaborate example of early earthwork construction is at the site of Poverty Point in Louisiana.[8] Poverty Point was a society sufficiently well organized to command the labor of hundreds of persons to construct a community. The central construction of Poverty Point is a large geometric earthwork, 3,969 feet across. In its original form it was comprised of six concentric octagons of earthen ridges, each nine feet high, with ditches between the ridges. The diameter of the innermost octagon measured 1,950 feet. The ridges may have been platforms supporting up to 600 houses. Associated with the earthen ridges were three mounds. These, together with the concentric octagons, utilized about one million cubic yards of earth. There was no other construction in all of eastern North America to compare with Poverty Point in the Archaic period.

Poverty Point has orientations in relation to the winter and summer solstices and to other astronomical factors, suggesting that it may have been a significant ceremonial center with cosmological concepts incorporated into the site planning. If so, this is the earliest site in eastern North America of this specialized type of construction. Poverty Point seems to have been short-lived, surviving as a community possibly no longer than 200 years, and at any one time it supported no more than a few hundred people.

It was upon this basis of horticulture, the domestication and use of starchy seed plants, that sedentary communities developed and populations increased. The period after 1000 B.C., until about A.D. 700, is known as the Woodland period. The general trend through the Woodland development is one of increasing dependence on horticulture and the establishment of large but dispersed communities centering on earthworks. These earthworks are largely tomb burial mounds but there are many earthen-walled enclosures as well. The climax of this development was between about 500 B.C. and A.D. 500 and is known as Middle Woodland or, more commonly, the Hopewell period.

The settlements in this period were of four types: base settlements, harvest-

---

8. Ford and Webb 1956.

ing camps, regional exchange centers, and burial maintenance areas. The regional exchange centers were large sites where exotic goods such as obsidian, copper, galena, grizzly bear teeth, and shells were found. These centers dictated the local cultural developments within the larger region.

Throughout the Ohio and Mississippi River systems and the Gulf Coastal plain, a special grouping of artifacts has been found over much of the area. These artifacts differ from the regional products of local cultural development. The exotic items include ceramics of distinct styles with broad pan-regional similarities. There are also copper items, raw mica and mica cutouts, pieces of lead ore, pipes made in a specific platform style from a stone quarried in the Ohio area, obsidian artifacts, grizzly bear teeth, conch shell vessels, and other objects.

These artifacts, which had a widespread distribution, are very similar in style and form. Yet they were found in a wide variety of local traditions that could clearly be differentiated from each other. This is compelling evidence that a cultural uniformity overlay a foundation of cultural diversity. Some sort of unifying belief system tied the different cultures of eastern and central North America together—much as Roman Catholicism overlay the nation-states of medieval Europe, from Italy to the North Sea.

The materials these objects were made from came from a wide area, implying an extensive procurement and distribution system for them. The main source of copper was the remote Isle Royal, an island in northwestern Lake Superior. Secondary copper sources were almost as distant, located in northern Wisconsin and Michigan.

Large quantities of obsidian have been found in Hopewell mounds in Ohio, where over 500 obsidian implements were placed on one altar in a mound. The main sources of obsidian on the North American continent are in Oregon, California, the Yellowstone region of Wyoming, and central Mexico.

It is this regional trade that is the most significant development in eastern North American prehistory in the Middle Woodland period. While Archaic peoples had procured items from outside their regions, they had probably passed them from locale to locale on a face-to-face basis of reciprocity. With the shift to a Middle Woodland culture, trading took on far different significance. Although important raw materials and even food items were procured through this trade, it was the goods that were associated with individuals of status that became important. A "status goods economy" developed.

The Middle Woodland materials have been found in large quantities and in very specific situations indicating a different societal context. Their distribution suggests a much more systematic mode of procurement and distribution. The fact that many of these items came from sources that were sometimes distant indicates specific and intentional procurement. The distribution is not random but is concentrated in areas manifesting the most complex cultures of the time period. This is most notably true in southern Ohio, which had the most complex earthworks and the largest quantities of exotic goods.

Just how this active trade was carried out is a matter for speculation. Some scholars have proposed a class of merchants who traveled from group to group with goods to trade. Others suggest the development of a system of trading partners between groups sometimes far distant from each other. These partners could visit each other and exchange "gifts." Thus, by a system of overlapping territories and a chain of trading partners, goods could have traveled over great distances. The exchange of these exotic goods would have cemented social and political ties between the areas.

The actual procurement of the materials may have been handled in a similar way. Copper and galena were actively mined. This could have been done by local people who then moved the metals into the system in exchange for other goods. Another possibility is that expeditions went from certain centers specifically to procure materials, such as obsidian from Yellowstone.

Most of the exotic goods obtained by a community had one primary purpose: to honor specific individuals. Who were these people that merited such wealth? There are two types of charismatic persons who might have received such treatment. One is the Big Man, who, though living in an egalitarian society, achieved his status during his lifetime by significant attributes such as valor in warfare, hunting prowess, and organizational ability to get needed goods from other groups. The Big Man gave feasts to assure his status and to distribute resources to other members.

The second type of individual is the chief. A chief functions in societies that are ranked, each individual having a well-defined position in the society. The ranking is in terms of the kinship group or lineage into which the person is born. The ranking of every person in the group is in relation to the chief, who is often thought to have descended from a mythical founder. (The French, in the late seventeenth and early eighteenth centuries, referred to their ruler as the "Sun King." While his subjects did not believe in the king's literal descent from the sun, his status was greatly enhanced by such a reference.) In such a chiefdom, wealth is funneled through the chief and redistributed by his power to the families, lineages, and individuals in the society.

The line between these two types of societies is not sharply drawn. Successful Big Men could pass their positions on to descendants and in this way establish their family as the ranked lineage. Most of the exotic goods traded in the Hopewellian Interaction Sphere, an exchange and trade network that had existed for nearly a thousand years, were destined for these status individuals. By burying these goods with the dead, the society was making a statement about the social organization of the people and reiterating the position of the person and his lineage.

Another type of "material" that may have been exchanged was the magico-religious concept. There is a surprising uniformity of art style over much of the area of the Mississippi and Ohio Valleys during this time period. The platform pipes and human figurines bear a strikingly similar style wherever they are found. They may have been connected with certain fertility, healing, or religious rituals that were meaningful to many of the societies.

The great trade network, which began in the first centuries before the Christian era, reached its peak around A.D. 300 It was during the next period, after A.D. 500, that the system of exchange of exotic goods broke down, not to reappear again until its resurrection by the mighty lords of Cahokia. The trade network was a piece of the complex ideological system that led to the growth and dominance of Cahokia in the American Bottom and throughout central North America.

THREE

Early Investigations into the Great Mounds

If it had not been for the imminent construction of the interstate highway in the 1960s, the Illinois Archaeological Survey would have shown little interest in Cahokia. Indeed, Cahokia had excited only slight local interest in the 150 years since Brackenridge had first written about it. If the mounds were thought of at all, they were considered impediments to progress. The great Monks Mound lay as it had for a thousand years, a mute feature on the landscape, subject to the pokes, prods, and speculation of the curiosity hunters, the looters, and the occasional passing student of antiquities.

In 1831 the tract containing Monks Mound was purchased by a mechanic named T. Amos Hill. Hill wanted to reside above the malarial bottomland so he cut a road up the side of Monks Mound and built his house on the summit, where he also dug a well, unearthing, as he did so, quantities of human bones, pottery, and stone implements. Hill's well was described by a Mr. Flagg in his journal, published as *The Far West* in 1838.

> Upon the western side of the Monks Mound, at a distance of several yards from the summit, is a well some eighty or ninety feet in depth; the water of which would be agreeable enough were not the presence of sulfur in some of its modifications so palpable. This well penetrates the heart of the mound, yet, from its depth, cannot reach lower than the level of the surrounding plain. I learned, upon inquiry, that when this well was excavated, several fragments of pottery, of decayed ears of corn, and other articles were thrown up from a depth of sixty-five feet; proof incontestable of the artificial structure of the mound. The associations, when drinking the water of this well, united with its peculiar flavor, are not of the most exquisite character when we reflect that the precious fluid has probably filtrated, part of it at least, through the contents of a sepulcher.[1]

---

1. Flagg 1838:166–167.

While from the top of the mound Hill drew water of dubious quality, down below, on the open spaces between the mounds, farmers grazed their cattle and plowed their fields, sometimes over the tops of the smaller mounds.

For travelers coming up the Mississippi, Cahokia provided a convenient opportunity to sketch one of the curiosities of the West. In 1834 an Austrian prince, Maximilian of Weid, sailed up the river on an expedition to the upper Missouri River area. A member of his party was the Swiss artist Karl Bodmer, who made two drawings of Monks Mound (he labeled one picture, in German, "Trappists Hill") and the surrounding area—showing it as open pasture land with a creek and scattered trees (fig. 1).

In 1841 J. C. Wild visited Cahokia and made some drawings that, while exaggerated, gave a view of Monks Mound and some of the surrounding mounds as they must have appeared in the early part of the nineteenth century. Wild also picked up artifacts. "From the surface of the small mound from which the view was taken," he wrote, "the artist and the writer, in the space of a few minutes, picked up about half a peck of broken bones and pieces of pottery and flint. One of the bones, which is nearly perfect, is evidently the arm bone of a human being."[2]

Beginning about 1860 several anthropologists visited Cahokia. Among them was Dr. Charles Rau, a curator at the Smithsonian Institution in Washington, D.C.[3] Rau had been born in Belgium and educated in Germany, where he received a Ph.D. degree from the University of Freiburg. In an article published in 1869 he describes the finding of a cache of unused prehistoric tools—50 flint hoes and 20 stone shovels—unearthed by workmen grading an extension to Sixth Street in East St. Louis.[4] Rau had a keen interest in Precolumbian artifacts and was the first to suggest that the oval-shaped stone objects with the notches on opposing sides might be agricultural implements.

The land containing Monks Mound was bought in 1864 by Thomas J. Ramey, whose heirs were to live on the property for the next 59 years. The Ramey family took a protective attitude toward the mound though they allowed local individuals to dig on the property. One who did archaeological investigations was William McAdams, a Missouri resident and a member of the St. Louis Academy of Science. He wrote a description of Monks Mound in 1887 and also dug there for treasure.[5]

"In excavating near the base of the great temple mound of Cahokia, whose

---

2. Wild 1841:52–53.
3. Rau 1867.
4. Rau 1869:402–405.
5. McAdams 1881, 1882, 1887, 1895.

Figure 1. Sketches of Monks Mound and other Cahokia mounds by the Swiss artist Karl Bodmer in 1840. Top: View of the east side of Monks Mound. A smaller mound in the right foreground has a Mississippian pot on its surface. Bottom: A view of the mounds and plaza area south of Monks Mound. In the right center are the flat-topped Fox Mound and the conical Round Top. Used with permission of the Joslyn Art Museum.

towering height of over one hundred feet gave a grateful shade for our labors,"
McAdams wrote, "we found in a crumbling tomb of earth and stone a great
number of burial vases, over one hundred of which were quite perfect. . . . Some
of these were painted and there were also the paint-pots and dishes holding the
colors."[6]

McAdams recorded Thomas Ramey's attempts to investigate the mound.
"About midway, on the north side, or face of the pyramid, and elevated 25 or
30 feet above the base, in a small depression, stands a pine tree. . . . There was a
story rife among the early settlers that this tree stood at the mouth of an opening or gallery into the interior of the mound. To ascertain the truth of the matter, Mr. Thomas Ramey . . . commenced a tunnel at this tree and excavated about
90 feet toward the center of the mound. When fifteen feet from the entrance to
the tunnel a piece of lead ore was discovered but no other object of interest was
found."[7]

By the end of the nineteenth century, Frederick Ward Putnam[8] and David
I. Bushnell[9] of the Peabody Museum of American Archaeology and Ethnology
at Harvard University were developing the techniques of modern professional
archaeologists. Bushnell made a detailed survey of the entire northern portion
of the American Bottom and published the results in 1904 in a paper entitled
"The Cahokia Site and Surrounding Mound Groups."

Impressive as the mounds themselves were, it was the vast quantity of artifacts lying about or just under the surface of the ground that continued to attract
visitors. In 1891 the Reverend Stephen Peet wrote about his visit to Cahokia.

> In the field adjoining one may find beautiful fragments of pottery, some of which
> bear the glaze and red color which formerly characterized the pottery of the
> Natchez Indians. There are also vast quantities of bones hidden beneath the
> surface and one can scarcely strike a spade through the soil without unearthing
> some token of the prehistoric races. Mr. Ramey, the owner of the mound, speaks
> about digging in one part of the field and finding heaps of bones eight feet deep
> and says that the bones are everywhere present. The workmen who were engaged
> in digging ditches for underdraining had a few days before come upon large
> quantities of pottery and skeletons of large size, but had carelessly broken them
> instead of preserving them.[10]

Two artifacts particularly engaged Peet's attention. One object "represented

6. McAdams 1895:179.
7. McAdams 1883:2–3.
8. Putnam and Patrick 1880.
9. Bushnell 1904, 1922.
10. Peet 1891a:10.

a squirrel holding in its paws a stick, the teeth placed around the stick as if gnaw-
ing it, the whole making a handle to the vessel. . . . The object which impressed
us most was a sand-stone tablet which contained figures very much like those
found upon the inscribed tablets taken from one of the mounds of the Etowah
group in Georgia."[11] Peet, who was editor of the *American Antiquarian,* was
sufficiently impressed by the tablet to publish a drawing of it in his journal.

One of the first since Brackenridge to conceive of the Cahokia site as the
remains of a prehistoric metropolis covering a large geographic area, rather than
just a likely place to collect Indian relics, was Dr. John J. R. Patrick, a dentist from
Belleville, Illinois. Though, like others of his time, Patrick assembled collections
of artifacts from the site, his interest went beyond the amassing of collections.
In the 1880s, at his own expense, he hired surveyors to make an accurate map
of Cahokia. Patrick regarded the site as a unit—a whole—a great mysterious
something that had once occupied more than six square miles near the banks
of the river. Whatever Cahokia was, and no one was quite sure what that might
have been, it was certainly more than a collection of mounds on a floodplain
salted with pottery and crumbling, ancient bones.

Patrick's surveyors did a remarkable job. While they were draftsmen, they
were also artists. With their fine-tipped pens they carefully drew in and numbered 71 mounds at Cahokia, shading the sides of the mounds to give an indication of height. Water areas of the map were colored with a pale blue wash and
the mounds were tinted gray to make them stand out from the background of
the map.

To complete the mapping of the site, the surveyors drew in the evenly spaced
mounds along the intervening area between Cahokia and East St. Louis, where
Brackenridge had once walked on the ridge that is now U.S. Route 40. The
Patrick maps covered an area from Cahokia Creek on the east all the way west
to St. Louis.

Patrick did not stop with making maps of the Cahokia site alone. He also
ordered maps made of the remaining mounds located in the growing city of East
St. Louis, where 17 mounds could still be identified among the city streets. Across
the river in St. Louis, Missouri, his surveyor marked the location of Big Mound,
the largest mound in the St. Louis group.

Big Mound, which was destroyed in 1869, was one of the last survivors of
what had been a group of approximately 26 mounds that had formed a rectangular enclosure or plaza on the west side of the Mississippi River within the city
limits of St. Louis.[12] The artist Titian R. Peale, who was traveling with an expe-

11. Peet 1891b:58–59.
12. Long 1903 [1823]); Peale 1862; Williams and Goggin 1956.

ditionary party up the Missouri led by Major Stephen H. Long, stopped in St. Louis in 1819 and reported Big Mound to be 319 feet long, 158 feet wide, and at least 34 feet high. As Big Mound was being torn down to provide fill for the extension of the North Missouri Railroad, Thomas Easterly, a local photographer who had an interest in antiquities, made daily visits and carefully observed it. He reported the mound contained a tomb about 75 feet long, 8 to 12 feet wide, and about 10 feet high. The tomb was built like a room with plastered floors and walls and a roof constructed of heavy timbers.

Inside the tomb, workers found about 30 burials (no one was trying to get an accurate count) laid side by side on the floor with their feet toward the west. Covering each body from the thigh to the head were thousands of shell beads, which, at the time of the burials, had probably been sewn onto fabric to make a kind of shell blanket. Each body was covered with about six quarts of beads, beads so tiny that they averaged 2,400 to the quart. Other bodies were also buried in the mound along with more beads, earspools, and copper artifacts. One of the more significant artifacts found in the Big Mound was a mask with a very long nose.

Most of the bones, beads, and artifacts uncovered in Big Mound—and the 25 other mounds in St. Louis—went into landfills. A modern city, the gateway to the West, was being built and the past was bulldozed aside to make way for the future. Finally, all that remained to mark the location of Big Mound and the Indian city that had occupied the same site as St. Louis was the small circle Patrick's surveyors drew on the map at Broadway and Mound Streets to mark the place where, they were told, Big Mound had once stood.

One who shared Patrick's interest in the totality of Cahokia was a fellow physician and contemporary, Dr. John Francis Snyder.[13] Snyder had been born in 1830 in a farmhouse built on the side of a mound (known in his time as Snyder's Mound) at what is now called the Pulcher site, just south of the Cahokia mounds. Though he was trained as both a doctor and a lawyer, Snyder disliked practicing medicine and was at heart an archaeologist and historian. He had spent his boyhood wandering over the Cahokia area and its history became his lifelong interest. Though the science of archaeology, dealing with prehistoric peoples and cultures, had not yet been developed, Snyder anticipated much of the methodology of modern archaeologists and kept careful records of his findings and their locations. He joined the scientific associations of his day, corresponded with the leaders in the field of anthropology, and wrote articles for the journals, even becoming the editor of a monthly archaeological magazine entitled *The Antiquarian*. Snyder's written descriptions of some mounds

---

13. Fowler 1962.

that were destroyed, such as the Beardstown mound and the charnel house mound near East St. Louis, are the only records of those unusual sites.

The greatest problem that would face archaeologists of the future, Snyder was convinced, was that irreplaceable sites were being destroyed by vandalism and the expansion of cities. He had been shocked to see the great Beardstown mound leveled to get fill for the city streets and the Mitchell mounds at Cahokia destroyed to make way for the railroad. To his dismay he saw that the general public was uninterested in saving these monuments. Instead of considering them as resources for the study of the past, they saw them as impediments to progress.

Snyder was a forceful man with strong opinions. He was scornful of the curio collectors who looted sites and was unhappy with the archaeological journals' common practice of carrying advertisements of Indian artifacts for sale, as he knew this only encouraged looting. He believed the state should sponsor archaeological fieldwork by professionals. He presented these views in a paper read on January 6, 1900, at the first meeting of the Illinois State Historical Society but there was no response. It would be twenty more years before any agency of the state of Illinois would sponsor archaeological work.

In 1911, as part of his attempt to change public attitudes, Snyder formed an organization called the Monks of Cahokia, to lobby the Illinois legislature to preserve the area and make Cahokia a park. Reflecting the times, the Monks were a supposedly secret organization of several hundred men (though everyone knew who the members were) who donned hooded robes and cavorted on the summit of Monks Mound before repairing to a local tavern for refreshments. A secret society was not the best means to arouse public and legislative support for the mounds and the effort failed.

While there had been little question in the minds of Brackenridge, Patrick, Peet, and Rau that the mounds at Cahokia were the works of American Indians, many other experts had serious doubts.

When the first Europeans invaded North America in the sixteenth and seventeenth centuries, they saw abandoned towns that had obviously been inhabited by hundreds of people. They also found thousands of large earthen mounds, some nearly as large as the Egyptian pyramids. They dug into the mounds, discovering sumptuous burials, carved stone statues, fine ceramics, and copper ornaments.

It was obvious that the civilization that had generated these monuments and artifacts had been here before Columbus. Though the Indians were the only known inhabitants of North American before the coming of the Europeans, few people believed the ancestors of the impoverished Indians they saw about them could have created these impressive monuments and works of art. Soon a belief developed of a separate "moundbuilder culture." The moundbuilders, the white settlers were convinced, must have come from Europe and been early Celts, Romans, or Vikings. Some even blamed the Indians for having killed off the extinct superior "moundbuilder race."

These speculations generated intense public interest. The Smithsonian Institution devoted early publications to the question of the moundbuilder culture as did the Bureau of American Ethnology and the American Philosophical Society. Most thinking people reached similar conclusions as to who the moundbuilders were. In 1787, Benjamin Smith Barton wrote that the moundbuilders were Vikings who had settled the New World and then died out. Josiah Priest in 1833 claimed the mounds had been built by Egyptians, Israelites, Greeks, Chinese, Polynesians, or Norwegians.

Noah Webster wrote a series of letters to Ezra Stiles, president of Yale College, in which he speculated that the mounds might be the product of Carthaginians or other Mediterranean nations. The letters were published between 1789 and 1790 in the *American Museum,* where they were apparently read by General George Rogers Clark, who had been a frequent traveler in the area of the American Bottom. Clark disputed Webster's claims and wrote a letter in which he quoted the Kaskaskia chief Baptist du Coigne, who asserted that the nearby mounds represented the palaces of his forefathers.

Clark's letter was not published until much later, and the belief that some group other than the American Indians had built the mounds persisted in most scholarly thinking. By the 1880s, scholars and lay people alike attributed the mounds to an array of ancient peoples ranging from the Vikings and Anglo-Saxons to the Lost Tribes of Israel. Most Americans were willing to believe any group could have built the mounds except the Indians, who were considered too unskilled and too lazy to have created such monumental constructions. The poet William Cullen Bryant suggested that the mysterious moundbuilders had been killed by barbarous American Indians and in a poem called "The Prairies" lamented that the industrious creators of the mounds had vanished from the earth.

Under the auspices of the American Ethnological Society, Ephraim Squier, a midwestern newspaper editor, and Edwin H. Davis, a physician, explored more than 200 mounds and 100 earthen enclosures in Ohio and published their findings in a series of books sponsored by the Smithsonian Institution. Although many of their conclusions uncannily anticipated the ideas of modern archaeologists, Squier and Davis also concluded that the earthworks displayed "a degree of knowledge much superior to that known to have been possessed by the hunter tribes of North America" and they referred to the Indians as "those hostile savage hordes."[14]

---

14. Squier and Davis 1848:42–44.

The issue was debated until the beginning of the twentieth century. The majority agreed with J. W. Foster, president of the Chicago Academy of Sciences, who wrote that to assume that the Indians, a people "signalized by treachery and cruelty," had built the mounds "is as preposterous, almost, as to suppose that they built the pyramids of Egypt." The Indian, he added, "repels all efforts to raise him from his degraded position and whilst he has not the moral nature to adopt the virtues of civilization, his brutal instincts lead him to welcome its vices. He was never known voluntarily to engage in an enterprise requiring methodical labor."[15]

J. D. Baldwin, in his 1872 book *Ancient America,* wrote, "It is absurd to suppose a relationship or connection between the original barbarism of these Indians and the civilization of the mound-builders."[16] Minnesota Congressman Ignatius Donnelly, in a popular book, announced that the mound builders were in reality survivors of the lost continent of Atlantis.

The belief that the mounds had been created by a superior, non-Indian race also had comforting political ramifications. If Europeans could convince themselves that the savage Indians were, in reality, interlopers who had overrun a prior advanced civilization, one founded by fellow Europeans, then they could feel justified in their persecution of the Indians and in the destruction of the Indian cultures.

The myth of the moundbuilders held popular sway throughout the nineteenth century and bolstered beliefs in the superiority of the Europeans. It was the foundation on which the revelations of Joseph Smith, the founder of Mormonism, were based and the focus of the main theme of the Book of Mormon. Even avocational archaeologists, including men such as Snyder and McAdams, stated that the American Indians could never complete a project the size of Monks Mound. The irregular second terrace of Monks Mound, they thought, had gained this shape because the builders had tired of the project and wandered off to hunt buffalo. Any explanation, no matter how strained, appeared to be more logical than the obvious one that Native Americans had built these mounds.

Not until the last decades of the nineteenth century was the moundbuilder legend put to rest. It was Cyrus Thomas, an Illinois native and natural historian, who did the definitive study to show that the moundbuilders were the ancestors of the American Indians. Thomas was an exceptional scholar with deep interests and abilities in a variety of fields. The official entomologist for the State of Illinois, he founded the University Museum at Southern Illinois University at Carbondale. While in southern Illinois he became interested in Indian mounds, including those at Cahokia, and took that interest with him when he

15. Foster 1843:800.
16. Baldwin 1872:61.

went to Washington, D.C., to work for the Bureau of American Ethnology. It was there that he conducted his massive study of thousands of mounds and other pre-European sites in eastern North America and published it in 1894 as the twelfth annual report of the bureau.[17] The moundbuilders, he declared, were the ancestors of the Choctaw, Cherokee, Osage, Quapaw, Shawnee, and many other Indian tribes. A decade later Thomas published one of the first professional papers on Cahokia and produced a schematic map of the mounds.

Where the Cahokia mounds were concerned, there was yet another explanation for their existence that did not involve Vikings, Phoenicians, or any other human group. These particular mounds could, after all, be the works of Mother Nature—natural products of glaciation or erosion from the bluffs above the river. One who believed this was A. H. Worthen, author of *Geological Survey of Illinois,* who wrote, "We infer that these mounds are not artificial elevations, raised by the aboriginal inhabitants of the country, as has been assumed by antiquaries generally, but . . . they are simply outliers of loess and drift, that have remained as originally deposited."[18]

Taking strong exception to such opinions was Wills DeHass, one of the first archaeologists to visit the Cahokia mounds, who had written in 1869, "The only charitable conclusion is they [the geologists] never examined the mound. No man whose opinions are worth quoting could have examined even one of these interesting monuments and not declared, unequivocally, in favor of artificial origin."[19]

DeHass may have thought he had settled the natural-versus-artificial controversy but he had not. A fellow geologist, Dr. A. R. Crook, then director of the Illinois State Museum, held the firm opinion that the mounds were naturally occurring. He had sunk borings with a 2-inch auger 25 feet into Monks Mound and was convinced, from this test, that the mounds were nothing more than natural hills.[20]

Crook's opinion created a major problem for Snyder and his associates, who had been campaigning to get the State of Illinois to appropriate funds to buy and preserve the Cahokia site for a park. As early as the 1890s, Thomas Ramey, who not only owned most of the mound land but also was a member of the Illinois General Assembly, had pushed for Cahokia's preservation. In 1913 Rep. Norman Flagg, of Moro, had introduced a bill into the Illinois legislature to purchase the site. The bill proposed spending $250,000 to buy 200 acres that would be set aside for a state park. The bill was defeated when "Bull" Burke of

17. Thomas 1894.
18. Worthen 1866:314.
19. DeHass 1869:291.
20. Crook 1915:74–75.

the Cook County delegation asserted, "my district needs parks for live people and the guys in that mound are all dead ones."

Despite the failure of the bill, support for the idea of a park was growing. A Cahokia Mounds Association was organized by supporters and incorporated in March 1914, under the laws of the State of Missouri. The association's goal was to convince the United States Congress to appropriate funds to buy 760 acres containing Monks Mound and 60 smaller mounds for a national park. When the association's members were unsuccessful in persuading Congress to appropriate the funds, they focused their efforts on the Illinois State Legislature, publishing a pamphlet stating, "Illinois should take steps to preserve the most interesting historical feature in its domain."

With the director of the Illinois State Museum declaring that the mounds were nothing more than hills, the natural product of erosion, there was little chance of convincing the state legislators to appropriate money to preserve them. Dr. John Snyder and his friends resolved on another tactic.

In 1921, they arranged to bring Warren King Moorehead to Cahokia in the hope that he would be able to provide sufficient archaeological evidence to convince the state to purchase the land. Moorehead was a professional archaeologist from the Robert S. Peabody Museum of Archaeology at Phillips Academy, Andover, Massachusetts. He had already excavated 15 of the more than 30 mounds on the Hopewell farm near Chillicothe, Ohio, to provide exhibits for the World's Columbian Exposition, held in Chicago in 1893. Moorehead arrived in Cahokia in June 1921 and when he looked over the site it was immediately apparent to him that this was the biggest collection of genuine Indian mounds that he had ever seen. He also saw that they were in imminent danger from commercial and industrial development. The railroads and factories were now less than a mile away from the largest mounds on the site.

Moorehead was politically astute. Working under the auspices of the Illinois State Museum and the University of Illinois, he immediately formulated a four-point program and began to implement it. His four points were: (1) get permission from landowners to dig on their land; (2) inform the press about Cahokia; (3) raise funds for exploration into the mounds; and (4) persuade some institution, such as a museum or university, to take charge of the work.

By August he had written and distributed a pamphlet entitled *Help Save Cahokia Mounds*. It read in part, "I know that you cannot conveniently spare a large sum, but if each museum or individual will send us a small contribution we shall be able to begin excavation. . . . From all I can ascertain, I feel safe in stating that once excavations are begun interest will be aroused generally throughout Illinois . . . and the legislature persuaded to pass a bill when it meets a year and a half hence. . . . The matter is very urgent and much is at stake."

Moorehead spoke to the Daughters of the American Revolution and to Rotary Clubs and the contributions began to come in. He urged a St. Louis group to save Cahokia, saying that the mounds are to America what Stonehenge was to England. He raised the question whether it would be the great Cahokia or factories on the east side of the Mississippi River.[21]

Moorehead's efforts raised $1,800 from individuals and local museums, and $1,500 from the Peabody Museum. Then the president of the University of Illinois, who was a Phillips Academy graduate, persuaded the university to grant $1,500 to the project and arranged for the materials from the excavations to be curated at the university and the Illinois State Museum. Moorehead sent editorials to newspapers throughout Illinois bringing the plight of Cahokia to public attention.

Still the question remained as to the origin of the mounds. Legislators needed proof that these were truly Indian mounds before they would appropriate money to buy them. Enlisting the help of a geologist, Dr. Morris M. Leighton, of the University of Illinois (and later director of the Illinois Geological Survey), Moorehead made three auger borings into Monks Mound. Then, with Crook himself observing, he and Leighton cross-sectioned Mound 33 and established to everyone's satisfaction that the mounds were totally artificial.

In 1923 Dr. Leighton made his definitive report to the president of the University of Illinois. By this time he had examined many of the mounds opened up by Moorehead and his evidence was overwhelming. Leighton wrote that the mounds

> are mainly of fine materials—silts, fine sands and gumbo—but unassorted lumps and masses of one kind being intercalated with materials of another kind, and bones, artifacts, flints, travertine fragments, charcoal and pottery being scattered throughout without any suggestion of a mechanical separation or orientation. . . . Salt-water shells from the Gulf of Mexico occur indiscriminately with local fresh-water shells; burned layers occur at various horizons; and a long series of holes with bone refuse in their bottoms was found in one mound. Such a mixture, such an arrangement, such a complex association of unusual materials, are characteristic only of man-made mounds.[22]

Even the doubting Mr. Crook looked at the evidence and concurred. This was proof enough for the members of the Illinois State Legislature. In 1923 Thomas Fekete of East St. Louis introduced House Bill No. 26, which called for the State of Illinois to buy a 235-acre tract surrounding Monks Mound, including 35 of

21. Moorehead 1921:2.
22. Leighton 1928:143.

the smaller mounds, for $250,000. The bill passed but only after the legislature had cut the offering down to $500 an acre for 100 acres. The Ramey family rejected the amount and filed suit. Finally, in 1925, $52,110 was paid for 144.4 acres of the Ramey land, and Cahokia Mounds State Park came into being.

Moorehead was the first professional archaeologist to spend any period of time at Cahokia. His career went back to the early years of archaeology when practitioners were part scientists and part relic-hunters and collectors. To Snyder's great disgust, Moorehead was also a pot collector who dealt in the commerce of artifacts. Though he was a champion for the preservation of the mounds, he was a careless archaeologist and Snyder grew to dislike him for his pothunting proclivities.

It appears that Moorehead began excavating at Cahokia before he had drawn up an adequate map. Later he made copies of sections of Patrick's map but he failed to understand the keys Patrick had assigned to connect the sections of the map. As a result Moorehead put the maps together incorrectly and so misinterpreted some of Patrick's data. Patrick had numbered the mounds he mapped, but Moorehead began his work using a different numbering system from Patrick's. Later he went back to Patrick's system but then got mixed up on which numbered mounds were which. Moorehead called Round Top mound number 57, instead of Patrick's number of 59, and he got mounds number 24, 25, and 26 confused. Some mounds show evidences of Moorehead's excavation—for which he left no explanation in his notes. And some of his notes on pottery finds are unclear as to which mound he was digging in when he found them. As a result there is considerable confusion as to which mounds Moorehead actually excavated. The maps Moorehead eventually published were poor copies of Patrick's to which additional mounds had been added.

Nevertheless, everything about Cahokia excited Moorehead. The size of the mounds and the vast number of them filled him with energy and enthusiasm. He was like a youngster in a candy store and, assembling a crew, he began taking bites out of as many mounds as he could. Despite the problems with his work, which are certainly irritants to archaeologists working today, Moorehead made an enormous contribution. His work provided the baseline on which future Cahokia archaeologists could establish their work. Many of the details published in his copious field notes, considered insignificant at the time, have since assumed importance.

Fortunately Moorehead found some good people to work with him. One was a civil engineer named Jay L. B. Taylor. Moorehead assigned Taylor ridge-top mound number 66, the Harding Mound, now called Rattlesnake Mound, to excavate for him. Rattlesnake Mound was an impressive size, 500 feet long and 30 feet high. Lying just south of the right-of-way of the Baltimore and Ohio

Railway, it was soon to be scooped up by steam shovels. Moorehead theorized that since the mound had a narrow ridge-top shape, it could not be the base for a temple and must have been a burial mound. He preferred to excavate burial mounds as they usually contained grave goods. Taylor was told to see what he could find in the mound before it was demolished by the railroad.

Taylor was a careful and methodical worker. His records are among the most concise and detailed of the time, and his excavation exhibited the most careful control of any done by Moorehead and his crew. Taylor's topographic survey revealed, to his astonishment, extraordinarily symmetrical contours. His field notes also relate some of his day-to-day problems:

> Our trench face now measured something more than six feet in height and a heavy rain that night caused the whole fifty feet to slide in on our working floor, an unexpected interruption that necessitated the removal of several tons of heavy muck before trenching could be resumed. The American Bottoms . . . were so completely inundated that numbers of blue racers and rattlesnakes sought refuge on the mound where they finally became so annoying that we postponed work in the trench long enough to mow and burn all the vegetation on such parts of the mound as we were camped on. A violent storm drove the crew out of the trench at 2 P.M. At 3 P.M. our supply tent and all our provisions and cooking utensils were blown off the mound, and the office tent, in which all our instruments and records were stored, was held in place through a driving rain and wind only by the united efforts of the crew who quit the shelter of their own tents and mounted the south end of the frame. But by five o'clock we had salvaged practically all of our equipment and supplies.[23]

Moorehead was correct in his assumption about the ridge-top mound. It contained at least 150 poorly preserved bundle burials—groups of bones from different bodies grouped together—interred in a layer about a meter below the ground surface. Each bundle consisted of "from two to six skulls with their corresponding limb bones and teeth" and Taylor located each burial in his notes and maps with precision and care.[24] On one of Taylor's maps he shows at least 35 discrete interments in the excavated area, one of which was a partly articulated individual. The bundles of crania and long bones covered an area of about 40 to 50 square meters. In the center of the bundled bones was a circular deposit of orange-yellow dirt, which may have been a fire-hardened layer of earth.

Taylor was impressed by the extent of Cahokia and urged that a new and more accurate survey be made of the entire area before more was lost to real-estate development. He and Moorehead were undecided even on how many

23. Moorehead 1928:70.
24. Moorehead 1928:72.

mounds to include within the Cahokia complex. If they drew a circle seven miles in diameter, centered on Monks Mound, they would encompass about 150 mounds. If the boundaries were extended about nine miles east and west and fifteen miles north and south from Monks Mound, many more mounds would be included. In a letter written February 1, 1928, W. J. Seever, one of Moorehead's coworkers, stated that he had been familiar with the Cahokia area for forty years and that he had counted nearly 300 mounds in the region, with more than 150 in the central group alone.

In his publication about his work at Cahokia, Moorehead wrote an introduction to Taylor's field notes on Rattlesnake Mound in which he noted, "It has been thought best to present complete details of the mound construction and its peculiar character, although we are quite aware that no persons except technical students will find much of interest in these succeeding pages."[25]

Moorehead could not have been more wrong. To give him credit, there was no way, in the 1920s, he could have known that ridge-top mounds would, four decades later, become the keys to an understanding of the organization of Cahokia.

Another mound that was to prove important years later was the Jondro Mound, named for the owner of the land, Tusant Jondro. The Jondro Mound was small, lying a mile and a half west of Monks Mound. It had been excavated by Seever, who found about 40 burials in the south end of the mound. On his maps of the burials, Seever had noted the depth below the surface at which he had found them. Later, Melvin Fowler was able to correlate the burials with the various mound stages.

Moorehead published often, and in considerable detail. His book on Cahokia is like an archaeological dig itself, and each generation of Cahokia archaeologists sifts through it for details that have suddenly become significant. Fowler spent hours poring over the field notes bequeathed to him by Moorehead, Seever, and Taylor.

Since he was also a collector, Moorehead interviewed local relic hunters and reported on their observations in his publications. Local collectors told him that the whole range of high land alongside the river from Alton to Cairo was one immense, ancient cemetery and that skeletons were plowed up each spring and fall. Another observer reported that large numbers of bones had been found by railroad crews and road builders, that the bones were loaded onto a flatcar with the soil and debris and dumped into the outlet of Long Lake. McAdams obtained some excellent specimens in flint, stone, and copper when two or three of the mounds were destroyed.

---

25. Moorehead 1928:65.

Little distinction was made in Moorehead's time between professional and amateur archaeologists. All of the people who worked to save Cahokia—for example, Snyder, McAdams, and Patrick—made their living at other pursuits. Occasionally a professional archaeologist from the East would visit Cahokia, look around for a few days, make some pronouncements, and then leave. This annoyed the local amateurs, who were experts in their own ways. They knew the locations of the sites and the peculiarities of the local terrain, and they knew the people. Unfortunately, among the local amateurs (and some of the professionals as well) were relic collectors who looted the mounds and went about the countryside offering to buy artifacts from the farmers. These people had no concern for the context of the items or the sites from which they had come. As a result valuable archaeological data were lost and hostility developed between the amateur and professional workers that took years to overcome.

Moorehead did make another major contribution by helping to convince officials of the State of Illinois that they had an extraordinary archaeological site in Cahokia (as well as in smaller surrounding mound groups), a third of which had already disappeared under the urban development of East St. Louis, and that they should act promptly to protect the mounds that remained. He was deeply concerned that the site would be lost to the encroachment of racetracks, railroads, and factories. He was horrified when private owners of the mounds contemplated dividing the mounds into small tracts and selling them off. Thanks to Moorehead, Snyder, Patrick, and a handful of others, the great mound of Cahokia was saved within the boundaries of the state park. The rest of the site, the rows of mounds that stretched for miles to the east, west, and south of Monks Mound, were in private hands and therefore still in jeopardy.

From 1811 until the afternoon Melvin Fowler stood atop Monks Mound in the early 1950s and wondered what he was supposed to do about it, everything that had happened at Cahokia was a kind of happenstance. No institution or governmental body had supported the antiquarians' efforts at preservation. Travelers wandered by and drew sketches of Monks Mound, collectors dug for artifacts, farmers plowed up bones and clay pots and discarded them, while small boys with shovels unearthed skeletons with copper serpents lying on their breasts.

Through the years a small group of concerned citizens and amateur archaeologists in St. Louis, some of them physicians, continued to watch over Cahokia. They knew, beyond any scientific verification, that here lay a sleeping giant—a colossal monument to antiquity—a key to the understanding of ancient American civilizations. They suspected that Cahokia had been a prehistoric metropolis, a political and religious center out of which had flowed the concepts that shaped the beliefs of the people over half a continent.

While most Americans were obsessed with the future and the western frontier, these believers in Cahokia knew that the past was also a frontier of knowledge that someday would be explored. The clues, they were certain, lay on the banks of the Mississippi River, hidden in the great mounds of Cahokia. It would take another generation of archaeologists to prove what they only guessed at, that Cahokia is the largest prehistoric site north of the Rio Grande and represents the most complex and elaborate achievement of Native Americans in what is now the United States of America. Monks Mound is the largest Precolumbian earthen construction in the Western Hemisphere.

FOUR

The Destruction of the Powell and Murdock Mounds

Though it was decades before the Illinois Archaeological Survey would be founded, both the University of Illinois and the Illinois State Museum took some notice of Cahokia during the destruction of the Powell and Murdock Mounds. Powell Mound was one of the largest mounds at Cahokia, second in size only to Monks Mound, and was located a mile and a half west along U.S. 40, or Collinsville Road. The haystack-shaped mound was owned by two brothers, William and Frederick Powell, for whom the mound—310 feet long, 45 feet high—was a colossal irritation. The Powells were horseradish farmers who wanted to level the mound and use it as fill for a nearby swampy area.

Because the Powell brothers realized that their mound had some archaeological significance, for three years in the late 1920s they had made a standing offer of $3,000 to the officials of any institution in the state who would excavate the mound and dump the dirt as fill in a low-lying area—a location about 200 yards away. For three years they waited for an offer and none came. No museum or university was interested in the Powells' mound—even with the generous bounty offered by the brothers. The public indifference and apathy so lamented by Brackenridge and Snyder continued.

The Powell brothers' offer did get the attention of some officials of the State of Illinois, however, who proposed that the state buy just the mound itself and a 50-foot margin around the base with a road leading out to the highway. This would have carved a lollipop-shaped piece of land out of the neat rectangle of the Powells' 50-acre farm. The Powell brothers rejected the state's proposal but responded with an offer to sell their entire farm to the state. The State of Illinois did not want the entire farm; it wanted only the area of the mound. The Powells and the state became deadlocked over the issue, and after a time, state officials began talking about initiating condemnation proceedings on the land where the mound stood.

The threat of condemnation proceedings thoroughly upset the Powell brothers, who thought they had been trying to do the right thing all along, and in December 1930 they hired a steam-shovel operator and told him to cut down the mound. They carefully placed the steam shovel on the north side of the mound, where the activity could not be observed by drivers passing on U.S. 40. The ruse worked for eight days. Then Dr. Paul F. Titterington, of the informal Cahokia protection network, got wind of what was happening and called the University of Illinois for help.[1]

Despite Titterington's frantic call, no one moved very quickly. Sixteen more days passed, days filled with steam-shovel activity, before the university sent Dr. A. R. Kelly to the Powell Mound. Kelly was to act as an observer and do whatever scientific hand excavations the contractor would permit. By this time the great mound had been sliced almost in half. The Powell brothers gave permission for the university archaeologist to observe the work so long as he did not interfere with the contractor.

The work was excruciating to watch. Titterington and his friends stood helplessly by as the shovel uncovered a four-inch-thick humus line that started at the base of the mound, rose 20 feet to about the middle, continued at this level for almost the entire length of the mound, and then dropped down again to the base. They were good enough archaeologists to know that they were looking at the cross section of an older flat-topped mound that lay inside the Powell Mound. At about the middle of the mound the steam shovel crashed into a cache of human bones. Beads and thousands of shells fell from the cut in the dirt. It appeared to the observers on the ground that a burial chamber about 30 feet long had been broken into. As they watched, the great shovel took massive bites from the side of the mound, rotated on its base, and dumped the contents into the bed of a truck to be carted off for fill. Nothing from the burial could be saved.

Later a second burial at the same 20-foot level was uncovered and a side of it torn out and exposed by the shovel. This time the contractor agreed to put Titterington and Kelly into the scoop of the shovel and raise them up to the level of the burial, where they could get a close view of it against the vertical face of the cut. Leaning over the side of the massive scoop and brushing away the dirt with their hands, they tried to determine, in the short time allowed them by the contractor, how the burials had been done.

---

1. Paul Titterington, a medical doctor, was among the most active avocational archaeologists in the United States. Living in St. Louis, Missouri, he acted as a sentinel to alert the few professional archaeologists as to the ongoing destruction of mounds. He was active in fieldwork and his seminal article on the Jersey Bluff culture in Illinois was selected for publication in the first issue of the professional journal *American Antiquity.* See Titterington 1933, 1935, 1938, 1942.

Figure 2. Two views of Powell Mound. Top: A 1922 photo of Powell Mound (Mound 86) taken by Lt. Goddard in the first successful attempt to get aerial photographs of the Cahokia site. Bottom: A view of Powell Mound in 1930 as it was being destroyed. Used with permission of the Illinois State Museum.

As near as they could tell, from their precarious position in the scoop, a layer of cedar sticks, about one inch in diameter, had been laid down parallel to each other about three feet apart on the top of the humus line. The sticks had been covered over with a layer of bark and the bodies laid on top of the bark. The burials were then covered with one to five layers of shells in such definite rows and over such a wide area that the men thought they must have been sewed to garments or robes. Another layer of bark covered the shells and over all lay 20 feet of dirt of the upper mound.

While Kelly and Titterington were able to make some observations of this burial before it was destroyed, they were able to save very few of the artifacts.

What they were able to recover were perforated shell beads and some copper-covered cedar ornaments that they salvaged from the general mound fill.

Titterington and Kelly also observed another feature that later was to be as significant as the beads and burials. It was a cedar post, about six inches in diameter, that was uncovered slightly west of the center line of the mound. The post was located three feet below the humus line of the flat-topped inner mound. The top of the post had been splintered by the steam shovel while the bottom was still sunk into the depths of the mound. The two men noted the location of the post in their field notes and then watched as it was scooped up with the dirt and hauled off as fill. By the time the razing of Powell Mound was halted in January 1931, only seven feet of the 45-foot-high mound remained.

The destruction of Powell Mound belatedly got the attention of the archaeology departments of the Midwest. In February 1931, Thorne Deuel, then a graduate student at the University of Chicago, and W. C. McKern, of the Milwaukee Public Museum, got permission from the Powell brothers to make some controlled excavations on the remaining seven feet of the mound.[2] They cut two trenches through the mound at right angles to each other and recovered pieces of broken pottery from the mound fill. They proposed that the entire mound belonged to the same general time period, which they called the "Trappist," or "Bean Pot," culture, the latter from the shape of the potsherds they found. The so-called bean pots were straight-walled, beaker-shaped pots with thick walls and a handle extending out from the side wall.

The University of Illinois also sent investigators to Cahokia under the direction of Kelly to excavate a small mound southeast of the big Powell Mound. Kelly and his field director, Gene M. Stirling, uncovered an earlier level under the mound, which they called Old Village—as it was obviously older than the Bean Pot culture. Potsherds from the Old Village culture were very thin, often black in color, and of a finer texture than the heavier bean-pot sherds. The finding and naming of these two distinctive pottery types marked the beginning of what was to later become an intricate ceramic sequence at Cahokia.

Archaeological time is based on the simple premise that what is found deepest in the ground is likely to be the oldest and that objects found nearer to the surface are apt to be newer. The layers of sediments in which objects may be found comprise the stratigraphy of the site. By maintaining strict vertical controls on an excavation, an archaeologist can tell which type of pottery was made earlier in time and which was made later. However, few excavations work out this neatly. There are refuse pits where all kinds of pottery and stone objects are tossed in together. Pottery was imported from other geographic regions and left

2. Ahler and DePuydt 1987.

at the local site. People in ancient times, as now, were fickle and changed their taste in pottery. New technologies arose that were adopted, at first by the elite or the pioneers in the culture and then, as the styles became more popular, by the rest of the population.

Once archaeologists figure out the chronology of a site they can then move on to reconstruct the lifeways of the past. How did ancient people spend their days, conduct trade, find or raise their food, engage in sports and play, defend themselves from their enemies, worship their gods? How did they organize their society?

When the lifeways are understood, archaeologists strive to elucidate the cultural processes that underlie human behavior—whether it be that of people who lived a thousand years ago, such as those at Cahokia, or people of the twenty-first century. This is a difficult goal, requiring archaeologists to go beyond particular artifacts that were made at a particular time in a particular place to gather information from other disciplines—ethnology, sociology, philosophy, economics.

The investigation of every site, however, begins with the question of time, with a chronology. Chronologies are based on two elements—the artifacts themselves and notations of the precise location where they were found. Of all the artifacts found at archaeological sites, ceramics are both the most numerous and the most significant.

One reason for this is that ceramics are the most malleable of all artifacts. While stone can be chipped into various shapes, there are limitations on what can be made from it. But when a potter makes up a clay mixture and adds the tempering (the ground stone, crushed shell, or grit that helps hold it together and keeps it from cracking), it can be formed into almost any shape desired. The potter can paint it in different colors, carve a design on the surface, or cover it with various colored slips. There are tremendous numbers of possibilities in ceramics. Stylistic differences take place in ceramics that allow archaeologists to separate the ceramics into different categories.

The big question always is, What are these categories? Should the categories be based on the shape of the rim or the body of the pot, on the materials used to temper the clay, on the color of the pot, on the way it was decorated, on the incising of the surface or the slip covering, on the type of handle—or on a combination of some or all of the characteristics?

The ceramics from the Cahokia area had not been studied by the 1930s. The research by Kelly and Stirling established that there was a premound culture whose pottery differed from that which they had found in the mound fill. The two-part division was published by Kelly and Fay-Cooper Cole[3] in a brief ar-

---

3. Kelly and Cole 1931.

ticle but it remained for James B. Griffin[4] to analyze the Cahokia material, document the sequence, and give some detail to it. For his part, McKern recognized that a type of ceramics found at Cahokia, named "Ramey Incised," was strongly similar to a type found at a Wisconsin site called Aztalan, and he raised the question of a possible relationship between the two.[5]

McKern was on to something significant but he was decades ahead of his time. The battles over ceramic analysis at Cahokia lay ahead. In the 1930s the sequence and categories were simple. There were only two, Old Village and the newer Bean Pot (or Trappist). The United States was in the grip of the Great Depression and few universities or museums had money to invest in the recovery of additional potsherds from the Indian mounds at Cahokia.

In 1940 the vigilant Dr. Titterington learned that the construction of the Mounds Acreage subdivision of houses southeast of Monks Mound was about to destroy another group of Cahokia mounds outside the park area. A builder named Harry Murdock had been leveling the land with a horse and scraper preparatory to building and had come across human bones.

Titterington immediately called Thorne Deuel, who was now the director of the Illinois State Museum. It was June 1941 before Deuel sent one of his staff, Harriet Smith, with a crew of a dozen Works Progress Administration (WPA) workers to see what they could salvage before Murdock built his ranch houses on the property.[6]

Harriet Smith was a rarity in archaeology at that time: she was a woman. She was a graduate of Fay-Cooper Cole's program at the University of Chicago and another of the people from that program who were dominating midwestern archaeology. Unlike most deans of anthropology at the time, Cole allowed women to participate on the University of Chicago digs. (John McGregor, at the University of Illinois, had not allowed any women on his crews until the late 1950s. He maintained that "women need more privacy and they aren't as strong as men. They should not be in a field situation.") It was to fall to Harriet Smith to conduct the first modern large-scale professional excavation at Cahokia.

Murdock was cooperative and lent tools and screens to Smith and her workers as they dug trenches to see what they could learn about the site. In all they determined 13 stratigraphic levels, five in a habitation area below the mound and eight in the mound structure itself. Working through the summer and fall with a steadily declining crew as the men left to take jobs in the defense industry, Smith was able to define six levels of occupation at what appeared to have been a densely populated residential area. Her workers uncovered the remains of many well-constructed wattle and daub houses.

---

4. Griffin 1941, 1949.
5. McKern 1946.
6. Smith 1969.

A wattle and daub house is one built from walls made of upright poles interlaced with vines or smaller sticks, called the "wattle." A mixture of mud mixed with straw and grass, called the "daub," is plastered over the wall to create a solid construction. Walls constructed in this way are relatively durable and provide insulation against both the heat and the cold. (A variation of wattle and daub construction, called "bajareque," is a traditional house style in Colombia, and hundreds built in the last century are still in use. Wattle and daub houses are still being constructed in rural areas of Central and South America.)

Smith discovered that the Cahokia wattle and daub houses were not built on the surface of the ground but in depressions, from one to three feet deep, called "house basins," scooped out of the earth (fig. 3). The roofs of the houses were made of thick bundles of grass and around the inside walls were built-in benches, about two feet across, constructed of clay. Every house also had a fire pit in a central location.

As Smith and her workers excavated house after house they came upon one that was different from the others. It was larger than its neighbors and had been constructed in association with a second house, this one built in a circle. All of the previous houses had been rectangles. The round structure, 16.5 feet in diameter, had been built in a house basin excavation about 10 inches deep, much shallower than the houses Smith had been excavating. The walls had been a foot thick, twice as thick as the walls of the other houses, and the outside of the walls had been covered with woven mats that had been carefully tucked into the edges of the excavated basin. The fire pit in the center of the room was more like a well, over 16 inches deep with perfectly vertical sides and a flat floor. The clay around the fire well had been intensely fired, suggesting that fires had burned

Figure 3. Mural in the Cahokia Mounds Interpretive Center, showing reconstruction of the northeast corner of the Grand Plaza with Monks Mound in the background. Note wattle-and-daub houses and methods of construction. Painting by Michael Hampshire used with permission of Cahokia Mounds State Historic Site.

continuously, or at least over long periods of time, in the circular room. A large rectangular house stood only seven feet from the round building. Could this have been the residence of a clan head or a priest of Cahokia? Smith wondered. And could the round building have been a sweat lodge or temple—a sacred space with an eternally burning flame?

Another unusual building Smith uncovered was a cross-shaped structure set in a circular pit. The saucer-shaped pit had a diameter of 27 feet. The double-walled building inside it measured 21 feet from one arm of the cross to another. The walls of the cross-shaped building had been two feet thick.

From the potsherds collected by her workers, Smith estimated that her site had been continuously occupied for 370 years—from A.D. 1000 to A.D. 1370. As she studied the locations of the houses and temple mounds, other peculiarities captured her attention. She noted that the Murdock Mound and all the houses she had excavated through five levels of occupation had been oriented on a north-south axis. In addition, their sides were all lined up parallel to the sides of Monks Mound. She found this orientation so frequent that she hypothesized that the builders of Cahokia had a city plan. Houses were not randomly scattered about, she insisted, but had been placed where they were according to some agreed-upon community design.

When she measured the sides of Murdock Mound and the other ritual buildings, Smith speculated that the ancient city planner or architect of Cahokia might have been working with a 16.5-foot module in mind. Distances between objects appeared to Smith to be either the 16.5-foot module or half of it. This became significant to her when she recalled that Precolumbian architecture at twelve Mexican sites, from that of the Olmecs to the Aztecs, was also thought to be based on the 16.5-foot module.

Using her 16.5-foot module, Smith began to experiment with angles and slopes to see if she could estimate the original height and shape of Murdock Mound. Her formula was complicated and based in part on predictions of how the mound might have slumped through the centuries. According to her calculations, the mound had once had two terraces, with the lower platform extending across the west face and a higher platform, which she called the Temple Platform, on the east half of the mound. She suggested that the original height of the mound had been about 33 feet and that the northeast and southeast corners of the mound had been faceted.

Harriet Smith's ideas were provocative, original, and controversial and were rejected by her fellow archaeologists. Most thought her ideas and charts did not make any sense. Nevertheless, believing that her work was truly pioneering, Fowler included her paper in Bulletin 7 of the Illinois Archaeological Survey.[7]

---

7. Smith 1969.

He was sharply criticized for this by other archaeologists, who thought Smith's paper was too speculative to be included in the official publication. Fowler, who was the editor, disagreed, pointing out that her fieldwork and archaeological controls had been excellent. The issue was not whether her theories on measurements were right or wrong but whether she should be recognized for incorporating other methodologies and novel ways of thinking in attacking the problems presented by archaeology.

Harriet Smith never received credit for her pioneering work. As a colleague, Joseph Caldwell, was later to observe about her, "It is all right to be ahead of your time so long as you are not too far ahead." While her associates rejected her theories on measurements and the possible connection with Mexican sites, they did agree that Murdock Mound had been a densely populated, elite residential area through several centuries of occupation and they recognized Smith's discovery of the distinctive round buildings in association with the larger square structures.

Smith's work came to an abrupt end with the Sunday morning bombing of Pearl Harbor, December 7, 1941. The next day the remaining members of her crew put down their shovels and departed—either to military recruiters' offices or to wartime jobs. Smith's friends drove over the following weekend from Missouri to help her pack up her equipment and the dig was abandoned. Archaeological work was on hold for the duration.

A short time after ending her work at Cahokia, Smith left the Illinois State Museum for a job in the education department of the Field Museum in Chicago. She had time to write her analysis of the structural features, but there had not been enough time for her to do an analysis of the potsherds her crew had collected.

When Fowler arrived at the Illinois State Museum in 1949 he found Smith's potsherds still in the bags where her workers had put them. They had never been analyzed since being dug up. Deuel agreed that something should be done about this and he and Fowler arranged for a student of Preston Holder's at Washington University in St. Louis, a young man named John S. Tarr, to do the analysis. Tarr had grown up in the East St. Louis area and, as a teenager, had been a daily visitor to Smith's dig and had helped her with the photography on the site. Fowler drove to Chicago to collect Smith's notes and took them and the potsherds to Tarr.

For some reason, Tarr never finished the job of analysis and had got the collections mixed up, which greatly upset Smith when she learned about it. Since nothing was happening with the pottery at Washington University, Fowler brought the potsherds back to the Illinois State Museum. Years later, when he was at another institution, Fowler reclaimed Smith's potsherds and assigned some students to try to straighten out the problem. As hard as they tried, from the information they had, the students were unable to tie the potsherds into the specific locations from which they had been excavated. Eventually the students gave up and Fowler once again sent the bags of potsherds back to the Illinois State Museum. After all the traveling of the potsherds it suddenly occurred to Fowler what Tarr's system had been. Tarr had assigned a color to each stratigraphic level of the dig and had painted a little dot of the appropriate color on each potsherd. If Fowler or the students had realized it in time, they could have determined at least the vertical distribution of the materials, if not the horizontal. To this day the ceramics Harriet Smith dug from the Murdock Mound have not been properly analyzed and identified.

Despite her problems with fellow archaeologists, Harriet Smith, through one of her colleagues, has had the last word. When Smith was at the Field Museum she received a grant to conduct summer archaeological field schools for high school students. One of her fellow instructors at the field school was a young woman named Margaret Brown who had earned her Ph.D. in anthropology. Brown was later to become the director of the Cahokia Mounds State Historic Site, and when Murdock Mound was reconstructed, she saw to it that the reconstruction followed the design, with two terraces, that Harriet Smith, in 1941, had determined it once had.

FIVE

The Hopewellian Ceramic Conference and Digging the Modoc Rock Shelter

Melvin Fowler had worked at the Illinois State Museum for two years when Thorne Deuel called a conference, in 1951, to deal with the Hopewellian ceramics in Illinois. Among the people invited was James B. Griffin, one of the leading authorities on ceramics in the United States.[1] Griffin had spent much of his career traveling to archaeological sites and collections, looking at pieces of pottery. He probably knew every potsherd that had been excavated from archaeological sites in eastern North America in the 1930s and 40s. Griffin was short, portly, and bald. He was also extremely bright, with a quick mind that was almost photographic in its ability to remember details. Griffin's outstanding mind and control of details give him a confident, if not cocky, attitude when dealing with his colleagues. As a result of his considerable skills and knowledge, Griffin published many papers on the prehistory of eastern North America.

Griffin grew up in Oak Park, Illinois, and began his academic work at Chicago at about the same time Fay-Cooper Cole was founding the anthropology department. After his falling out with Cole, Griffin went to the University of Michigan, where he set up a ceramics repository, a collection of ceramic types from all over the eastern United States.

Griffin completed his graduate studies at the University of Michigan, writing his dissertation on the ceramics excavated by WPA crews in the Tennessee River area. He later wrote on the Fort Ancient culture of the Ohio River Valley. This monumental volume is still a basic reference in eastern United States archaeology. In later years, when statistics became a major tool for archaeologists, Griffin would point out that he had been called "a master of the statistical technique," by a contemporary reviewer of his book. With a twinkle in his eye he would point to the vast appendices to his volume, which contained nothing

---

1. Green 1997.

more than the numbers of various types of pottery he had observed in different collections.

Fowler had met Griffin while Fowler was a graduate student at Chicago. Griffin had come to participate in a ceramic conference at the university in 1948 and the students had listened in on what was, in essence, a conversation among Griffin and their professors. Griffin was from the old school of archaeologists and had little time for lowly graduate students.

Two weeks before the 1951 ceramic conference was to begin, Griffin came to Springfield to examine the State Museum's potsherd collections and do an analysis of them—sorting them out according to a predetermined classification of categories or types. (The term "type" has a specific meaning in archaeology, referring to abstract, ideal constructs created by archaeologists to make sense of their material. Since archaeologists cannot pore over each of thousands of individual items, they usually create a few carefully chosen typological categories—or types—and divide their artifacts among these.)

Within the profession, an argument was raging as to whether archaeologists were constructing types for their own convenience or whether they were trying to construct models of what the Native Americans may have had in their minds when they made the ceramics in the first place. The majority, represented by Griffin, were of the first school. Typological analysis was primarily for the benefit of the archaeologists.

Deuel assigned Fowler to work with Griffin. For two weeks the men emptied bags of pottery that had come from the field—some of it dating back to finds in the mid-1930s—onto tables and sorted it out. Fowler learned a great deal from Griffin about his system. Griffin would pick up a potsherd, give it a quick glance, and toss it onto a pile. The bases for his sorting were the shape, the decoration, and the kind of clay used to make the potsherd. Surface decorations were lumped into a single type even though they may not have been found on a single complete vessel. Sorting potsherds according to his own system was easy for Griffin. "If you can recognize the different years and models of cars," he said, "you can learn to recognize differences in pottery." For two weeks prior to the conference, Fowler and Griffin stood at the tables, discussing and sorting hundreds of potsherds (fig. 4).

The ceramic conference lasted for three days, with the visiting scholars delivering papers that would later be published by the museum in a report entitled *Hopewellian Communities in Illinois.*[2] Griffin presented the results of his analysis categorizing the ceramics into different types. Fowler, who was considered a mere technical assistant to Griffin, did not present a paper nor did he comment

2. Deuel 1952.

Figure 4. Dr. James B. Griffin (second from left) discusses pottery with Dr. Thorne Deuel (far right) during the 1951 ceramic conference. Listening in are Melvin L. Fowler (left) and Dr. Georg Neumann (center). Used with permission of the Illinois State Museum.

during the discussions following the presentations. However, he was impressed with a paper presented by Richard (Scotty) S. MacNeish about his work at a site in central Illinois.

MacNeish did not sort his potsherds in the typological manner favored by Griffin but instead used a method called *seriation*. Seriation was a method that enabled an archaeologist to monitor artifact changes through time. It was based on the observation that changes in the style or shape of an object begin gradually and then increase as the change becomes popular with more and more people. Eventually, after the popularity of the new style peaks, the use of it will drop off until it disappears entirely from the archaeological record. When this distribution of ceramics is drawn on a graph, the shape often looks like the outline of a battleship. MacNeish used bar graphs to illustrate his innovative method. MacNeish's paper generated a great deal of argument at the conference. Griffin vociferously opposed it and when the book from the conference was published, MacNeish's paper did not appear.

When the conference was over, Fowler began thinking about MacNeish's ideas. While in graduate school at Chicago he had heard a lecture on seriation from Dr. Kenneth Orr, who had suggested this method as a way to deal with the possibilities of ceramic variation. Orr had also lectured about modal analysis, developed by Professor Irving Rouse of Yale University, and seriation as applied by James Ford to ceramic studies in the lower Mississippi Valley and northern South America. Fowler decided to apply the seriation approach, which separated decorative techniques from other categories, to the ceramics he and Griffin had just analyzed. He went into the laboratory, opened all the bags of potsherds, examined each one from his new perspective, and recounted them all, describing and seriating the ware groups and attributes using MacNeish's method rather than Griffin's typology. Then he wrote a paper explaining his analysis and illustrated his findings with bar graphs. When it was finished he gave a copy to Thorne Deuel. Deuel would have nothing to do with it. "This conflicts with Griffin's paper," he said.

Fowler then sent a copy to Griffin, expecting to receive an objective critique of his work and perhaps some suggestions for improvement. Instead he received a tirade by return mail. Griffin was incensed that an alternative or a modification of his analysis was being proposed. Fowler should not have been surprised. Many archaeologists, including Griffin, jealously guarded their methodologies and were quick to attack anyone who challenged them. During Fowler's years at the Illinois State Museum he had attended archaeology conferences and had observed that Griffin made a practice of sitting in the front row and uttering critical comments, *sotto voce,* out of the side of his mouth during the presentation of papers.

Griffin was both feared and respected by younger archaeologists, who, irreverently but with admiration for his acumen, referred to him as "The Pope." Griffin understood this reference. He often recounted a story about the time he had spent in Mexico working on Mesoamerican ceramics with Mexican colleagues. When the final report was published, Griffin's name as coauthor was listed as *Jesus* B. Griffin. Whether it was done in jest or was a simple mistake, he never said.

Occasionally, young students would travel to the University of Michigan to talk with Griffin. He would attack their ideas, putting them through what Fowler called a "test of fire." If they withstood it, Griffin would work with them and perhaps even visit their archaeological sites. If they did not, he would have little or nothing further to do with them.

Despite this controversial aspect of his personality, Griffin was a compelling individual. At the informal gatherings that formed during conferences, Griffin always had a circle of students and colleagues gathered around him, listening to every word that he said.

Though Fowler, who was soft spoken and good humored, knew Griffin's reputation for making caustic comments and had observed him acting in destructive ways, he was unprepared for the fury with which Griffin responded when his work was challenged. Refusing to be daunted by Griffin's attack, Fowler submitted his paper to *American Antiquity*, the journal of the Society for American Archaeology, where it was published as a lead article.[3] Despite Griffin's criticism, Fowler would come to use general artifact categories and attribute analysis rather than types, along with seriating materials from stratified contexts, as an integral part of his approach to analyzing archaeological remains.

From June through August each year the Illinois State Museum conducted archaeological research, which meant that every summer Fowler was away from his family directing fieldwork at different locations in the state. Field projects were planned on the basis of tips Deuel received from his strong collector network. The targeted sites were investigated through the use of summer "field schools" sponsored jointly by the museum and the University of Chicago. The field schools, with students from Chicago and other universities attending, were directed by Fowler.

In 1952, while supervising a field school at Kaskaskia Indian Village in Illinois, Fowler investigated the Modoc Rock Shelter, a site located beneath a sandstone overhang on the Mississippi River bluff at the southern edge of the American Bottom, near Barbeau Creek in Randolph County, Illinois. Among his crew were Stuart Struever, who had received his undergraduate degree in English from Dartmouth; Howard Winters, a graduate student in anthropology at Chicago; and Dan Morse, a young man who had just graduated from high school but who had excavated skeletons with his father from a mound first dug by Titterington.[4]

As happens so often in research, Fowler discovered the Modoc site almost by accident. Irvin Peithman, an amateur archaeologist who was among Thorne Deuel's network of informants, pointed out to Fowler a place under the bluff where the highway department had removed about 10 feet of dirt to use in rebuilding the highway.[5] When Fowler looked under the rock overhang he could see the remains of fire pits in the walls of the earthen banks left by the highway crew. That season, whenever it was raining and his crew could not work out in the open at the Kaskaskia site, Fowler took them under the rock overhang where they dug a few test pits, expecting to reach the bottom of the site very soon. The season ended before the bottom of the Modoc Rock Shelter could be reached.

The following spring, in 1953, Deuel summoned Fowler to his office. "I have arranged with the University of Chicago for Howard Winters to go back to the Modoc Rock Shelter this summer and do some digging," he told the surprised Fowler. Winters had been one of Fowler's student workers for two years.

---

3. Fowler 1952.
4. Titterington 1935, 1942.
5. Fowler 1959a, 1959b; Fowler et al. 1956.

Fowler protested. "That is a project I started and I want to do that."

"Oh, you will still be in charge," Deuel explained. "Howard will just be running the fieldwork." By being "in charge" Deuel meant that, since Howard did not drive, Fowler would have to transport all of the heavy equipment from Chicago for him, help him get set up, and then visit him regularly to see what else he needed. There was no possible appeal, or even discussion, of Deuel's decision. Fowler helped Winters (whom he personally liked) set up at the rock shelter site and worked with him through the summer.

Fowler faced one perplexing problem during his work at Modoc. Before he began work, he obtained permission to test the site from the landowner of record, who lived on top of the bluff and, according to the English common-law system, owned the land from his boundaries to the center of the earth. However, the owner of the land on the floodplain below was relying on the French land-ownership system, which said he owned the land to the edge of the valley, which included the shelter under the overhanging bluff. The dispute among the landowners and the Illinois State Museum went on for years and became so bitter that, for a time, Fowler was refused permission to set foot on the site where he was directing excavations.

When Winters arrived that summer, he dug and dug. Almost single-handedly he made a five-by-ten-foot excavation, digging down very carefully in six-inch and sometimes three-inch layers and recording and bagging everything he found. He went down 18 feet before he hit what appeared to be sterile soil. Adding in the 10 feet previously excavated by the highway department, Winters and Fowler found that the Modoc Rock Shelter was 28 feet deep, with each layer showing signs of human occupation.

Willard Libby, the developer of radiocarbon dating, was at the University of Chicago and he sent a specialist, Dr. Fred Matson,[6] of Pennsylvania State University, to collect samples from the Modoc Rock Shelter to run through the radiocarbon dating process in one of the early tests of Libby's system. When the results came back, they were a shocker. Radiocarbon dating indicated the site had been inhabited as far back as 7000 B.C.

The radiocarbon dates from the Modoc Rock Shelter challenged all of the current archaeological thinking. The whole chronology of eastern United States archaeology was believed to be very short. Everyone in archaeology at that time assumed that the Archaic period went back to 2000 B.C. at the earliest. If Winters and Fowler were correct, they had come up with an astounding revelation. They wrote a paper about their work and had it published.[7] Shortly thereafter Griffin wrote a review of it.

6. Matson 1955.
7. Fowler et al. 1956.

The review was scathing. Despite the radiocarbon dating and the careful work Winters and Fowler had done, Griffin did not believe the Modoc site could have been inhabited 9000 years ago. How could these two young archaeologists have discovered evidence that contradicted the conclusions of the most eminent scholars in the field, including Griffin himself? Griffin had consulted a geologist friend who told him the Modoc Rock Shelter would have been under water during the Archaic time period. (Fowler and Winters had also checked their data with a geologist, Morris Leighton, before publishing their paper.)

In an advance copy of his review Griffin wrote that the people who had lived at the Modoc Rock Shelter "must not have been mere-men but must have been mermaids," claiming that "the bottom level of the shelter was under 28 feet of water at 8700 B.C."[8] It was a silly way to write a review. The offensive phrase was removed before publication of the piece. Though angered and perplexed by Griffin's response, Fowler continued to excavate at the Modoc Rock Shelter and wrote up more detailed reports on the environment, settlement, and subsistence changes from early through late Archaic times in Illinois. As a result of his work, the Modoc Rock Shelter was recognized as a nationally important site in the American Bottom and was purchased by the State of Illinois and designated a National Historic Landmark. Griffin, however, never changed his mind. A decade later he wrote in an article, "There is the Modoc Rock Shelter but we don't really know what happened there."[9] Other reviewers were more accepting of the early Modoc finds.[10]

----

8. Griffin 1957.
9. Griffin 1978:225. Despite Griffin's skepticism, evidence from the Modoc Rock Shelter about human adaptations and paleoenvironmental change during the Archaic period in the American Midwest would not go away. Thirty years later, Fowler, under the sponsorship of the Illinois State Museum, the National Science Foundation, the National Endowment for the Humanities, and the University of Wisconsin, Milwaukee, returned to re-excavate at Modoc. That research, done under the field and laboratory direction of Steve Ahler, a UWM Ph.D student, and Dr. Bonnie Stiles at the Illinois State Museum, confirmed and greatly expanded the earlier conclusions. In the summer of 1980 the deep excavation areas from the 1953 and 1956 seasons were reopened and a working field conference was held at Modoc, which drew more than 100 visiting archaeologists from all over the United States.
10. Mayer-Oakes 1960; Williams 1958.

SIX

Chaos and Confusion at Cahokia

While Deuel and McGregor chased after tips sent in via their collector networks, the largest archaeological site in the entire United States and Canada was essentially ignored. The university archaeology departments of the Midwest tried to pretend that Cahokia wasn't there. One of the problems may have been the size of Cahokia. An archaeology department or a museum could cope with a single burial, or a rock shelter, or even a village site. But how could it approach a site that covered more than six square miles? University departmental and museum budgets could support the digging of a trench or two but full-scale investigation of a site the size of Cahokia staggered the imagination and, as a practical consideration, was beyond reach.

Though the Illinois Archaeological Survey had been formed by the mid-1950s, it had not yet taken action at Cahokia. Even the small portion of the site that had been purchased by the state was not protected from unauthorized digging. The remainder of the site, available for commercial and industrial development, was subjected to a confused series of excavations and bulldozing. Frustration over the state's inability to do anything and regret over lost opportunities hung like a cold fog over Cahokia until it was eventually dispelled in the 1960s by the juggernaut of the federal highway program. In the meantime, Cahokia struggled to survive the 1950s.

Each decade had seen a little more investigation carried out at Cahokia. Kelly, Deuel, and Stirling had worked at the Powell Mound in the 1930s. Harriet Smith had excavated the Murdock Mound in the 1940s. The 1950s, however, was a discouraging decade at Cahokia. The site was looted, concerned amateurs and professionals tried to do salvage archaeology on their own on weekends, retail stores were built over mounds despite anguished protests from archaeologists, and the meager research that was done was underfunded.

The academic institution geographically closest to Cahokia was Washington University in St. Louis, Missouri. In 1952 the university had hired Preston Holder, an archaeologist from the University of Buffalo in New York, to teach in its Department of Sociology and Anthropology.

Holder was an iconoclast—a former telephone lineman, a chain smoker and tobacco chewer (he died of lung cancer), and a breaker of conventions in both his personal and professional life. As a naval officer in the Pacific during the Second World War, he had encouraged Pacific Islanders to reactivate their head-hunting activities and practice them on the Japanese. A small man physically, Holder wore a ponytail and owned a single tweed suit. He was a forceful personality who, though he antagonized many of his colleagues, nevertheless did careful archaeological work.

Most of Holder's work at Cahokia was what he called "crash-program salvage work." Washington University, like most of the academic community, had little interest in the Cahokia Mounds as its attention was focused on classical archaeology in the Mediterranean. When an Illinois farmer's plow turned up a burial, the farmer would call Washington University and Holder would go out on weekends with a girl friend to investigate.

As Holder wrote in a letter to Fowler:

> *All* of the work which I did was of an urgent, salvage nature and was not part of any archaeological "program." It was all done on request. The rest of the profession seemed to be sitting around and letting the stuff go down the tube. So as long as I had the expertise and was on hand I felt some moral obligation to get what could be got, which turned out to be considerable. The work was done during spare time and on regular vacation from my teaching task at Washington University. I received no remuneration for the work and much of the necessary labor was volunteered.

On one occasion Holder recruited two Catholic nuns and their students from a nearby girls' school to excavate a human burial. Among the sites that he investigated at or near Cahokia were a burial near some radio towers at Horseshoe Lake, mounds number 10 and 11 of the Kunnemann Tract—a group of mounds a little more than a mile north of Monks Mound—and a junkyard that later became the location of the Indian Mounds Motel.

When he arrived at the Indian Mounds Motel site, southwest of Powell Mound on the south side of Collinsville Road, Holder found that most of the mound had already been destroyed by a bulldozer in site preparation activities.[1]

---

1. Holder's work was never published due to a variety of circumstances. A summary of Holder's discoveries at the Indian Mounds motel site is included in an article by George Milner (Milner 1984d).

The mound remnant, consisting of at least three building stages of Mississippian affiliation, with an underlying Woodland occupation, had been badly disturbed over the years. In its passages over the site the bulldozer had unearthed a burial with many shell beads and conch shells.

When he investigated, Holder found the complex to be a single interment of at least 175 individuals. Some were secondary bundle burials but others were primary burials placed carefully on the flank of the initial mound just prior to the building of the next stage. Some of the burials had mutilated teeth—the upper incisors having been notched along the biting edge. Nelson Reed, a young volunteer who was working with Holder, examined the skeleton of a woman bearing an unborn child. In her ear she wore a bone ear plug with copper wire coiled around it. Holder interpreted the burials as dedicatory offerings to the "new" mound that had been built above them.

Holder excavated what was called the Kunnemann Mound after he heard rumors that the mound was about to be leveled for use in the construction of a bridge where Sand Prairie Creek crosses Cahokia Canal. For this project Holder got a grant of $2,000 from the American Philosophical Society and some assistance from Washington University.[2] With a few students and volunteers, Holder spent the seasons of 1955 and 1956 working at the Kunnemann Mounds 10 and 11, as they were designated on the Patrick map, which were actually one mound. The six mounds of the Kunnemann group, which marks the northern boundary of the Cahokia site, are aligned on an east-west line along a ridge that is all that remains of an ancient oxbow of the Mississippi River.

Holder was not the first to examine the flat-topped Kunnemann Mound—the largest mound of the group of six. Warren King Moorehead had dug there in the 1920s, and before him, in 1904 and 1905, a St. Louis antiquarian group called the Knockers had excavated at the Kunnemann site. The Kunnemann Mound was one of those examined by Morris Leighton in his work with Moorehead. The mound had suffered insults over the years from farmers excavating dirt to fill low places in their fields. By 1955, when Holder began his work, the mound measured approximately 408 feet east to west by 246 feet north to south, about half of its original size, and its estimated prehistoric height of 36 feet was down to about 23 feet.

Holder had his own ideas about what he was looking for and how excavations should be carried out. He had little interest in digging five-by-five-foot test pits, what he called "the telephone-booth-excavation mentality." He insisted that, to reconstruct the way of life of the indigenous peoples of the Mississippi

---

2. For a excellent summary of Holder's work at the Kunnemann Mound see the analysis by Timothy Pauketat (Pauketat 1993).

valley, he needed a wealth of knowledge regarding settlement patterns, status relations, technological traditions, and patterns of labor expenditure.

To learn this, he believed that he had to excavate large areas. Frustrated at working with hand tools through a rainy spring in search of a "status burial" that he believed had to be there, Holder removed the plow zone, the area that had been disturbed by local farmers, and cleaned out Moorehead's excavation on the west edge of the big mound.

He had uncovered only a portion of the top of the mound when he saw evidence of a great many structures. The flat top of the mound had once supported an array of buildings—temples, residences, store houses, and sweat lodges—presumably for the use of the chiefs and priests. There was historic precedent for what he was looking at. Garcilasco de la Vega, the chronicler of the travels of De Soto, had written of the Indians of Florida, "[O]n the top of these [platform mounds] they construct flat surfaces which are capable of holding the ten, twelve, fifteen or twenty dwellings of the lord and his family and the people of his service."[3]

Among Holder's findings was evidence that the Kunnemann Tract had been a major manufacturing center for shell, bone, and sandstone beads; carved walnut; and implements of granite and flint. Holder unearthed bone awls and hundreds of shell fragments. It appeared to him that at least four kinds of mollusk-shell beads and pendant forms had been manufactured at this one site. Earlier relic hunters at Kunnemann had reported finding 1,197 flint implements, 52 pearls, and 100 celts in various stages of manufacture. Celts are highly polished oblong axes of gray or black igneous rock, such as granite, with rounded ends. One was found that weighed 25 pounds.[4]

Much of the material was recovered within and near a large Mississippian house, evidence that the inhabitant of the house was a craft specialist. The house was standing at the same time that the Kunnemann Mound was begun and it had an unusual L-shaped extension with a central hearth that had been cleaned out and relined several times. After a period of time the residence had been burned, the house basin filled in, and a new structure built in its place. Again, this evidence reflected the historical record. The first Europeans to visit the southeastern Indians reported that when a chief or other important man died, his house and all of his possessions were burned and a new house for his successor was built in the same location.

While Holder was digging on the Kunnemann Mound, Fowler had been at work on the Modoc Rock Shelter. The two men had met at a spring meeting of

3. De la Vega 1962:265.
4. Mason and Perino 1961; Holley, 1990.

the Society of American Archaeologists where Fowler had introduced his assistant, Dick Kesslin, to Holder and arranged to bring the students working with him at Modoc to Holder's excavation for a professional site visit. Fowler often took his field school students to other sites to enlarge their experience.

When the group arrived at Cahokia, Holder greeted Fowler warmly. "Hi, Mike," he said. "Glad to see you." Kesslin, who had met Holder at the conference, stepped forward and held out his hand. "I'm Dick Kesslin," he said. "We met before."

Holder ignored the outstretched hand. "Goddamn, I don't have time for any graduate students," he exclaimed, turning away from Kesslin. The crusty Holder, like James Griffin, was from the old school of archaeologists. Throughout their visit, the only person Holder would speak to was Fowler.

It was the equally testy Griffin, who had known Moorehead, who secured the first grant to do archaeological research at Cahokia. The grant Griffin received came from the Viking Fund—in later years known as the Wenner-Gren Foundation.[5]

In the summer of 1956 Fowler and Thorne Deuel drove down to St. Louis to visit Griffin's project. Griffin was working on Mound 34 to the east of Monks Mound and was also testing at other places on the Cahokia site and at the Pulcher site to the south. Griffin was not a fieldworker. He spent most of his time classifying potsherds in his laboratory, set up in the basement of the Old Federal Building near what later became the site of the St. Louis arch designed by Eero Saarinen. To do the fieldwork Griffin had brought in Al Spaulding, who was an excellent surveyor, statistician, and archaeological fieldworker. Spaulding supervised the fieldwork and made the maps while Griffin studied the ceramics.

Every day Griffin waited eagerly in his laboratory to see what pottery pieces came in from the field so he could put them in order and classify them. The two-phase system, Old Village and Bean Pot or Trappist, was still in use but Griffin was seeing more complexity that, he began to think, might warrant the addition of a third classification.

Among the areas Griffin and Spaulding tested was the Pulcher site. Griffin noted some distinct differences between the pottery from Cahokia and that from Pulcher. The Pulcher pottery was tempered with crushed limestone instead of the crushed clamshells used in the Cahokia pottery. The limestone-tempered pottery was often covered with a red slip, similar in type to what Griffin had earlier named "Monks Mound Red." It was the only non-shell-tempered pottery listed in his earlier papers on Cahokia ceramics. Griffin also began to notice sherds that were tempered with crushed pieces of pottery, called grog. These were similar in

---

5. Griffin and Spaulding 1951.

form to the "Bluff" pottery that had been found earlier by Titterington in Jersey County, Illinois, where he defined a pre-Cahokian culture he had named "Jersey Bluff" or "Bluff" culture. This similarity raised the idea in Griffin's mind that there may have been a pre–Old Village phase at Cahokia and made him doubt more and more the usefulness of the simple two-part division.

At the end of the year the Viking Fund grant expired. Griffin and Spaulding applied for funds to support a second year of work but were turned down. Unfortunately, very little in the way of publications came out of this effort, though Fowler, editor of the *Journal of Illinois Archaeology,* published one article on their work. Many years later Griffin published an article pertaining to this work in *American Antiquity* but a full analysis of these materials has never been made.[6]

Griffin's crew also excavated on sites in Saint Charles, Missouri, which were scheduled to be destroyed by the building of Interstate 70. The fieldworkers found ample evidence of Mississippian occupation but they were digging in the traditional five-foot-square method. After the crews left, Holder moved in with a big earth-moving machine and cleared off a large area to get the big picture. He uncovered several house basins and storage pits and learned much more about the site than had Griffin's crew. That too has never been published.

In 1948 Walter W. Taylor, an archaeologist with a freshly minted Ph.D. from Harvard University, had published a book called *A Study of Archaeology.* The book was a frontal attack on the elders of American archaeology and it caused a sensation in the field. Taylor assaulted every archaeologist of any repute at the time. His basic point was that renowned archaeologists, such as A. V. Kidder of Mayan fame, had been looking at monumental structures and not paying enough attention to the way the ordinary people lived. Instead of studying temples, glyphs, and fancy potsherds they should have been looking at the minutiae of a settlement to see what the people ate and wore and how they lived. Only by studying the garbage dumps, he was saying, could an ethnography of ancient people be constructed. He called his new orientation to archaeology the *conjunctive approach,* by which he meant to emphasize the interconnection of archaeological objects with their cultural contexts.

Taylor had some good ideas, ideas that have since been accepted by the profession, but in presenting them he attacked honorable people who had been working within the constraints of their times. It was true that Kidder emphasized monuments over village life but those were the kinds of projects favored by the Carnegie Foundation and the National Geographic Society, institutions that provided his financing.

---

6. Griffin 1977.

Archaeologists hated Taylor's book but they all read it. One of the people Taylor mercilessly attacked for his limited outlook was James Griffin, who immediately became Taylor's bitter intellectual enemy and a foe of the conjunctive method. Griffin acidly referred to Taylor's approach as "conjunctivitis." On one of Griffin's visits to Springfield, Thorne Deuel invited him, Fowler, and J. Charles Kelley from Southern Illinois University to Deuel's home one evening to discuss Griffin's Cahokia project. Kelley was a Harvard graduate, a contemporary of Walter Taylor, and knew the ideas behind the conjunctive method very well. He was also aware of the attack Taylor had made on the irascible Griffin. Late in the evening, when the men were sitting in Deuel's den, Kelley leaned over to Griffin, slapped his knee and asked, "Well, Jimmy. Are you going to apply the conjunctive method at Cahokia?"

There was a long silence. Griffin visibly struggled for control and Fowler wondered if he was about to witness the verbal tearing apart of Kelley. Then Griffin leaned back in his chair and growled, "I am going to do good archaeology," and let the moment pass.

While James Griffin was doing good archaeology at Cahokia in the 1950s, others were doing more problematic archaeology on their own or for collectors. One of these amateur archaeologists was Gregory Perino, from Belleville, Illinois.[7] Perino was a first-generation American of Italian descent who developed a keen interest in archaeology. Though he had no formal training in archaeology, he learned from observing other people's work, and, over time, became a proficient field technician.

Exceptionally skilled with his hands, Perino was a fine cabinetmaker and craftsman and could operate many kinds of machinery with ease and precision. He was part of Thorne Deuel's network of amateur archaeologists and, on his own, had learned the archaeology of the American Bottom exceedingly well. He had a good grasp of artifact types and their relationships to each other.

Gregory Perino had grown up in the American Bottom area and had been interested in the remains and artifacts of the Native Americans all of his life. A boyhood friend recalled how Perino would show up for school in the morning for the roll call and, after he had been recorded present, would skip school and hop a freight train to an area where he knew Precolumbian materials could be found. He would dig most of the day, uncovering bones and artifacts, before hopping another freight train back to his school in time for the end-of-the-day roll call. Perino's talents were just what Thomas Gilcrease, a wealthy oil man and collector from Tulsa, Oklahoma, was looking for.[8]

---

7. Perino 1947, 1957, 1959, 1968, 1971a, 1971b, 1971c.
8. Thomas Gilcrease Institute of American History and Art 1984; Morand 1990.

Gilcrease was a Native American. Born in 1890 in Louisiana, he grew up in nearby Indian Territory where, in 1899, each member of his family was given an allotment of 160 acres of land in the Creek Nation. The land Thomas received lay near the center of what was to become a major oil-producing field southwest of the present city of Tulsa. Gilcrease used his early oil earnings to educate himself and later amassed a fortune trading oil leases and drilling for oil in Oklahoma and Texas.

Gilcrease was proud of his Native American heritage (he was one-sixteenth Creek) and to reflect that he began collecting art that dealt with the West. Within the amazingly short span of two decades, during the 1940s and 50s, he amassed what is generally recognized as the largest and most varied collection anywhere of North American Indian and Western art and artifacts, consisting of 8,000 artworks, 41,000 Indian artifacts, and 81,000 archival and library items. Gilcrease was an energetic collector who bought everything he could find relating to the West and to American Indians. He did not buy individual pieces; he bought whole collections. A dealer remembered this conversation with Gilcrease.

The dealer: "Here is the entire list of the Moran estate collection."

Gilcrease: "Hmmm. Let's see. One hundred, two hundred, three hundred, four hundred items. I'll buy them all. I have to go now." And he left.

In May 1949 in Tulsa, Gilcrease opened the Thomas Gilcrease Institute of American History and Art, a museum based on the collecting activity of one man, where his collections are housed. Several years later, showing remarkable civic foresight, the citizens of Tulsa taxed themselves to acquire most of the collections and keep them in their city. Gilcrease bequeathed the remainder of his collections to the city and made arrangements for income from his properties to be used to maintain the museum after his death, which occurred in 1962.

To acquire his thousands of Indian artifacts Gilcrease bought collections from individuals who had looted mounds. Though Gilcrease may have been unaware of the effect of his collecting activities, from an archaeologist's perspective he was the worst kind of collector and antiquarian because his activities encouraged the destruction of Indian mounds. When word got around that Gilcrease was paying substantial sums of money for Indian relics, people also began manufacturing them and, before long, Gilcrease found that he was getting fakes in his collection.

Gilcrease solved the problem of fake artifacts by sponsoring digs of his own. If he could get his own artifacts out of mounds, he would know they were authentic. But he needed someone with a knowledge of archaeology to do his digging for him. When he made inquiries around the state of Illinois for the name of a good field archaeologist, Fowler was recommended to him. Melvin was astounded, one day at the Illinois State Museum, to receive a job offer from

Gilcrease that would pay him a higher salary than he was getting at the museum to do a form of archaeology that Fowler considered to be little more than the looting of mounds. Though Fowler had a growing family and thus a constant need for money, he turned down the offer.

Though an unselfish and honest man, Gregory Perino did not have the professional scruples that Fowler's academic training had given him, and Perino accepted Gilcrease's offer, going to work in that gray area between the collector's arena and the professional world. Perino knew in general how archaeologists excavated and he understood the soils and internal construction of mounds. When he excavated a site, he knew how to draw profiles. He was also skilled in the use of heavy equipment such as bulldozers. Perino's skills gained him a grudging acceptance from academics and when Perino needed a fieldworker, James Griffin recommend Dan Morse, who had worked for Fowler at the Modoc Rock Shelter and was now an undergraduate student in anthropology at the University of Michigan.

Perino was excavating a site called the Bedford Mound, in the lower Illinois River Valley. Gilcrease and Griffin had urged Perino to hire Morse to take notes, photograph the excavations, and, incidentally, help ensure a more scientific dig. Perino soon encountered a burial in the mound and, as was his habit, simply troweled the dirt away. Morse, though only an undergraduate, had learned field techniques from Fowler and he was appalled by Perino's crude methods and lack of controls. Morse remembers becoming angry at Perino and vowing that if they found another burial and it was treated in the same manner, he would quit. Perino observed Morse's distress and when another burial was discovered he allowed Morse to excavate it in a proper manner by himself. Perino was impressed with his young employee's work and soon put him in charge of all the burial excavations.

Even so, they had to make compromises. On one occasion the two men were working together on an impressive burial that contained silver earspools and a necklace of grizzly bear teeth. Because they were running out of time Perino worked on one side of the burial, exposing the bones and burial goods, while Morse worked on the other. When they were finished, Morse's side of the burial was completely exposed so the features could be photographed, while Perino's, in Morse's words, "looked like a pile of dirt." To Perino's credit, he recognized the differences in their work and vowed to improve his technique. Within a short time he could clean up a burial as well as his student worker Morse could.

Though Perino had learned the accepted methods and standards of excavation, since he was working for Gilcrease he could not take the time required to excavate a mound carefully by hand, starting from the outside, slowly working in, keeping careful vertical controls, and writing up everything he found.

Like many contract archaeologists today, he had the attitude that he worked for a client. Perino did what Gilcrease wanted, which was to produce artifacts as quickly as possible for his employer. To do that Perino convinced Gilcrease to buy him a bulldozer. With the bulldozer Perino could slice a mound in half and get the profile. Once he reached the base of the mound he would give his workers shovels to dig through the dirt and look for burials and pots.

Perino's method was successful in that he uncovered a quantity of grave goods and other artifacts. When Griffin failed to get his Viking Fund grant renewed for a second year and left Cahokia, Perino moved his bulldozer onto Griffin's Mound 34 site and cut into the same mound that Griffin and Spaulding had spent weeks carefully sectioning with their trenches. Where Griffin and Spaulding, with their painstaking excavation, had gotten only small potsherds and tiny fragments of artifacts, Perino, with his bulldozer, pulled out whole pots from the center of the mound. There was no one to stop him. The land on which Perino was excavating was private property, the piece of land known as the Ramey Tract, to the east of Monks Mound. Although the State of Illinois had bought a portion of the tract in 1925, it had not yet gotten around to purchasing the remainder.

When Fowler learned of Perino's activities he went to visit him at Cahokia. Perino had been digging in the Ramey field area as well as conducting a minor examination of an area of erosion on the southwest corner of the first terrace of Monks Mound, and he was happy to show Fowler the pottery he had found. One pot looked to Fowler very much like a pot illustrated in the Bodmer sketch, made when the artist was looking at Monks Mound from the east. In the foreground of the Bodmer drawing is a little mound with some pots sitting on it. The mound that Perino had excavated was not the mound Bodmer drew in his sketch but one very close to it. Perino also showed Fowler some unusual black-and-white pottery that had come from his Cahokia excavation. It seemed to Fowler that this was more like pottery found in the Southwest than pots he had seen from Cahokia. Fowler took pictures of the pots and showed them to colleagues working in the Southwest but no one could positively identify them. So where had they come from? No detailed analysis of the pots dug by Perino has ever been done.

While excavating at the edge of Monks Mound, Perino found some charcoal. He gave it to Morse, who was working for him during the summer, with the request that when he went back to school at the University of Michigan, he give it to Griffin and have it dated. Morse did so and the test resulted in the first radiocarbon date (C^{14}) to be made on Monks Mound.

At the University of Michigan, Morse studied lithic (rock) technology and, while looking over the Cahokia material Preston Holder had donated, thought he recognized some blade cores. Blade cores are the residual portion of a nodule of chert, a kind of flint, after blades have been removed by the artisan. Blades are a special form of rectangular chert flakes with parallel sides. The original piece of stone required special preparation before blades could be recovered from it. Once formed, the blades were used for the manufacture of specialized cutting tools, one of which was a microdrill. It is believed that microdrills were used to perforate shell beads.

Morse surmised that the blades must have been made into something and he contacted Perino to get his opinion. Perino replied that he did not know anything about cores or blades but he knew where there were microdrills at Cahokia. Morse arranged to meet Perino at the Cahokia site where the microdrills had been found. When they arrived at Perino's location, to Morse's astonishment, he found that he was looking over a sea of cores, blades, and microdrills. In a paper written by Perino and Ron Mason, one of Morse's classmates, this microblade industry and the possibility of a specialized shell-working area at Cahokia were first defined.

After excavating at Cahokia, Perino moved his operations into eastern Arkansas and excavated mounds there, continuing, on a fixed salary, with the Gilcrease museum as a curator of the archaeological collections. Fowler visited him in Tulsa and admired his truly impressive collection of Mississippian materials. Perino was forthcoming and lent Fowler slides of all of the artifacts he and Gilcrease had collected from Cahokia. Fowler made copies of the slides and placed them on file at the Cahokia Mounds State Park headquarters building.

Unfortunately the copies of Perino's field notes have been lost and Perino destroyed the originals after writing up his reports. Even many of his Illinois manuscripts and illustrations have disappeared as they were left in the care of professionals who evidently thought other copies were available.

Perino worked with Titterington, Griffin, and Spaulding at Cahokia at a time when most professionals in Illinois ignored the site because of its complexity. He was among the early people to recognize the archaeological deposits at Cahokia and the potential that was there for major work. Perino was also familiar with Titterington's earlier work on "Bluff" culture in Jersey County. Perino recognized a similar group of ceramics in the American Bottom. In his discussions with Griffin and others, Perino proposed that the Bluff culture could have been contemporary with early Cahokia, or might even represent a stage that preceded Cahokia and Old Village. Perino was the first to use the term "Bottom Bluff" to describe this early Cahokia culture.

In his relic-hunting activities Perino would have been right at home with Moorehead, but as the field became professionalized he was left more and more on the periphery. Professionals, such as Fowler, though they recognized Perino's skills, were dubious about his activities. Nevertheless they tried to maintain skeptical but friendly contacts as people like Perino knew the local territory and artifacts better than many a theoretically trained professional and could be invaluable partners in archaeological research.

The 1950s were turbulent not only for people who worked around Cahokia, but also for Fowler. He had spent six years at the Illinois State Museum and he wondered if he was getting anywhere. One spring night he lay awake in a hotel room in the small Illinois town of Harrisburg, distracted by thoughts of his career. He was in Harrisburg to supervise the excavation of a burial mound in southern Illinois near the town of Cave-in-Rock on the Ohio River. There had not been enough time during the previous summer to complete work on the burial mound and Deuel had sent Fowler back in March with a local crew to finish it.

Fowler stared at the ceiling in the middle of the night, thinking that he had to make a change. This was no way for him and his family to live. He got out of bed and wrote a letter to Deuel asking for a sabbatical leave so he could go back to school and get his Ph.D. Despite the "terminal" on his diploma from the University of Chicago, Fowler had always intended to go back. Deuel responded that the museum did not have a sabbatical program but that he would discuss Fowler's request with the museum's board of directors.

The president of the museum board was Professor Sol Tax, from whom Fowler had taken courses at the University of Chicago. Tax urged Deuel to allow the sabbatical leave. The arrangement Deuel worked out was a novel one. He would allow Fowler to live in Chicago for a total of six months. If he could fit his Ph.D. classwork into six months of time, that would be acceptable to the museum. It happened that the University of Chicago was on a quarter system in which students went to classes for eight weeks and then were given four weeks off to write their papers. Fowler could spend eight weeks in Chicago attending classes and then return to Springfield to write his papers and work for the museum. The six months of research leave was enough to cover all of his classroom time. His thesis topic was the Modoc Rock Shelter, which his museum job required that he write up anyway. His museum work and his Ph.D. studies meshed perfectly. Fowler had to retake all the exams he had done so poorly on eight years before. This time he was the highest scorer of all the Ph.D. candidates taking the examinations. Professor Tax sent him a note of congratulations (which Fowler still has) and he was awarded his Ph.D. degree from the University of Chicago in 1959.

During one of the four-week periods when Fowler was in Springfield between class sessions at Chicago, Thorne Deuel came into his office and sat on the corner of his desk. Deuel had the habit of going into the office of one or another of his staff at a quarter to five in the afternoon and, sitting on the corner of the desk, he would make conversation until five. Then he would leave. He knew that staff members tried to leave a few minutes before five to catch the elevator down to the parking lot.

Deuel settled himself and said, "You know, Fowler, you need help. You need an assistant and I think we should hire one for you."

"Fine," said Fowler. "This young man, Dick Kesslin, who is working as my field assistant at Modoc, is pretty good." "All right," replied Deuel, who, seeing it was now five o'clock, got up from the desk. "We'll think about making him an offer."

When Fowler left for his next eight weeks of classes at Chicago, Deuel hired Joseph Caldwell,[9] without discussing it with Fowler. Caldwell was hired not to be Fowler's assistant, which would not have been appropriate, but to be curator of anthropology, the job Fowler held. Fowler was demoted to assistant curator. Caldwell had preceded Fowler by a year in getting his Ph.D. from the University of Chicago. He was ten years older than Fowler and was married to the daughter of A. R. Kelly, the archaeologist who had done the work in the early thirties at the Powell Mound complex at Cahokia. Though Fowler liked Joe Caldwell and worked well with him, he could not understand Deuel's reasoning in hiring him as his supervisor.

The final outrage of the 1950s at Cahokia took place in July 1959. Caldwell received a call from Dr. Paul Titterington that a commercial establishment called "Grandpa's Store" was scheduled to be built directly east of Monks Mound on the site of two sizable mounds. Titterington was trying once again to raise an alarm. Despite all of his efforts, the public was still indifferent to the fact that two ancient Indian mounds, numbers 30 and 31 on the Patrick map, were about to be leveled to make way for a discount store and an asphalt parking lot. What, he asked, could the Illinois State Museum do about it?

On the Patrick map, Mound 30 was shown as a platform mound with the long axis running east and west. It stood about 20 feet high and was 180 feet long. Close to it was Mound 31, a rectangular platform mound 25 feet high and approximately 270 feet long. A former owner had dug a mushroom cellar into the side of the mound and discovered pottery and artifacts. This was probably the same mound where another former owner had dug an ice house and uncovered handsome pottery vessels ornamented with animal-shaped handles. Since the land was not owned by the state of Illinois, the construction could not be stopped.

In response to Titterington's call, Caldwell came down from Springfield and, with the help of a group of local avocational archaeologists, did some test ex-

---

9. Caldwell 1958, 1964.

cavations in Mound 31. From his testing, Caldwell was able to get a stratigraphic sequence of the construction of the mound as well as the occupation beneath it. The mound had been built, as had been many Mississippian mounds, by starting with a small mound and then adding layers or stages of enlargement (fig. 5). Caldwell's excavations showed this mound to be unusual in its large number of building stages—ten in all. Each stage was carefully capped with a special clay mixture to plaster the surface and protect it from erosion.

After Caldwell returned to Springfield, the volunteers continued working and were able to open up an additional area underneath the mound where they found some larger features—very similar to what Harriet Smith had found. It was obvious that this had been another elite residential compound consisting

Figure 5. Three views of the Mound 31 excavation conducted by Joe Caldwell in 1959. Top left: A view of tree-covered Mound 31 from the south. Right: A view of Mound 31 excavation in progress. Joe Berta stands at the upper right. Dark circular marks near the bottom of the photo indicate the locations of house wall-posts. Bottom left: Joe Caldwell points out the earliest construction stage of the mound. Four of the ten mound construction stages are marked in the walls of the excavation. Used with permission of the Illinois State Museum.

of many more stages of occupation than had been found at other archaeological sites at Cahokia. Before they could learn anything further, both mounds were destroyed and the area was paved over with asphalt.

The work of Caldwell and his dedicated crew of volunteer archaeologists confirmed Smith's findings of twenty years before. In both locations residential compounds were found that were later built over by a sequence of platform mounds. These platform mounds were probably the foundations of elite residences. While Caldwell's excavations had revealed an unusually large number of building stages for a single mound, Smith's work had shown more detail about the premound occupation. Smith had had a larger crew of workers and more time to devote to the project. Both of these projects, along with the contributions of Preston Holder, were the beginnings of the understanding of just how complex and sophisticated a community Cahokia must have been.

The wanton destruction of Mounds 30 and 31 shocked and galvanized Caldwell and he began to lobby in Springfield for the state to purchase more acreage around the Cahokia site. He was particularly concerned about the Ramey land where Perino had dug and which lay just east of Monks Mound. Thanks in large part to Caldwell's efforts, an addition of land—the first since Moorehead's time—was made to the Cahokia site. Caldwell stayed at the Illinois State Museum for several years before moving to the University of Georgia, where his father-in-law, A. R. Kelly, had gone after leaving the University of Illinois.

There was one additional outcome from Joe Caldwell's work that was appreciated by the archaeologists. Excavating is thirst-provoking work and at the end of the day Caldwell and his volunteers would repair to the Horseshoe Lounge on Collinsville Road, where they received a friendly reception from the owner, Pearl Stabile. Caldwell spread the word to Fowler that the Horseshoe Lounge was a welcome watering hole for archaeologists.

One of the volunteers who worked with Caldwell was Joe Berta. An avocational archaeologist, Berta had, on his own, rescued a quantity of skeletons from an ossuary that was being demolished on the cliffs above Cahokia. The bluff line is composed of loess deposits, wind-blown dust that formed deep drifts up against the cliffs. This loess soil is light beige in color, very soft and clean, and is useful for landfill. Several companies had heavy equipment up against the bluff, mining this soil. They would dynamite it at the bottom to break it up and then scoop it up, load it into dump trucks, and haul it away.

As they dug into the cliff they moved further and further into the bluff line, which rose higher and higher. At a point east and about midway between Cahokia and the Mitchell site, a collection of mounds seven miles north of Monks Mound, the workers came upon a big ossuary, a pit about four feet deep and twelve feet long stacked full of skeletons. Because the pit was about 75 feet up the face of the cliff and the loess was unstable, there was no easy way to get to it.

Joe Berta heard about the ossuary and talked the machine operator into telling him when the workers were planning to dynamite the cliff wall. When they did, he went there and saw that the burial site had been destroyed and the skeletons had all fallen down the face of the cliff into a heap at the base. When the loaders got a bucketload of bones and dirt, Berta talked them into backing up and shaking it—winnowing it out by bouncing it up and down. Berta ran around picking up bones from the loose dirt on the ground. Then the loaders would go back for more dirt, jiggle it, and let Berta gather up as many bones as he could.

Berta put the skeletons he had recovered in boxes to deliver them to Washington University, where he hoped the anthropology department might find them of interest. Berta owned a black 1949 Packard and he filled his car with boxes of bones. The trunk was full, the back seat was full, the passenger seat—every space was filled with boxes all the way to the ceiling of the car. Then Berta set off for the university. On the way he had a terrible thought. What would he say to the police if he was stopped for a traffic violation? How could he explain having hundreds of human skeletons inside his Packard?

SEVEN

The 1960s Highway Salvage Program Begins

THE federal interstate highway program shifted into high gear at the end of the 1950s. Representatives of the three major partners in the Illinois Archaeological Survey met at the University of Illinois at Urbana-Champaign to divide up the archaeological salvage project among themselves and decide how to proceed. This investigation was going to be a major one—the largest such salvage effort that had ever been attempted in the United States. The great site of Cahokia was to be investigated on a scale that approached its size. None of the three archaeologists involved had ever run a project of this size before.

While the highway department was providing the money for the investigation, it was also putting obstacles in the way of the archaeologists. They were told that they had to work on the contractor's time schedule and had to restrict their work to the highway right-of-way. Where the highway property ended, they had to stop, no matter how significant the material they were uncovering might be. Technically, the crew members doing the archaeological work would be union employees of the contractor, not of the institutions directing their work. Even the land along the right-of-way belonged to the contractor until the work was finished and it was turned over to the highway department. Every detail of the archaeologists' work would have to be negotiated with the highway contractor.

Fowler and McGregor reported back to the Illinois Archaeological Survey that, according to information from the highway department, four areas at or near Cahokia would be affected by the construction of Interstates 55, 70, and 270. One of the affected areas was a tract of about 15 acres, 300 yards directly west of Monks Mound. They named this Tract 15B. A similar plot 700 yards further west they called Tract 15A. On 15B, a country lane, called Sand Prairie Lane, was slated to be transformed by the highway department into an overpass that would carry traffic over I-55 and I-70. An interchange was planned for the site of 15A. There were no mounds on these sites but the archaeologists wanted to see what, if anything, was under the ground before it was graded and paved over with concrete. Preliminary testing had indicated there were signs of habitation in the locations of 15A and 15B.

Area three was the horseradish field near where the destroyed Powell Mound had once stood, a mile west of Monks Mound. The fourth area was the Mitchell site, seven miles north of Monks Mound, which had largely been destroyed by the railroad. Though many of the mounds were gone and others would soon be destroyed, the archaeologists believed there was much to be learned from a study of the land under and around the mounds.

The three archaeologists studied maps and staked out their claims. Fowler wanted the Illinois State Museum to take over the work at the Mitchell site at the northern border of Cahokia, which, he believed, presented some unusual problems and would be totally destroyed when the interstate went through it. Deuel did not agree. He insisted that the museum work on the main Cahokia site. Fowler had no choice but to accept Deuel's dictates and the museum was assigned to excavate tracts 15A and 15B. The University of Illinois took the Powell tract on the far western edge of the site and Southern Illinois University was assigned the Mitchell site. Excavation was set to begin on 15B in the summer of 1960.

Before work could begin, however, Fowler was offered a professorship in anthropology at Southern Illinois University. His change of jobs also changed the area Fowler was supervising at Cahokia. Now Fowler was in charge of the work at Mitchell—a project he had wanted to do all along.

In early 1960, three archaeologists were selected to direct the Cahokia fieldwork for the three principal member institutions of the Illinois Archaeological Survey. Fowler hired Jim Porter, from the University of Wisconsin, Madison, to direct the fieldwork for Southern Illinois University at the Mitchell site. Charles J. Bareis was put in charge of the fieldwork for the University of Illinois, and Deuel hired a young archaeologist named Warren Wittry to take Melvin Fowler's position at the Illinois State Museum and to supervise the museum's work on tracts 15A and 15B at Cahokia.

Warren Wittry had grown up in Green Bay, Wisconsin, and, as an eleven-year-old, had belonged to a Cub Scout pack. A fellow member of the pack was a boy named Bob Hall whose mother was an enrolled member of the Wisconsin Stockbridge band of the Mohican nation. Bob's mother and her family collected Indian relics and one day, for an outing, she took the entire Cub Scout troop out to collect arrowheads. Every youth came home from the field trip that day with a chip of flint or an old piece of bone. Warren and Bob were thrilled to hold in their hands an object that an Indian had held a thousand years before them.

The two boys, Warren Wittry and Bob Hall, became best friends and whenever they had any spare time they would ride their bicycles out into the country to investigate archaeological sites they had learned about. When both were 16 and in high school, they went on a longer expedition. They had heard of a cave, about 12 miles outside of Green Bay, where, three centuries earlier, Indians had taken refuge. They decided to try to find it. Peddling off on their bicycles, they found the cave and discovered that it was still being used by Indians. Digging in the cave, the two boys found an ancient burial as well as more recent artifacts: an old alcohol lamp, a trowel with a soft, rotting wood handle, and a burlap bag.

Back in Green Bay the boys wrote up their discovery. Their paper was read at a junior science conference and eventually was published in the September 1945 issue of the *Wisconsin Archaeologist*. Their careers were set. Both Warren Wittry and Bob Hall determined to become archaeologists. Bob won a Westinghouse Science Talent Search award and on his prize trip to Washington, D.C., he met Dr. Waldo Wedel at the Smithsonian Institution. Wedel was impressed with the fledgling archaeologist and told him that when he was through school and ready for a job, he should give him a call.

Warren and Bob went into the navy together, were discharged at the same time, and entered the University of Wisconsin. When they graduated in anthropology, Bob made his call to Wedel, who hired them both to do river basin surveys in South Dakota for the Smithsonian. Though Bob was cheery and talkative and Warren a man of few words, people thought they were brothers. Both left South Dakota at the same time to return to Wisconsin, where they got their M.A. degrees together doing work on the same cave. Wittry worked as curator of anthropology at the Museum of the State Historical Society of Wisconsin while he earned his Ph.D. degree. Hall worked on his dissertation while director-curator of the Rock County Historical Society and Lincoln-Tallman Museum in Janesville, and he went on to direct the Institute of Indian Studies at the University of South Dakota. Wittry and Hall received their Ph.D. degrees from the University of Wisconsin within a year of each other. Hall then attended Harvard University for a year and moved on to a project in Venezuela while Wittry stayed in Wisconsin. It was at this point that Deuel hired Wittry to replace Fowler at the Illinois State Museum and to be in charge of the fieldwork at 15B in Cahokia.

Wittry needed supervisors for his work crew and he hired three young men to help him. One was a college junior at Western Illinois University named Pat Munson. Pat had grown up at Lewistown, Illinois, a small town about five miles north of Dickson Mounds, and was a distant cousin of Don Dickson, the man who had developed the Dickson Mounds site.

Dickson Mounds[1] was a Mississippian cemetery located on land owned by the Dickson family. Don was a chiropractor who, when he discovered the hundreds of Indian burials on his land, decided that instead of looting them, he would make them into a tourist attraction. He had them excavated and developed an informative exhibit and tour, running it as a family business for years before it was eventually purchased by the State of Illinois.

The presence of the Dickson Mounds in the area had a tremendous influence on a whole generation of young people growing up in the small town of Lewistown. Pat Munson, while still a boy, became a surface collector of arrow points and potsherds. When workers at Dickson Mounds or the nearby Mississippian village site of Eveland, the excavation of which was directed by Joe Caldwell, needed help, Pat and his friend Alan Harn volunteered. The two boys became sufficiently skilled at archaeological work that they were able to get themselves excused from weeks of high school to work on the Eveland site. Every summer they were the "local boys" who found jobs working at the two sites.[2]

Though Pat Munson had been powerfully attracted to archaeology from boyhood, he did not major in it as an undergraduate in college. Like Melvin Fowler, he had been told that he could never make a living at archaeology, and, unlike Fowler, he looked on it as "a silly game." Despite his disdain he found that he was continually getting caught up in archaeological projects. When he heard that Warren Wittry and the Illinois State Museum were going to excavate 15B for the Illinois Archaeological Survey, he rushed over to Springfield and talked Wittry into hiring him for the summer as his third assistant at Cahokia.

Munson's buddy, Al Harn, was also interested in working at Cahokia. Harn had been born on a farm a mile west of Dickson Mounds. While a small child, before he had even started elementary school, he was roaming through the fields looking for arrowheads. "I was regularly crossing a substantial creek, two pastures and some fields to get to a place where my father and brothers had found arrow points. I would come back with little chips that were not anything—but to me they were treasures," he remembers.

Unlike Pat Munson, after high school Al Harn was unable to go on to college. "It was a funny thing," Harn said, "but I was never aware that our family was very poor. We had food all of the time and I wore my brother's clothes and he wore a cousin's clothes that were handed down to him. Though I never felt

---

1. Harn 1971, 1980.
2. The two were not alone in their interest in Indian mounds and burials. Two other youths from tiny Lewistown, Larry Conrad and Ann Cyphers, would, like Pat Munson, eventually go on to earn graduate degrees and have professional careers in anthropology—Conrad at Western Illinois University and Cyphers at the National University of Mexico in Mexico City—as a result of having grown up in proximity to Eveland and Dickson Mounds.

poor, there was never a question of having money to go to college. There just wasn't any."

Despite the fact that his formal education had ended with high school, Harn found that he was in demand because of his experience as a youth working at the Eveland and Dickson Mounds sites. In late winter 1960 Joe Caldwell called from the Illinois State Museum and asked Harn to go with Wittry to Cahokia to help with the site testing.

Harn drove to Cahokia on March 20 in an old panel truck that he planned to sleep in while working at the mounds. He was 19 years old and on his first trip off the family farm. Wittry, who had driven down from Springfield the same day, met him at the little museum building beside Monks Mound and together they drove in Wittry's car down Collinsville Road (U.S. 40) to a nearby motel, called the Danny Boy, where Wittry had made reservations to stay for the summer.

They were met at the motel by Joe Stabile, the owner, who was hard of hearing. Wittry introduced himself. "I am Dr. Wittry from the Illinois State Museum. I believe you have a room reserved for me." "No," replied Stabile, looking from Wittry to Harn. "It's only for one." Wittry nodded toward Harn. "He is with me but he is staying somewhere else," Stabile ignored him. "Price I quoted is only for one. If he stays, five dollars more a week." Wittry turned to Harn. "Al, do you want to stay with me for five dollars a week?"

"Sure," replied Harn. Stabile relaxed. "Okay" he said. "Now it is okay."

The two men were hungry and had noticed a restaurant that looked interesting just down the road. "What about that place?" Wittry asked Stabile, pointing back toward Collinsville Road. "Is that a good place to eat?"

"No," replied Joe. "Youse guys don't want to go near that place." When they had gotten back into the car Wittry and Harn looked at each other. "Where do you want to go?" asked Wittry.

"That first place down the road sounds kind of intriguing," Harn replied.

"That's what I thought," said Wittry.

The two men went into the restaurant and sat down. It was very dark, with tiny blue lights the only illumination. As their eyes became accustomed to the gloom they saw that what they had thought was a restaurant was really only a bar. A woman approached them, and Warren asked to see a menu.

"Are you pulling my leg?" the woman asked. "No," replied Wittry. There was a long silence. Then the woman asked, "Do you want to see a girl?" Harn looked around. Is there another waitress? he wondered.

Wittry suddenly smiled and ordered them each a beer. "Do you have any kind of snack food to go with it?" he asked. The woman rolled her eyes and left to bring them their beers. As they drank, Wittry and Harn saw that the only other occupants of the establishment, a man and a woman at the bar, were having an argument. The disagreement grew louder and as Harn watched, open mouthed, the man began hitting the woman.

Harn had never seen a man strike a woman in Lewistown. After a few minutes the woman got up from her bar stool and left. Wittry and Harn finished their beers and followed her out. As they got into their car they noticed the woman pulling a long object from the back seat of a white Buick in the parking lot. Whatever it was, it was rolled up in a blanket. As they drove out of the parking lot the woman walked back into the bar, poked the long object—a shotgun—into the stomach of the man she had been fighting with, and blew him in two.

If Wittry and Harn had stayed in the bar for two more minutes they would have been eyewitnesses. The shooting was a dramatic introduction to the Cahokia Mounds region. They soon learned, in fact, that the episode in the bar was not unusual. Knifings, beatings, robberies, and shootings occurred in Cahokia on a regular basis.

Though they had not known it when they first arrived, the archaeologists quickly became aware that there was something unusual about the political situation in the area around Cahokia. Collinsville Road, or "the strip," runs east-west in front of Monks Mound, cutting the site in two and forming the county line between Madison County to the south and St. Clair County on the north. The area was unincorporated and the nearest law enforcement was the St. Clair County sheriff, based in Belleville, or the Madison County sheriff, in Edwardsville.

Lining the strip were approximately 20 bars and other institutions of dubious reputation. A race track anchored the east end of the road. The authority in the area was wielded by Buster Wortman, a gangster who had been awarded the territory by Chicago gangster Al Capone. The bars, lounges, night clubs, race tracks, vending machines, houses of prostitution, and gambling establishments in East St. Louis and the Cahokia Mounds area were controlled by Wortman and his associates, a spinoff of the Chicago-based Capone gang.

Episodes of violence were common. Richard Bakos, the second-generation owner of Bakos Hardware store on Collinsville Road, remembers that "bodies were always being found in trunks" at the Red Rooster tavern across the street from his store. The county line ran through the middle of the tavern (the road turned at that point while the county line ran straight) and when the owner of the Red Rooster would get a tip that he was about to be raided by the sheriff of one county, he would move his gambling equipment to the other side of his building, thus putting it in the next county and out of the sheriff's jurisdiction.

The woman who owned the bar next to the hardware store maintained order in her establishment with a baseball bat she kept under the counter. If she thought someone was beginning to get out of hand she would take her bat and, without saying a word, hit the offender over the head with it. Amazingly, it worked and her bar was one of the quieter ones in the area. Down the street, the misnamed Friendly Tavern was the scene of violence almost every night.

Bakos remembers making a delivery of lumber to a house of prostitution. The owner had a stage set of a little coffee shop in the living room for a front and was pacing back and forth in front of the windows. When Bakos asked her what was wrong, she replied that she was "waiting to be raided by the Madison County sheriff any time now."

Thanks to Joe Caldwell's recommendation, the Horseshoe Lounge at the Danny Boy Motel became the bar favored by the archaeologists, who frequented it almost every night. The lounge manager, Pearl, was Joe Stabile's wife. An attractive, slender woman of about forty, Pearl kept her own bottle behind the bar and drank from it regularly throughout the night. Though the contents looked like vodka, just a few people knew that the bottle contained only water. Pearl ran a bar but she did not like to drink.

At the end of a day digging test excavations, Wittry and Harn were walking down Collinsville Road toward the Danny Boy Motel and Pearl's Horseshoe Lounge. As they drew near, they saw ahead of them a car that had run off the road into the ditch. As they approached to offer help, the driver, instead of appearing relieved, looked at them suspiciously and locked his car doors.

"Do you need some help?" called out Wittry. "We can give you a push." The man reluctantly nodded assent and they pushed his car back on the road and into the lot of the Danny Boy. The man got out of his car and pulled some bills from his pocket.

"Here's a ten spot for each of you," he said. Wittry and Harn backed away. "We don't want that," they said, embarrassed at the gesture.

"Well, can I buy you a beer?" the man asked.

"Sure," the two men replied. When they went into the bar, Pearl met them and said to Wittry, "I didn't know you knew Buster." "I don't," Wittry said. "We just pushed him out of the ditch."

"Pearl," Buster broke in, "who are these people?"

"This is Dr. Wittry from the State Museum and these people are archaeologists," Pearl explained. After a few beers Buster invited the two men to a barbecue he was giving the following Sunday. Wittry declined, saying he had to return to Springfield over the weekend, but suggested that Harn attend.

Harn was delighted. "How do I get there?" he asked. "Don't worry," replied Buster. "I'll send a car for you."

The car that came for Harn was long and black. When he arrived at the barbecue he saw that all the cars there were long and black. Visitors were gathered around a pool and there were tables on the lawn with more food than Harn had ever seen in one place in his life. Several houses were arranged in a cluster or compound, and one house in particular caught his attention. It was very large and built on an island in a small body of water, looking very much like a castle surrounded by a moat. Wow, Harn thought, these people must have a lot of money.

It was not until a year later when Harn was in a barbershop on Collinsville Road that he learned where he had been. Waiting for his haircut he overhead the barber talking with another customer. The customer was describing his flight in a small plane over a compound with a big house surrounded by a moat. "Man," said the barber, "you could have been shot. That's the Wortman complex." Harn slid down in his seat. "I know that house," he thought. "I've been there."

Despite the fact that Pearl Stabile was tied into the gang and her husband was an enforcer and collector for the mob, she looked after the archaeologists. Word soon spread that the archaeologists were under Pearl's, and therefore the gang's, protection. Fowler was drinking in the lounge one evening with one of his long-haired archaeology students when a group of bar patrons began to harass the young man.

"Goddamn hippie," they grumbled. When they began to crowd around the student, Pearl intervened. She said only a few words before the men backed off, the situation suddenly becoming clear to them.

On another occasion, Wittry and Harn were in the Horseshoe Lounge and talking with a local person when the man suddenly looked up with a scowl on his face. Though he went on talking, other heads began to come up. After a few minutes the man turned to Harn.

"Say, you fellows should probably step outside for a while."

"Why? I don't want to leave." Harn protested. "We're having a good time."

The man persisted. "You really need to step outside. There is going to be trouble here in a little bit and you shouldn't be part of it." Wittry and Harn understood the message, got up, and left.

Despite such experiences, Harn, still in his teens, did not grasp the full extent of the vice around Cahokia. He went into a little restaurant next to Monks Mound for breakfast one morning. A woman came in and asked, "What would you like, honey?"

"Do you have any Wheaties?" asked Harn. The woman looked at him strangely.

"Where are you from?" she asked.

"I'm one of the people digging at the mounds."

"Oh," she said. "You are one of those arch . . . arch . . . " She stopped. "I think I could probably get you something." The woman disappeared into a trailer and reappeared in a few minutes with a bowl of cereal, milk, and orange juice. Harn was enjoying his breakfast when Wittry walked in.

"Al," said Wittry, "what are you doing here?"

"Eating breakfast," replied Harn. Wittry and the woman looked at each other and smiled. When Harn reported for work at the site, the workmen greeted him with jeers. "Where have you been, Al?" they asked him. "What were you doing?"

"I just had breakfast," the puzzled Al responded.

"Sure."

Wittry spoke up. "Honest to God. I saw his car in front, walked in, and there he was, eating a bowl of Wheaties."

Wittry and Harn completed their testing in late spring and archaeological work on Tract 15B, a flat section of land measuring 400 feet wide and 900 feet long, began on August 1, 1960. Harn returned to work at the Eveland site near Dickson Mounds and Wittry stayed on at Cahokia. Wittry had until October 31 to complete his task. On November 1 construction of the overpass would begin. Wittry and his three young assistants, Pat Munson, Robert Salzer, and Bill Hurley (fig. 6), stood in the dry grass and looked over their project. Wittry was pleased it had been a dry summer. That would make the work easier.

Wittry's first task was to find some workers. He sent Munson down to the

Figure 6. Dr. Warren Wittry (second from right) with his crew chiefs (left to right) Robert Salzer, Patrick Munson, and William Hurley on Tract 15B, west of Monks Mound. Used with permission of the Illinois State Museum.

local union hiring hall with instructions to hire 27 unskilled laborers. While these were individuals with very little education (few had completed high school), they were men who knew how to use shovels and they were capable of working for eight continuous hours under the hot Illinois sun. A few of them had worked for archaeologists before, had become interested, and were excellent fieldworkers. The hourly union wage was $3.45 an hour, to be paid by the contractor of the highway.

Wittry and his crew began by removing the topsoil down to the bottom of the plow zone. Though there were undoubtedly artifacts in the plow zone, they had been so mixed up through the years of plowing that they were no longer very useful to archaeologists, for whom the precise location of an artifact was of great importance. Besides, time was short. The men had time only to uncover whatever major features might be under the soil.

Wittry arranged for the contractor to bring in a huge earth-moving machine called a Caterpillar DW21 and his very best operator. The machine was called a 21 because its cubic capacity was 21 yards of dirt. A cubic yard weighs, depending on the water content, anywhere from 3,000 to 4,000 pounds. The DW21 could pick up from 31 to 42 tons of dirt on each pass before it had to dump it into trucks to be hauled away.

Wittry lined the DW21 up at the east end of 15B and told the operator to lower the eight-foot blade and take off a foot of the plow zone. The operator had gone about 300 feet when Wittry yelled at him to stop. The topsoil had rolled up like a carpet, revealing an astounding sight. The bare earth was full of features that were being scrambled into each other as the blade scraped across the top. There were house basins, pits of all sizes, walls extending under and over other walls, scattered artifacts and relics. Everything just popped out before the eyes of the astonished Wittry and his helpers. The light-beige silt of the soil was marked everywhere with the dark stains of archaeological features. None of the men had ever seen anything like it before.

They had to change their plan. Wittry and his helpers marked off the area of 15B into blocks 100 feet wide and 200 feet long, approximately one-half acre each. From now on they would excavate only one rectangular block at a time. The machine operators were not pleased at this. They liked making long swaths and could not understand why the archaeologists wanted to work in smaller units. But they were expert operators. Instead of one deep cut, Wittry had them take the plow zone off a few inches at a time so as not to damage the material underneath. The final cut was only one-half inch deep. The operators were so skilled they could put the blade down and for 200 feet take off exactly one-half inch, no more, no less, without skipping. The end result was a plot as flat as a table, perfectly smooth and slick, without a crumb of soil marring the surface.

The only marks on the plot were the broad tire tracks of the massive Caterpillar DW21 vehicle.

With the plow zone carefully removed, Munson, Salzer, and Hurley, the three supervisors, staked the plot out into a grid. They put stakes at 10-foot intervals and staked out rectangles 30 feet wide and 40 feet long, stretching tapes across to mark the grid. Then they numbered each square in the grid to identify it.

This done, they gave every man a trowel and lined up the 27 laborers at the end of the plot. They had them get down on their hands and knees, each man about four feet from the man beside him, and told them to "trowel off the surface." Troweling off the surface meant digging down one-tenth of an inch to rid the surface of smears caused by objects that the blade had picked up and dragged. There were potsherds, stones, clods. It took half a day to trowel it all down. Walking behind the line of men was Pat Munson, scribing in the soil with the tip of his trowel everything he could see: house basins, wall trenches, and pits. Walking back and forth behind the advancing line of men, Munson marked features as fast as he could. Meanwhile the other two supervisors were working at the plane table, a drawing board on a tripod with a surveying instrument mounted on it, which allows an archaeologist to construct maps in the field. One of the men would measure the features as Munson scribed them in the dirt and the other would enter them on a map and assign them numbers. The numbers were either an F number, for "feature number," or an H number, for "house number."

By the time the troweling and scribing were finished, the supervisors had a map completed. It was a crude map, in pencil, but it allowed them to assign numbers to every feature and house they had uncovered. Then the workers were called back to the beginning line and the real work of excavation begun. Each supervisor was assigned nine men who carefully excavated each feature that had previously been assigned a number. A heavy sack with the date and the number of that feature on it was laid out and the men were told to put anything they found in that feature into the sack. They found potsherds, bones, rocks, and pieces of flint. If it wasn't dirt, it went in the bag.

Slowly, as the trenches and pits and superimpositions were dug out, the outline of the area began to show more clearly. The workers had to get the fill out before they could get the definition of the wall trenches and see where the houses had been. While the men dug and cleaned out, the supervisors mapped. It was a constant struggle to keep up with the mapping, to draw the cross sections and the profiles, and to keep things going. Each supervisor had a section of the block to complete and had to keep his nine-man crew working. "You dig that house pit," Munson would tell one man. "And you dig that basin," he would direct another, "and tell me when you've got it done."

Some house basins were only 12 or 18 inches deep. Clearing these out was not too difficult. In other places there were bell-shaped storage pits that went down three feet below the plow zone. As the men dug out the outlines of houses—blocks and blocks of houses and pits superimposed on pits—it became apparent that Cahokia, or this part of it at least, had been thickly populated (fig. 7). At some point in the past, 15B had been a crowded urban neighborhood filled with hundreds of houses.

As Wittry looked out over the intricate patchwork of excavations the 27 workers had dug, he realized that 15B was going to change radically the prevailing conception of Cahokia. Up to that point Griffin and others had insisted that

Figure 7. Crew members of the first highway project at Cahokia hand excavate house wall trenches and storage pits after the area had been scraped by heavy equipment. In the wall behind the shovel can be seen the dark humus line that was the ground surface before excavation began. Used with permission of the Illinois State Museum.

Cahokia was a ceremonial center to which the Indians came only on ritual occasions. Very few Indians, Griffin believed, had actually lived there for any period of time. Cahokia, Griffin insisted, was a ritual center where a few inhabitants lived for brief periods of time in insubstantial temporary housing. The hundreds of sturdy house walls, storage pits, burials, and other features Wittry and his workers saw spread out over every square foot of 15B sharply contradicted that idea. This was not a place where Indians had come once a year to do a rain dance. Cahokia was vastly more complicated than that.

There was another puzzling feature to this excavation. The diggers could find no "midden." "Midden" is the archaeologists' term for trash. Usually when a house site is excavated the diggers also find the household trash heap, usually not far from the front door. Midden contains such revealing objects as discarded bones, potsherds, seeds, ashes from fires, pieces of flint—anything and everything people living in a place threw away.

Munson and his coworkers were perplexed. Here they had 15 acres covered with hundreds of houses, some built and occupied over several generations, thousands of pits, and no trash. Was it possible that hundreds of people had once lived here and not one had thrown anything away? The workers would dig down to the floor of a house and find nothing—just bare ground. It was uncanny. There was, Munson knew, a lot of midden that had been tossed over a nearby slope into a slough. Had the residents of Cahokia been that neat on their own or was the cleanliness the reflection of a strong political organization?

There was something else perplexing about this site—some strange pits that, for want of a better term, were called "bathtubs." Wittry had never seen anything like them before. They were elongated oval pits, about eight feet long and usually from five to six feet deep. One end was shallower than the other—giving them a very real resemblance to deep bathtubs. They were not bathtubs, of course, but what were they? Wittry found traces of charcoal in the bottom of some of them but that did not solve the mystery. Moorehead had also noted the pits and suggested they might be mini-quarries where clay had been dug for pottery making. If so, why the bathtub shape, and why did they all look more or less alike? Some had an extension, like a wing, on the side. Wittry and his young assistants puzzled over their strange discovery, gave them each a feature number, and moved on.

When one 100-by-200-foot unit was completed, the crew would move on to the next. The DW21 would scrape off the plow zone soil and the dirt would be trucked off for highway fill. Munson and his two associates would establish and number the grid. The 27 workers would trowel and excavate while the three supervisors rushed to get it all mapped and the artifacts bagged and labeled. None of the dirt that was dug out was put through a screen—the usual procedure at an archaeological site. There was no time. The October 31 deadline was approaching.

With two days left before the deadline, and the contractor refusing to grant an extension or more money, Wittry and his workers had one more 100-by-200-foot block to complete. The next-to-the-last day they scraped off the plow zone, got it troweled down and cleaned off, and drew the grid lines. When the sun came up on the last day they had hundreds of pits, houses, and burials exposed and numbered but only 10 hours to excavate and complete the job. Everyone started out that morning with the knowledge they had to get the job completed that day.

Munson directed the crew, put the numbers on the bags, and put a bag by each feature with a clod of dirt on it to keep it from blowing away. Calling the men together he explained the plan for the day.

"Go to the nearest bag, excavate the feature, put the stuff you find in the bag, fold it up, drop it in the pit and go on to the next bag," he told them "Don't bring it to me. Don't ask questions. Don't even talk to me." All day the 27 men, the three supervisors, and Wittry worked their way down the plot. Munson directed the men and Wittry, Salzer, and Hurley mapped. The last section contained over 100 pit features, about 40 houses, and 10 burials. The workers used shovels to dig out the houses—digging out three feet on one corner and three feet on the opposite corner to indicated the outline of the house, and then went on. But when the 10 hours were up they had finished the job. The 27 workers had exceeded all expectations. While some were better workers than others, all had risen to the occasion and, because of their efforts, Tract 15B was mapped.

Early the next morning the heavy equipment of the highway department was on the site digging seven-foot drainage ditches through what had once been a densely populated prehistoric neighborhood. Within hours the excavated houses, storage pits, burials, and bathtubs were obliterated.

The following summer, 15A was scheduled to be excavated. This time Wittry decided to hire college students for his crew. He put advertisements in college newspapers that workers were needed for an archaeology dig. They would be paid above minimum wage but less than the union wage, and they would have to provide their own food and housing. Pat Munson was hired again as a supervisor.

The plan of attack was the same. The workers would open up the 100-by-200-foot blocks, trowel them down, grid and excavate them. They had the same machine operators, the same machines, and the same contractor. What was different were the college students and the weather.

While a few of the students were very good (James Anderson, who would become a key investigator of the site, had his first archaeological experience at

Cahokia as part of the 15A crew and was one of the good ones), most were dreadful. Many had never so much as spaded a garden before and were physically and mentally incapable of doing the work. Others thought an archaeological dig was going to be a big party and it was not. It was hard work. Some of the students could work all day, drink all night, and still put in a day's work on the site, "bleeding from their eyeballs," as Munson put it. Others were totally worthless.

Because he needed experienced help and he had some extra money, Munson looked up four of the best men who had worked on the crew the year before and offered them jobs at the same rate the student's were earning. Though it was below union wages, because the men were out of work, they took it.

A few weeks later Wittry had a visit from the union representatives. Munson spotted the union men, four burly workers, as they walked onto the site looking for Wittry's little 10-by-10-foot office, where he was busy sketching maps. When Munson noted that one of the union men was armed with a pistol, he suspected trouble and suggested to several of the more able-bodied students that they find an excuse to sharpen their shovels and to drift over to the office. Munson joined them there.

The union officials were angry that nonunion men had been hired to do the excavating on 15A. Wittry patiently explained that these were not ordinary workers; they were college students who were learning their profession. He talked for a long time and eventually the union leaders were convinced, or at least mollified. As they were walking across the field to leave the site, they came upon the four laborers Munson had hired to supplement the student crew. One of the laborers, Frank Bodine, was at the bottom of a six-foot-deep bathtub pit, digging it out.

The union official recognized him and, leaning over the edge of the pit, called down, "Hey, Frank, what college do you go to?" Frank looked up. "If I had gone to college," he replied, "do you think I would be down in the bottom of this fucking hole?" Despite the union officials' skepticism about the workers excavating 15A, they stayed away from the site and did not cause further problems during the twelve weeks of the project.

On another occasion Munson was walking by Bodine when Bodine looked up from his digging and remarked to Munson, "We don't have to worry about Indians sneaking up on us, do we?" Munson glanced around.

"What are you talking about, Frank?" he asked. Bodine gestured toward a college student who was leaning on his shovel and gazing off into space. "That guy over there," Bodine said. "He is watching for them." Munson looked. The student, his shovel shiny and clean, was rocking gently back and forth, his gaze dreamily fixed on the horizon.

Annoying as the student labor problem was, the greater difficulty was the weather. While the summer before had been dry, this summer was wet. When the DW21 was brought onto the site it sank into the wet earth. When the operator tried to strip off the plow zone he found that the machine's wheels would catch on the archaeological material and slide it underneath them, deforming the features below. A house wall that had obviously been constructed in a straight line would come out with a jog in it. Instead of cuts they got ruts. Many of the machine passes were total disasters. Finally, digging by hand because the big machines were ripping the site apart, the workers managed to excavate a complete 100-by-200-foot section. This location had many of the peculiar bathtub pits, some of them 11 feet deep.

They had no sooner gotten a portion of the site excavated and cleaned out when a torrential rain hit. It was shortly after eight o'clock in the morning and Munson had just gotten to work. The sky looked as if it had been painted. There was a strip of gray, then a strip of yellow, and above that a strip of black. The black was the cloud and the gray was the rain. Within an hour almost five inches of rain fell on the newly excavated site, filling the bathtubs and the entire excavated area up to the level of the surrounding soil. Instead of an archaeological site they had a big rectangular pond.

The night before, the workers had covered much of the site with 30-by-30-foot sheets of black plastic. When the storm hit, the wind blew the sheets of plastic off the site and onto nearby U.S. 40. Drivers trying to navigate their way through the driving rain suddenly had to swerve and zigzag to avoid huge airborne sheets of plastic blowing across the highway.

Getting rid of the water was a major problem. Cahokia is flat and there was no slope to drain the site for more than 200 feet. In the middle of the site were all the bathtub holes full of 11 feet of water. Munson put his crew to work digging trenches down the south side of the site. Eventually, because the rains continued, they ended up digging three-foot-wide trenches every 30 feet—partly to give the workers something to do. It was too wet to do much of anything else.

Despite the problems, most of Tract 15A was eventually excavated. What the archaeologists found were hundreds of bathtubs and all kinds of other pits and house basins.[3] Pits and house basins they understood, but what were the bathtubs? Everyone speculated on what they could be until one day that summer, during the excavation at the Mitchell site, the mystery was suddenly solved.

Mitchell was a cluster of ten mounds on the bank of Long Lake, a stagnant body of water in an ancient channel of the Mississippi. A large burial mound at the site had been destroyed by the construction of the railroad in 1877 and the

---

3. For a detailed description and analysis of the work at Tract 15A see Paleolithic 1992 as well as Wittry 1969, 1980, 1996.

remaining mounds covered an area of between 80 and 100 acres now dotted with roads, houses, businesses, and industry. Four of the mounds appeared to define a kind of public square or plaza with living units scattered around it. The location of Mitchell, halfway between the north limestone bluffs of Alton, Illinois, and Monks Mound in "Downtown Cahokia," made it a key strategic position for control over the confluence of the Mississippi, Missouri, and Illinois Rivers. Any prehistoric traders or warriors passing that point on the rivers would have had to contend with the residents of Mitchell.

James Porter,[4] whom Fowler had hired to direct the fieldwork at Mitchell for Southern Illinois University, was a large man, a former football tackle with narrow hips, powerful thighs, and shoulders so broad he appeared to be still wearing his shoulder pads. He had curly, reddish brown hair and an extremely volatile disposition. A geologist as well as an archaeologist, he was a field archaeologist who was constantly getting into fights. Though everyone who worked with him found that they learned a great deal, they also learned to gauge his moods and, when he was in an ugly one, to stay out of his way. When he drank, Porter became unruly and mean, fighting and drinking as hard as he worked. Porter kept his workers busy washing potsherds far into the evening, and on weekends he volunteered himself (and them) to excavate the "fill site," an area for which there had not been money appropriated to excavate. Though archaeologically significant, the fill site was land the highway department was using as a source for fill dirt for the road construction.

The Mitchell crew was a large one, at times numbering 45 men. Al Harn had come back from working for Joe Caldwell at the Eveland site near Dickson Mounds to be one of the five field supervisors under Porter. The workers were all union men, earning their $3.45 per hour, and after a few who could not get the hang of the job were weeded out, the remaining men were, in Harn's words, "the most productive people I have ever worked with."

The supervisors taught the men how to excavate by demonstrating how they wanted the work done. Because of the union rules, Harn and his fellow supervisors could not touch a shovel unless the worker to whom it belonged stood idly by. Harn borrowed the shovel of a worker named Charlie Copeland, a man in his sixties, to show him how he wanted the floor of a 45-square-foot excavation cleaned off. Harn was proud of his skill. With a flat-bladed shovel he could make an excavated floor surface perfectly level, as smooth and flat as a table top. He demonstrated to Charlie what he wanted and left him to get started. When he estimated that Charlie would have completed about a third of the job, Harn came back to check on him. To his amazement the entire area was completed

4. Porter 1969, 1974.

as neatly as the best Harn could do. The vertical walls of the excavation looked as if they had been polished.

"Who helped you with that, Charlie?" Harn asked.

Charlie spit out a big splat of tobacco. "Nobody," he replied.

Charlie was typical of the Mitchell site workmen. They detected early on that Porter and his young field supervisors respected them and wanted to involve them in the project. When they understood that, they became intensely interested and worked twice as hard despite work conditions that approached the intolerable. Temperatures often reached 100 degrees, with high humidity. One day more than a third of the crew passed out from the heat. Their coworkers carried them down to Long Lake and revived them in the water. Harn lost 27 pounds in six weeks.

Doing salvage archaeology for an interstate highway that was under construction meant that the men were working on their hands and knees next to dozens of massive road scrapers and bulldozers. The contractors filled areas almost as soon as the archaeologists exposed them. There was time only to draw the maps and move on. The machines ran from morning until late at night, enveloping the workers in clouds of dust and deafening noise and causing the earth to tremble.

Despite the working conditions, the crew's enthusiasm grew to where they became competitive with Wittry's men working on Tract 15A. The rivalry began with friendly banter during the nightly visits to the bars when workers from Porter's site would brag to workers from Wittry's about the materials they were finding. A chess contest sprang up between some of Porter's and Wittry's men and finally one group challenged the other to a basketball game.

The basketball game was not really a basketball game but an excuse for a war. Someone found them a local gym. Porter's team could field only five men so they went in search of a sixth. They were discussing their problem in the Horseshoe Lounge when Pearl overheard and volunteered her 14-year-old son, Joey. Joey became the sixth man. As a smoker, Porter could make only a few trips up and down the court before he would be winded. While Porter rested on the bench, they sent in Pearl's Joey. Predictably the game got rough. Wittry, who was the referee, let matters get out of hand, and when Porter's team finally won the game the losers challenged them to step outside and continue the rivalry.

Porter's and Wittry's crews were not the only ones working at Cahokia that summer. Charles Bareis was directing the University of Illinois's work on the Powell tract at the western edge of Cahokia. Bareis was a small man with dark hair who, to keep cool, cut the sleeves out of the shirts he wore on excavations. Unlike Porter and Wittry, Bareis discouraged (and at times prohibited) contact between his field assistants and the others working at the site. The result was that he and members of his crew held themselves apart from the others and were not part of the rivalry.

While the competition between Wittry's and Porter's men had been fierce over basketball, it was almost as intense over what each day's excavations revealed. Porter and his men were excavating the area he had decided, from the placement of the four mounds, must be a plaza area. Porter knew from historic records that the Indians had customarily swept their plazas clean and sprinkled them with white sand for ceremonies. Porter had stripped off the plow zone over the plaza expecting to find sterile soil with a sprinkling of white sand over it, but right in the geometric center of the empty plaza the workers encountered a huge stain on the soil. Harn was in charge of that area of the excavation and thought they had come upon a house because the stain was so large—over 20 feet long and 8 feet wide. He instructed his workers to dig down through the area of the stain. They had dug down about four feet when one of the workers called to Harn to tell him there was some reddish-brown wood sticking up from the bottom of the excavation.

At that news everyone stopped work and gathered around. More workers were assigned to the digging. Excavating around the edges they discovered a massive bald-cypress log, about three feet in diameter and ten feet long. It lay at an angle, the same angle as the slanting pit. The pit grew deeper and deeper as they dug down around the sides of the massive log. Finally only one worker, a slim youth named Gary Orr, would go down in the pit and dig for fear of the walls collapsing. Eventually the bottom of the log was uncovered and they were able to drag it to the surface (fig. 8). The wood had become waterlogged and in that anaerobic environment had not decayed. The bottom of the log still showed where it had been burned and chopped off with stone tools.

In an instant the mystery of the bathtubs was solved. They were post pits. The shallow end of the bathtub was a ramp down which the heavy log was slid. When it reached the bottom, men with ropes could pull it upright. The wings that had been observed on some of the bathtubs were extraction ramps, dug when a post was removed from a pit, perhaps to replace it with a new post. The cypress log in the Mitchell plaza had originally been standing upright. It appeared that the Indians had tried to remove it, broken it off, and decided to leave it in place in the pit.

Because the post was in the exact center of the plaza, Porter reasoned that it must have been a marker of some sort. He carefully noted the location of the cypress post on his maps and continued working. Interstate 270 would soon be coming through the middle of the Mitchell site and time was running out.

Porter's men were jubilant. They gloated over finding the log. That night Porter and Harn decided to celebrate by having a drink in every bar on the strip.

Figure 8. Log measuring 2.8 feet in diameter found in the post pit in the center of the plaza at the Mitchell site. The base of the log, which had been rounded by charring and chopping, is at the left. Used with permission of M. L. Fowler.

They started out at the Northgate Bar in Collinsville and had gotten only to the second, the Glen Carver, when they met a man who insisted on buying them drinks. The man claimed he was running for sheriff and bought them what Harn later estimated were 20 mixed drinks apiece. While they drank they composed a song in honor of their Mitchell site, to the tune of "Home on the Range," and sang it, repeatedly, to everyone in the bar. It was sometime after midnight before they finally drove home to the Danny Boy to find Wittry drinking alone in the deserted Horseshoe Lounge. Taking the 20-dollar bill Wittry was holding in his hand, they lit it with a match and, as the bill turned to ashes, they sang him their song.

> *At the Great Mitchell Site,*
> *In 1020 A.D.*
> *There lived a Mogul on the Mound.*
> *He was preaching the word*
> *About shell tempering and sherds*
> *And the dropping of grit on the ground.*

The refrain went:

Mounds, Mounds, there you are.
You surpass anything thus far.
When it comes to the new,
It takes Mitchell and you,
To get what's been missing from view.

Though Porter got an amazing amount of work from his crew, they also let him know when he had crossed a line in dealing with them. One day he went up to a worker in his middle fifties and brusquely ordered the man to give him his shovel. Instead of handing it over, the man, Valle Suggs from Pocahontas, Illinois, replied, "Why don't you try and take it from me, Jim?"

Porter looked at Suggs, a small man with a little beer belly hanging over his belt who had been a ranger in World War II. Then he grabbed for the shovel. Suggs hung on and the two men went round and round. Work stopped as everyone watched. When the contest ended, Suggs still held the shovel.

About two weeks later Porter and his field supervisors arrived for work in the morning to find the men standing in a cluster talking. "What's going on," asked Harn. "Has something happened?"

"We had a little trouble in the coffee shop this morning," one of them explained. "But we let Suggs take care of it for us."

The men were in the habit of stopping for coffee and doughnuts at a local establishment before coming to work. They had been sitting at the counter, nursing their coffee that morning, when a man had come in brandishing a knife. He had ordered the men to put their wallets on the counter. Then he went down the line, picking up wallets—until he came to Suggs, who still sat hunched over his coffee, smoking a cigarette. Suggs had not taken out his wallet.

"Where's your wallet?" the man asked. Suggs looked up at him. "Son," he said softly, "you made two mistakes today. One was robbing this place and the second was fooling with me." With that he grabbed the man's arm and in one quick movement snapped it like a twig over his knee.

On the last day of work, with the bulldozers poised to overrun their site, Porter bought a case of beer and, taking Harn with him, went to the fill site. The heavy equipment had destroyed everything except one little wall and a few pits they had exposed. They started early in the morning digging pits and drinking the case of beer. In the middle of the afternoon Porter got up and staggered over to the edge of the woods. "Boy," thought Harn. "Porter's really drinking a lot of beer. I wonder why I don't feel anything. I've been drinking beer all day too."

A few minutes later Harn exposed a large fish bone sticking straight up in the air. He reached for it, lost his balance, fell, and rammed the bone so deep into the palm of his hand that Porter had to dig it out with a knife. When the two men finished the day, the bulldozers came at them over the top of the mound, pushing great piles of dirt ahead of them. Porter and Harn grabbed their tools and scrambled out, the bulldozers at their heels.

A continual source of conflict between the archaeologists and the highway department was the highway department's source of fill dirt. The highway engineers needed vast quantities of dirt for fill and saw the mounds on private property as ideal sources. So did the owners of these mounds, who were eager to sell their mounds to the highway department. When the archaeologists heard about the proposed sale of the mounds for fill dirt they protested. After lengthy negotiations with the state and federal highway officials the archaeologists were granted a veto over the use of the mounds for fill. Property owners in the area were not pleased. Some of them threatened the archaeologists with physical harm for preventing them from selling their mounds. Fortunately, the quick action by the archaeologists saved some of the mounds from being destroyed, but not all. The archaeologists' veto applied just to mounds. One wily owner sold the dirt surrounding his mound. The heavy equipment from the highway department excavated a moat several feet deep all around the mound, leaving it standing—an isolated promontory in the middle of a pit.

Large as the highway salvage project had been, the main highway right-of-way was never examined for archaeological remains. The four areas investigated were only those places where interchanges were planned. It was as if the highway department was giving lip-service to the concept of salvage archaeology but was ignoring the meaning and purpose of the activity. This was painful for the local archaeologists, who could do nothing but stand helplessly on the sidelines as one side was cut off Mound 5. One Sunday, Wittry took part of his crew and cleaned off the cut the machines had made in the mound, much like surgeons examining and cauterizing a wound. Mounds 3, 79, and 46 were buried and Mound 45 was bulldozed away. Nelson Reed, an amateur archaeologist who had worked with Holder, visited the highway construction site and asked the members of a construction crew if they ever found artifacts.

"Oh yeah," they replied. "We find stuff."

"What sort of stuff?" asked Reed. "Oh, we found a bunch of copper tubes joined together like this." One worker pantomimed a set of pan pipes. "What did you do with them," asked Reed.

"Oh," said the worker, "I gave them away to a fellow." Though Reed made inquiries, the pan pipes were never recovered.

The haphazard and desultory activity of the 1950s at Cahokia had given way to a frenzy of activity in the 1960s—research driven by the engine of interstate highway construction. With the universities and the Illinois State Museum now deeply engaged in the project, the members of the Illinois Archaeological Survey were determined to maintain the momentum of their investigations of Cahokia. Though the highway money had been spent and the salvage archaeology work had ended, they resolved to look for other funding to support their research. Cahokia, they now understood, was a site of national, if not international, significance—a prehistoric metropolis on a scale unsuspected north of the Rio Grande. Though the archaeologists received a small grant to support laboratory analysis of data, it would take a detour through Mexico by Fowler to bring resources and the investigators full circle back to Cahokia.

EIGHT

The Emerging Picture of a Complex Cahokia

When the highway salvage project drew to a close, the members of the Illinois Archaeological Survey were faced with a mass of raw, undigested data collected from its four Cahokia sites. As they would soon learn, some of the most significant discoveries would be made not in the field but back in the laboratory when the data was analyzed. The highway department had financed the collection of the data but had appropriated nothing to pay for the task of analyzing it.

This was not unusual in archaeology. When the Tennessee Valley Authority was founded, archaeologists were hired to do salvage archaeology in the reservoirs. The notes they wrote from their fieldwork and the specimens they gathered are, to this day, still stored in warehouses waiting for someone to do the analysis. Preliminary reports have been written in some cases, but decades later large amounts of data are still totally unanalyzed.

The members of the Illinois Archaeological Survey did not want to make the same mistake as had the Tennessee Valley Authority and decided to seek funds to analyze the data that had been collected during the highway salvage program at Cahokia. One possible funding source was the National Science Foundation. By 1962 the NSF had established its anthropology program and the members of the Survey decided to apply there for assistance.

The Survey, in the meantime, had experienced a kind of palace revolt among its members. John McGregor had been running the organization as if it were a department of the University of Illinois instead of a cooperative venture among three coequal state institutions. This had begun to rankle the other two institutional members and, when they had a chance, they ousted McGregor and elected Fowler as president. Shortly afterward, McGregor left the chairmanship of the Department of Anthropology at the University of Illinois, and Joseph Casagrande, a linguistics expert, took his place.

The members of the Illinois Archaeology Survey board were sitting in the Survey office at the University of Illinois, discussing their request for funds from the National Science Foundation, when Fowler remarked, "Someone has got to coordinate this. We can't go to the National Science Foundation without having named someone as principal investigator."

Casagrande spoke up. "Well," he said, "you are the president of the Illinois Archaeological Survey, so you should coordinate the grant." As a result of Casagrande's remark, Fowler was named principal investigator of the first National Science Foundation grant to be awarded for Cahokia. The grant was approved for three years. While most of the money went for data analysis and reports, Fowler managed to set aside small amounts for his colleagues to conduct small-scale excavations in the Cahokia area.

Al Harn was hired, through Southern Illinois University at Carbondale, to do an archaeological survey of the southern half of the American Bottom, and Pat Munson was engaged to do essentially the same thing at the north end of the Bottom at the Wood River Terrace. These surveys provided information on the types of smaller communities that might have supported the great Cahokia center.

As Munson explained, "Cahokia and Mitchell and Dupo (the Pulcher site) had so dominated the archaeological scene down there that nobody had ever looked at anything other than those three big sites. Those sites were contemporary with Woodland and Mississippian. No one knew a thing about anything earlier. I was hired to survey as much as I could between March 1 and June 15 in the northern part of the American Bottom and put the sites in a geographic and temporal context."

Munson concentrated largely on the bluff line and the base of the bluff rather than on the floodplain. He documented whole cemeteries above the Mitchell, Cahokia, and Dupo sites (which are now covered by housing developments), mapped individual burials, and, significantly, believed he was starting to see populations coalesce into cities.

When Warren Wittry returned to his laboratory at the Illinois State Museum in the fall of 1961, he brought with him the maps he had made of 15A and 15B. Tract 15B was clear in his mind. The entire plot had been excavated and he had been able to study it all of a piece. His goal had been to see the overall plan of settlement of this section of the Cahokia site, to try to understand the special patterns the houses and pit features might have taken and if they had been laid out with some system in mind.

This had been relatively easy to see in 15B, but 15A was another matter. Because of the summer's wet weather the archaeologists had never been able to open up the entire site as Wittry had wished. He had to settle for trenching by shovel on the edges and excavating bits and pieces. The big picture had never been revealed, as he felt it had at 15B.

As Wittry studied his map of 15A in his office at the Illinois State Museum, the site looked like nothing more than a great sea of confusion. There were 171 houses and 384 pits in the northeast quadrant of the site alone. These pits, he knew, were burial pits, storage pits, refuse pits, and fire pits. From the finding of the cypress log at the Mitchell site he now knew that some of these pits, particularly the bathtub-shaped ones, were also post pits where posts from 18 inches to more than three feet in diameter had been buried in the earth.

Wittry took a piece of paper and began to plot just the post pits, leaving out all of the other pits on the map. Suddenly he noticed that the elongated bathtub/post pits were all angled as if toward a central spot and when he plotted them on the map, rather like the child's game of connecting the dots, he found that the locations of the pits formed an arc. Arcs are parts of circles. As he plotted the location of more and more post pits he found that he had parts of not one, but several circles. Because of the wet season, not all of the pits had been uncovered. By projecting where the circle might be, and noting the regular distances between the posts, Wittry believed he could predict where more post pits could be found.

Wittry numbered his circles as 1, 2, 3, and 4. Circle 1 was on the eastern edge of the salvage site with part of it running underneath a medium-sized mound. Circle 2 was 410 feet in diameter. Wittry called his circles "woodhenges," after the Stonehenge site in England. The posts at Cahokia's woodhenge had been erected in precisely the same manner as those of the late Neolithic stonehenges in England and Western Europe. The western side of Circle 2 was missing because the highway crews had scooped up tons of dirt from that location to build the interstate highway. No one, including the archaeologists, had any idea that a woodhenge was there when the dirt had been removed.

Through radiocarbon dating of a fragment of post found in a hole, Wittry estimated Circle 2 to date from about A.D. 1000 and Circle 3 to A.D. 1045. The post pits averaged 7 feet long, 2.2 feet wide, and a little over 4 feet deep. Impressions at the deep ends where the weight of the posts pressed the ends into the soil showed that the posts had been about 2 feet in diameter. How high were they? No one knows. Judging from the diameter of the logs, Wittry guessed the height was about 30 feet. Circle 3 looked to be a little larger than Circle 2, with its center southwest of the Circle 2 center. Circle 4, about the same size as Circle 2, was south and east of Circles 2 and 3 but intersected them both, with part of its circumference lying under the four lanes of U.S. 40.

Wittry had made a major discovery. The ancient Cahokians had a science. Like other early agricultural peoples around the globe, Cahokia's priests had been astute observers of the sky. These circles were some sort of seasonal or astronomical observatory. The question remained, What kind? Wittry asked himself, What movements of heavenly bodies were the Cahokians marking with these massive circles of logs? Could they predict dramatic astronomical events such as eclipses? Were the circles sighting devices? Columbus had once astounded the natives of the New World with his ability to predict an eclipse of the moon. Had the leaders of Cahokia maintained their power over their subjects by similar demonstrations of esoteric knowledge?[1]

For the next twenty-five years Warren Wittry would match wits with the brilliant person who lived a thousand years before him, a person Wittry called "this priest-astronomer, this genius." If he could figure out the meaning inherent in the alignment of the woodhenge posts—why they were placed where they were—Wittry was convinced he would understand a great deal about the culture and the beliefs of the people who once lived at Cahokia.

Before Wittry could pursue these ideas he changed jobs. He left the position he had taken over from Melvin Fowler at the Illinois State Museum to accept an appointment at the Cranbrook Institute of Science at the Cranbrook Museum in Detroit. Taking his place at the Illinois State Museum was his old Green Bay and Boy Scout friend, Robert Hall. Wittry showed Hall his maps of the posthole sites and urged him to continue the search for more segments of the circles and to prove, conclusively, that these were not figments of Wittry's imagination, that there really had been a series of giant log circles constructed on site 15A.

Hall was happy to take up the task. The next summer he found more posts of Circle 2 and projected that it would contain 48 posts evenly spaced about the circumference. He found there were posts at the exact cardinal points of the compass (north, south, east, and west) and when he explored in the center of the circle he found the center post. To his surprise, however, he discovered that the center post was not in the exact center of the circle, as he had projected it would be, but five feet east of the true center. What was going on? The circle was laid out with such precision (the posts were set to within tolerances of tenths of a foot) that the location of the center post could not be an error. Wittry's ancient genius was too good for that. There had to be a reason. When Wittry and Hall measured angles and consulted astronomy charts, they figured out that an observer at the off-set center post in A.D. 1000 would see the sun rise on Midsummer's Day, the summer solstice, directly over one of the posts in the circle.

This was strong evidence to suggest that the woodhenges at Cahokia were sun calendars by which priests or chieftains observed the equinoxes and the summer and winter solstices, the places where the sun appeared to stop before

---

1. Pauketat 1996; Wittry 1996.

returning in its path through the heavens. If Wittry and Hall were right about this, then the Cahokia woodhenges were the only known devices of this sort in ancient America north of Mexico.

Wittry had found something else that reinforced his and Hall's belief that the giant log circles were sky observatories. When excavating near one of the post pits in 1961, the workers had found a fragment of a ceramic beaker with an elaborate design carved into the side. The design is of a cross within a circle, with rays radiating out from the circle. To ethnologists familiar with ancient Indian designs, it was a well-known pattern.

Wittry proposed that the rays on the outside of the design represented the sun, the circle was the old Indian symbol for the earth, and the cross represented the four cardinal directions. On the right side of the design, the circle was open and showed a path leading downward, which could represent the sun at the winter solstice sunrise, the place where the sun stopped moving south and turned back north again—a very important event for prehistoric agricultural peoples. On the left side of the design, the path was closed, perhaps signifying the winter solstice sunset with the rays of sunlight streaming toward the center of the earth.

Wittry found it particularly significant that the beaker fragment had been found near a post pit that was later determined to be a winter solstice sunrise sighting post. Along with it were fragments of other important objects: part of a fired-clay ball, grinding stones, hematite and red ocher, the only Busycon shells found on Tract 15A, galena and quartz crystals, wolf teeth, and seven arrowheads. These seven arrowheads, found in the pit with the beaker fragment, were more than were found in the entire excavation of 15A.

Cahokia's woodhenges were undoubtedly more than calendars or sighting devices. They were elements in the culture's sacred geography that joined nature and society together. These great circles of massive cedar posts inspired a religious transformation of the landscape that connected the people of Cahokia to the enduring gods of the cosmos.

Another, more macabre interpretation of the woodhenges occurred to Wittry and Hall. They were familiar with a sketch made in 1564 by Jacques Le Moyne de Morgues of Timucuan Indians in Florida. The sketch depicted a village in which there was a similar circle of tall posts, and hanging from the tops of the posts were war trophies of body parts—scalps, arms, and legs of vanquished foes. The only human bones found in 15A were three adult legs and one adult arm, all from different individuals and all buried in one pit.

Besides making possible the recovery of thousands of artifacts (one of the largest collections of Cahokia materials in existence), the highway salvage program slowly changed the understanding of Cahokia. The conventional wisdom had been that Cahokia, as large as it was, was essentially a vacant ceremonial center to which the Indians had come only for special occasions. Moorehead had interpreted the site as a series of sequential encampments along the banks of Cahokia Creek.

The attitude of most mid-twentieth-century archaeologists toward Native Americans was formed by the ethnographic studies made in the late nineteenth and early twentieth centuries, studies written long after smallpox and other diseases introduced by the Europeans had decimated native populations and, to a great extant, destroyed the Native American social organization.

The highway salvage excavations showed that Cahokia, instead of being a region populated by wandering clans of hunter-gatherers, had been a place of densely concentrated structures, residences, religious buildings, mounds, and post circle monuments. All were laid out in an orderly manner indicating complex systems of organizing society and planning construction. As only Brackenridge had noted, this could not have been the work of "thinly scattered tribes." The houses were superimposed on one another, suggesting that they had been rebuilt on the same spot for generations. The varieties of ceramics that were discovered gave strong indications that the old two-part division of Cahokia's time span would have to be reconsidered, if not abandoned. Like a ship coming into port through a fog, Cahokia was emerging from the mists of time with a shape and definition that, year by year, came more clearly into focus.

To cope with the overwhelming number of ceramic artifacts that were coming into the Illinois State Museum from the densely occupied areas of Cahokia, the museum was named the third recipient of the National Science Foundation grant money. With Wittry and Hall occupied working on the problem of the woodhenges, Joseph Vogel, a young graduate student from California, was hired to help in the study of the ceramics.[2]

Vogel had worked with Fowler at the Modoc Rock Shelter in the 1950s and had gone on to do advanced studies in archaeology. He had also been a member of Wittry's 15A crew during the summer of 1961.

Griffin, in a seminal paper published in 1949, had described a series of ceramic types as subcategories of the Old Village and Bean Pot, or Trappist, divisions. Vogel utilized a statistical modal analysis and came up with categories that both overlapped and subdivided Griffin's types. Vogel also suggested, as did many others at the time, that the division between Old Village and Trappist was no longer useful.

Vogel urged dropping the dichotomy of Old Village versus Trappist and proposed that the Mississippian occupations were historically continuous, as he

---

2. Vogel 1975.

could see little evidence in the ceramics of rapid displacements or sudden shifts in the population. Vogel also raised pertinent questions about the relationships of the Bluff culture, first defined by Titterington, to the formation of Mississippian culture in the American Bottom and at Cahokia. Without subdividing his continuum into a set of phases, as others would later do, Vogel named a whole series of newly recognized ceramic types and showed the changing styles from about A.D. 600–700 to A.D. 1400 at Cahokia. Vogel tentatively suggested that there were two pre-Mississippian phases, which he named Loyd and Merrell.

In response to the growing understanding of Cahokia's complexity, Robert Hall[3] also proposed an early phase that overlapped Vogel's pre-Mississippian phases. Following Griffin's earlier thoughts about the different kinds of ceramics from the Pulcher site and noting that similar materials were being found at Cahokia, Hall proposed a pre–Old Village Pulcher phase.

As president of the Illinois Archaeological Survey, Fowler was responsible for this ongoing NSF-funded research but he was not directly involved. During the spring months of 1961, 1962, and 1963 he was in Mexico. Despite his work in Illinois archaeology, Fowler had never lost his interest in Mexico or Mesoamerica, which originally impelled him toward archaeology. Though his church leaders privately told him to consider the Book of Mormon stories about the origin of Native Americans as fables, he was now professionally interested in the complex societies that had emerged in Mexico before European contact. Fowler's work in Mexico, though he could not know it at the time, would provide the impetus for the major future discoveries at Cahokia.

In Mexico, Fowler worked with Richard MacNeish at a site near Tehuacán, Puebla, Mexico. It was MacNeish's analysis of potsherds that had impressed Fowler years before at the Illinois State Museum ceramic conference. MacNeish put Fowler in charge of excavations at the Coxcatlan Rock Shelter. Although not as deep as the Modoc Rock Shelter in Illinois, the Coxcatlan shelter was similar in that it encompassed the same time period, primarily the time of the Archaic adaptations of post-big-game-hunting peoples in central Mexico. A major difference between the two sites was that Coxcatlan was located in a very dry area so that there was good preservation of plant remains such as seeds, stems, and leaves as well as sandals, fragments of basketry, and woven fabrics. Desiccated human coprolites (feces) were also recovered from the deposits. Accompanying the organic materials were abundant stone projectile points, stone bowls, and other artifacts of nonperishable materials, which gave a more complete picture of subsistence than had been obtained at Modoc.

Of primary interest in these preserved organic remains were cobs and other remnants of Indian corn. In the upper levels these cobs were very similar to the

---

3. Hall 1975.

maize grown by the modern Mexican farmers in the fields surrounding the site. But in the lower levels of the excavation Fowler found tiny cobs, only a few centimeters in length. These were quite different from the later remains but were clearly a form of Indian corn. The tiny cobs, it turned out, either were the remains of the plant from which maize was originally domesticated or represented maize in its very earliest stages of domestication. The changes revealed in the stratigraphic deposits of Coxcatlan and other archaeological sites near Tehuacán showed the step-by-step progress of maize development from a minor food plant in its early stages of domestication (perhaps as early as 5000 B.C.) to its position as the mainstay of subsistence in Mexico in later times.

MacNeish's project demonstrated that the Tehuacán Valley was a major area where Indian corn had been domesticated. Corn had gradually spread from there to other areas of North and South America, finally reaching Cahokia about A.D. 750–800.

Since maize is a tropical plant fine-tuned to the equal amounts of daylight and dark of the Tropics, it took hundreds of years for it to become adapted to the relatively long hours of daylight during the growing season north of the Tropics. When a plant is first domesticated it rapidly spreads laterally in the same latitude as its native habitat. Indian corn probably spread southward into South America quickly as there is not that much variation of daylight hours within the Tropics. It was the spread north of the Tropics that took a long time. Though maize was utilized to a certain extent in the lower Mississippi Valley and in the Southwest as early as 100 B.C., it was not until about A.D. 750–800 that it became an important food-producing plant in the Midwest.

Because of its sensitivity to cold, for a long time corn was a staple only in the southern regions where there are at least 200 frost-free days a year. During the Mississippian period, corn was further domesticated and newer strains appeared that could survive further north where there were only 120 frost-free days. Through the gradual evolution of subsistence systems, maize finally became the dominant source of food for sedentary village farmers throughout the lower latitudes of eastern North America. Corn continued to be modified to accommodate the climate, temperature, and day length, so that by the time of the European contact in the sixteenth century, corn had become a staple as far north as Ontario, Canada.

The spread of corn farming has been tracked by analyzing carbon isotope concentrations in the bones of ancient Native Americans. Corn contains relatively high amounts of C^{13} so people who eat corn have high concentrations of this isotope in their bones. Skeletons of people who lived before A.D. 1000 tend to have little C^{13} but beginning at about A.D. 900 this isotope is found in radically higher concentrations in the bones of Native Americans.

It was while he was working in the Tehuacán area in 1962 that Fowler learned about yet another site, called Amalucan—a prehistoric city in the state of Puebla. Though Amalucan was a thousand years older than Cahokia, both sites were classified as preclassic or formative, one of the major stages in the development of culture in the New World. The formative stage is an identifiable one that leads, in many cases, to the later classic period. Amalucan had mounds, although not as many as Cahokia, but they were scattered over almost as large an area. The mounds at Amalucan had been faced with stone but, in modern times, soil had drifted over the mounds so that the stone faces were covered and, like Cahokia, the mounds resembled hills. The two sites were similar in that they were both at a pre-urban stage of development and were probably at the same level of social and political organization. This prelude to urbanization is what interested Fowler. He wanted to conduct a comparative study of how these pre-urban sites developed, examining both of the sites at the same time and noting any similarities or differences they might have had.

When Fowler went home to Carbondale for the 1963 fall quarter at Southern Illinois University he resolved to seek support for excavations at Amalucan. The American Philosophical Society gave him a grant and he was awarded a Senior Post-Doctoral Fellowship from the National Science Foundation. He moved his family to Mexico City and began intensive work at Amalucan. It was while working in Mexico in 1964 and 1965 that Fowler got the ideas that were to provide a great leap forward in Cahokia archaeology. Some of those ideas came from a colleague named Rene Millon.

Millon was a small man with an owlish expression who wore dark wire-rim glasses and had a sardonic sense of humor. The two men had met when both were attending the University of Chicago field school in 1949. Millon was a few years older than Fowler and had been a student at Columbia University. That institution had not had a field school and so he had gone to the one at Chicago.

Millon was a student of Julian Steward, who was among the first to propose the ecological approach to anthropology. This approach looked at the way people interacted with each other as well as with the landscape, the climate, and the natural resources. It led to a particular method called the "settlement pattern analysis" in which archaeologists, instead of excavating and concentrating on an individual site, looked at an entire area and tried to figure out the distribution of settlements over the landscape and then relate them to the resources available to the inhabitants. The concept was based on the idea that ancient peoples, for the most part, did not live in isolated settlements but occupied large areas in a complex pattern of relationships with each other and the physical resources that surrounded them.

The way to understand a culture, Steward believed, was not to concentrate on just one isolated site, but to look at the patterns of settlements over a whole range of sites representing different activities of the same culture. One settlement might be on a bluff above a major river, another on a floodplain where irrigation would be practiced; still another site might be a fort built for protection in a wooded area. These sites, all functioning differently, would be aspects of the same culture. Their relationship to one another had to be examined if the cultural system was to be understood. This was a new idea in archaeology and was in sharp contrast to the accepted practice of archaeologists, which was to spend all of their time digging and collecting artifacts from a single location. Steward's approach had been utilized by Gordon Willey, a professor from Harvard University, in a project in the Viru Valley area of northern Peru. John McGregor had also done a small study based on these principles in the central Illinois River Valley.

After receiving his doctorate from Columbia, Millon received some small grants to go back to Mexico and work at Teotihuacán—the largest urban center in pre-conquest America. In the 1920s the Mexicans had dug some tunnels into the giant Pyramid of the Sun and then not paid much attention to them. Millon was interested in those tunnels. He worked laboriously for months in the tunnels, drawing profiles and collecting shard samples. When he was finished he was able to demonstrate that the Pyramid of the Sun, unlike most of the other pyramids in Mesoamerica, had been built as one unit. The Pyramid of the Sun was a single, massive, planned construction, erected at the same time that the entire city had been redesigned. It was obvious to Millon that at some time in the past an unknown but powerful architect-leader had instituted a form of city planning and imposed a grand design over the entire Teotihuacán metropolitan area.

Millon went on in 1957 to get a National Science Foundation grant to produce the first comprehensive map—a settlement survey map—of the Teotihuacán site. Because he had such a large area to cover he decided to experiment with mapping it in a new way—by aerial photography. Gordon Willey had been the first archaeologist to do mapping by using aerial photographs taken of western Peru during the Second World War. Millon knew about Willey's work and decided to see if aerial photography might not be a cheaper and faster way to create maps of Teotihuacán.

Fowler, who was in Mexico at the time, was immediately interested. He remembered his Purdue engineering lectures about how aerial photography could reveal past disturbances of the ground and provide clues to subterranean features that were not apparent in surface observation.

In 1963, through the University Museum at Southern Illinois University, Fowler had experimented with taking pictures from airplanes himself to see if he could develop some simple techniques of aerial photography that would be within the budget and technical capabilities of a working archaeologist. The opportunity had come when SIU was asked to do some salvage work where a big reservoir was being built about 50 miles east of St. Louis. On the ground Fowler could detect a large dark area that, he believed, had to be some sort of prehistoric occupation. He decided to get aerial pictures of the entire site as a guide for excavations.

Fowler asked a friend, the curator of history at the University Museum who flew a small Cessna 150 plane, to take him up to get some pictures. "I need vertical shots, pictures taken shooting straight down at the ground," Fowler explained. "How can I do that out of this little window in the door?"

"Easy," replied his friend. "We'll just take the door off." The friend removed the passenger door from the airplane and the two men took off. When the plane was at a proper altitude and positioned over the area, Fowler extended his seat belt and put one foot out onto a little platform on the landing gear. His friend reached over and with one hand grabbed Fowler's belt, while with the other he banked the plane in a steep turn over the site. Fowler was looking through his 35 mm camera lens straight down at the ground.

Though he later thought he had no reason to be alive, the photographs turned out beautifully. As Fowler studied them in his office he noted faint white lines running parallel to each other in the pictures, like rungs set close together on a ladder. His students began excavating and plotting the location and distribution of artifacts and, when they compared the chart of artifact distribution to the photos with the white lines, they found that they matched one for one. The lines, he realized, were the furrows of ancient cultivated fields.

The prehistoric farmers in southern Illinois had planted their crops, probably corn, in deep furrows or else on ridges that they created by piling up dirt. The furrows were widely spaced, from 8.2 to 10 feet apart. Some of the ridges were 2 feet high and 3 feet wide. To do their cultivating and digging, the farmers used hoes made out of chert. Through use—as in hoeing a crop—this chert developed an unusual polish. This patina is so distinctive that archaeologists who are specialists in stone implements can look at the polish on a piece of chert and tell what the tool was used for. As the Indians worked their fields, digging the furrows and piling up the dirt, they would stop from time to time to sharpen their hoes. In doing so they would knock off little chips of polished flint. These little polished chips were the artifacts found by Fowler's crew excavating the reservoir site.[4]

There are good reasons why digging furrows and creating ridges would have been effective agricultural practice for the hoe farmers. Planting on the ridges

---

4. Fowler 1969.

would have made planting and weed control easier. In low-lying and water-saturated swampland, by building up the earth into ridges, the seed bed could be kept above the water level. Also, by creating a high ridge it would be possible to extend the growing season a few more weeks each fall, an important consideration when growing corn at its northern limits. When a light frost hits, the cold air literally slides down the surfaces of the ridges and collects in the furrows, keeping the upper portions of the ridges frost-free for a longer period of time.

The process of locating these ancient fields at the reservoir site by aerial photography was so successful that Fowler decided to experiment with the technique again at the Pulcher site, a compact site 10 miles south of Cahokia that had been mapped by Patrick at the same time he had mapped Cahokia. Industrial development had not yet reached the Pulcher area and the land was still being used for agriculture. Fowler went to the local airport and rented a plane. This pilot refused to take off the passenger door. "That's against FAA regulations," he said. "But if you need vertical shots I can go up high and we can dive straight down. You can shoot your pictures through the windshield."

That sounded fine to Fowler so they went up as high as the small plane could go. Then the pilot aimed the plane at the earth, and down they went, rushing headfirst at the ground while Melvin clicked the shutter of his camera. Again, the pictures turned out well and he found the same striations, alternating light and dark bands of soil in square and rectangular patches, like garden plots divided by paths. In the middle of one garden plot was a square discoloration he thought was probably the location of a prehistoric house.

Fowler remembered a visit he had made to the museum at the Ocmulgee site near Macon, Georgia. The site had been excavated as a WPA project under A. R. Kelly (Joe Caldwell's father-in-law and the archaeologist the University of Illinois had sent to observe the destruction of Powell Mound) and under one mound the team had exposed a curiously undulating ancient surface. The undulations were the ridges and furrows of ancient fields, and right in the middle of one of the patches were the wall trenches of a Mississippian house. The photos in the Ocmulgee exhibit, filed away in his mind, were the clues Fowler used to interpret the aerial photographs he later took in southern Illinois.

These experiences had convinced Fowler of the value of aerial reconnaissance in archaeology. As a civil engineer and surveyor he knew how slow and expensive land surveying could be. If aerial photography could be used by archaeologists to make accurate detailed contour maps, it would be a valuable breakthrough. A contour map represents differences in elevation through the use of curving lines, with one line connecting all points of the same elevation.

During his 1964–65 stay in Mexico, Fowler went every week to Teotihuacán to talk to Millon and follow the progress of the mapping. Millon had hired a professional aerial photographic firm from the United States and by using their pictures he found that in a few weeks he could map an area of Teotihuacán that would have taken months or years to map by conventional surveying techniques. Renting the planes and equipment was costly, but over the long run it was much less expensive. Moreover, his aerial pictures were changing the way archaeologists thought about Teotihuacán.

Millon was facing the same problem that Fowler and others would later face at Cahokia. Teotihuacán was turning out to be larger and more complex than earlier archaeologists had realized or would accept. The conventional wisdom had held that Teotihuacán had been a sparsely occupied ceremonial center, inhabited principally by priests, to which the masses of people came only on special occasions. Millon's aerial photographs were revealing that the pyramids were surrounded by miles and miles of residential neighborhoods that few had suspected were there. Those who had previously excavated residential compounds had referred to them as "palaces." A new picture of Teotihuacán was emerging from the aerial mapping—that of a crowded city whose residents had once numbered in the hundreds of thousands.[5]

Another of Fowler's archaeologist friends at Southern Illinois University was Pedro Armillas, who was using aerial photography to discover and map the ancient drainage system built by the Aztecs at Xochimilco. At the time of the European conquest, Xochimilco and the Chinampas had been a vast agricultural area covering many square miles—the breadbasket of the Aztec empire. The Aztecs had drained and irrigated the land through a complicated network of hundreds of miles of canals and ridges. Following the Aztecs' defeat by the Spanish, the canals had been filled in and most of the gardens abandoned. From the ground there appeared to be no way to tell where the old canals had once been.

When he examined aerial photos of the Xochimilco area, Armillas discovered lines of vegetation that were different from the weeds growing over most of the area. Those lines were made up of broad-leaf vines that he deduced were growing on the sites of the ancient canals. Though the canals had been filled in for hundreds of years, the moisture content of the soil where the canals had been was still sufficient to support vines instead of dry-land weeds. By tracing these rows of vines on his photographs, Armillas was able to map the locations of the Aztec's waterways at Xochimilco.

As Fowler observed the mapping process at Teotihuacán and Xochimilco, he thought of the mound complex at Cahokia. Why couldn't that site be mapped from the air as well? The old Patrick map, while skillfully done, was clearly in-

---

5. Millon 1973.

adequate for contemporary work. As was the case at Teotihuacán, no one yet knew how much area the city of Cahokia had once covered.

Moreover, Fowler remembered, Cahokia had a history of being photographed from the air. The first aerial photographs of an archaeological site in North America had been taken of Cahokia in 1922 by army pilots from Scott Field in Belleville, Illinois, at the urging of David I. Bushnell, who was researching the area for the Smithsonian Institution. The pictures had not been clear and the pilot explained that the mounds were surrounded by factories burning soft coal, which created a blanket of smoke extending from the ground up to 400 feet in the air. Nothing, observers decided, could be seen in the photographs that was not more visible from the ground.

Despite this discouraging result, Dr. A. R. Crook, then director of the Illinois State Museum, persisted in calling for aerial photos to help resolve the question of the geology of the mounds, whether they were natural or manmade. He got his opportunity when General Pershing visited Springfield. Crook carried his request for photographs directly to the general.

Pershing was intrigued and agreed to help. He ordered an army pilot, Lieutenant G. W. Goddard, and his assistant to fly over Cahokia and take pictures. The weather for this flight, made in April 1922, was far better than it had been for the previous flight. A fortuitous wind may have blown away the smog, for the pictures Lieutenant Goddard brought back were clear and sharp and provided excellent views of all kinds of soil patterns that were not visible at ground level.[6]

Black-and-white film has an emulsion of silver salts on it that become black when they are activated by light energy. The light reflecting off a surface onto a sheet of film consists of energy from all manner of sources, light energy as well as energy that reflects the absorption and reflective characteristics of the land. Dry soil reflects light differently from wet soil and once soil has been disturbed it absorbs moisture differently, a difference that cannot be seen with the human eye but is recorded by the sensitive silver eye of a sheet of film. If a graph of the entire electromagnetic spectrum were enlarged to three times the circumference of the earth, the portion representing the part the human eye can see would be no wider than a pencil line.

The more Fowler observed the activities at Teotihuacán, Mexico, in the mid-1960s the more he wanted to use aerial photography to map and study both Cahokia and Amalucan. While still in Mexico he began writing a grant proposal for submission to the National Science Foundation. Rene Millon read it over and made suggestions. Fowler reworked it, explaining that mapping the sites was

---

6. Crook 1922; Goddard 1969.

the necessary first step to gaining an understanding of the communities as a whole. He wanted to be able to look at the surface distribution of features and try to figure out how the community might have functioned. On the basis of that understanding he would then select a few key locations to excavate.

Fowler finished writing his Cahokia-Amalucan proposal when he returned from his summer's work in Mexico in the fall of 1965 and submitted it. It came back from the National Science Foundation with the notation that the NSF would fund work at one site but not at two. He would have to make a choice, Cahokia or Amalucan.

Fowler's title at Southern Illinois University was "Curator of North American Archaeology." Since he had more experience with the Midwest, and Illinois was where his paycheck was coming from, he decided on Cahokia. He resubmitted his proposal to the National Science Foundation emphasizing Cahokia. In his request he included funds in the budget for making an aerial photogrammetric map of the Cahokia Mounds area at a scale of 1:2000 with a one-meter contour interval. These were the same specifications that Rene Millon had set for his map of Teotihuacán and it would result in the first map made of Cahokia since the Patrick map in the nineteenth century.

It was a major proposal, the largest request for funds for Cahokia since the highway salvage operation. This project would be the opposite of what the salvage project had been. There would be no more working within a contractor's time schedule, no more being restricted to the highway right-of-way, and no more excavations dictated by the locations of overpasses. When the archaeologists made the next excavation at Cahokia, it would be where their professional judgments dictated they should dig, not because the site was in the way of a new discount store or housing development. Fowler spelled all of this out in his request to the NSF and in 1966, after Southern Illinois University signed off on the papers, he was awarded the grant. The decades-old dreams of Patrick, Snyder, and Moorehead would, at last, be partially fulfilled.

Before the project could begin, Melvin Fowler's career took another turn. He received a letter from the chairman of the anthropology department at the University of Wisconsin, Milwaukee, asking him to apply for a professorship that was open. Though he was reluctant to leave Illinois, Fowler applied and was offered the position. He and his family moved to Milwaukee in the summer of 1966. The National Science Foundation grant to map Cahokia, along with a cadre of graduate students, followed him to Wisconsin.

Fowler's first task, after moving to Wisconsin, was to organize the big Cahokia project. He divided it into three phases. A major goal, phase one, would be the mapping of the site and an attempt to understand the relationships among the major visible features of Cahokia. The second phase would be an investigation of some faint white lines he had observed on the Goddard air photos, and the third phase would be the investigation of a small ridge-top mound, Mound 72.

He would begin with the mapping project. Fowler's undergraduate training in civil engineering at Purdue University had taught him how to make and read maps as representations of three-dimensional space as well as to use and interpret aerial photography. At the University of Chicago, Professor Rexford G. Tugwell had taught Fowler to look at space and its use in terms of its social implications.

Fowler decided to hire the same aerial photography firm from New York to do the mapping of the Cahokia site that Rene Millon had used to map Teotihuacán. The maps they had produced were excellent, though Fowler later wished he had used a local firm so he could have worked with its staff more closely and continued the relationship over the years.

Because of a photograph's ability to show alterations in the soil that had taken place centuries before, Fowler hoped to find evidence for early changes at Cahokia. Beginning around A.D. 750, agriculture based upon Indian corn became a major subsistence source at Cahokia. While the maize plant had been known to the Native Americans for centuries before it became a major food crop, it was the Mississippians who spread maize agriculture over much of eastern North America.

Maize grew well in the hot and humid summers in the American Bottom. Barring a drought, corn harvests were bountiful and the caloric content of corn, compared to that of the smaller-seeded native plants, was enormous. Of special significance, corn could be stored in large enough quantities to provide a food source through the winter. It could support the construction of public works such as mounds, the clearing of fields, or the building of fortifications. Corn that was not needed for food could be traded for other goods and services or used as gifts to religious or social elites. Because of its abundance, nutritional content, and durability while in storage, corn played a major role in the economy and culture of the Mississippians of the American Bottom.

Fowler suspected that the development of maize agriculture may even have been a cause in the breakdown of the Hopewellian Interaction Sphere. Supported by agriculture, communities became more localized and independent and developed more complex community hierarchies and organization. Labor became more specialized. In the Cahokia area there are large numbers of hoe-like implements made out of Mill Creek chert, from the Mill Creek quarries of southern Illinois. The fact that so many hoes were found suggests that a specialized production of hoes developed along with the extensive cultivation of corn.

The landscape around Cahokia in A.D. 500 was filled with small villages surrounded by outlying farmsteads. While the settlements were more or less independent, the residents interacted. Their subsistence was largely based on the starchy seed plants but with the rapid addition of maize to their diet. There was not the widespread distribution of exotic goods that had been present in earlier periods nor were there any large community earthworks. These village farming communities slowly grew in population and expanded into the river bottoms, becoming the foundation upon which Cahokia would be built.

The American Bottom provided an almost inexhaustible supply of plant and animal resources for both the prehistoric Cahokia population and the later European settlers. On the floodplain next to the river willows, cottonwoods and herbs such as sedge, nightshade, and knotweed grew in abundance while fish and mussels lived in the ox-bow lakes and sloughs. Water-loving plants such as cattail, arrowhead, American lotus, and wild sweet potatoes grew in the wet areas, along with pin oak, honey locust, and persimmon trees. Back from the river, where the land was better drained, were the wetland prairies observed by Brackenridge. There prairie grasses flourished with a rich variety of sedges and small legumes such as wild beans and prairie clover—largely the starchy, small-seeded plants that had been domesticated in the Archaic period. In the higher areas along the base of the bluff were silver maple, box elder, American elms, hackberry, and pecan trees. Grapes and other vines grew in abundance.

Along the top edge of the bluffs grew stands of oak, elm, ash, sugar maples, pawpaw, black walnut, butternut, and mulberry. On the ground, flourishing in the shade of the trees, were herbs such as bloodroot, jack-in-the-pulpit, and wild ginger. Behind this were the rich growths of the upland prairie. These diverse plants flourished on the American Bottom within a very short distance of each other—no more than a half day's walk from any human settlement.

Animal life too was abundant. The Mississippi was a major flyway for waterfowl while beaver, mink, and muskrat lived in the sloughs, backwaters, and abandoned river channels of the floodplain. Catfish, sunfish, sucker, gar, and bowfin were plentiful in the rivers and streams. In the nearby woods lived white-tailed deer, raccoons, wolves, bears, and squirrels. The weather was temperate with long summers marked by frequent rains and high heat and humidity. Everywhere the soil was fertile and, during the wet and humid summer months, plants grew with a tropical intensity.

The area Fowler planned to photograph from the air in 1966 bore only the slightest resemblance to this Eden. The area around Cahokia was a flat, biologically monotonous, agro-urban environment littered with the detritus of American economic life. Gone was the network of wetlands, swamps, and sloughs that had once supported that great diversity of plant and animal life. Drive-in theaters, carpet sales outlets, trailer parks, asphalt parking lots, weed-choked empty lots, and oil storage tanks lined the highways and interstates. In the midst of this wasteland, the mounds rose suddenly from the flat land like islands of calm, their mysterious presence a radical contrast to the urban frenzy surrounding them.

Despite the contrasts between Cahokia and modern-day St. Louis, it is not an accident that the largest city in ancient North America was located on the same site as a major city of the modern world. Ancient Cahokia and modern St. Louis developed in the same place in response to the same realities of geography—though the people who made the decisions were separated from each other by centuries and by cultures that would have been mutually unintelligible.

Both cities were gateways to a vast and rich hinterland. St. Louis had its beginnings as much on the east side of the Mississippi, in Illinois, as on the west where the downtown of St. Louis now stands. Both cities depended on the great network of rivers. In later years the direction of frontier movement for St. Louis became east to west, while Cahokia remained the gateway to a north-south fan-shaped land dependent mainly on transportation by waterways.

Despite their differences from the European settlers, the Native Americans had responded similarly to the geography of mid-America, to the pounding rivers draining the heart of the continent. Both societies, for reasons they may have only dimly understood, built their metropolises on the banks of the Mississippi, almost equidistant between the Great Lakes and the Gulf of Mexico.

And both cities grew large. In terms of influence, public works, technology, ceremonialism, and population density, the Mississippian peoples at Cahokia represent the high point in the cultural evolution of Native Americans in North America. By A.D. 1000 they were practicing intensive corn and squash agriculture, and they had a complex social organization, chiefs who could control vast amounts of the society's wealth and power, a theocratic organization with leaders having both religious and political power, towns in which thousands of people lived year round, specialized craftspeople, and monumental architecture. Lastly, they established a network for the procurement and distribution of status goods.

As Fowler studied the Patrick map, he could see that the Cahokia site was shaped like a broad diamond or wide kite that covered about six square miles. Approximately in the middle stood Monks Mound. A mile and a half west of Monks Mound was the Powell group of mounds, which had been largely destroyed, although Charles Bareis continued excavations in the area for a number of years. A mile and a half east of Monks Mound was the East Group, which was still mostly intact though a modern-day house had been built on top of Mound 1. The Kunnemann Group was at the northern point of the diamond, and 2.25 miles to the south was the Rattlesnake Group.

It would eventually be determined that at least 120 mounds had once lain within the boundaries of that diamond. Patrick had found 71. With his new maps, Fowler would eventually locate 92 but be unable to determine the original shape of 47 of them. Of the other 45, 28 were single-platform mounds and 4 were double platforms, all of which had probably once had buildings on top of them.

Fowler marveled at the prodigious amounts of communal labor that must have gone into building the mounds. There was the initial planning of the structures, the excavating, the carrying of the dirt to the construction site, the piling up of sediment loads so as to create the final form and elevation, and then the finishing off of the surfaces to prevent slumping and erosion.

The size of the platform mounds and their location, Fowler thought, probably implied their relative importance to the community. The residences of the bulk of the population were built on low platforms. The residential structures found on the top of the higher platform mounds had probably been the homes of the community leaders. Monks Mound, near the geographic center of Cahokia, was undoubtedly the central focus of the community.

The shape of the mounds, Fowler surmised, must have been deliberately chosen by the builders to conform to the purpose for which they were built. The most common mound form, the platform type, was built in the shape of a truncated pyramid with a flat top. Mounds of this form were common in sites first visited by the De Soto expedition and were described as platforms for important buildings.

Many of the residences of the bulk of the population at Cahokia were built on low platforms. Brackenridge had observed such platforms, surrounded by residential debris. Harriet Smith concluded from her excavations in the Murdock Mound that the area had first been a residential area with structures built on low platforms. Later a large mound with a building on top of it had been built over the area. Her interpretation of this sequence was that the area had changed from being a general residential area to an "elite" neighborhood, and then to a "temple" location on top of the mound.

Eleven mounds were conical or chocolate drop in shape. The bases of these mounds were circular and they rose to a point with no platform on the top that could have held a residence. The best-preserved conical mound is Round Top, number 59. Round Top Mound was never cultivated and so has consistently maintained its height of 40 feet and diameter of around 80 feet. Another conical mound, the James Ramey Mound, number 33, was not so well preserved. The mound, originally 35 feet high, had been greatly reduced by plowing and removal of earth from its summit to fill in nearby low spots. The Jondro Mound, number 78, a conical mound, was partially excavated by Moorehead's crew, which found forty complete burials as well as other fragmented human remains.

A characteristic of the conical mounds is that seven of the eleven examples were found in association with platform mounds and there may have been ramps or causeways that connected the two. Fowler wondered if the conical mounds might not be burial mounds. Eyewitness accounts from the early historic period in the southeastern United States record the Indian practice of storing human remains in charnel houses. These mortuary warehouses were emptied from time to time and the remains buried in mounds. Could the platform mounds be the location of charnel houses and the associated conical mounds the burial mounds? Might the chocolate-drop mounds not be the graves of select individuals of the society?

Eight mounds were classified as ridge-top, also called "hayrick" mounds, after the distinctive shape of the wagons farmers used to haul hay. The wagons were longer than they were wide and, when filled with hay, rose to a narrow ridge on the top. Moorehead had noted the mounds' rectangular base outlines and the fact that they rose to a ridge "too narrow on top for large wigwams or temples." The two best examples were Rattlesnake Mound, number 66, and Powell Mound, number 86. Rattlesnake had been one of the largest mounds at Cahokia, measuring 170 feet north to south and 430 feet east to west. It was about 30 feet high and its present form is marred by the unfilled trench that Moorehead and Taylor cut through the center of it in the 1920s.

Powell Mound had been almost destroyed for landfill in 1931 but fortunately the 1922 aerial photos show its undisturbed form. The final destruction of Powell Mound took place in the 1960s when the Gem Store was constructed on the site. The only remains of the huge mound are north of the store where about two feet of the northern third of the mound can still be seen. The other six ridge-top mounds were much smaller mounds that had been plowed over. Fowler identified them by their rectangular base outlines and the fact that some had been mapped as ridged mounds by Patrick.

Five of the eight ridge-top mounds were at the extreme limits of the mound area, from 1,000 to 2,000 meters (3,280 to 6,560 feet) from Monks Mound, while one, Red Mound, number 49, was located about 150 meters (1,875 feet) south of Monks Mound. Mound 72, a ridge-top mound, was in the south-central portion of the site, about 860 meters (2,821 feet) south of Monks Mound. Because of their locations, Fowler theorized that these mounds might be marker mounds of some kind, delineating the peripheries of the site and other critical points within the community.

In addition to the mounds, there were 19 borrow pits. "Borrow pit" is the quaint name (used by archaeologists but "borrowed" from highway engineers) given to the large holes created by the Indians when they dug (borrowed) dirt to build the mounds. There were undoubtedly many borrow pits scattered over the Cahokia site that were filled in by the ancient Cahokians during their process of city building. The largest and most obvious pit is an area south and west of Fox and Round Top Mounds, about 750 meters south-southwest of Monks Mound.

In the 1922 aerial photographs the borrow pit shows up as a large white area, apparently completely filled with water. In later years a large stand of trees and brush grew up in it though it contains standing water in the spring and early summer. Fowler doubts that the Cahokians dug their borrow pits much deeper than six feet for practical reasons. Three feet below the surface is a stratum of silty clay that has a high water content and slumps very easily. Most of the borrow pits, which usually fill up with water and acquire a population of fish and ducks, look like large ponds.

The 1966 aerial mapping proceeded on schedule, using a 1:2000 scale with a one-meter contour interval, as planned. The plane, with a camera mounted in the bottom, flew sight lines, much like a farmer plowing a field, back and forth over Cahokia. Each series of pictures overlapped the previous set by a third. Within the series for the flight line, the photos overlapped by two-thirds. When the overlapped pictures were put into a viewer, somewhat like a stereopticon, they produced a three-dimensional image. It was these three-dimensional images that enabled technicians to create a contour map showing elevations.

Though it is now done by computers, at that time the contour maps were made by a technician focusing a beam of light on a known elevation and following that elevation with the light beam. The light beam was attached to a pantograph that traced the lines. When one elevation was complete, the technician would reset the light on an elevation one meter higher and do it all over again. When Fowler finally received the maps in the fall of 1966 they were in huge sheets to show the detail. It took six of them to register the entire site.

The aerial photographs revealed the locations of mounds that had never been mapped and were now totally destroyed. The photographs also helped relocate mounds that had appeared on Patrick's map but could not be found later. One set of three mounds was supposed to be in the area just north of Monks Mound. There was nothing to be seen on the surface in that location when Fowler walked over the ground, but the aerial photographs showed three white soil scars in exactly the places Patrick had mapped (fig. 9).

Lost mounds were found in subdivisions and farmer's fields, under the asphalt of streets and public school parking lots. One residential street has an abrupt hump in the middle of it where the street was constructed right over the top of a mound. Patrick's 71 mounds had grown to 120 and Fowler was sure there were more still to be discovered.

Besides the pictures taken to create the maps, Fowler arranged to photograph the entire 4,000-acre site at different times of the year, from different altitudes

Figure 9. Aerial photo of Monks Monks from the southeast, taken by M. Fowler in 1968. The large building in the lower right is the Ramey farmhouse. Interstate highways 55 and 70 are in the background and Collinsville Road is in the foreground. The circular white spots near the interstate are the plowed-down remnants of mounds. The Washington University excavations can be seen on the top of the mound. The curving white strip on the left of Monks Mound is the road to the summit first used by Hill. Used with permission of M. L. Fowler.

and with different films. Pictures taken in February with standard panchromatic black-and-white aerial film were the most useful as the vegetation was largely gone and soil marks, indicating subsurface features, stood out most clearly. Mounds that had been leveled and plowed as part of a farmer's field showed up on this film as distinct white squares. When the photographer used infrared film to take pictures in the morning, an archaeological feature on the ground would show up dark on the film because it was absorbing energy. An infrared picture taken of that same feature in the afternoon, after it had already built up heat, photographed white.

Once arrangements had been completed for the mapping project, Fowler moved on to the second phase of the NSF grant—an investigation of some faint white lines that Bob Hall had pointed out to him on the 1922 Goddard photos. The lines had appeared again on pictures taken in 1933 by Dache Reeves, an army air corps lieutenant who was interested in archaeology, and they appeared again, though more faintly, in recent pictures. The persistence of the lines over time gave them credibility and Fowler determined to find out what they were. The lines ran north and south, just to the west of Monks Mound. There were also faint lines on the east side of the mound and to the south. Could there have been an enclosure of some kind—such as a wall? If so, the wall would have enclosed about 200 acres of the central portion of Cahokia, including Monks Mound and 17 additional mounds, some of them the largest platform mounds on the site.

Though Fowler had to be at work in Mexico during the summer of 1966, he arranged for James Anderson to be his field director at Cahokia to test in the area of the faint white lines Fowler had seen on the Goddard and Reeves aerial photographs.

Anderson was a tall, big-boned man from Iowa. While an undergraduate at the University of Iowa he had worked on Wittry's 15A highway salvage crew. Anderson was one of those individuals who could drink most of the night and still put in a full day of good archaeological work in the field. Anderson would wear only starched white dress shirts and black pants in the field and he never tied his shoes (fig. 10). Fowler had gotten acquainted with Anderson when Anderson was a graduate student at Southern Illinois University at Carbondale and believed that, despite his idiosyncrasies, he was an excellent field technician.

Figure 10. James Anderson (left) and Melvin Fowler at the palisade excavation, 1971. Used with permission of the Illinois State Museum.

Fowler sent Anderson, with a crew of students from the University of Wisconsin, Milwaukee, to dig test trenches about 200 meters east of Monks Mound across the area where the white lines showed up on the photographs. They had not dug very far before they came upon the characteristic dark stains in the yellow soil indicating archaeological features. The features were a series of trenches that had once held the logs of a great wall or palisade. As they dug further, they found evidence of not one but four palisades. Anderson and his crew of students worked for six weeks that summer and found not only the palisade but the outlines of bastions as well. At that time, the only other Mississippian site where a palisade had been excavated was the Aztalan site in Wisconsin. Evidence of palisades had been noted in the contour maps of the Angel Mounds, a site in southern Indiana, and at the Kincaid site in southeastern Illinois.[7]

Through work done that summer and in 1967 and 1968, Anderson and his crew learned that the Cahokia palisade was made by standing logs upright side-by-side in the ground. At regular intervals there were bastions, portions of the palisade wall that projected outward from which archers could shoot arrows in three directions. Along the wall between the bastions the archaeologists found L-shaped gates. The Indians had built the palisade walls by digging four-foot-deep trenches in the ground, setting logs upright in them, and then immediately backfilling around the logs. The logs used for the bastions were larger than the wall logs and were set deeper into the ground, suggesting that they were load-bearing posts designed to support raised platforms constructed in the bastions. Larger load-bearing posts had been placed at intervals along the wall and set deeper into the ground to provide support. Once the uprights were in place, cross pieces of poles had been lashed, like lath, to both sides of the walls and the whole plastered with a mixture of mud and straw to protect it from fire and weather. The wall probably stood four to five meters above the ground.

A description exists of a similar wall that was seen by members of the De Soto expedition as they fought their way across Florida and up the Mississippi River in the mid-sixteenth century. It was written by Garcilosa de la Vega, the son of an Inca princess and a Spanish conquistador, who had interviewed members of De Soto's company:

> Situated upon a very beautiful plain, the town of Mauvila was surrounded by a wall as high as three men and constructed of wooden beams as thick as oxen. These beams were driven into the ground so close together that each was wedged to the other; and across them on both the outside and inside were laid additional pieces, not so thick but longer, which were bound together with strips of split

---

7. Anderson 1969.

cane and strong ropes. Plastered over the smaller pieces was a mixture of thick mud tamped down with long straw, filling up all of the holes and crevices in the wood and its fastenings, so that properly speaking, the wall appeared to be coated with a hard finish such as one might apply with a mason's trowel. At every fifty feet there was a tower capable of holding seven or eight persons who might fight within it, and the lower part of the wall, up to the height of a man, was filled with the embrasures of a battery designed for shooting arrows at those outside. There were only two gates to the town, one on the east and the other on the west, and in its center there was a great plaza around which were grouped the largest and most prominent houses.[8]

Anderson's excavations exposed 120 meters (394 feet) of the palisade line beside Monks Mound and short segments near U.S. 40 and on the edge of Cahokia Creek.[9] It was obvious that the palisade was a long one. Estimates of its length range from 2,800 meters (9,186 feet) to 4,000 meters (13,123 feet). Even at the conservative estimate, 9,186 feet is 1.75 miles.

When one palisade wall weakened with age, after a period of years, a new one was built in front of the old one so that a continuous barrier was in place at all times. Bastion styles changed, however. The first palisade had round bastions, 12 feet in diameter; the second building of the wall featured large square bastions about 20 feet across. By the time the third and fourth walls were built, the bastions had become smaller open-backed rectangles.

How long did it take the Indians, with stone tools, to build such a palisade with its accompanying bastions and gates? William Iseminger, who worked on the palisade excavations beginning in 1968, has made some guesses based on certain assumptions. He estimates that 20,000 logs (the trunks of full-sized trees) would have been required to build each of the four palisades. This would have included 9,800 logs for the main wall, 5,880 logs to construct 112 bastions, 2,240 logs for 112 bastion platforms, 750 logs for 30 gates, and a minimum of 1,120 logs used to make an estimated 5,600 meters of horizontal lath to lash to both sides of the tops of the posts in order to hold them together.

If a person with a stone ax can fell two trees in an hour (a questionable assumption), then it would take 10,000 person hours to cut down all 20,000 logs. Trimming all the trees would take another 20,000 to 40,000 person hours. Another 20,000 person hours would be required to dig the trenches to hold the logs. To move the logs from where they were cut to the job site would take another 40,000 to 80,000 hours. Additional tasks such as erecting the posts, backfilling, making ropes, tying the crosspieces to the uprights, and plastering the whole

8. De la Vega 1962.
9. Anderson 1969.

construction would take at least another 60,000 hours, bringing the grand to-tal to something like 190,000 hours, or 23,750 eight-hour days. The true number of hours could easily have been double Iseminger's estimate. He allotted no time for planning, for organizing and directing the labor, or for making increasingly longer trips in search of trees of a suitable size.

The existence of the palisade raised many questions. Was Cahokia under attack from outside groups? Were the walls constructed for protection or as a kind of deterrent to enemies? Were the palisades intended to demarcate the center of the city as an elite residential or ceremonial area? The building of the palisade indicated that Cahokia was a highly organized community with levels of authority and a population willing to follow the direction of its chiefs. The palisades meant that workers had time to spare, time that could be marshaled toward a civic purpose. There is no indication that the palisades were ever burned, though there is ample evidence that residential neighborhoods were destroyed when the palisades were built. The palisade, along with the mounds and woodhenges, speaks to the organizing abilities of an elite group of rulers who could conceive of monumental architecture and communicate that vision to the masses of people needed to accomplish it.

In the summer of 1968 Fowler decided to investigate an area where, according to the lines on the photographs, the palisade turned toward the southwest, south and east of the two big mounds called Fox and Round Top. He put a crew to work on the area called the south palisade. Its excavations were successful in that the workers found several stages of construction similar to what had been encountered in the north, sufficient to prove that the palisade did make the turn that was indicated by the lines on the photographs.[10]

Not all of Fowler's excavations resulted in the conclusions he anticipated. While working at the south palisade area, Fowler had his crew investigate a ridge that Nelson Reed had pointed out to him. During a picnic at Cahokia, Reed had been lying on the ground with his head propped up on his hand. From that vantage point he thought he could detect a slight ridge that ran from Rattlesnake Mound in the south all the way up to Fox and Round Top Mounds. Could this be an ancient causeway?

To test the causeway theory the students cut through stands of poison ivy. One student, though his hands were swollen from ivy poisoning and swathed in gauze, refused to stop and kept on digging. The students cut a trench all the way through the causeway and near the bottom they unearthed an artifact. It was an iron railroad spike—not the artifact Fowler had expected.

10. For a more complete discussion of the palisade see the reports by Iseminger et al. 1990 and Holley, Dalan, Lapinot, and Smith 1990.

From information sent him by Bob Hall, Fowler belatedly learned that at some time in the past the railroad had proposed running a track from near Rattlesnake up to Fox and Round Top Mounds to facilitate cutting down the mounds and hauling them away for fill dirt. Apparently a tramway had been constructed but then later was dismantled and forgotten.

Despite such occasional false steps, knowledge of Cahokia was growing at an exponential rate. From Wittry's discovery of the woodhenges to Fowler's aerial mapping and unearthing of the palisades, the mysteries of Cahokia were being revealed at an ever accelerating pace. Word of what was happening on the American Bottom spread throughout the archaeology departments of the country and students began competing for places at Fowler's field schools at Cahokia. Their instincts were not misplaced. The greatest discovery ever made at Cahokia was about to unfold.

NINE

The Excavation of Mound 72

While work continued on the excavation of the palisades in the summer of 1967, Fowler decided the time had come to begin the third part of the NSF project—the investigation of a mound so small it had not even appeared on Patrick's map. Moorehead had put it on one of his later maps and given it the number 72.[1]

At the time of the aerial photogrammetric mapping, Mound 72 had trees growing on top of it and, even though it was about three meters high, it had been missed by the mappers. Fowler had to survey it himself and add it to the map. His interest in Mound 72 had been rekindled during one of his Illinois Archaeological Survey site visits. Charles Bareis had been driving him around Cahokia and as they passed Mound 72 Bareis had remarked, "Here's a little mound that is quite different." It was a ridge-topped mound similar to Rattlesnake and Powell Mounds. When Fowler later examined the mound more closely he noted that it was 30 degrees off the east-west line. Almost all of the other mounds at Cahokia were oriented on north-south and east-west axes. He chanced to mention that fact to Warren Wittry.

"That's interesting," said Wittry. "That's exactly the alignment of the summer solstice sunset and winter solstice sunrise in this latitude—depending, of course, on which end of the mound you are looking from."

There was another reason Fowler chose Mound 72 for study. It was the only ridge-top mound within the protective boundaries of the park. As a result of the highway program, the depredations of looters, and the state purchase of land for the park, private landowners now saw the appearance of archaeologists on their property as the first step in the process of losing their rich farmland. Ar-

---

1. These investigations and the projects they have led to have been reported in several publications reviewing Mound 72 and its relationships to the larger community. See Fowler 1969, 1974, 1978, 1991, 1996a, 1996b; Fowler et al. 1998; Fowler and Anderson 1975; Fowler and Krupp 1996; Fowler and Watson 1997, 1998; Fowler et al. 1998.

chaeologists were not welcome on private property, a point the owners often made clear, not just with threats, but with a display of firearms. What little remained of Powell Mound was on private land, which, as far as Fowler was concerned, put it off limits, and Rattlesnake Mound was owned by the railroad. Getting permission to excavate on park land was simple in those days. Fowler had only to inform Park Superintendent Joe Webb where he was going to dig and Webb would say, "Fine, I'll help you in any way I can."

The first step in the 1967 investigation of Mound 72 was to expand the site grid. As noted earlier, an archaeological site is laid out in grids to locate it in space and so that the places where artifacts have been found can be precisely recorded. In the days of the earlier excavations at Cahokia each project director had laid out a grid of his own for project control. When James Porter was working on Monks Mound he decided that a grid should be established that could be extended to cover all the projects at Cahokia. Fowler agreed and since he had a student who had just completed his mapping course, he sent her to help in the project. The beginning point, or 0 north-south and 0 east-west (labeled 0:0), was established just southwest of Monks Mound. With the grid established, it could be expanded to any location on the site and reduced to one-meter or even smaller squares if necessary.

Mound 72 was in a low-lying section of the park, in an area of sand ridges and clay swales left by ancient channels of the Mississippi River. Because it was a picnic area, Joe Webb mowed it periodically and there were tables and pit toilets nearby.

James Anderson was the field director and he got the crew busy removing the plow zone from the top of Mound 72 in preparation for digging a test trench while other crew members continued their excavations in the palisade area. Fowler sat in the old Ramey farmhouse they used for an office at Cahokia, studying his maps. Something about the placement of the mounds was bothering him and he could not figure out what it was. He sensed that he might be looking at a pattern but, as hard as he tried, he could not see it. He walked out to Mound 72, where his crew was busy removing the top layer of soil, and stared at the mound. Then he went back and studied the maps. And studied. His crew members began to chide him.

"Dr. Fowler," they said, "don't you ever do any digging?" It was June and growing hot and muggy. The crew was contending with poison ivy and mosquitoes.

"My job is not to dig but to think great thoughts," replied Fowler, an edge of impatience in his voice, as he headed back to his office. Once again he spread a section of the Cahokia map out on his desk. He could view only a section at a time because he did not have a table large enough to hold the entire map. Taking a long ruler, he began to draw lines (fig. 11). He drew a line along the ridge

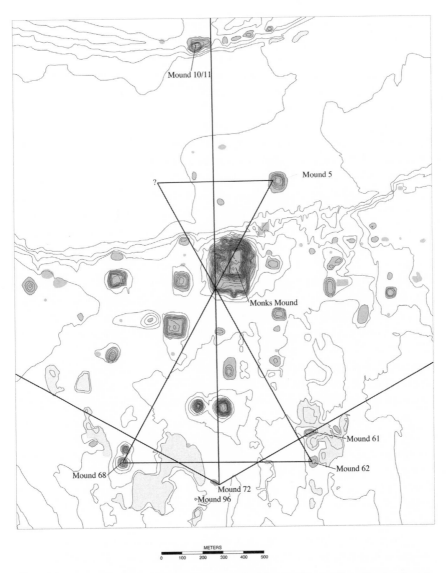

Mound 10/11

Mound 5

?

Monks Mound

Mound 61

Mound 62

Mound 68

Mound 72

Mound 96

METERS

0   100   200   300   400   500

Figure 11. Contour map of the core area of Cahokia showing the lines Fowler drew to discover a north-south axis of the site and to locate Post Pit 1 on Mound 72. Used with permission of M. L. Fowler.

of Mound 72 and extended it into the distance to see if it would cross any mounds. It didn't. (Actually, as he later learned, it did. The mound that it crossed was further off in the distance. He had not extended his line far enough.) Then he tried drawing a line perpendicular to the ridge line and sliding it up and down on the map in the area between Mound 72 and Monks Mound. When he did, he found that the line simultaneously crossed points on the southwest corner of Monks Mound and a mound to the northwest of Mound 72. Then he wondered what would happen if he flipped his lines over and got a mirror image. When he did that he found that he had two lines crossing at the southwest corner of Monks Mound and two 30-degree-angle lines coming together at the southeast end of Mound 72. When he ran a line from the southeast end of Mound 72 through the southwest corner of Monks Mound, he discovered he had a line that ran straight north and south. Furthermore it was true north—not magnetic or grid north but a true north-south line. That same line, extended 600 yards south, hit Rattlesnake—another ridge-top mound.

Fowler sat back and thought. Was it his imagination or was he on to something? Could it be that ridge-top mounds were marker mounds of some sort and that Mound 72 had been carefully calculated and placed where it was to mark the north-south center line at Cahokia? Porter had found that big post in the geometric center of the plaza at the Mitchell site. Could the Indians have been marking critical points of the site with big posts? And if they had done it at the Mitchell site, wouldn't they also have done it elsewhere—perhaps on Mound 72? A post pit on the southeast end of Mound 72 would be a powerful confirmation of his hypothesis.

Fowler, the most cautious, professional, and circumspect of scientists, was excited. He began making calculations, drawing grid lines on the map of Mound 72 and doing the complicated arithmetic. At last he had it. He rushed out to the field where his workers were stripping sod and told them to put in a one-meter trench at south 862.5 and east 83.5 on the grid. He marked it in and told them to start digging, keeping a straight profile on all three sides.

Like Babe Ruth pointing to where he was going to hit his next home run, Fowler announced to his skeptical crew, "Put a trench in right here and I predict we will find a big post pit." This was an extraordinary pronouncement. Archaeologists seldom announce in advance the features they expect to find.

Anderson and the students began to dig. They dug one meter into the mound. Nothing. They went in a second meter. Still nothing. Fowler couldn't understand it.

"Wait a minute," he said. "Let me go back and check."

Fowler went back to the farmhouse and carefully recalculated all of his numbers. To his chagrin, he found that, in his excitement, he had made a simple error in arithmetic. Though a skilled civil engineer, he could become befuddled over arithmetic and on more than one occasion had made simple errors. He had been off his target by exactly three meters. Fowler hurried back to the mound and told his sweaty workers to move south three meters and start all over again. They did, and this time they hit the big dark circular stain that told them they had found the post pit. Fowler had indeed been thinking great thoughts.

Finding the post pit was like opening up a master plan of the Cahokia Mounds. Suddenly this was not a random collection of mounds, scattered haphazardly over the American Bottom, but a city with a plan, built by people who understood angles and units of measurement. Fowler was certain he had stumbled upon the north-south center line, the main street of Cahokia. As he studied his maps he could see evidence for an east-west line as well. Harriet Smith, too, had observed the regular alignment of mounds when she had worked on the Murdock excavation in 1941, and now Fowler was asking if there might have been an organizational plan for the entire area. As had been the case with the Modoc Rock Shelter, what he was finding was upsetting all of the previously held dogma about Cahokia.

Fowler decided to hold a field conference about the finding of the post pit. He had proposed a hypothesis, tested it, and proved it. Conceptually at least, his work on Mound 72 was completed. Interest in Cahokia was high and about sixty archaeologists from all over the Midwest came to learn about the new discoveries. Among those who came was James B. Griffin. A few years before, Griffin had received a fellowship to go to Paris for a year's study of Paleolithic artifacts. When he came back he was wearing a jaunty beret, which he continued to wear as a personal trademark, along with his customary dark blue suit, white shirt, and tie.

Fowler began the field conference by taking the visitors on a tour of Monks Mound and the second season of palisade excavations. Then he brought them to Mound 72 by an old road that went around a borrow pit. He had set up his easels and chairs at the western end of the mound, on the side away from the excavation. When the group had all gathered, Griffin in his beret, the curmudgeon of eastern archaeology, was in the front row.

Fowler had prepared several easels with sections of the 1967 maps of the site and sheets of drawing paper. He began with a lecture on his theory, illustrating it by drawing the lines on his maps as he had drawn them back in his office. He drew the line along the ridge of Mound 72 and showed how it did not go anywhere. Then he drew his perpendicular line and slid it up and down, showing the connection it made with the southwest corner of Monks Mound and another mound.

As he built up his theory he could see Griffin thinking, "Fowler has really flipped this time. Where are his potsherds, dammit." Fowler persisted, turning pages and drawing lines with his felt-tipped marker until he had a pattern of lines that converged on the southeast corner of Mound 72.

"We predicted that there should be a marker post at exactly this point." Fowler put an X on the southeast corner of Mound 72 on his map. The group was silent. Fowler gestured. "Come around here," he said, leading the way around the side of the mound to where they could see the excavation. As was his custom, Griffin was in the front rank. Fowler pointed to the dark circular stain on the cleaned-off floor of his excavation. "This is exactly the point we predicted," he said. "And there it is."

Griffin stared. "Oh, for Christ's sake," he exclaimed. Fowler believed that was the only time in his life he had ever really impressed Griffin. The timing and presentation had been perfect. Fowler had succeeded, in a small way, in tracking the thinking of the ancient people who had built the mounds. He was convinced that the Indians had been acting with a plan—a concept—and he had discerned a part of it. With the discovery of the Mound 72 post pit, archaeologists began conceiving of Cahokia as an organized community and developing new ideas about its level of complexity.

When the conference ended, Fowler had his crew excavate the post pit (fig. 12). They left the north side of the pit in place and excavated only the south half, making drawings all the way. What they did not realize until later was that 1967 was a dry year and it had been dry the preceding three years. As a result they were able to dig down the entire nine feet to the bottom of the pit and get a unique sequence without the walls caving in. The walls started to bulge when they got close to the bottom but a four-by-four-foot plywood panel put in the hole kept the walls from collapsing. Not until they reached the bottom of the pit did they find a bit of moisture in the sediment.

In later years they learned just how unusual their experience had been. The gumbo-like clay at Cahokia is very fine grained so that when it rains and water begins percolating down from the upper strata, the clay begins flowing like a liquid. The one particular stratum of the clay soils that had this tendency to flow was in the upper half of the excavation. For lack of a better term, and lacking

---

Figure 12. Excavation of Post Pit 1 in Mound 72. Top: The circular area of dark lumps of earth indicates the presence of Post Pit 1 in Mound 72. The vertical string in the center marks the point at which the post location was predicted. The white sloping surface in the upper center is the plastered surface of 72Sub1. Bottom: The lower meter of the excavation of Post Pit 1. In the bottom of the pit, near the vertical string, are the impression in the natural sandy sediments left by the post and the dark remnants of the cribbing logs. Used with permission of M. L. Fowler.

technical training in soils analysis, the crew referred to this as the "buttery clay" soil. Fortunately, in 1967, the walls of the post pit remained solid and they made their second discovery. Though they did not find the remains of the post, as Porter had at Mitchell, they found something equally interesting. In the bottom of the post pit lay the remains of two cribbing logs, lying at right angles, which the Indians had placed to help hold the upright log in place. The wood from the cribbing logs yielded the first radiocarbon dating of Mound 72. The tests were run by the University of Wisconsin laboratory and came back with readings of A.D. 950, plus or minus 50 years, and A.D. 930, plus or minus 50. These were raw, or uncalibrated, radiocarbon dates.

Analysis of the pit, called Post Pit 1, revealed that at least three different posts had been put in this same hole, two of them before Mound 72 had been built, and one or more afterward. The original pit outline the workers had discovered turned out to mark the extraction pit for the removal of the second post and the insertion pit of the third. Fowler was getting his first inkling of the complexity of Mound 72.

One of the workers on Mound 72 was a young man named Kenneth Williams. As a fourteen-year-old, Williams had gone with his parents to visit Dickson Mounds. After touring the museum Williams was walking around the grounds, scuffing his shoe in the dirt in hopes of finding a potsherd or artifact, when Don Dickson came out of his house. He saw the boy fruitlessly looking, walked up to him, and gave him a prehistoric chert knife. Williams was thrilled and excited.

"How can I get into archaeology?" he asked Dickson. Dickson replied that some archaeologists were working on Monks Mound and if he was interested he could volunteer. When the Williams family returned to their home at Granite City, near St. Louis, Ken persuaded his father to drive him to Monks Mound, where Porter was doing some work for Nelson Reed.

"How can I help?" he asked Porter. Porter pointed to a free-standing wall between two trenches and told the boy to knock it down.

"Don't stop unless you see a whole pot," Porter told Ken, figuring the hard work in the hot sun would wear the boy out and that would be the last he would see of him. He was wrong. The next day Williams was back, and every day thereafter. Williams went on to major in anthropology and was working with the University of Wisconsin students who excavated Mound 72.

When the post pit was excavated, Fowler had his crew start a new trench, again coming into the mound from the south side. The trenches were to be dug down to undisturbed soil and then moved slowly into the mound, keeping the walls vertical. The crew had moved in only a short distance when they encountered a smaller mound inside the large mound. The students called it the "black mound" because it had been covered with a heavy black clay mixture that was very resistant to erosion.

The students had exposed a portion of the black mound when Anderson told Williams to take his mattock (a tool with a two-and-a-half-foot handle and blade about four inches wide that makes a flat, straight cut) and cut a trench into the black mound. The surface of the mound was hard and Williams swung his mattock, bringing it down about a foot into the mound. A chunk of black clay flew off, uncovering three perfect projectile points, gleaming white in the morning sun. Williams stared at them in shock. He had come within an inch of shattering the points with his mattock.

The mattocks were laid aside and the students picked up, instead, spoons, dental picks, and orange-wood sticks. Carefully they cleaned off the three arrowheads and found another, and then another. Soon Williams realized that he was uncovering an entire cache of arrow points, numbering in the hundreds. Anderson called Fowler.

"Mike, you've gotta see this," he said. Fowler looked. "Yeah," he replied, "that is really different. Let's keep working."

Besides arrow points the students began finding human bones. The students rushed for their cameras and sketch pads and Anderson went in search of Fowler. Again everything stopped while Fowler determined what part of the body a bone was from, which would determine how they would approach excavating it. A call went out to the dentists in the area for their used dental picks and orange sticks. The bones were so fragile that when the workers tried to lift the dirt away from them, fragments of the bone would come away as well. In an attempt to stabilize the bones the students coated them with Elmer's Glue thinned with water. When that did not work, they tried hot wax, or hot wax with fabric embedded in it. This was only partially successful. In many cases they resorted to following the edge of the bone with the tip of a knife and gently carving the dirt away.

The students were concerned when they were not able to salvage more of the skeletons. Fowler reassured them. "I have dug burials in the Ohio Valley," he told them, "where all that was left was a smiling row of teeth. The Indians made finger rings of copper and there would be the rings where the hands once were in the burial." The skeletons at Cahokia were not that far gone, but they were close to it.

When a layer of bones was encountered, the soil on top of it had to be removed. The excavators could not just shovel it off. Instead they removed each layer slowly and carefully, keeping control of the levels, taking photographs and making detailed drawings. Despite the slow and painstaking pace, an undercurrent of excitement was coursing like electricity through everyone, from the eager students to the cautious Fowler. They came to work early and stayed late. Security became a problem. During the day there were always students at the site. At night they covered the mound with large plastic sheets, anchored with sand bags, and Anderson and Fowler took turns sleeping in their cars at the site to protect it.

Williams's blow with his mattock on the hard clay had revealed not just arrow points but an enormously complicated Mississippian burial, one that was to occupy Fowler's team for the next four years and would further change anthropologists' ideas about the lives of the people who had once lived at Cahokia.

The students carefully removed the dirt from around one set of bones only to find more and more skeletons below, until it became apparent that Mound 72 was a complex mortuary site holding the remains of hundreds of individuals. At a point about 1.5 meters west of the post pit they found two groups of burials. The main figure was a man, laid out face-up on a platform of about 20,000 cut-shell beads, which were drilled and ready to string. While most of the beads were about one inch in diameter, some beads from other areas of the mound had been made from very thick marine shell, up to two inches in thickness, indicating that the shell they had been cut from had grown to more than two feet in diameter. Shells no longer grow that large on the Gulf Coast because of pollution.

The man on the shell-bead platform was obviously a high-status individual who appeared to have been buried shortly after his death. Lying near his body was a quantity of bones that make up what archaeologists call "bone bundles." A bone bundle may consist of all leg bones or all arms or ribs bundled together in one group. In addition to the bone bundles were found the disarticulated remains of several other individuals.

Near the group burial were the remains of three men and three women who had been buried at the same time as the man on the beaded platform, leading Fowler to suspect they were retainers who had been sacrificed at the time of the burial of the man on the beads. Buried with them was a wealth of grave goods (fig. 13). There was a three-foot-long sheet of rolled-up copper that had come from the area around Lake Superior, several bushels of sheet mica that must have been imported from North Carolina, and hundreds of exquisite arrowheads that showed no sign of ever having been used. Each arrowhead was an object of art, a gem of the flint-knapper's craft.

The arrowheads had been carefully sorted into types and by material in the way that any modern archaeologist would recognize. There were arrowheads made of a black chert from the Caddoan area of Arkansas and Oklahoma and of Kaolin chert from southern Illinois. Others were made from stone mined in Tennessee and Wisconsin. Approximately 1,200 arrow points were eventually found in Mound 72.

Figure 13. Artifacts associated with burials in Feature 102 of Mound 72. Arrowhead caches are in the lower left and in the central right area. Chunky stones are in the center. Above these is a pile of mica. To the right of the chunky stones are rolls of hammered sheet copper and strings of large shell beads. Used with permission of the Illinois State Museum.

The arrow points appeared to have been carefully placed in the burials. One cache contained over 300 arrowheads of various types that had been placed pointing northwest, near the head of one individual. In a second cache, more than 400 arrow points were laid across the lower legs of another person and were pointing southeast (fig. 14). Though the wood shafts of the arrows had long ago decayed, the ways the points were grouped suggested they had been put into the grave on shafts and in bundles, as if prepared to be placed in a quiver.

The grave goods Fowler found most impressive were 15 beautifully polished double-concave stone discs made of granite, four to five inches in diameter, called "chunky stones." There is abundant ethnographic evidence that the Indians used chunky stones in a kind of sporting event. Chunky stones are highly prized by collectors, and though Moorehead had found one when he excavated Rattlesnake Mound to the south, no one had ever found a cache of them at Cahokia before.

Figure 14. Projectile point caches from Feature 102 of Mound 72. Left: The projectile points at the northwest end were placed between the skulls of two burials and were pointing to the northwest. The arrowheads were mostly made of local chert from quarries near St. Louis and are typical Cahokia triangular forms. Right: Projectile point cache (pointing southeast) found lying over the legs of the southeastern-most burial of Feature 102. Cache includes black arrowheads native to Arkansas and Oklahoma as well as projectile points from other areas outside the American Bottom. Used with permission of the Illinois State Museum.

The first European visitors to the southeastern United States reported seeing the Indians playing a game they called "chunky" with similar discs. According to the descriptions, two men would be standing in a kind of outdoor bowling alley. One man would send a stone rolling down the line and then would run alongside it and cast his spear at the point where the stone was expected to stop. Another version had the players throwing a spear and trying to knock the stone over.

Though the stones were highly polished and smooth, Fowler noted little peck marks breaking through the polish. On the edge, where the stone came in contact with the ground, it was smooth, but on the sides were the little marks, which, he believed, was where spears had hit them. Some of Fowler's colleagues disagreed, saying the peck marks were there because the Indians had not polished them well enough. To Fowler, that was the "crude savage Indian" idea coming out again.

"These guys were artisans," he insisted. "They were not going to leave little blemishes on their stones." In Fowler's opinion the peck marks indicated the chunky stones had been used and were already old when they were buried. In the 1700s an Englishman by the name of William Burtram was traveling through the Southeast and wrote in his journal about chunky stones among the Cherokee and Choctaw—noting that the stones were the property of the community and were exempt from being buried. They were the possessions of the corporate group. The chunky stones went to the grave in Mound 72 with an individual who may very well have embodied in his person the corporate identity of a group.

To the students digging that summer, and through the four following seasons, there seemed to be no end to the bodies they were discovering and to the resultant mysteries. They uncovered another small mound within Mound 72 and under this mound the bodies of four men had been laid side by side with their arms overlapping each other. The mystery was that all four men were missing their heads and their hands.

In a nearby pit the students uncovered the bodies of more than 50 individuals. These bodies, too, had been placed side by side, and when those placing them ran out of space, they had stacked the bodies on top of each other in layers. Al Harn was called in to help determine the sex of the skeletons. Harn lay on his stomach on a plank over the pit, studying the rows of bones in the excavation. From time to time he would get up, shaking his head. From his analysis they were all turning out to be women. All were between the ages of 18 and 23. How could that be? Harn took a break and began to question his judgment. Was it reasonable that all 50 or more skeletons would be of young women? Harn had years of experience studying bones at Dickson Mounds and he could recognize the wider pelvis and smaller bones of women. "Reasonable or not," he finally told Fowler, "these are all bones of young women."

Though there was no physical evidence of it, Fowler was sure the young women had met an untimely death. Their closeness in age argued against their having died from disease or some common disaster. There is a description of the Natchez Indians, made in the 1720s by a French man who had observed the burial of an important leader. As part of the burial rites women were lined up along the ceremonial route, each given a large quid of tobacco, perhaps to dull their senses, and then garroted from behind. It was difficult for Fowler to avoid the conclusion that the four headless and handless men and the fifty or more young women had all been sacrificed, probably as part of some kind of funeral ritual. Their bodies lay very near that of the man on the beaded platform. Could their deaths, Fowler wondered, have been part of a sacrifice for him?

One of the graduate student workers who came to work on Mound 72 in 1970 was Jerome Rose, a young man who had earned his B.A. degree in anthropology in 1969 at the University of Colorado at Boulder. Rose had gone on to the University of Massachusetts for graduate work in osteology and paleopathology when he heard, from another graduate student, about the extraordinary burials that were being found at Cahokia. When he learned that Fowler was looking for an osteologist he applied for a summer job. Fowler hired him and Rose drove from Boston to East St. Louis, arriving on a hot summer day.

His first reaction to Cahokia was astonishment at its massive size. Rose recalled, "I was totally amazed at the gigantic size of the site and the mounds. Coming from Colorado, I had absolutely no idea that there was any archaeology east of the Mississippi River. Finding these huge mounds of such cultural complexity was staggering to my imagination. There were 100 people working at four or five projects. Yet you would never know anyone else was there. We were all working on widely scattered sites spread over a large area." Within a couple of hours Rose was sharing a cookout with the crew on top of a mound while they watched a storm roll in and a tornado touch down not far from where they sat.

Rose's specialty was bones, but the bones at Cahokia gave him challenging problems. He had come from archaeology in the Southwest, where bones were perfectly preserved in the sand of a semiarid region. Here the workers were digging in very hard, compact clay material that was so difficult to excavate they had to hack it away with pick-axes and mattocks, shovel it into wheelbarrows, and carry it away. Skeletons buried in this material were squashed down to pancake dimensions. Rose studied the fragile bones, saw that the glue and wax processes had not worked, and realized that he did not have a clue as to how to get those poorly preserved skeletons out of the ground. He ultimately decided they should remove the clay material as best they could, make as many observations as possible in the ground, and go on from there. To excavate the burials, students lay suspended on boards so they could work over the pit, reaching down with dental picks as they tried to clean the hard mud off the skeletons.

When torrential rains came, they were disastrous. The burial pits were the lowest points in the excavation and they filled up with rainwater. Rose remembers that he would see kneecaps and other bones floating around on the top. Eventually, when most of the water had drained away, the students would sop up the remaining moisture from the bones with sponges and then try to remove the mud. The wheels on the wheelbarrows would get so covered with mud that they would bog down and could not be pushed. The workers walked around with five pounds of mud clinging to each shoe.

The temperature went up to 109 degrees and stayed there. When the sun shone on the clay it turned it into a material as hard as concrete. Anderson rigged up sump pumps to cope with the rains, and when the students began falling behind in their work, he went to an army surplus store and bought flood lights salvaged from a PT boat, set up a generator, and organized two eight-hour shifts. One shift worked from 7 A.M. until 4 P.M., when the second shift started and worked until midnight or one in the morning. Anderson worked both shifts.

Excavation of burial pits where women had been carefully laid out required extraordinary care as the workers found evidence that the layers of bodies had been separated by woven mats. The mats were gone but the impressions of the matting remained on the sand at the bottom of the pit. One of the students found the remains of pieces of string, which she meticulously excavated, one grain at a time, using sewing needles. At one corner of the pit workers found a bone pin that may have been used to hold the mats together.

When the first season for archaeological work on Mound 72 was coming to an end, the man on the beaded platform had still not been completely excavated. Fowler had hoped to remove the entire clay platform and take it to his laboratory in Milwaukee where it could be carefully excavated during the winter. The workers began undercutting the slab and covering the clay itself with strips of cloth soaked in plaster of Paris. The piece was large, at least eight feet long, four feet wide, and four feet thick. The plaster added more weight. When they finally had it ready to remove from the mound they found it was too heavy to take back to Milwaukee with the equipment they had and they decided to store it for the winter in a barn on the park property. There it could stay until the next summer, when Fowler and his students would set up lights and cameras and complete the excavation.

They loaded the beaded burial onto a tractor and moved it slowly and carefully to the barn, where it was placed on a sturdy platform and left until the following summer. The only thing they had not anticipated was a hungry raccoon. When they opened the barn doors the next spring, they found that a raccoon had eaten a hole down through the middle of the beaded burial. It had not occurred to them to put plaster strips over the top of the skeleton.

In the fall of 1967, at a midwest archaeology conference, Fowler gave his first report on the Mound 72 discoveries. He put a slide on the screen of the beaded burial and told the assembled archaeologists that the skeleton had been laid out on a beaded cape with some sort of hood extension. He had gone on to other slides when Pat Munson suddenly shouted from the back of the room, "My God, Mike. That is a bird. A beaded bird."

Munson insisted that Fowler back up his slides to the shot of the beaded burial. Fowler was skeptical. How could a youngster like Munson see something at first glance that Fowler had missed during weeks of scrutiny? But sure enough, the more they looked at it, the more they could see that the beads were laid out in the shape of a bird, possibly a falcon. Even the wings and tail feathers were evident. Though Fowler admitted he was a hard sell on the concept, the beaded burial became known thereafter as the "Beaded Birdman Burial" (fig. 15).

Excavation continued at Mound 72 for four years with students supplying the labor. Anderson, the field supervisor, was conscious of the image the students projected while they were working. Tourists were coming in droves to see what was going on at Cahokia and he insisted that the students take breaks to answer questions—no matter how foolish or poorly phrased they might be. He reminded the students that they were working with human remains and to show the proper respect.

Anderson's reminders were necessary. The students were working eight-hour shifts, many in cramped holes in the ground, in 100-degree temperatures, and high jinks were both inevitable and necessary to relieve their stress. Anderson understood, but he did not encourage them.

While the students dressed in shorts and T-shirts because of the heat and humidity, Anderson wore his usual dark trousers and starched white shirts with

Figure 15. The Beaded Birdman of Mound 72 was laid out on a platform of 20,000 shell beads arranged in the form of a bird. The white arrow indicates north. Used with permission of the Illinois State Museum.

the sleeves rolled up. Rose remembers Anderson giving an interview to reporters from national television. He was standing on Mound 72, gesturing and explaining the dig, his trademark white shirt buttoned crookedly up the front, sleeves rolled up, and untied shoelaces trailing on the ground about his feet. If he had a life away from Cahokia, no one ever knew about it.

As Barbara Vander Leest noted, "Anderson just ate, drank, and lived Cahokia Mounds." Vander Leest, a graduate student from the University of Wisconsin, Milwaukee, was one of the students working in a pit. Among her tasks was accurately counting and sorting shell beads—more than 36,000 of them—as she and fellow workers removed them, one by one, from their thousand-year deposit in the clay.

Three more female mass burials were found with, respectively, 19, 22, and 24 individuals in them. Above one group the pit had been partially redug and grave goods deposited, including the 36,000 marine-shell beads, 400 perfect arrowheads, an antler harpoon and spear points, and five broken vessels. Another burial pit had 40 individuals, of mixed ages and both sexes, tossed in haphazardly, while about six inches above them there were 14 individuals who had been carried to their graves on litters made of six-foot-long cedar poles and shorter cross pieces. Because cedar is more resistant to decay than other woods, the poles were still there, though the fabric that had once been stretched between them was gone.

Mound 72, barely seven feet high, had turned out to be an enormously complex burial site used for the interment of elite individuals of Cahokia or, perhaps, even several generations of the same prominent family. Back in his laboratory, as Fowler studied the field notes and maps made by his crew, he identified a sequence of building phases on the mound that included six separate burial episodes involving approximately 272 individuals. He estimated that the entire sequence covered no more than 100 years and probably less.

The first episode, which was contemporary with the erecting of the marker post in Post Pit 1, began with the construction of a timber building on level ground. Because there was little household refuse around the building, Fowler deduced that it was a charnel house—a building for the storage of bodies. Near the charnel house was another large post pit, Post Pit 2. The charnel house building was later dismantled and a mound raised over a group of burials that included the burial of two males who had just died, and the bundled bones of others who had been dead for a long time. These burials were laid out precisely above the wall trenches of the dismantled charnel house. This kind of interment suggests a ritual that postpones the burial of lesser relatives until the kinsman of high status dies, when all are buried as a group. To the south side of these bundle burials were a male and a female burial in extended positions.

The earthwork that was built over this first mass burial was a small, two-level platform mound measuring about 46 square feet at its base. The square mound was oriented to the cardinal points of the compass with the lower terrace on the east. The second large post was standing in the northeast corner of the platform. Nothing was added to the mound for some time, except for one pit that was dug on the east side and another on the south to accommodate some female burials.

These pit burials were the second episode of burials in this inner mound, which, along with its later stages, was called Mound 72Sub2. It was given this designation for convenience and not in reference to its sequence in mound construction or when it was discovered. There is little doubt that it was one of the earlier constructions at Mound 72 but whether it was earlier, later, or contemporary with the burial mound at the other end of Mound 72 has not been determined.

The third episode involved two further excavations and additional construction. One of the excavations was a pit that intruded into the fill covering of the pit dug earlier in episode two on the south side of the mound. No bodies were buried in the new hole. Instead the diggers had placed pottery, shell beads, and projectile points in the pit and then filled it up again. At about the same time a rectangular pit was dug at the southeast corner of the mound and 24 females were buried there. Work did not stop with the refilling of the pit but was continued until a platform or ramp was raised above it, extending the initial platform mound to the southeast.

Another complex burial group was placed to the southeast near Post Pit 1. These burials were later covered over and became part of what was called Mound 72Sub1 (fig. 16). Mound 72Sub1 was a low, flat-topped mound with the long axis north-south and small platform extensions on the east and west sides, giving it a unique cruciform shape. The large Post Pit 1 was at the center of the east end of this mound. Central to this group was the Beaded Birdman Burial—the burial of the individual who was placed upon the elaborate platform of shell beads. Later analysis would disclose that the Beaded Birdman Burial was, in reality, two burials. One individual had been placed under the shell beads, face down, and a second had been placed on top, facing up. These individuals were accompanied by a number of bone bundles and the partly disarticulated remains of other individuals. Nearby were the remains of the three men and three women who had been buried with the great wealth of grave goods—the arrowheads, copper, mica, and chunky stones.

The next stage in mound construction was the extension of 72Sub2 in the direction of 72Sub1 and the covering over of the burial pit and platform that had been placed in the southeast corner of 72Sub2. This extension of 72Sub2 took place in at least three stages, ending up as a long platform mound with a ramp at

Figure 16. Field-crew members, foreground, excavating Features 101 and 102 in Mound 72Sub1. Melvin Fowler (background, left) points out details of the excavation to Thorne Deuel (center) while Al Meyer puts finishing touches on a drawing. Used with permission of the Illinois State Museum.

its southeast end. A large pit was excavated about ten yards southeast of the extension that had earlier been added to the platform mound. Between the pit and the mound extension a small earthen mound had been raised and the bodies of four men, the ones with their heads and hands missing and arms interlinked, were placed on top of it. In a pit beside that containing the four men, the bodies of the more than 50 young women were placed side by side. Earth was heaped over both group burials so that the platform mound was extended still farther to the southeast. This construction was called by the archaeologists Mound 72Sub3 (fig. 17). Mound 72Sub3 filled in the area between 72Sub1 and 72Sub2, with its highest point in the geometric center of the complete Mound 72.

Along the south side of 72Sub3 several rectangular pits had been excavated and burials placed in them. One of these, Feature 229, was of particular interest in that it contained two layers of burials. The lower level was a jumbled mass, as if the bodies had been thrown in helter-skelter, perhaps as a sacrifice. Over these burials was the group of individuals who had been tightly wrapped and carried to their graves on litters. The cedar poles of these litters yielded a radio-

Figure 17. The surfaces of Mounds72Sub1 (top) and 72Sub3 (bottom) as they were exposed in the Mound 72 excavations. The triangular cut areas are where test excavations were dug to locate the mounds. Note the thin white cap over the mounds and the mottled profile in 72Sub1 indicating basket loading. The fill in 72Sub3 is comprised of laminated bands rather than basket loading. Used with permission of M. L. Fowler.

carbon date of approximately 1030 radiocarbon years A.D., or about 100 years after the age estimates for Post Pit 1.

Altogether, ten oblong pits had been dug near the southwestern edge of the multiple mound. The pits were used for mass burials and in some instances the individuals were buried soon after death. In others, bundles of bones were included. When the last oblong grave was filled, the builders of Mound 72 covered the multiple structure with fresh earth, giving it the ridge-top form that had initially attracted the archaeologists' attention. Some burials were included in the mound fill and others were found in pits that were probably dug after the mound was finished.

What had appeared in the beginning as a simple ridge-top mound had turned out to be an exceedingly complex sequence of mounds. The form, orientation, and interrelationships of the mounds comprised a carefully planned program. Each of the submounds was related to a grouping of burials and offerings and each of the mounds had been carefully constructed and capped with specially prepared erosion-resistant materials.

Gradually, as Fowler and his colleagues analyzed their data, the sequence of the buildup of Mound 72 could be seen. The first features in place had been the two post pits with, at one time, large posts inserted. Next came the construction of the two primary mounds, one over each of the post locations. The next stage was the construction of several modifications and extensions of 72Sub2 in the direction of 72Sub1, culminating in the building of the third mound, 72Sub3, over the headless males and the female burial pit. The final stage was the shaping of Mound 72 to cover all three submounds. Even after Mound 72 had received its final shape, it was not left alone. Along the southwest margins of the final mound was the series of rectangular pits with burials in them.

By 1972 about two-thirds of Mound 72 had been excavated, leaving the northeast portion of the mound largely untouched. A north-to-south trench had been run through the area along the east 75 grid line from south 845 to south 859. The profiles in this trench showed a different kind of fill from what had been observed in the other excavations. This fill was largely basket loading of a more sandlike material and the basket loading was clearly defined. No burial or other features were encountered in the trench. Fowler believed this represented the last construction phase of Mound 72, in which the three primary or submounds had been covered and the orientation of the final mound to the 30-degree or solstice axis of the final ridge-top form had taken place. Though nothing had been encountered in the test trench, this did not mean that there was nothing to be found in the unexcavated area. In the southwest portion of the mound, burials and burial pits were found that had been sunk into the final ridge-top of Mound 72. Fowler had to decide whether to seek additional funds to continue or to cease excavations. Certainly he had already acquired enough data to keep archaeologists busy analyzing it for years to come.

Fowler, with Anderson's help, considered his decision very carefully. A primary factor in their consideration was the rapidly growing American Indian Movement (AIM), some members of which held that archaeologists and academics were disrespectful of the Indians' heritage and beliefs and, by excavating Indian sites, were desecrating sacred areas. In their frustration, members of AIM had shut down some archaeological digs in the United States and destroyed the painstakingly accumulated notes of archaeological field projects.

A major AIM premise was that everything in prehistoric North America represented the Native America heritage and should not be tampered with by archaeologists. Even the process of investigation, they believed, showed disrespect for Native Americans and their sacred places. Some Native Americans felt that they knew their own history from creation stories and had no need for archaeology.

Fowler and Anderson were sympathetic with the Native American philosophy and, up to a point, agreed with it. Archaeological sites that dated within the past two or three hundred years could possibly be tied to contemporary Indian groups. Work in these areas should be attempted, they believed, only with the approval of the Native American groups involved as the work had a direct impact on the remains of their ancestors.

Archaeological sites before that time period, however, were much more difficult to match with any living group of American Indians, either cultural or linguistic. The more ancient the archaeological site, the more difficult the problem, as there were undoubtedly population movements before the European arrival. A site such as Cahokia, which was a thousand or more years old, was even more difficult to tie to any historically known groups. Ancient communities as large as Cahokia must have attracted peoples of diverse cultural and linguistic backgrounds who became allied with the ruling power of Cahokia and blended into the total population.

At the time of the first European contact with the Indians of eastern North America there was a tremendous disruption of Native American cultures due to the introduction of deadly diseases to which the Indians had no biological immunity. Populations were reduced by 60 percent or more in just a few decades—within one person's lifespan. Pandemics spread these diseases and their consequences far beyond the face-to-face contacts that first introduced them.

As a result, great dislocations of populations took place when remnants of one group joined forces with remnants of other groups to produce viable societies. Ancient tribal identities were blurred or lost and new ones formed. Populations were forced from their homelands, which further dislocated other groups. The debilitated Native Americans were no match for the onslaught of European colonization and conquest that followed. The history of the period after A.D. 1500 would have been quite different if the Indians had had biological immunity to European diseases such as smallpox and measles.

The question for archaeologists, as Fowler saw it, was how to make connections with these pre-European peoples—a process that he felt could be accomplished, in part, through archaeological research. The concepts of pan-Indianism, which tended to homogenize the native cultures, were a major impediment to making these connections with the past. In the end, out of empathy for but not in total agreement with Native American concerns, Fowler decided to discontinue the Mound 72 excavations. The northeast portion of the mound was left untouched. This portion of the mound could be excavated at some time in the future when questions of Native American concerns had been addressed and resolved.

During the excavation of Mound 72, 25 "burial units" or features containing 272 individuals were recovered. Numbers were assigned to 252 skeletons but when they were analyzed in the laboratory, some units were found to contain more than one individual. At the end of the last two field seasons, in 1972, Rose, who had two more years to go to complete his Ph.D., took the skeletons back with him to the University of Massachusetts.

For the next two years Rose spent all of his spare time going through the thousands of bags of bone fragments from Mound 72, working to determine the sex and age of the bones and anything else he could learn about them. No money had been allocated for analysis. Rose was given a total of 500 dollars to be used for supplies. Because of the poor preservation of the bones, he found that the best material he had to work with was the teeth. There were hundreds of teeth in the bags and before long Rose found that he had fallen in love with teeth. Inspired by his work on the teeth from Cahokia, Rose became a dental anthropologist and continued to work on teeth throughout his entire academic career. Every year he teaches a course on dental anthropology at the University of Arkansas and the vast majority of his publications are in that area.

When Rose graduated with his Ph.D. and was offered a teaching position at the University of Alabama at Birmingham, he took the hundreds of boxes of Cahokia skeletons with him and continued to work on them in his spare time. He wrote a draft report on the skeletal remains in 1974 but kept revising it and adding bits and pieces of new information. In 1976 he moved to the University of Arkansas and took the boxes of bones along with him.

Fowler's original agreement with the Illinois Department of Conservation, which was originally responsible for the Cahokia site, had stated that these collections could be kept by the scientists until the analysis was completed. That agreement was changed, however, when Illinois state officials shifted responsibility for archaeological sites on state land to a new agency, the Illinois Historic Preservation Agency. The formation of the IHPA was a critical step in the state's taking responsibility for its archaeological resources. New policies for managing collections were designed to recover dozens of "neglected" collections that had been acquired in the 1950s and later. The collections were neglected because although excavations and fieldwork had been done and artifacts collected, few reports or analysis of the work had ever been published. The problem developed because institutions had found that, while they could get money to conduct fieldwork, it was very difficult to find funds for the less-glamorous but equally essential work of data analysis and publication. Contributing to the problem was the fact that many of the individuals involved in the original research, such as Rose, had moved on in their careers.

Not all institutions, however, were equally guilty of this neglect. The University of Wisconsin, Milwaukee, had received grants from the National Science Foundation and the Illinois Department of Conservation to prepare the first edition of Fowler's *Cahokia Atlas: A Historical Atlas of Cahokia Archaeology*, which nevertheless languished in the offices of the IHPA for ten years before publication.

The greatest controversy arose when the IHPA demanded that collections be returned to the State of Illinois. After much acrimonious debate and threats from all sides, notes and collections were shipped to the Illinois State Museum, which had been designated the official repository for collections. At the time the debate was raging it was unclear if the collections could be utilized for further analysis by the original investigators. Later a policy was developed that allowed Illinois institutions to borrow and work with collections. This was later broadened to allow material to be sent beyond the borders of Illinois.

It was in response to this controversy that Fowler, in 1986, drove down to Fayetteville, Arkansas, with a trailer and collected the Cahokia skeletons from Rose, who had continued to work on them, and took them to the Illinois State Museum at Springfield. Rose estimates that there are still thousands and thousands of hours of work to be done to complete the analysis.

Rose's analysis of the skeletons was severely hampered by the poor bone preservation, which was due to a variety of causes. The high moisture content of the gumbo river clays in which the burials were deposited produced rapid decomposition of the bone. Rose found that the weight of the overlying clay and the soft consistency of the moist bone had resulted in all the bone being crushed and flattened to the extent of reducing the diameter of long bones by 50 percent. The soft bones had been difficult to remove and only a few were removed intact. The hardening and cracking of the clay as it dried further fragmented the bone and contributed to the difficulty of burial removal. Additional deterioration resulted from torrential rains that would frequently flood the site and expose the burials.

Determining the sex and age of the burials was a difficult task and many could not be identified. Despite the problems, Rose's analysis revealed a great deal of information about the people who had been buried in Mound 72. He divided the adult burials into the following age categories: young adult (20–25 years), midadult (25–30 years), mature adult (30–35 years), and old adult (35+ years).

The central figures in Mound 72Sub1 are the two individuals (probably males) who were lying in extended positions above and below the beaded falcon. Burials of young adults, of both sexes, lie nearby. One is a completely disarticulated bundle burial and another lies face down with the right leg drawn up to the chest, indicating he may have been thrown down or was not dead when positioned.

Mound 72Sub2 had a "pile burial" containing approximately 21 individuals with their bones partially sorted out. This indicated that the bodies had been stored separately between disarticulation and burial and had been transported to the burial site in three loads, long bones in one load, skulls in another, and flat bones in the third.

The burial pits had been carefully prepared, lined with a thick layer of fine white sand and woven mats. Grave construction followed a sequence of a layer of sand, then a layer of woven matting, a layer of corpses, a layer of matting, a layer of corpses, and a final layer of matting. The individuals in several of the mass burials, including one of 19 females with a mean age of 19.5 years, appeared to have been sacrificed.

Mound 72Sub3 contained the headless and handless men. All showed evidence of mutilation. The first cervical vertebrae of one man between 25 and 30 years of age had five shallow and narrow cut marks on the ventral surface while the second cervical had 14. This indicated that the heads were removed by repeatedly cutting at them with a small, sharp instrument from the front or as close to the base of the skull as possible. Rose concludes, "The absence of heads and hands on otherwise completely articulated skeletons indicates ritual mutilation and sacrifice."

The same was true of the 50 or more young women, mean age 21.2, who were buried in a mass grave in two layers with matting arranged over and under each layer. Though they were not mutilated, the women were close in age, substantiating Rose's hypothesis that these were sacrificial burials.

At some time prior to the completion of the final mound, a mass burial of 40 men and women took place under violent conditions. Some had projectile points in their bodies. Though the pit was lined with fine white sand, the arrangement and condition of the bodies indicated that they were thrown in haphazardly. The individuals were in various positions, almost always face down, but with their arms and legs sprawling in various directions.

From the position of many of the bodies, Rose suggests that the victims were lined up at the edge of the pit before being struck from behind with a heavy blunt instrument. The feet were close to the edge of the pit, as if the bodies had fallen and the feet then slid down the side. Three males had been decapitated prior to being thrown into the pit and the heads were thrown into a corner before the burials were covered. Another male appears to have been incompletely decapitated, as the atlas and skull are separated by 10 centimeters from the rest of the vertebrae. The fracturing of the mandible and its separation from the skull indicates that considerable force supplied by a heavy implement such as a stone ax or mace was used in the decapitation. From the vertical position of some of the fingers, which appear to have been digging in the sand, it is apparent that not all of the victims were dead when they were interred—that some had been trying to pull themselves out of the mass of bodies.

The only consistent burial pattern within Mound 72 as a whole is found in the four mass graves of young females arranged in two layers and separated by mats. Rose believes that this limitation of age and sex and the care with which the bodies were interred suggests that these were ritual sacrifices whose deaths were an honored occasion. Almost 62 percent of all the dead in Mound 72 are believed to be sacrificial. Twenty percent were primary burials, meaning they were laid out face up, with their bodies intact, while almost 16 percent were bundle burials. Partially disarticulated skeletons were the least frequent and accounted for less than 3 percent of the burials.

Of the skeletons that were determined to be male, half were primary and half were bundle burials. When they were sorted by age, 70 percent of those under 25 years were found to have had a primary burial while 30 percent were bundle burials. For those over 25 years of age, 70 percent were bundle burials and only 25 percent were primary burials. If increased age is related to greater status, then bundle burial was the preferred method for interment. However, the Beaded Birdman and most of his retainers were primary burials, as were most of the burials on the litters. It is probable that for the highest-status individuals in Cahokia at the time, a primary burial was the preferred method of interment, with bundle burial a close second.

Rose suggests that the operation of two distinct mortuary programs could resolve the questions of burial type and status, based on what is known of the Natchez burial ceremonies. When an important person, such as the Beaded Birdman, died, he was buried with his wives and retainers and a mound was constructed over his grave. The bundle burials may have been the bones of those who had been chosen to accompany the great man in death but who had, themselves, died earlier. Their bones would have been stored in a charnel house until his death, when they would have been moved and reburied with the leader.

Rose theorized that the mortuary program would follow a specific calendar date. If the period of time between death and burial was long enough, the body would decompose. It is known that some groups of Indians had a specific group of people, called the "flesh pickers," who grew their fingernails very long and whose task it was to strip the flesh from the bones of human corpses and clean and store them until burial. If the deaths were random and burial dates occurred three to four times a year, then the proportions of completely decayed to partially decayed bodies would be about equal, which was the proportion of primary to bundle burials found in Mound 72.

Rose's hypothesis is supported by the seven partially articulated skeletons found in Mound 72. In their cases, the interval between death and burial may not have been sufficient for complete decomposition. Only one group of bodies in Mound 72 appeared to have come from the emptying of a charnel house. It is possible that they represent the final transition between a charnel house program and the new calendrical system.

Because of the poor preservation of the bone, Rose could make only a few observations as to the health of the individuals buried in Mound 72. Two pathological conditions were noted. One was possibly caused by an iron deficiency anemia and the second was periostitis, or inflammation of the long bones. No severe case of either condition was observed. The high-status individuals showed the least evidence of illness, as did the sacrificial women victims. Since periostitis of the long bones in the legs is due to soft-tissue infections, women with skin imperfections may not have been chosen for sacrifice.

As Fowler, Rose, and others compared the burial types, they wondered if the individuals might have come from different social groupings. Some sacrifices had been shown respect in the laying out of their bodies. They were laid out in neat rows with the arms at the sides. Others appeared to have been thrown carelessly into their graves. Could the female sacrifices have been drawn from a different social group than the mid-ranked individuals? And how can the litter burials be explained?

Rose got at this problem by studying the teeth. The shape of human teeth has been shown, through family and twin studies, to be genetically controlled. Three traits of the incisors and canines show high heritability: the cusp number, groove pattern, and a trait called Carabelli's cusp. These traits were studied in four groups of burials: 44 of the female sacrifices, 23 individuals judged to be of a mid-rank social position, 13 of the litter burials, and 29 of the litter-burial sacrifices.

The litter burials and their sacrifices were the only two groups that showed no significant differences in the morphology of their teeth, indicating that they were undoubtedly from the same gene pool. The mid-rank burials differed from the litter burials in three independent traits and from the sacrificial burial in only one independent trait, not enough to indicate that they were from a different population.

The surprising finding was in the great differences between the female sacrifices and everyone else. The women differed significantly from the mid-ranked burials, the litter burials, and the litter-burial sacrifices, raising the intriguing possibility that they may not have been from Cahokia at all. The sacrificed women, all unblemished specimens who appeared to have been buried with great care, may have been tribute paid to Cahokia from distant societies it dominated.

One other problem perplexed Fowler as he studied his data. He had accurately predicted the location of Post Pit 1 but he had not expected to find Post Pit 2. What was Post Pit 2 all about? The answer lay in a little mound, number 96, that had not yet been discovered. Mound 96 lay precisely 410 feet from the location of Post Pit 1 in Mound 72. The rise of Mound 96 was so slight that it was hardly noticeable to the workers digging on Mound 72. Occasionally a crew member would look over to the southwest and ask if the gentle swelling of the earth in that place could be a mound.

Fowler, intent on keeping his workers focused on Mound 72, discouraged their speculation. "Nah," he told them, "that's too low to be a mound. Besides, with all the loiterers around here, I'm not going to check it out." It would be 30 years before Mound 96 would be investigated.

From the day young Ken Williams swung his mattock to break through its clay seal to the present, Mound 72 has been providing archaeologists with a wealth of material for both speculation and insight into the activities of Cahokia's leading citizens. Originally thought of as an elite mortuary site, Mound 72 has provided clues to the political and economic structure of Cahokia and to the strategies Cahokia's chiefs may have used to maintain their power.

In a complex chiefdom, where power and allegiances continually shifted from one chief to another, preserving status was essential. One way the elite men and women at Cahokia may have maintained their status was to acquire surplus human and nonhuman resources and display them to the community. The sacrificed women in the mass graves in Mound 72, though they were undoubtedly killed, may not have been sacrifices as such are thought of today, but were conspicuous displays of surplus wealth. The power of the individual came from the fact that his goods represented the sacred and unique relationship that existed between him and the "outerworld."

The goods displayed in Mound 72 impressively communicated the relationships this chief and his elite kinship group had with a variety of "outerworld" places. Both the raw material and finished products in Mound 72 (fig. 18) came from distant places, among them the Lake Superior region, central Wisconsin, northeastern Oklahoma, southern Illinois, the lower Mississippi River Valley, and the Gulf Coast. The many thousands of locally manufactured marine shell beads and projectile points in the mound demonstrated the power the chief had

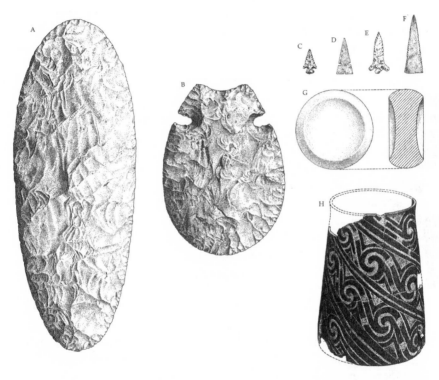

Figure 18. Artifacts from Cahokia indicating interaction with other areas. The flint tools (A, B) were made of chert from the Mill Creek quarries in southern Illinois. The larger of the two is 13 inches long. The projectile points are from Mound 72. Point C was made from a black chert from Oklahoma. The more common Cahokia form is the small triple-notched triangle (D), about 1.5 inches long and made from a local chert quarried near St. Louis. Point E is from Arkansas. The triangular point (F, 2.5 inches) was made of flint from southern Illinois. The chunky stone (G) is identical to those used in historic times by Indians of the Southeast. The beaker (H), 9.5 inches high and found in the palisade excavation, has an unusual scroll decoration similar to that of the Braden style of the late Mississippian cultures of the Southeast. These drawings first appeared in *Scientific American* 22, no. 5 (1975); used with permission of the estate of the artist, Tom Prentiss.

to control the labor of craftspeople. When these objects were buried with significant individuals, the display of wealth could create powerful ancestors. At Mound 72, the mica, copper roll, chunky stones, and even the young women sacrifices created a politically potent ancestor and maintained and legitimated a politically influential descendent kin group. While supplies of maize and other food staples might have been used to influence the populace, the manipulation of exotic goods was the primary leverage used by aspiring Mississippian leaders. They were as aware as any twentieth-century leader of the ideological benefits of conspicuous consumption.

Based on the stratigraphy and radiocarbon dating, it appears that most of the construction and burials in Mound 72 took place in the first half of the eleventh century. Within two to four decades after A.D. 1000, the charnel house was emptied, taken apart, and the area cleaned. Mound 72Sub1 was built over Post Pit 1 and several different burials of human remains, including the Beaded Birdman Burial, and assorted exotic materials (rolled copper, mica, chunky stones, beads, and four bundles of hafted projectile points) were placed in the mound.

Most of the grave goods within Mound 72 are not directly associated with any single individual. Instead, the focus seems to be on the group. Many of the caches of exotic materials and the four mass female burials appear to be separate dedicatory offerings, perhaps relating as much to the beginning and end of mound construction, ritual, and ceremonial activities as they do to the status of individuals. Mound 72 may have served as a showpiece of an elite lineage's wealth between mortuary events. The creation of Mound 72 may have been a family's calculated strategy to establish a political position for itself at Cahokia.

The last stages of Mound 72 construction did not contain the large caches of exotic goods that were found in earlier stages. This could suggest that, while the group still had political influence, expensive displays of surplus were either no longer possible for them or may not have been necessary. Since Mound 72 was not included within the limits of the later palisade wall, over the intervening years the Mound 72 kinship group may have lost much of its influence and political power.

Human bones are powerful symbols. The bones of saints have been preserved in reliquaries in European cathedrals for centuries. In the context of Mississippian ritual, bones may have represented social identity and social history as well as a concept known as "inalienable wealth." Inalienable wealth refers to the power of an object to define a person in a historical sense. The object, such as a bone of an ancestor, serves to bring past time into the present, so that the history of ancestors becomes a part of the present. In a preliterate society, objects such as human bones could have had immense symbolic power, thus justifying the additional effort required to store and treat bodies before their secondary interment. Some of the people buried at Cahokia may have been from other communities and it was their membership in an elite group that gave them access to Mound 72.

Little is done in a mortuary situation that is accidental. The placement of bodies and bundle burials, their orientation and relationships, the accompanying grave goods and caches of exotic materials all suggest mysteries that will not soon be resolved. Mound 72 is an ancient text with its own set of Rosetta stones and is slow to give up its secrets.

Excavations on Monks Mound

Fowler's discoveries of the palisade and burials at Mound 72 not only energized the institutions concerned with archaeology but strengthened working relationships with nonprofessional archaeologists as well. Nelson Reed was not an archaeologist but a businessman whose heart was in archaeology. He had worked as a volunteer for Preston Holder and had written a book, *The Mayan Caste War*, about the revolt of the Yucatán Indians against the Spanish.

Reed was concerned that so many of the mounds at Cahokia were still in private hands and could be destroyed at any time by their owners. He was also upset with the State of Illinois for not moving faster to buy up the land containing the remaining mounds. In an attempt to spur the state to action, Reed planned to excavate the top of Monks Mound to find the remains of the chief's residence that most archaeologists believed had once crowned the summit. If he could find evidence of the temple, surely the most dramatic single structure at Cahokia, the attendant publicity, he hoped, would encourage the state to appropriate funds to expand the park.

The park had few restrictions on who could dig. The Illinois Archaeological Survey acquiesced to Reed's project as did Washington University, though neither institution contributed any money. It was up to Reed to raise private funds for his project.

Reed's first money came from appearing in a cigarette ad. Though he had stopped smoking himself, he earned 500 dollars for his project by putting on the photographer's coat and posing with a cigarette in his hand. A Collinsville bank gave him 200 dollars and eventually he raised 2,000 dollars. In 1964 Reed hired James Porter and recruited Charles Bareis and his University of Illinois field school to begin digging. At the end of the first season Reed organized a cocktail party at the top of the mound, hauling up picnic tables, food, ice, and drinks. He had invited 70 local politicians to attend. The most notable guest was the elderly Paul Titterington, now almost blind but still committed to the preservation of the Cahokia Mounds. Though Reed had not yet found the temple, at the cocktail party a new generation of politicians was introduced to Monks Mound and some of them began to give the project serious attention.

In the fall of 1965 Reed and his associates, John Bennett and James Porter, received a one-year National Science Foundation grant to sink test cores into Monks Mound. Bennett was another of Fay-Cooper Cole's Ph.D students from the University of Chicago. Although he had done archaeological work under Cole and Deuel in Illinois, Bennett was primarily a cultural anthropologist. At the time of the Monks Mound project Bennett was chairman of the anthropology department at Washington University in St. Louis and it was his association with the project that made the National Science Foundation grant possible. Though Bennett was the titular head of the project, the fieldwork was under Reed's direction, with Porter in charge in the field. Porter's background in geology made him the best possible person to direct the day-to-day operation of the coring project.

Using a big coring machine, Porter supervised the excavating of a total of nine cores. One each was done on the first and second terraces and the remaining seven on the third and fourth. When the cores were laid end to end they produced a stratigraphy of Monks Mound. As they examined the cores Porter and Reed noticed dark bands of limonite at various levels. Limonite is a hydrated ferric oxide that forms on the surfaces of soil with a high iron content when the soil is exposed to the weather for a period of time. This characteristic made it a good indicator of time intervals between periods of mound construction, except that limonite has other properties as well. It will dissolve in water and seep down through the soil until it hits some sort of a barrier, such as heavy clay.

Despite the difficulty of making judgments based on the bands of limonite, Reed and his associates were able to identify 14 stages in the construction of the mound and speculated that each stage had lasted about 18 years. Radiocarbon dates from the cores indicated that Monks Mound was begun about A.D. 900 and completed about 1150.[1]

Excavation on the top of Monks Mound continued through the summers of 1965 and 1966 with mixed results. On the third terrace the archaeologists found the remains of a house, possibly Amos Hill's, and, in the northwest corner, Hill's grave. But Reed was not satisfied with his workers' progress. Though they had found some features, no overall plan had emerged and they had not found what he could identify as the remains of the temple. As Reed explained it, "We nibbed and nabbed and sort of chopped at the top of the mound, here and there without much success."

---

1. Reed et al. 1968.

In 1970, as part of an Illinois Department of Conservation project, Reed reopened his old excavations and, with his workers, continued digging for a few weeks using the traditional hand-excavation procedures. Then he became impatient. He had accumulated 1,788 feet of profiled walls, found out all he wanted to know about the stratigraphy, but had still uncovered nothing that would define, for him, the big picture. Where was the temple he was sure had been up there? Reed told his workers to put down their hand tools while he brought a backhoe up onto the summit of Monks Mound. Within a short time, using the backhoe, he had excavated several 16–foot squares to a depth of 17 to 24 inches. Immediately the pieces of the puzzle began to come together. Reed found more features and wall trenches with the heavy equipment than he had in all the previous years combined, including a large feature that he promptly identified as the temple he had been seeking.

In the summer of 1971 Reed went back with his backhoe, reopened his old excavations, dug out new squares, and exposed the foundations of what had been three structures, three rebuildings of those structures, another outbuilding, a wall, and a pit that had once contained a massive post. This was the summer Fowler had called a ceramics conference at Cahokia and the assembled archaeologists were invited to inspect Reed's work on Monks Mound. The day before the tour, Reed had his workers carefully clean up the excavations and stretch strings along the grid lines. Reed, the nonprofessional, wanted to impress the professionally trained archaeologists. It was not to be. During the night, someone (there were strong suspicions as to the identity of the culprit) climbed the mound and tore out all the carefully stretched strings and stakes and threw them down the coring holes, which were still open.

When the archaeologists toured the site the next day, most were not impressed. Reed had conducted unconventional archaeology and it was much criticized by Holder and others. (In a letter to Fowler, Holder called it "the terrible rape of Monks Mound. When I saw it more than a year after the fact it looked like a movie set for the destruction of Vietnam.") A great deal of information was lost in the mechanized earth stripping. Nevertheless, with the top layer of soil gone, dramatic evidence of the buildings that had once stood on the summit of Monks Mound stood out clearly to the disapproving observers.

One of the workers Reed had hired was an archaeologist from the South who was accustomed to post pits that were no more than six inches in diameter. He had trouble imagining the size of the posts that were used at Cahokia. The archaeologist was standing in the hole that had been dug for the prehistoric post, which must have measured over three feet in diameter. When he looked around and exclaimed, "I don't see any post pit," his fellow workers told him he was standing in it.

Despite Reed's questionable methods, there was no doubt that he had found the "temple" that had once crowned the summit. It was located on the northeast corner of the fourth terrace and measured 104 feet long by 48 feet wide, was probably about 50 feet high, and was the largest building yet found at Cahokia. The politicians were suitably impressed. Plans for the park expansion were submitted to the Illinois Department of Conservation and Reed went with the delegation to Springfield to help promote it.

As Reed told the story, "I worked my way up past the Chamber of Commerce and this branch and that branch of government. Finally we went to Springfield and got to meet the governor. Each room got bigger and bigger and finally we got to a tremendously big room and there was this little man. He kept shaking hands. It turned out he was the governor. Afterwards someone said, 'Well, you got it.'"

"'What do you mean, we got it?' I asked."

"'He says he will do it. When the governor talks like that he means he is going to put your request to expand the park in the budget.'"

While the excavations on the summit of Monks Mound were going on, Charles Bareis was digging at the intersection of the first and third terrace of the mound for the University of Illinois, with startling results. He uncovered a series of steplike plateaus rising toward the third terrace. Each of these steps was made of a yellow-brown sand that appeared to have been deliberately covered with a dark-brown heavy clay. At the bottom of the plateaus or steps he found a feature made of a heavy blue-gray clay that functioned much like a buttress.

Bareis's discoveries indicated to him that a kind of structural engineering had been used in building the mound. Interfill areas composed of different soils, as opposed to one solid mass of clay, would provide good drainage and give stability to the mound. The significant implication from Bareis's work is that the various stages of Monks Mound were carefully planned and engineered. It was not a matter of people throwing basketfuls of dirt onto a pile and adding to it whenever they felt like it. A group of individuals with a specialized knowledge of soils was responsible for directing construction of the mound. Bareis also found evidence that the basic part of Monks Mound had been built as a single unit with the first terrace added on much later, perhaps to prevent slumping.

Fowler had predicted the location of the massive Post Pit 1 in Mound 72 by noting where a north-south line crossed the southwest corner of Monks Mound. If his analysis was correct, there should be another post pit at that location on Monks Mound. The summer of 1968 he assigned one of his graduate students, Elizabeth Benchley, to excavate the southwest corner of the first terrace of Monks Mound.

Elizabeth Benchley was a petite woman with long blond hair who looked a decade younger than she was. A granddaughter of the writer Robert Benchley, she was working on her Ph.D. in anthropology at the University of Wisconsin, Milwaukee, when Fowler hired her to supervise the work on Monks Mound. Jim Anderson was again the field director, responsible for overseeing the digging on Monks Mound as well as the continuing work on Mound 72 and the ongoing palisade excavations.

Benchley's first problem was finding a place to stay. Crew members had to find their own lodging and Benchley drove up and down Collinsville Road looking for a place to rent for the summer. Eventually she found modest accommodations that included a bedroom and kitchen facilities. A student on her first field experience was coming from Milwaukee in a few days to stay with her and Benchley thought one of them could sleep in the living room. The apartment was dirty, with holes in the floor. It was located behind a restaurant and the area was surrounded by bars and houses of prostitution.

When the parents of the young woman who was to stay with Benchley delivered their daughter for her summer's work, they took one look at the apartment and its surroundings and said, "This won't do." They found the women a trailer to rent in a trailer park east of East St. Louis in a residential area. Though it was located in an economically depressed neighborhood, they believed it would be a safer place for two young women to live than in the apartment behind the restaurant.

The two had been in their trailer for a month when they received an eviction notice from the manager of the trailer park. No reason was given and they wondered what they had done wrong. They had not been noisy. They worked hard all day at the dig and were usually exhausted by nightfall. When they inquired they learned that the park was reserved for people who owned their trailers. An exception had been made in Benchley's case because the owner of the trailer had murdered his wife there and then committed suicide by ramming his car into a bridge abutment. The bank had taken possession of the trailer and was now selling it.

Benchley and the student gave up trying to find a place to rent near the Cahokia Mounds. They went to a discount warehouse and bought themselves a tent, which they pitched on the east side of Monks Mound. They were not alone. Other crew members had also pitched tents and a small camping community had sprung up. Altogether, about 100 archaeology students from five institutions were camping on the east side of Monks Mound in the late 1960s. Five-gallon drums of water, wrapped in black plastic, had been set up at the camp site for showers and the students worked out their own cooking and sleeping arrangements. Some had traditional camping gear and shopped for food at the local grocery stores. Others, living more like the original hunters and gatherers, caught rabbits, plucked ducks from the ponds, scrounged corn from neighboring fields, and, on one memorable occasion, found a crate of cabbages, which they hauled triumphantly back to the camp. One man had brought his dog, a retriever, with him. One evening the dog came trotting back to the camp bearing a full bucket of hot Kentucky Fried Chicken, which his appreciative owner and friends promptly ate.

The location Fowler wanted Benchley to investigate was a spot on his north-south axis line that crossed a small rise on the southwest corner of the first terrace of Monks Mound. Her job was to investigate the rise and find the proposed marker post. The first terrace was a level area about 650 feet wide by 330 feet deep. On the southwest corner of the terrace there was a peculiar elevation, about ten feet in diameter and ten feet higher than the rest of the terrace. The area where Fowler predicted the marker post would be was at the peak of this rise.

Benchley and her crew dug two intersecting trenches, a little over six feet wide, toward the center of the mound so they could understand the stratigraphy of the mound before they began to dig into the critical central area. The plow zone was four inches deep and they shoveled that off and screened the dirt. Using their shovels they went down about six feet. Then, with their mattocks, they began moving the six-foot walls of the trenches into the mound toward each other until they intersected at the center—where Fowler had predicted the post pit would be.

When they reached the center, there was no post pit. Instead they found garbage; plates, bowls, jars, bottles, and the bones of deer, fish, and swans. The material, and the little mound it came from, dated from A.D. 1150 to 1300, 200 to 300 years after Mound 72 had been constructed. Rather than the single marker post they had expected to find, they found evidence of intense construction activity, which included large buildings, fences, posts, and a small platform mound. This level of building activity had not been found anywhere else on Monks Mound. Benchley's data suggested that the southwest corner of the first terrace of Monks Mound had been a focal point at the Cahokia site from A.D. 900 to 1200 and perhaps continuing into the 1500s.

The profiles of Benchley's excavation trenches showed that the flat-topped mound had been constructed on top of all the debris and other structures she found in the bottom of her trenches. The mound had obviously been built after the complex buildings underneath it had been abandoned or destroyed. When the north surface of the mound was cleared of later debris, Benchley found the post pit she had been looking for. When the pit was cross sectioned Benchley discovered that it was not a single post pit but a series of superimposed post pits that were very close to Fowler's predicted location.

Benchley's cross trenches eventually reached a depth of 13 feet, where she found that posts, 12 inches in diameter and probably made of cedar, had been set into the ground. She would have had to excavate down an additional 36 feet to reach the level upon which Monks Mound had been built. It is that lower elevation that was probably contemporary with Mound 72 and its post pit. The smaller post pits in the platform mound on the first terrace indicate that this was still an important point in the site perhaps as long as 300 years after the north-south centerline had been established.

The presence of the large quantity of potsherds and animal bones around the building sites puzzled Benchley because in earlier times that never would have happened. The excavation of Tracts 15A and 15B had suggested that early Cahokians kept their living areas very clean. They apparently had specific places where they put their garbage and they did not litter around the mounds. Benchley wondered if in later prehistoric times the social and political controls had relaxed, become less rigid, and that the presence of the trash reflected those changes.

Another theory for the presence of the debris came from ethnographic records of the Indians of the Southeast. Once a year the Indians held a renewal and cleaning-out-of-houses ceremony, accompanied by a feast. After cleaning their residential areas, people brought their broken pots and other debris to the temple and left them as part of the ceremony or else spread them on the ground to seal off the underworld influence and to purify the area for further use. Was a ritual community-cleansing ceremony the reason for the unusual amount of debris at this place on Monks Mound?

Not all of the buildings Benchley uncovered had litter associated with them. She called these "special purpose" buildings because they had none of the storage pits or domestic and craft debris associated with a house. They were also large. While the average size of a house in Tract 15B was 31.4 square meters, the largest building Benchley found on the First Terrace was 192 square meters, six times the size of the average Cahokian dwelling. The special purpose buildings had been burned, and the absence of artifacts, other than a few chips of pigment, a persimmon seed, and a pair of earplugs, indicated that the buildings may have been cleaned out before being intentionally torched.

Benchley was finding something else that interested her—finely made plates, almost black in color and slipped and polished. Plates are different from jars, which tend to be cooking and storage vessels. Plates, she thought, implied that people were serving and eating from them and not just dipping into a common pot. Plates also suggested a fixed place to eat, such as a special eating area. She wondered if this implied a society of the type in which archaeologists begin to find the use of tableware.

In the top levels of her excavation Benchley also found glass beads, a cast copper bell, and other historic material, along with the remains of an unusual building that had not been constructed in the usual wall-trench method of Mississippian Indians. Near the remains of the building were a few burials. Later research revealed that the French had constructed a chapel on the southwest corner of Monks Mound in the mid-eighteenth century and that native people, who may have been caretakers of the chapel, had been buried nearby.[2]

Further excavations on the southwest corner of the first terrace of Monks Mound indicated that the corner was made up of a series of platform mounds on which buildings had once been constructed. Below the platform mounds was a series of extensive superimposed floors, suggesting that the first terrace had been built up by having large structures, built around patios, constructed on them. The entire area showed signs of intense activity. At some point most of the structures had been burned. Radiocarbon dating indicates that much of the first terrace mound building occurred during the twelfth century, contemporary with the construction and utilization of the building Reed had excavated on the fourth terrace.

Though Benchley found the archaeology she was doing exciting, her first summer at Cahokia was a trying experience for her. Her mostly male crew had dug before, thought they knew what they were doing, and found it hard to take direction from a new graduate student who looked like a younger sister. James Anderson, both hard working and secretive, had three sites to supervise and was not always a good manager of people. Anderson was a large man, over six feet tall, with a full beard and bushy hair that he cut on an indeterminate schedule. Benchley thought that Anderson failed to supply her with wheelbarrows, screens, and cameras when she needed them, and he criticized what he believed to be her lack of progress. Benchley, who was basing her Ph.D. thesis on her Cahokia work, proceeded slowly, making careful notes, screening the dirt as it came out of the excavation.

Anderson complained. "You have to move more dirt," he insisted. "We don't have time to do the detail work you are doing." Benchley told Fowler that she would not work under Anderson another year. If she were going to continue she would have to be in charge of her own site. Fowler concurred, ordered more equipment so there would not be problems over the sharing of wheelbarrows and cameras, and put Anderson to work in another area. The two eventually got to know each other and became friends though they never worked on the same specific location together again.

While Benchley was working on the first terrace of Monks Mound, Ken Williams, working under Fowler's direction and financed by the Illinois Department of Conservation, was supervising his first excavation as a field director on

---

2. Benchley 1974, 1975; Walthall and Benchley 1987.

a lobe on the east side of Monks Mound. The department wanted more information on the original appearance of the mound for a possible reconstruction project.

Ever since Moorehead's time, archaeologists had speculated on the nature of the lobes that projected out from the east and north sides of Monks Mound and on the northwest corner. Two lobes on the east side ran parallel to each other. What could they be? Fowler, who had spent considerable time studying the pyramids of Mexico, thought they might be a pair of ramps leading to the summit of Monks Mound.

To determine how the lobes had been formed and to investigate their function, Fowler put Williams to work digging an exploratory trench on the southern of the two east lobes. His goals were to determine whether the east lobes were wash deposits, slumpage, or manmade features. If they were manmade, what was their purpose, when were they built, and what had been the aboriginal appearance of Monks Mound?

Williams's plan was to dig a north-south trench, two meters wide, parallel to the east side of Monks Mound to establish the vertical stratigraphy in the area. He would then section the lobe lengthwise with an east-west trench, joining the north-south excavation in a T.

When Williams began digging he immediately found signs of basket loading as well as cultural material through 14 feet, a surprisingly long chronology. When Fowler saw the basket loading he took this as evidence that the lobes were manmade and could not be the result of erosion of the mound. Fowler's interpretation of erosion involved the usual concept of dirt and sediments, what archaeologists call "slope wash," washing off the side of the mound during a heavy rain and being deposited in separate layers. One would never expect to find undisturbed basket loading in an area affected by erosion. Or so he thought. Nelson Reed argued with Fowler over his interpretation. Reed had consulted a geologist who had told him that it was possible for large blocks of earth to slump or cave in as a unit without showing any disturbances of the materials within them.

Fowler was still not convinced. With his limited experience in erosion, he believed that when a hillside eroded it would not be in huge slumps such as the lobes on Monks Mound. Williams continued digging until he reached a level that was underneath the lobe and here he found a small mound containing a burial. He called in Jerome Rose to give his opinion of the age and sex of the skeleton. After examining the bones Rose pointed out something strange about one of the arms of the skeleton. The radius and the ulna of the left arm were rotated to an unnatural extent, inconsistent with the laying out of a body after death. Though no one realized it at the time, the twisted arm of the burial under the east lobe was the first clue that Fowler was wrong in his interpretation of the lobes. Rose puzzled over the position of the arm but could not come up with an explanation. Williams noted the curiosity in his field notes and then forgot about it.

Williams had cut into the wall of the trench, about a meter from the burial, when his trowel hit what he first thought was a rock. He was about to make a startling discovery. Digging around the object, he saw that it was in fact a sandstone tablet sticking out of the dirt. He could see that the side of the tablet that was facing up had crosshatching on it. While pleased, Williams did not get too excited over his find as several crosshatched tablets had been found before. He sent word to Benchley to come down with the camera to take a picture. Benchley brought the camera but, being something of a perfectionist, she refused to take the picture until Williams had cut his trench walls perfectly vertical. When he had straightened up his excavation to her satisfaction, Benchley took the picture.

At that point Williams carefully pulled the tablet from the dirt wall. When he turned it over, instead of seeing the additional crosshatching he had expected, he saw an engraving of an eagle dancer—the only such representation to have been found in good context at Cahokia (fig. 19). (The first stone tablet from Cahokia had been found by Thomas Ramey in the late 1800s in a field very near where Williams was digging.) Williams's tablet measured about four inches long by three inches wide and depicted a masked figure with a diamond eye and a

Figure 19. The birdman tablet found in the east lobes excavation of Monks Mound. Used with permission of the Cahokia Mounds State Historic Site.

hook nose and wearing an oval piece on its chest. The arms were feathered wings. Williams was both stunned and ecstatic. He remembers that his field notes "waxed poetic that morning." The drawing of the birdman on the tablet has since become the logo of the Cahokia Mounds Interpretive Center and is reproduced on everything from literature about Cahokia to highway overpasses in the area.

At the end of the 1971 season Williams wrote up his field notes on Monks Mound, and in 1975 his preliminary findings were published by the Illinois State Museum. He concluded, first, that there was a thick Late Woodland/Emergent Mississippian midden accumulation in the area dating A.D. 800–900. Second, the midden was overlain by several meters of fine silt layering interspersed with features dating to A.D. 900–1500. These bands of silty sediments represented stages of the construction of Monks Mound and were slope wash from those surfaces. Third, he identified several later occupation surfaces, which he dated to A.D. 1150–1300.

Williams noted the discovery of the burial on the premound surface under what was the tip of the east lobe. The burial pit did not appear to have been filled in, which he thought was unusual. Instead, a kind of ridge seemed to have been constructed that ran parallel to the east side of the mound and crossed under the tips of both lobes. Williams suggested that the ridge must have been built over the open burial pit and that a similar burial might be found under the tip of the other east lobe. Charcoal from the pre-lobe surface, directly under the small mound, yielded a date of A.D. 1310.[3]

Williams's final conclusions about the east lobes were that they had been manmade no earlier than A.D. 1300, were probably used as ramps, and had suffered no major erosion. The lobes look today, he wrote, essentially the way they did when they were built. That conclusion would go unchallenged until the spring of 1984 when persistent heavy rainfall again focused the archaeologists' attention on the lobes of Monks Mound. What Williams would discover then was that his earlier conclusions had been dead wrong.

---

3. Williams 1975.

ELEVEN

New Sequential Ceramic Phases Defined

Fowler's National Science Foundation grant and the subsequent discoveries at Mound 72 had awakened the archaeology departments of the Midwest to the extraordinary research opportunity that lay in their backyard. Cahokia went from being an ignored and neglected site to one crowded with archaeologists. Between the summers of 1969 and 1972 five institutions conducted research on Cahokia.

The Illinois Department of Conservation provided money for what it called "interpretive excavation," meaning excavations that would provide data that would be useful in developing interpretations of the site for visitors. It was a multi-institutional project, coordinated by the Illinois Archaeological Survey. The students' tent city expanded into an annual summer colony.

One of the repeat campers was Barbara Vander Leest, who was part of Fowler's hired crew. Her father had given her the family camper, which he parked for her under a mulberry tree on the east side of Monks Mound. The camper, known as Barb's Bar and Grill and later simply as the B & G, became the social center of the camp. When the students finished their work at the dig in the evening, they would drink rum and cokes at the B & G, bring their grills over to cook their dinners, and later depart for Pearl's Horseshoe Lounge, where they drank beer and cooled off in the air-conditioned bar.

Parties were frequent. Fowler's visits and tours by visiting archaeologists, photographers, and writers from *National Geographic* magazine were always occasions for a get-together. When Fowler was coming the sites were cleaned up, field notes completed. The crews looked forward to Fowler's visits, in part because of the discussions he would lead, but also because it would be the occasion for an especially good party that would last most of the night.

Jim Anderson, too, enjoyed the parties. Though he did not plan them, he encouraged the students to do so and he would be the last one to leave, in the early hours of the morning. Anderson's expertise in the field was never questioned by the students. Vander Leest remembers that he solicited the opinion of all the workers, even the novices, on the features they were uncovering and was open to talking about interpretations—asking the students what they saw in the walls of the excavations as well as explaining what he, with his longer experience, could see.

One evening a young woman who was camping in the tent village came up to Benchley and complained of feeling ill. Benchley had her taken to a local clinic where she was diagnosed with scarlet fever. The young woman was immediately quarantined and approximately 100 students on the dig were ordered into the Southern Illinois University clinic at Edwardsville for shots.

For days Benchley organized the making of appointments and the transporting of waves of students to get their shots. When her own crew from Wisconsin returned from the clinic she had planned to put them back to work on her Monks Mound site, but when she saw them sitting on the ground, hot and dizzy from their shots, she took pity and instead bought ice cream all around. A few days later a public health nurse came by the camp to check up on the girl with scarlet fever and discovered the archaeology students' informal living arrangements.

"Do you mean you live outdoors?" she asked. "And all these young people, who are not married, are living together and sharing food?"

"Don't worry about it," said Benchley. "We do this all the time. Besides, I'm here." The nurse looked at her skeptically. Though Benchley was in her twenties, she did not look to be older than 16.

The end of the season was always an occasion for a banquet. Anderson would arrange for a dining room at a local hotel, the students would dress up in the one dressy outfit each had brought, and they could show each other what they looked like cleaned up. Awards were given for Rookie of the Season. One memorable year, the season ended with a wedding on top of Monks Mound. Two student crew members from the University of Wisconsin, Milwaukee, were married on the top of the mound with their fellow workers in attendance. A pig roast at the foot of the mound followed the ceremony.

Though all of the projects underway at Cahokia uncovered valuable data, one in particular added crucial data for a later development of a ceramic sequence and information on the specialized communities that made up Cahokia. That project was Charles Bareis's excavation into the borrow pit under Mound 51.[1] Mound 51 was one of the mounds that had been destroyed by its

---

1. These excavations are summarized in a Ph.D. dissertation by William Chmurny (see Chmurny 1973).

owner, though Bareis and Porter had managed to salvage some archaeological information from the site in the 1960s.

When Wittry, Bareis, and Porter had first arrived at Cahokia to begin the highway salvage project, Mound 51 had been largely intact. But there was a large sign on it ominously stating, "Indian Mound for Sale." The private owner had been selling the dirt from the mound to anyone who needed fill. Bareis had been conducting his University of Illinois field schools at the Mound 51 location when he discovered that there was a large borrow pit under the mound that had been filled in during early Mississippian times.

At first he thought the borrow pit was on the south side of Collinsville Road. But the more his students dug, the bigger he found the pit to be. When he excavated on the north side of the highway he found that the pit was there as well— one huge borrow pit that had probably been dug as a source of dirt to build the early stages of Monks Mound. When Monks Mound had been partially constructed, some kind of land-leveling program was begun, the pit was filled in, and Mound 51 constructed over it.

The fill from the pit was extensive and well preserved because the area had been filled in and then covered with the mound. As a result Bareis was able to find preserved organic remains such as remnants of insects that had been in the house thatch that the Indians had thrown into the pit to fill it. William Chmurny, a graduate student from the University of Illinois who went on to become chancellor at the University of Wisconsin, Platteville, wrote his doctoral dissertation on the materials found in the fill from the borrow pit.

Chmurny found an incredible amount of floral and faunal remains, including insect fragments, preserved in the pit below Mound 51. Besides analyzing the physical remains, Chmurny interviewed retired farmers who had been active in the early part of the twentieth century, before extensive mechanization, the use of chemical fertilizers, and the drainage and irrigation of fields had become common. These farmers had to deal with yearly variations of rainfall, soil differences, and areas that were either saturated with water or well drained. Although many changes had taken place in the landscape since Mississippian times, the farmers had been working under conditions similar to those faced by the ancient Cahokians. The only nonvariable factor was the soil type. The rainfall patterns and the amount of soil saturation or drainage could not be predicted from year to year.

His ethnographic survey suggested to Chmurny that the most successful modern-day farmers were those who minimized their risk by planting a variety of crops in more than one niche, for example, different crops in both wet and dry soils. He believed this same strategy could have been used by Mississippian peoples. Fowler's discovery of the ridged fields revealed a technological adaptation by Mississippian farmers to drain their fields and add to the potential for better yields in wet soils.

Chmurny correlated this strategy of minimizing risks in food production with a hierarchy of settlements that were spread over the landscape of the American Bottom but centered in Cahokia, with smaller subcommunities of varying types subsidiary to it. In Chmurny's view, numerous specialized production communities funneled specific goods and services into the center. In return, the chief of Cahokia, who sat at the top of the hierarchical social organization pyramid, sent back status objects and favored the villagers with his beneficence and promises of protection. Chmurny found strong evidence that special food was brought into Cahokia for the use of the city dwellers. Only the choice portions of deer were represented in the bones recovered from the pit under Mound 51. The deer must have been butchered outside the city and the prized haunches carried in for the dining tables of the elite.

A wealth of material was being dug from the ground at Cahokia but the archaeologists were handicapped in their discussion of it because they were still using the two-part division of potsherds into either "Old Village" or "Trappist" and the binomial type names, such as "Monks Mound Red," that James Griffin had published in his 1941 and 1949 papers. These classifications had served well in the past, but the complexity of the potsherds they now had required a new definition of phases.

Discussion of a possible pre-Mississippian occupation of the American Bottom had been going on for some time. Griffin had begun to recognize signs of it and Hall had earlier proposed a Pulcher phase as representing the transition between the Late Woodland Bluff culture and the Mississippian as it was presently represented by the two-part classification.

Joseph Vogel, while analyzing pottery from Tract 15A for the Illinois State Museum, had come up with a detailed breakdown of the ceramic sequence into several periods. Ken Williams and others working at Cahokia were also seeing subdivisions, particularly in the earlier part of the sequence.

Another person who was working on this problem of ceramic sequence was Patricia O'Brien.[2] O'Brien was working under Donald Lathrap, a specialist in South American archaeology at the University of Illinois, who had been involved with some of the early salvage excavations at Cahokia. He suggested to O'Brien that she do her doctoral dissertation on the ceramics from the Powell tract of the highway salvage work done in 1961. O'Brien had not excavated at the site nor had she yet seen the Powell tract.

Despite O'Brien's lack of experience at Cahokia, Lathrap suggested that she

---

2. O'Brien 1969, 1972.

use a different method of ceramic analysis developed by an Andean archaeological expert from the University of California at Berkeley. While working at the Powell tract, Bareis and his crews had come up with archaeology almost as complex as that at tracts 15A and 15B.[3] The major features found at the Powell tract were superimposed house basins from different time periods. These basins had been filled in with debris including potsherds. O'Brien felt that she could develop a sequence of house types from the stratigraphy of these features. She could then analyze the ceramics found with each of these features and present a changing picture of ceramics through time.

In the end her analysis recognized five periods, designated by Roman numerals rather than names, covering the total time period for the Cahokia site. These periods were similar, in most respects, to those described by Vogel in his earlier analysis. It was the differences that later became a point of controversy among archaeologists.

Most of this data was unpublished but that did not prevent its being vehemently discussed in hotel rooms at professional meetings. To end the confusion and to create a new chronology for Cahokia that would have everyone's agreement on the different phases, Fowler and Robert Hall, the latter now at the University of Illinois, Chicago, called a Cahokia ceramic conference for July 19–23, 1971, at the Howard Johnson Motel in Collinsville, Illinois.[4] The conference was a continuation of the field conferences that Fowler and others had called in previous years. This conference, however, was organized to focus on a special theme—the ceramic chronology of Cahokia.

Invited to attend were all of the archaeologists who had conducted direct research at the Cahokia site and had collected archaeological data with stratigraphic and radiocarbon dating controls. Among those who attended, with their trays of potsherds and notes, were James Anderson, Charles Bareis, Elizabeth Benchley, Melvin Fowler, Glen Freimuth, Alan Harn, Frederick Matson, Patrick Munson, Patricia O'Brien, James Porter, Nelson Reed, Robert Salzer, James Schoenwetter, Harriet Smith, and Warren Wittry. James Griffin, the expert on Mississippian ceramics, was present and agreed to act as secretary.

For four days they looked at potsherds and examined the detailed stratigraphic contexts of the data and the supporting chronological information. After each individual had made his or her presentation, they all came together in a summary session to define the phases. They looked at data on settlement patterns, on ceremonialism, on outside contacts and relationships. They listed pottery traits and descriptions of associated artifacts. When they were finished,

---

3. Bareis 1964.
4. Fowler and Hall 1972, 1978.

they had reached agreement on five major phases, which they named, and one transitional phase, left unnamed. (See fig. 20.)

The first phase was the Patrick phase, named for Dr. John J. R. Patrick who in 1876 had made the first accurate map of the Cahokia Mounds. The Patrick phase ran from A.D. 600 to 900? and represented the early pre-Mississippian occupation at Cahokia by people identified as Late Woodland. The phase bore similarities to the Jersey Bluff culture Titterington had described thirty years earlier. The pottery from this period was cord-marked up to the rim, and houses associated with it were small semisubterranean dwellings made with a single-post wall construction. Single-post construction refers to the insertion of one

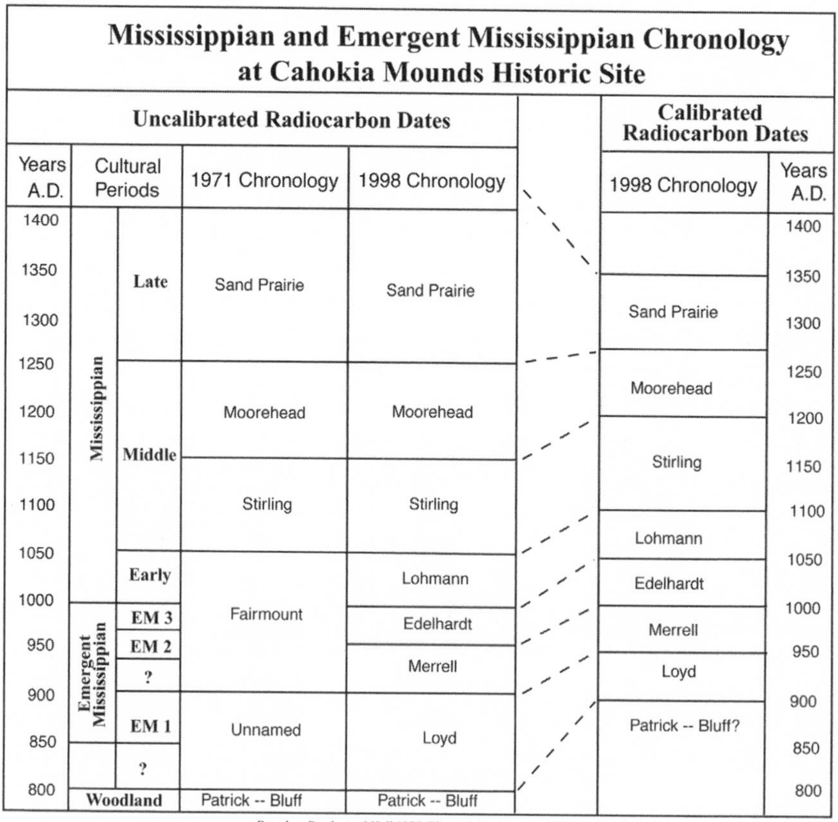

Mississippian and Emergent Mississippian Chronology at Cahokia Mounds Historic Site

		Uncalibrated Radiocarbon Dates			Calibrated Radiocarbon Dates	
Years A.D.	Cultural Periods	1971 Chronology	1998 Chronology		1998 Chronology	Years A.D.
1400	Mississippian / Late	Sand Prairie	Sand Prairie			1400
1350						1350
1300					Sand Prairie	1300
1250		Moorehead	Moorehead		Moorehead	1250
1200						1200
1150	Middle				Stirling	1150
1100		Stirling	Stirling			1100
1050	Early		Lohmann		Lohmann	1050
1000		Fairmount	Edelhardt		Edelhardt	1000
950	EM 3 / EM 2		Merrell		Merrell	950
900	?				Loyd	900
850	EM 1	Unnamed	Loyd		Patrick -- Bluff?	850
800	? / Woodland	Patrick -- Bluff	Patrick -- Bluff			800

Based on Fowler and Hall 1975: Figure 1; Pauketat 1995: Figure 3.3; Pauketat and Emerson 1997: Figure 1.3

Figure 20. Chart showing the 1971 chronology of the Cahokia area and a 1998 chronology. The phases were defined largely on the stylistic changes in pottery and were given time frames based upon radiocarbon assays of materials associated with the potsherds. Used with permission of M. L. Fowler.

post at a time in separate holes as house walls are built. The later technique was to dig a trench for each wall rather than individual post holes.

The second phase, A.D. 800–900, was left unnamed because it represented a possible transition phase between the Late Woodland Patrick and the next phase, the full-blown Mississippian phase called Fairmount. The conference participants recognized that with more time and study this unnamed phase might be incorporated into either the Patrick or Fairmount, or, if more evidence was discovered, elaborated into a named phase of the sequence. In any case, as they studied their potsherds, they believed they could see a change in the ceramics that preceded the major technological transition in house-building techniques that would come in the third phase.

Number three was the Fairmount phase, which ran from A.D. 900 to 1100. This phase saw the beginning of the construction of Monks Mound, the planned alignment of the community center at Cahokia, and the construction, late in the period, of some of the large woodhenges, or sun circles. Mound 72, with its human sacrifices and elaborate burial ceremonialism for an elite class, was in the Fairmount phase. It is the Fairmount phase, named for a jockey club nearby, that contains a variety of arrowheads, chunky stones, and flint hoes for the cultivation of corn.

Bareis's buried borrow pit that extended on both sides of what is now U.S. 40 was crucial in establishing the time period for the Fairmount phase. During the Fairmount phase the Indians had filled the borrow pit and built Mound 51 over part of the earth-fill area. It was one of several examples of their practice of a kind of renewal and reuse of land at Cahokia. In excavating the pit, Bareis had found ceramics associated with materials that could be radiocarbon dated. Comparable pottery had been found by Wittry, by Fowler at Mound 72, and by O'Brien in her analysis of ceramics excavated at the Powell Mound area. The finding of the pottery fragments along with material that could be radiocarbon dated anchored the Fairmount phase in a provable segment of time.

The Fairmount phase pottery had shell, limestone, and grog-grit temper, though shell temper was gaining in popularity. A red finish over a smooth surface was common, as were pots with rolled rims and pottery with a polished black surface, called "Powell Plain." Contacts outside the Cahokia area were indicated by sherds and other artifacts from the lower Wabash and Ohio River Valleys, the lower Mississippi Valley, southern Illinois, Oklahoma, and Wisconsin.

During the Fairmount phase, there was a shift in house styles, from the single-post rectangular pit house to the small wall-trench construction. The walls of a wall-trench house were constructed of upright posts, placed in trenches, and interwoven with smaller strips of willow that were plastered with mud. Interior walls and floors were lined with cane mats. The hipped roofs were covered with a thatch of grass. The conferees recognized that the Fairmount phase might be subdividable into two subphases. The earlier would be represented by the fill from under Mound 51 and the later represented by the material from Mound 72.

Next came the Stirling phase, which ran from A.D. 1100 to 1200 and included the completion of Monks Mound and extensive mound construction on the rest of the site. Some of the palisades were built around the central portions of the site and more woodhenges were constructed. The phase was named for Gene M. Stirling, who had excavated the small Powell Mound in the summer of 1931 for the University of Illinois. In this phase there is solid evidence of the extension of Cahokia's influence to other parts of the Midwest.

In the area of ceramics during the Stirling phase, shell temper continues to increase in popularity at the expense of limestone, grit, and grog. Rolled-rim and Ramey Incised pots are present as are new forms of jars and bowls. Pottery pieces from outside the Cahokia area are also present.

The next phase, A.D. 1200–1275, named for Warren K. Moorehead, represented what was believed at the time to be the highest point of development attained by the residents of Cahokia. Houses were larger. Single-post houses and rectangular refuse pits of the previous periods were a thing of the past. Stumpware, popular in past phases, was gone. Shell-tempered pottery replaced the earlier grit- and grog-tempered pottery except for crucibles and tall, narrow pots called "juice presses," which continued to be made with an all-grog temper. Limestone temper disappeared altogether. The black polished plates that Benchley had found at Monks Mound became popular and the red-finished pottery waned in popularity. Jars got taller rims and long-necked bottles appeared.

On the first terrace of Monks Mound, the Cahokians built a succession of platform mounds topped by timber buildings. Construction went on elsewhere on the site, including the last of the solar observatories and the rebuilding of the elaborate palisade that surrounded Monks Mound and 16 other mounds in its vicinity. The conferees believed the population had reached its peak in the Moorehead phase with houses organized into clusters around platform mounds, plazas, and structures that were probably burial mounds.

The last phase before the historic period is the Sand Prairie, dating from A.D. 1275 to 1350. The time period is named for Sand Prairie Lane in Tract 15B, which is now an overpass crossing Interstate 70. The lobes on the east side of Monks Mound date to this time. The plaza on 15B, which had been used for 200 years as a ceremonial space, reverted to housing. The sandstone tablet of the birdman was dated from this period. The pottery of the Sand Prairie period is characterized by deep, wide, cord-marked bowls; effigy-head bowls; pans with vertical sides; bean pots with fine incising; and plates with medium-high rims.

There was not total agreement among the conferees on these phases. As Bob Hall pointed out during the conference, the work of Joe Vogel had been ignored. Vogel's analyses had much to offer, particularly regarding the earlier unnamed phase, which covered the time of transition from the Bluff culture into Mississippian (Vogel's Loyd and Merrell phases).

Ken Williams felt that he had found sufficient evidence in his deep excavations into the east lobes area of Monks Mound to define and name this phase. He and other archaeologists suggested that the name "Jarrot" be applied to this phase. Nicholas Jarrot was the French landowner who gave the title to the land he owned around Monks Mound to the Trappist monks.

The conferees decided, much to Pat O'Brien's dismay, that what she called "Period V" had been misplaced and should be moved to an earlier time, to about the equivalent of the first Unnamed phase and the Fairmount phase. Donald Lathrap, O'Brien's professor, argued vociferously that since the analysis had been based upon the fill in the house basins and the assumption was that the basins had been filled rapidly, her analysis was correct.

Fowler countered with the argument that one really could not tell from fill what the actual date of the feature was since the fill could have been scooped up from any location. There was no way to know if the basin had been filled in slowly or rapidly. "Unless the sherds were 'glued' to the floor of the pit," Fowler insisted, "one did not have proper context." Lathrap eventually concurred.

Hall said later, "There may be reasons [O'Brien's] sequence is correct . . . because Cahokia is an enormous site and the situation is further confused by the coexistence of parallel Woodland and Mississippian traditions." In the end, Hall agreed with the final results of the 1971 Cahokia ceramic conference. "[Archaeologists], when discussing ceramic chronology and phases at Cahokia, sometimes seem to be talking about different sites," he said. "It is not that the Almighty, seeing men of science ascending Monks Mound, was displeased at their efforts and inflicted upon them a babel of tongues."[5] Hall concluded, with some reluctance, that the 1971 conference provided a new beginning and a new language for discussing the development of Cahokia. Porter, disgruntled with the results of the conference, muttered, "You can't legislate ceramic chronology."

The phases developed by the 1971 conference were widely accepted and used for a number of years. As new information came in from later investigations, the sequence was elaborated and refined. But, as of 1971, the conference's conclusions represented a major advance in understanding the development of Cahokia.

---

5. Hall 1975:30.

TWELVE

The Second Highway Salvage Project

The 1960s and early 1970s had been a period of activity, optimism, and discovery at Cahokia. The national media had printed major stories about the site, and scores of aspiring young archaeologists had moved into the tent city by Monks Mound. By the mid-1970s, however, everything had changed. The archaeological community that worked in the American Bottom had split into warring factions. There were now professional and personal conflicts over turf, money, and control of research at Cahokia, as well as philosophical differences over the propriety of doing archaeology on state-protected lands.

In the early days almost anyone could dig and conduct studies wherever he or she wanted. Nelson Reed, an avocational archaeologist, had been permitted to use earth-moving equipment on the summit of Monks Mound. When the Illinois Archaeological Survey was organized and took over the direction of the highway salvage program in the 1960s it became, in effect, the manager and gatekeeper of research at Cahokia. Later the Illinois Department of Conservation received state funds for research and divided the money among several institutions, including the Universities of Illinois and Wisconsin, Washington University, and Beloit College. The archaeologists involved, particularly those working with the Illinois Archaeological Survey, came to see Cahokia as their private preserve.

When the Illinois State Museum moved into management of the site in conjunction with the conservation department in 1971 and hired James Anderson and William Iseminger, procedures changed. Now there was a staff archaeologist on site, a position Anderson filled, and his authority challenged that of the archaeologists from the Survey. Anderson insisted that the scientists who worked at Cahokia follow certain procedures, make copies of their field maps and notes, and put the records in a central repository at the State Museum. Some of the archaeologists resisted. The data they had gathered was theirs, they said, and they did not want to share it. They could not countenance the idea of someone else's seeing and working with their hard-earned research. Though Anderson and Iseminger worked to get the information centralized, they were only partially successful as some archaeologists simply held back their information.

Cahokia went from being one of the most active research sites in the country to one of the most inactive. The conflict even slowed down the development of the long-awaited interpretive center. Archaeologists either dropped out or did work on the peripheries of the site, maintaining that more could be learned by studying the many communities surrounding Cahokia than by working in Cahokia itself. For several years the only archaeological work done at Cahokia was in a public field school, conducted by Anderson and Iseminger, to work on the east palisade.

Leading the opposition to Anderson's efforts were James Porter and Charles Bareis, members of the Illinois Archaeological Survey. Ill will had developed between the Survey members and the staff at the State Museum. Porter and Bareis were opposed to archaeologists' doing work on state lands, which were protected, while the area of Cahokia outside the park was being destroyed by urban development.

Eventually, Porter and Bareis sent a letter to the state conservation department calling for a moratorium on work at Cahokia. To the other archaeologists it looked like an attempt to shut them out. Porter and Bareis reasoned that Cahokia was a protected site and that other, unprotected, archaeological features were being destroyed. Work had been done (including their own earlier work) and not yet written up. Other archaeologists countered that this was no reason for not doing research at Cahokia, where only a fraction of one percent of the site had ever been investigated.

Many archaeologists believed that there were legitimate research questions that could be answered by investigations at Cahokia and other, equally significant, research questions that could appropriately be applied to sites outside the Cahokia park. A complicating factor for archaeologists who wanted to work outside the boundaries of the state park was the fact that landowners in the American Bottom had become hostile to archaeologists because so much of their rich farmland had been taken by the state for highways and for the Cahokia Mounds State Park. Gaining access to land not owned by the state was difficult and at times even life threatening.

The continuing controversy drove a wedge into the community of archaeologists who had worked at Cahokia. Porter and Bareis had strong personalities and, while they did good archaeology, egos and personalities got in the way. A sense of tension was present when they came to Cahokia. According to some of their colleagues, Porter and Bareis were "really antiacademic." They were committed to fieldwork and were antagonistic to the theory-driven approaches of archaeologists like Fowler and Hall.

The differences were presented as a dichotomy between people who did archaeology for field schools and research and those who did it full time for a living. The "real archaeologists" were scornful of the academics' fieldwork, claiming that they did archaeology "like teachers." In their view, the academics taught for nine months of the year, then went out and played in the field with their students during the summer before going home.

Porter and Bareis argued that the resources directed toward field schools and research should be used to salvage sites about to be destroyed, although they neglected to mention that the moneys for schools and research came from totally different sources with very different goals. Bareis's position on this question was particularly contradictory as he had for years run University of Illinois field schools at Cahokia and in the surrounding area directed at answering specific questions as well as salvaging data before its destruction.

Porter and Bareis made remarks about professors who do "telephone booth archaeology in the summer, then go home and think they know everything." Both Porter and Bareis did large-scale excavations but little writing or reporting of their results. Bareis and Porter appeared to be antiacademic in that they believed that highway construction shouldn't be held up to "wait for people to write up a site and put artifacts in sacks."

Some of his colleagues believed that Bareis's attitude resulted from insecurity over not having earned a Ph.D. himself. This did not seem important to others as Bareis went on to become a full professor of anthropology with tenure at the University of Illinois. Porter got his Ph.D. in 1974 from Wisconsin for work he had done on the Mitchell site in the 1960s.

An early incident that may have shaped their antiacademic bent was the National Science Foundation's refusal to fund a grant request they had submitted earlier to do work at Cahokia. The fact that neither Bareis nor Porter had their Ph.D.'s at the time had been a factor in the denial of their request. Whatever the source of the problem, the unintended result of this bias was to create a division between academics and those who thought of themselves as "real archaeologists."

During the mid-1970s the federal government and the Illinois Department of Transportation finalized plans for another interstate highway through the American Bottom that would move traffic to the east around East St. Louis. The bypass around St. Louis could not be built where it had been originally planned, across the 15A tract. The extensive archaeological finds that had been discovered there and during the nearby salvage operations had caused officials in the federal government to reconsider the antiquities laws regarding federally funded projects. The result was a new regulation that stated that federal funds could not be used to destroy archaeological and paleontological sites without adequate and proper mitigation of the impact.

It was apparent that there was no place at Cahokia where such proper mitigation could take place. The archaeological zone of Cahokia had proved to be so large and complex that mitigation would be excessively expensive and, even with mitigation, the site's integrity would be ruined. Alternative routes were proposed though each one would impact large numbers of archaeological sites. Finally the highway department, faced with the necessity of making a decision, selected a route east of Cahokia, nearer to the eastern margins of the American Bottom.

This section of highway, called I-270 (later renamed I-255), was a six-lane facility that traversed approximately 1,000 acres of farmland beginning just northeast of Cahokia and continuing southwest for 20 miles to the town of Dupo. In 1977 the Illinois Archaeological Survey, led by Charles Bareis, secretary-treasurer and the most influential officer of the organization, signed an agreement with the Illinois Department of Transportation and the Federal Highway Administration to supervise the testing and salvage mitigation of 59 archaeological sites that initial testing showed would be affected by the highway. The affair was called the FAI-270 project.[1]

The Survey immediately set up an advisory board, signed up other Illinois educational institutions to act as subcontractors, and divided up the sites. There was no question of moving the highway. The American Bottom was so rich in Archaic, Woodland, and Mississippian remains that any location chosen for the highway would have destroyed valuable archaeological sites. The only solution was the one selected, to do salvage archaeology ahead of the bulldozers.

Initially, of the 59 sites identified, 20 were chosen for more or less total excavation. (Before the project ended over 120 sites were identified, approximately 92 were investigated through excavation, and more than 1,000,000 square meters of site area were exposed revealing 12,000 features and hundreds of artifacts.) Before they began work Porter, Bareis, and their associates identified four research problems on which they planned to focus their efforts. These were (1) the shift from Late Archaic to Early Woodland; (2) the nature of the Late Woodland and Mississippian community plans and what this represented in the cultural evolution to complex society; (3) how the rise and fall of Cahokia was

1. This project ended with an enviable publication record as can be seen from the following list, especially the first item, an overview edited by Bareis and Porter: Bareis and Porter 1984; Emerson et al. 1983; Finney and Fortier 1985; Fortier 1985; Griffin 1984; Johannessen 1984; Kelly et al. 1984; Kelly and Cross 1984; Milner 1983a, 1983b, 1984a, 1984b, 1984c; Milner and Emerson 1984.

reflected in sites on the American Bottom outside of Cahokia proper; and (4) the significance of climatic changes in the American Bottom area over the past 3,000 years.

Overall, the primary goal of the fieldwork was to define the community plan at each site. The methods used would be those utilized by Wittry and Porter two decades before at the Mitchell and Cahokia 15A and 15B sites; they would bring in bulldozers, paddlewheel scrapers, and backhoes to do large-scale stripping off of the plow zone and see what features lay beneath.

There was much discussion among the members of the advisory committee regarding the appropriateness of Porter's and Bareis's plan to do wholesale stripping of undisturbed archaeological sites. During the 1960s highway salvage projects, there had been little choice. Archaeologists then had to strip the top soil and look for features or lose the data altogether.

But it had now been 20 years since the early work of Wittry, Bareis, and Porter on tracts 15A and 15B, the Powell tract, and the Mitchell site, and a new system was proposed. The new plan envisioned a three-phase process for the archaeological recovery of data from government-sponsored programs. Phase 1 would be the surface survey to locate sites. Phase 2 would be the testing of selected sites to determine if they were appropriate for final mitigation. If a site qualified, it was determined to be eligible for listing on the National Register of Historic Places. Phase 3 would be the full archaeological investigation and excavation of the chosen sites.

It was in the first two phases that strong disagreement among the archaeologists took place. Several approaches for doing phase 1, the initial survey, and phase 2, the testing, had been developed. Lewis Binford[2] proposed statistical probability sampling as a way of examining an area to find sites and other archaeological data.

In Binford's approach the archaeologists would survey only carefully designated areas that had been chosen through a meticulously designed strategy so that the materials found would be scientifically representative of the whole. For phase 2, Binford recommended sampling a selected site through controlled surface collection, a good beginning for a project that would be looking for distributions and community organization. Controlled surface collections had been done on smaller Mississippian sites in Illinois, Missouri, and Tennessee, and Fowler had used the method in southern Illinois before the concept came into the literature.

A controlled surface collection is based on the idea that materials found on the surface are representative of the materials that would be found beneath the

---

2. Binford 1964.

surface of the soil. A concentration of pottery and other artifacts on the surface might indicate a pit or a house below the surface. An area to be sampled is marked off into numbered squares. When the material has been collected from each of the squares, the distribution of various classes of materials can be plotted to look for concentrations. The concentration areas can then be tested by excavation to determine their nature. For large sites, statistical sampling of squares within the grid can be utilized. A controlled surface collection is a noninvasive way to get archaeological data. This method required plowing, but almost all of the sites in the American Bottom had already been plowed by local farmers so it was assumed that the upper several inches had been disturbed.

The debate, in part, revolved around the question of whether the plowed zone had been too disturbed to be representative. Bareis and Porter argued that it had and, furthermore, that there was not enough time or money to follow these new approaches. Over the objections of many on the advisory committee, they decided to proceed with the earth-moving equipment and stripping of large areas.

As it turned out, controlled surface collections, sometimes multiple ones, were made on every FAI-270 site over a period of years but they were not the statistical sampling strategies that were proposed by Binford to decide whether or not to excavate the upper levels or "plowed zones" of the sites. The results of the surface collecting have never been published.

The archaeologists were in an exciting position. Sufficient funds were available from the highway department to bring in enough heavy equipment of the right kind to do the work. All of the archaeological remains would be destroyed by the resultant highway construction and the land would never again be used for agriculture. The settlement plans they hoped to find were an important subject of interest because nobody had any idea what they might look like for any of the periods from Late Archaic through Mississippian times. Instead of studying Cahokia itself, they would be studying the settlements around it, using the suburbs and small towns to draw conclusions about what the large city itself must have been like.

Porter and Bareis may have been correct in their choice of methods given the timetable for constructing the highway. As with the 1960s salvage program, no one will ever know how much data was lost using heavy equipment to remove the plow zone and deeper layers from these sites. Except for Porter, the field director, the only crew member who understood and had experience with this kind of archaeology was Thomas Emerson. By going to work on the FAI-270 project, Emerson was drawn into the orbit of Porter and Bareis.

Thomas Emerson was from Chippewa Falls, Wisconsin, and had earned a B.A. in sociology and political science from the University of Wisconsin at Eau

Claire. Following college he served two tours of duty in Vietnam with the United States Navy, which gave him a lot of time to think about what he wanted to do with his life. He decided it was cultural anthropology. Not until he enrolled in the graduate program at the University of Wisconsin at Madison did he discover that the kind of cultural anthropology he was interested in had not been taught there for three decades. He was, he discovered, out of sync with the times. Though he had absolutely no interest in collecting arrowheads and other artifacts, an activity that had inspired most of his fellow students to go into archaeology, he entered the field almost by default.

Another happenstance brought Emerson to Illinois and Mississippian archaeology. While at Wisconsin he met a fellow graduate student, Larry Conrad, who had worked briefly with Nelson Reed on the fourth terrace of Monks Mound, with Fowler on a site survey, and on the controlled surface collection of Ramey field. Conrad was interested in beginning salvage archaeology on a large Mississippian site near the Dickson Mounds called Orendorf. He told Emerson that if he would come help him he would guarantee him at least enough money so he could eat while they dug.

Orendorf was slowly being destroyed by a coal mine. It was 1971 and the federal government had not yet written rules to protect sites or mandated funding for archaeological salvage. The two men organized a not-for-profit corporation called the Upper Mississippi Valley Archaeological Research Foundation and ran field schools to pay for the excavation. They tried to interest the University of Illinois and the Illinois Archaeological Survey in the project, without success. No one had any money. Emerson worked at Orendorf through 1974, using large earth-moving equipment and digging about 1,300 pit features and 200 houses. Since the money raised paid only for the summer digging crews, the results of the project have never been published and the site was eventually destroyed by the mine.

When Emerson returned to the University of Wisconsin, this time at Madison, to talk with his adviser about beginning work for a Ph.D., he happened to meet John Kelly, who was working in western Illinois. Kelly advised Emerson to write Jim Porter to see if he could get a job. Emerson did and was hired. The year was 1979.

After Emerson moved his wife and five children to Belleville, Illinois, to begin work under Porter on the FAI-270 project, he found himself enmeshed in what he characterized as a "prison camp mentality." Despite his years of experience, Porter started him at the bottom of the crew, digging features for five dollars an hour. Though the university contracted only for five days of work a week, Porter made his crew work seven days a week (which he later reduced to six), extra work for which they did not get paid. After six months of shoveling dirt, Emerson was made a crew leader along with Andrew Fortier, Dale McElrath, George Milner, and John Kelly.

Milner, who had been hired at the beginning of the FAI-270 project, recalled,

> The fieldwork, in 1978, started out as a debilitating rush to get as much done as possible. Many of us worked long seven-day weeks that first season. I held the record for working 75 days straight without a break. The enthusiasm for the work wasn't matched by an appreciation that we were in for the long haul. We were treating things as if it was just a long field season. For some reason, the fieldworkers simply didn't comprehend that we were facing several long years of fieldwork. But this atmosphere of rushing at all times would later carry over into the initial years of analysis and report preparation.

The unstated policy of Bareis and Porter was to hire nonacademics, former graduate students who were not in school any longer or did not have the mind-set of academics. They also focused almost exclusively on people from the University of Wisconsin at Madison. Emerson can remember only one who was not involved in some way with that campus.

Porter, who had not mellowed from his days at the Mitchell site, was one of the most colorful archaeologists working in southeastern archaeology and his idiosyncrasies quickly became legend throughout the archaeological community. Stories circulated about his having become enraged with the telephone company when service was discontinued because of nonpayment of a bill. Porter was said to have ripped the phone from the wall, then taken a shotgun and blasted a transformer off a pole in his yard. He lived in his emotions with the result that he lost some teeth in a fight in a bar. Porter would be in the laboratory at 7:30 in the morning when the crew members came to get their equipment, shouting at them that they were not working fast enough, not moving enough dirt. By 2:00 in the afternoon Porter would be in the Fountain Bar, drinking with the local men, and on Thursdays he left the site to go to his home in Wisconsin.

Emerson remembers that he saw Porter only a few times on the site while he was working and that was usually when someone, such as James Griffin, who had been appointed by the National Park Service as the official monitor of the program, was coming to visit. Milner had more site visits from Porter but recalls that Bareis spent most of his time in Urbana dealing with the Illinois Department of Transportation.

Despite Porter's erratic and emotional management, he set the psychological tone for the 100 crew members and their young supervisors. He made them feel that they were pitted against the rest of the world, that it was their task to show up the slow-moving academics from the participating institutions who, in Porter's opinion, were squandering money and accomplishing little. Porter's approach may have been the only way to have gotten so much work done in so little time.

In Emerson's view, Porter brainwashed people to get them to work themselves to death. When Emerson looks back at his experience he finds it unbelievable. Though the project went very fast, excavating a hundred sites in just three years, he still feels as if it consumed his entire life. Those years of intense fieldwork were, in Emerson's opinion, more than many professionals do in a lifetime, and he has no regrets. He worked on FAI-270 from May 1979 through June 1982. When he left, he was earning $14,000 a year. He and his wife had spent their entire life savings so he could work on the FAI-270 project in the American Bottom. Fortunately, Emerson was later able to use his highway salvage work as the basis for his Ph.D. dissertation.[3]

Bareis's and Porter's relations with the other universities participating in the FAI-270 work did not go well. In the estimation of the two men, digging sites was not a high priority for the professors who had classes to teach and other commitments, though each institution had hired qualified archaeologists to head the excavation projects. When Porter and Bareis judged that Southern Illinois University at Edwardsville was falling behind, they sent Milner to reorganize that portion of the project. He removed site director Ken Williams and replaced him with Bill Woods, who had broken his leg and hobbled around the site in a cast. Shortly thereafter, Southern Illinois University at Edwardsville dropped out, followed by Western Illinois University, which was to have excavated the borrow pits.

When the two universities withdrew, Porter and Bareis, headquartered at the University of Illinois at Urbana-Champaign, took over those projects. Besides the University of Illinois at Urbana-Champaign, the only institution remaining in the project was the University of Illinois at Chicago. Robert Hall refused to be shut out and did his part of the fieldwork. However, Porter and Bareis later refused to publish that campus's report in the series of site papers so Hall published it independent of the other reports. Emerson's evaluation of the whole unfortunate situation is that "people in general shot themselves, but there was no lost love." Despite the domination of the FAI-270 project by a clique and the continual internal bickering, the excavations revealed significant information about the countryside around Cahokia and the influence of that political and religious center on the hinterlands.

---

3. Besides the previously cited site reports on the FAI-270 project, Emerson has published extensively on the nature of Cahokian rural communities and art. See Emerson 1989, 1991b, 1997a, 1997b, 1997c; Emerson et al. 1999; Emerson and Lewis 1991.

When the FAI-270 work was begun the archaeologists had a model in their minds, first articulated by Fowler, of a system of four levels of community.[4] Fowler had always been fascinated by the kinds of information he could get by studying maps. By examining the map of Cahokia, the layout of the surface materials, the locations of the mounds, and their relationships to each other, he proposed a hypothesis of how Cahokia and the surrounding countryside might have been organized. It was obvious to him that the community had been designed around a central area that he called "Downtown Cahokia." Other mounds clustered around open spaces could, he suggested, have been subcommunities of the greater Cahokia area.

Fowler envisioned the American Bottom area as a four-tiered hierarchy of sites differentiated by size and the number of mounds. The division of the sites into the different levels was based solely on the obvious surface features of the site: the mounds, the arrangement of mounds, the absence of mounds, the surface extent of debris, and other above-ground characteristics.

The first-line community was obviously the six-square-mile massive mound center of Cahokia itself, which controlled social and economic relations among the three lower-ranked localities. The second level was the ring of multimound clusters of 124 acres or more. These included Mitchell, about seven miles north of Cahokia; the Pulcher site, near the southern end of the American Bottom; the East St. Louis site; and the St. Louis site. Third-line communities were identified as those having only one mound surrounded by habitation debris, while fourth-line communities were those localities without mounds that could be considered farmsteads or hamlets.

Were these outlying communities political outposts of Cahokia or were they separate chiefdoms of their own? Did they function as food-producing centers for the urban residents of Cahokia? What kind of political or religious domination did Cahokia exert over the hinterlands, or if it did not exert control, what was its influence? Where did the Mississippian characteristics of these outlying communities come from?

Fowler's model was designed to present an ideal of how Cahokia and its hinterlands might have been organized. Before the research of the FAI-270 project there had been little data to go on to analyze the settlements around Cahokia. Al Harn, in his surveys done in the early 1960s, had noted something peculiar—a distinct absence of later Mississippian pottery at many of the sites. He and his colleagues had speculated that this might be due to the fragile nature of the shell-tempered pottery, which would have made it vulnerable to weathering and the effects of intensive cultivation.

---

4. Fowler 1974, 1978.

Howard Winters suggested another possibility to Harn. What if there had been a nucleation process and many sites in the American Bottom had been abandoned when Cahokia became dominant? This was consistent with ideas that Rene Millon had talked about in his Teotihuacán studies.

When Fowler published his settlement pattern model he proposed two alternative interpretations. One held that all the sites had been occupied at the same time. The other, called the nucleation model, suggested that there had been a temporal shift in settlement concentration through time. As the temple-towns grew, the people moved from their rural farm sites into the larger centers.

After Emerson and others examined their FAI-270 data on the movement of people in the rural areas and the differences in the artifacts and structures they left behind, they began to formulate a model different from Fowler's.[5] Along with other researchers they saw the beginnings of Cahokia around A.D. 600, with intense transformations of the social, political, religious, and economic organization taking place between A.D. 900 and 1050. In this account, by A.D. 1000 the American Bottom had become the setting for a cluster of civic-ceremonial centers, headed by chiefs, which exerted influence over their neighboring smaller communities. These chiefdoms were unstable and competitive and survived through shifting networks of treaties and alliances. Around A.D. 1050 one chiefdom or ruling elite was able to consolidate its power and achieve dominance over all of the others. That chiefdom was Cahokia and its dominance changed not only the central city but life in the rural areas as well.

When Emerson and the others began excavating the isolated sites of the I-270 project, they were surprised to find that many were not simple farmsteads or hamlets, as they had thought they would be, but complex sites with buildings that had served different, perhaps ritualistic, functions. They found that the rural sites had sweat lodges and community houses associated with them and that they were surrounded by farmsteads. While these were not large population centers, it was obvious that someone with political or religious power was positioned in the center of these rural sites. This series of semiautonomous settlements in the countryside, wherein workers were busily producing foodstuffs for the great center of Cahokia, looked to Emerson like a tightly organized system that directly resulted from Cahokian intervention.

Emerson named these settlements "dispersed villages" and he identified three specialized forms: nodal households, civic nodes, and ceremonial nodes. He found that he could identify each of the nodes by their unique artifacts and architectural styles. What were these miniceremonial centers doing out in the countryside? This was a major shift in the way people had visualized rural Cahokia.

---

5. Emerson 1992, 1997c; Milner 1984d, 1986, 1991a, 1996.

In the late Archaic period (3200–600 B.C.), communities were characterized by a low labor investment in shelter or storage facilities. Houses were not permanent and few pits were dug to store food or tools. By the late Woodland period (A.D. 300–800), however, rural buildings in the American Bottom had become substantial semisubterranean pit houses, built inside basins dug below ground level. House sizes ranged from 5 to 12 square meters. The walls were of posts, set solidly into the ground, and the buildings were arranged around a central courtyard. The area around the houses was pockmarked with storage pits.

By the Emergent Mississippian period (A.D. 800–1000), the community design had become more formalized. The courtyards now had a central post, like a flagpole, surrounded by four large storage pits. Often a large communal building was constructed nearby along with sets of earthen ovens. The houses were larger, averaging 40 square feet, which represented a substantial investment of labor and materials, and they were rebuilt time and again on the same site, demonstrating a long-term commitment to the location. The largest house in a village had an open courtyard, which may have been dedicated to rituals overseen by a leader with central authority who lived in the large house.

Storage pits were everywhere. Storage pits in association with houses defined a household and were an indication of the wealth of the people living there. The fact that a household was able to produce storable surpluses of food, beyond that needed for day-to-day subsistence, was the foundation of social relations in the American Bottom. Early storage pits were placed outside of the houses. By the Stirling phase, when corn came into widespread use, storage pits of various sizes were placed both inside and outside of the houses and were used as places to deposit trash as well as to store grain, tools, and exotic goods.

While there were above-ground granaries as well, underground pits were efficient ways to store grain for long periods of time. The most successful were large bell-shaped pits with small openings at the surface. When the pits were filled with grain and sealed, the stored grain used up the available oxygen and then went dormant, prolonging the fertility of the seed.

The Stirling phase (A.D. 1100–1200) households typically had two large wall-trench structures with central hearths and large, deep, inside storage pits as well as outside hearths and pits. The houses had individual standard-bearing poles and lean-to additions. The houses were built over and over again on the same sites, suggesting that families had long-term rights to specific lots. Unlike at Cahokia, where houses were sited according to a master city plan, residents of the rural areas and smaller villages oriented their houses to the natural landscape and not to monuments or the cardinal directions.

Among the many changes observed in the Moorehead phase (A.D. 1200–1275) was the fact the houses continued to grow larger. A household was apt to consist of three buildings instead of two, with a fourth off to the side that may have been a smokehouse or hide-processing building. The buildings also occupied the highest ground. Although there was less than a meter's difference in elevation over much of Cahokia, Moorehead phase buildings have been found only on the highest sites.

The largest and most complex site excavated in the FAI-270 program was the Range site at Dupo, near the south end of the I-270 corridor. The Range site was a village on Prairie Lake, another of the Mississippi River channel scars, 12 miles south of Cahokia. Range had been occupied from the Late Archaic period through the Emergent Mississippian. The archaeologist in charge of excavating Range was John E. Kelly.[6]

Kelly is a tall, slender man with close-cropped dark hair who became involved with Cahokia in 1969 following his graduation from Beloit College in Wisconsin. Along with Robert Salzer, he had joined Fowler's summer crew to try to find the location of the western wall of the palisade in the Merrell Tract near 15B, excavated by crews from Beloit College in 1969–71. A few years later he was one of the residents of the tent city along with fellow Beloit College graduate Elizabeth Benchley.

Though Range never reached a stage where it had a mound, it was a complex site because it had been occupied for such a long period of time. The problem in sorting it out was that the different levels and time periods are mixed together. Houses and other features are stacked on top of each other. At one point Kelly estimated that he had to deal with 5,000 features. Despite the quantity of features, the largest number of houses that were occupied at any one time period was about 150 at around A.D. 900. If each house sheltered six people, Range had a population of about 900 people. Strangely enough, this was followed, a decade or so later, by an occupation of about six houses and Range never grew large again. What happened? Unless the people were stolen by aliens, as Emerson remarked, something very dramatic took place.

The dramatic event was a migration. A mass migration took place in which the people from Range, along with residents of almost the entire rural area of the American Bottom, packed up and moved to Cahokia. "You cannot get internal growth at Cahokia fast enough," Timothy Pauketat and Tom Emerson argue, "to grow that community from a small population of a couple thousand people to one of fifteen thousand or more without drawing them in from the countryside."

This is what Pauketat calls the "suction power" of Cahokia, or the "big bang in the American Bottom," and it was one of the major insights to come from the

---

6. Kelly 1990a, 1990b.

FAI-270 program. Something about Cahokia was pulling hundreds of people into its population center. While the mound centers of Mitchell, St. Louis, East St. Louis, and Pulcher remained the regional foci of social integration, after A.D. 1000 there were no longer the small, nonmound villages to stand in the social hierarchy between the large temple-towns and the rural homesteads. The countryside around the great mound center was emptied of its rural residents while Cahokia itself grew rapidly as it absorbed a five- to ten-fold increase in its population.

Because they were seeing dramatic changes through short periods of time in the American Bottom, Bareis and Porter added new divisions to the Mississippian ceramic chronology that had been established at the 1971 ceramic conference. They not only felt that they could subdivide the periods more precisely, they also decided to change the names of many of the phases. They preferred German names, substituting "Lohmann" for "Fairmount," for example.[7]

The continuum was first divided into "periods." The pre-Mississippian period, before A.D. 1000, they designated "Emergent Mississippian." Bareis and Porter called the succeeding period "Mississippian," and they divided the Mississippian period into three parts: early, middle, and late.

The fifty-year period from A.D. 1050 to 1100 they called the Lohmann phase, or Early Mississippian. The next 100 years was the Stirling phase. The Moorehead phase ran from A.D. 1200 through 1275, followed by the Sand Prairie phase, which continued until A.D. 1350. After a slow start through 200 years of what they called Emergent Mississippian, A.D. 800–1000, the Mississippian period exploded onto the American scene and lasted about 400 years.

During the Emergent Mississippian period the American Bottom had been populated with independent villages, farmsteads, and hamlets, each probably tied to some sort of kinship group. Within the smaller villages all of the people were probably related to each other. When Cahokia rose to dominance, it was important for the smaller communities to establish ties to the central authority or paramount chief. They did this by stressing their actual kinship ties with the chief or, if they did not have any, by establishing fictive ties. Ties were also probably established by offering women as brides to the paramount chief, a practice that would establish the "kinship" of the outsider group to the center.

At some point the belief systems that had long been held in common were taken over by the elite at Cahokia. They expropriated the symbols of the folk cosmology, sacralized the landscape, and through the sheer magnitude of their architecture achieved ideological and political control of the rural areas. Power

---

7. Additional refinements were made to the ceramic sequence for Cahokia and the American Bottom starting with Kelly's Ph.D. research (Kelly 1980) and continuing with the outstanding work of George Holley (Holley 1989).

moved from the hands of the commoners to the newly crowned elite, who used the idols and monuments to legitimate their authority.

Starting with the Lohmann phase, another dramatic change took place. The rural outposts were rebuilt and repopulated, but this time they were each headed by a political operative surrounded by the family-centered farmsteads. Each village became a centrally controlled political-religious center set up to ensure that ample foodstuffs were produced and transmitted to Cahokia.

The sheer size of Cahokia required new systems for provisioning the city. The combined power of fertility ceremonialism and community political activities dominated the tightly controlled rural networks and guaranteed that supplies would continue to move into Cahokia. The countryside was literally remade by the new philosophy emanating from the central political complex. This domination continued through the Stirling and into the Moorehead phase, when even more highly organized and controlled communities with temples appear. The rural communities with their binding ties to Cahokia did not begin to disintegrate until the late Moorehead and Sand Prairie phases.

As evidence for this theory, Emerson points to the Cahokian figurines, which he believes exemplify political and religious power. While supervising the work at a FAI-270 location called the BBB Motor site, he had been excavating a hamlet built on a ridge surrounded by marshes. The workers were digging out the house and pit features and Emerson had already cleared a wide area around the houses when he decided to clean off the remaining area between the house sites and the edge of the highway.

The road scraper was moving back and forth, shoving tons of dirt, and Emerson was walking across the site, talking with his supervisor. Suddenly, out of the corner of his eye, he saw what he thought was a soft brick that had been turned up by the road scraper. He walked over, picked it up, and found that he held in his hand a finely carved figurine in a red stone called flint clay (fig. 21). The machine had destroyed the top part of the head but the rest was intact.

Analysis of the piece, now known as the Birger figure, would take anthropologists a long distance toward understanding the complex belief system that underlay the organization of Cahokia. The carved stone figure is of a kneeling woman, dressed in a short wrap-around skirt, with a cord at her waist. She wears moccasins, and on her back is a flat, square pack held in place by a strap around her shoulders. In her right hand she holds a hoe while the other hand rests on a serpent that has the head of a cat or jaguar, with the requisite number of teeth for a feline. The serpent wraps around the woman, dividing into two vines at the woman's left side. One vine with three fruits—probably squash—runs along the women's feet and around her side. The other, with three fruits, trails up her back and over her left shoulder.

Figure 21. Front and back views of the Birger figure. Used with permission of the Illinois Transportation Archaeological Research Program, University of Illinois.

When the figure had been photographed it was sent to Don Lathrap at the University of Illinois for analysis. Lathrap was an advocate of the idea that Mississippian peoples had had contact with the great civilizations of Mexico and South America. This concept had been readily accepted in the early years of American archaeology, but it later fell into disfavor with the influence of Griffin and others who pointed out there were few Mesoamerican artifacts among Woodland or Mississippian materials. Most archaeologists were in agreement with this position, believing that if there had been contact with Mexico it had not been important and that anthropologists had to look at the internal history of southeastern peoples to understand how they had developed.

But how to explain the Birger figure, and other similar figures that were being found in the American Bottom? When Lathrap unwrapped the figure in his laboratory his first reaction was that his colleagues, knowing his minority position on contacts with Mexico, were playing a joke on him.

"Someone has faked this to try to make a fool out of me," he exclaimed.

"Not so," replied Emerson, who had been as surprised by the Birger figure as anyone. "I found it and it has good context." Emerson explained the circumstances of finding the figure and Lathrap was impressed. To Lathrap, the figure clearly represented the Mexican mythology of the Green Corn and serpent gods, perhaps even Quetzalcoatl, the feathered serpent.

There may not have been material culture going back and forth between Mexico and the American Bottom but here in Illinois was evidence in stone of concepts and ideas similar to those in Central America. The Indians of the Southeast, like those of Mexico, had myths about underwater panthers and monsters, composite beings, and snakes with feline faces. Could they have come from some ancient foundation myths that were common to all the people in North and Central America?

Emerson believes the figures represent the Green Corn symbolism, embodying the concept of fertility and rebirth. The figures appear at the beginning of the Stirling period, the period of greatest central control at Cahokia. This is also the time when the Ramey Incised pottery, a ware produced for the elite, appears. Emerson is convinced that the Ramey iconography was a symbolic portrayal of the cosmos and of elite-commoner relationships.

Around A.D. 1050 the central elite at Cahokia appropriated symbols—images of raptors, snakes, fertility, and gender—that had their origins in Archaic times, 2,000 to 2,500 B.C., and started making images containing these symbols for distribution to the rural centers. Emerson says it is significant that the figurines—carved of quartz crystals, mica, and galena—"were not found in the big chief's house at Cahokia. They were out in the rural centers. The chiefs were saying, 'We will help you deal with the world. Look at our power. We make these symbols. We make these earth mothers and we control them all.'"

The fertility symbolism complex was part of the shared cultural milieu of both the elite and the commoners. With the onset of the Stirling phase, however, the elite of Cahokia took these shared beliefs and made them into something that enabled this elite to dominate the rest of the populace.

The designs on the Ramey Incised pottery are remarkably homogeneous and they all deal with the theme of fertility and life-regeneration. The pottery and other elite goods may have been centrally manufactured at Cahokia and used in ceremonies where sacred objects were then carried from the central place to outlying areas. Historic accounts tell of new pottery being made for special ceremonial events, such as the Green Corn ceremony, and of people carrying away materials such as medicine in special pottery vessels.

The control that Cahokia exerted over the surrounding countryside, in many archaeologists' thinking, was not economic or military; it was religious and political. Cahokia, in this view, was not an economic empire. Certainly there was trade, but trade based on relationships. "Cahokia was exporting ideological power and there is no doubt that people all over the Midwest were looking up to Cahokia," says Emerson. "My God, it was impressive. But control? I don't think they controlled much beyond the American Bottom."

George Milner,[8] one of Porter's FAI-270 supervisors, proposes another variation on Fowler's four-tiered concept of community organization. Milner was a freshman at Beloit College in Wisconsin in 1971 when he chanced to attend a guest lecture by Fowler on his work at Mound 72 in Cahokia. The discussion fascinated Milner and, though he did not suspect it at the time, it was to set the direction of his career. That summer he signed up for Bob Salzer's field school at Cahokia and moved into the tent city on the site. There he soon met most of the principal actors on the Cahokia stage, including Jim Porter, who later hired him to work on the FAI-270 project.

During the five years he spent on the project, Milner's own ideas about the Cahokia hinterlands began to change. Much of his work was concentrated in a nine-mile segment of the American Bottom immediately south of Cahokia, especially at the Julien site, a location on the I-270 right-of-way that had been assigned to Southern Illinois University at Edwardsville for excavation. This area, like the rest of the American Bottom, was a floodplain filled with ridges, terraces, and alluvial fans situated near marshes, sloughs, and creeks that drained the uplands and meandered through the Bottom before emptying into the Mississippi. While the land was well adapted for the cultivation of maize, squash, and the starchy seed plants of goosefoot, knotweed, and maygrass, Milner estimated that only about 37 percent of the area south of Cahokia was habitable. The rest of the land was under water much of the year.

Houses had been constructed along the flanks of ridges. As time passed, the Indians had moved their houses to higher and higher ground. Milner speculated on the reasons for the moves. There may have been a decrease in the amount of bottomland suitable for farming because of the intensive cultivation in the area, a change in the flood patterns of streams, or an increase in soil-laden runoff from an overexploitation of forests on the bluffs above the river. Houses built during the Emergent Mississippian period were generally small and dug into basins with wall posts set into pits. By A.D. 1000, the beginning of the Mississippian period, the houses had grown larger, increasing in size from 9.5 square meters in the Lohmann phase to as much as 24 square meters by the Sand Prairie phase. Some of these special-function buildings were round, reminiscent of Harriet Smith's round building, which archaeologists surmise may have been sweat lodges.

---

8. George Milner has contributed extensively to the study of Cahokia and the American Bottom. His early emphasis, other than the FAI-270 project, was on bioanthropology and Precolumbian cemeteries. His more recent work has emphasized settlement organization and distribution as well as the fluctuating nature of power and populations of chiefdoms. See Milner 1982, 1984a, 1984d, 1985, 1986, 1990, 1991a, 1991b, 1992, 1996; Milner and Emerson 1984.

One of the large special-function buildings had been constructed in a rectilinear shape with paired hearths. Inside was cultural debris—projectile points, including one oversized white chert point covered with traces of red pigment. Many of the special-feature buildings were located on sites that were also distinctive, such as a high point on a ridge, near Range, or where two ridges intersected, at Julien. The many widely distributed farmsteads appeared to have been affiliated with their own special-feature site, a group of buildings with distinctive architecture indicating that they were used for some kind of ritual or community integrating function.

As Milner studied the field reports from the five years of work on FAI-270, he envisioned a more decentralized, socially segmented, and dynamic cultural system. He saw the American Bottom settled by more-or-less equivalent social units centered on locally prominent town-and-mound complexes. These sites may have served as residences for the elite who dominated a particular territory and its surrounding farmsteads. Mound centers may have been nearly autonomous politically and exercised control over the affairs of the people in their immediate vicinity.

Cahokia itself also directly controlled a territory of unknown size and, in Milner's model, had forged alliances with the elite of the other mound centers. These alliances, he believes, were fluid and shifting, the fluctuations in power resembling the maneuvers of medieval knights of Europe as they sought to maintain control over their castles and territories.

Milner saw the Mississippian cultural area as a virtual cauldron of volatile polities, alliances, antagonisms, and dominance relationships. The Cahokia palisade is evidence of Cahokia's response to its uneasy relations with the leaders of other mound centers. The palisade marked off the heart of Cahokia. Even when it was not needed for defense the palisade served as a graphic demonstration of the social distance that members of the elite group at Cahokia maintained between themselves and the rest of their society.

In Milner's opinion it was through these alliances with regional chiefs that the leaders of Cahokia were able to move exotic raw materials such as various types of chert, galena, hematite, copper, mica, whelk shell, and ritual artifacts throughout the area; commandeer labor to build the mounds and palisades; and, perhaps, even demand maidens for sacrifices.

In Milner's reading of the evidence from FAI-270, Cahokia's peak of development was not the Moorehead period, as was once thought, but corresponded roughly to the Stirling phase, A.D. 1100 to 1200. By A.D. 1150 Cahokia was a bustling, sprawling city of residential, public, and sacred areas. New mounds were being built. Monks Mound was crowned with the ruler's temple. Cahokia's interactions with people of distant regions and cultures were being expanded.

High-status goods were moving through trade networks over great distances. Despite its organizational complexities and its many impressive achievements, Cahokia's governance was an unstable system over the long term. By the beginning of the Moorehead phase, even though the people were living well and the trappings of high office were in place, Cahokia, the urban behemoth, was beginning to fail.

THIRTEEN

The Struggle to Build a New Cahokia Museum

In early 1971 the Illinois State Museum entered into a joint agreement with the Illinois Department of Conservation, which managed the Cahokia Mounds State Park, to develop an interpretive and education program at the site and to improve the museum facilities. Student groups and visitors had begun touring the site and, except for the grass-covered mounds, there was little for them to see.

The museum building was not really a museum. It had been built in 1930 as the ranger's residence, with one room set aside for a "relic room." Most of the relics, which had been contributed or loaned by local people, had been lost or had otherwise disappeared. Joe Webb had lived there since the early 1950s. Now he moved into one of five houses the state had acquired on the site and Anderson and Iseminger took over the building.

Bill Iseminger had become interested in archaeology as a young boy when relatives he was visiting in Illinois took him out into the fields to collect Indian artifacts. While an undergraduate he took a summer job at Dickson Mounds, the site that had been the training ground and fired the enthusiasm of so many other young archaeologists. There he met Bob Hall, Warren Wittry, Al Harn, Joe Caldwell, Pat Munson, and Howard Winters, all members of the informal network of professional midwestern archaeologists.

When the summer job ended, Iseminger and a friend attended the annual meeting of the American Association of Archaeologists, where Bill Gardner, a Ph.D. in anthropology from the University of Illinois, introduced the two students to Melvin Fowler, who was looking for workers for the next summer. That was what Bill was hoping to hear and he signed on to work on the 1968 south palisade project at Cahokia.

The field director under Fowler for the palisade project was Jim Anderson. When the summer ended, Bill stayed in touch with Anderson and in 1971, when he was finishing his master's degree at Southern Illinois University, he went to the meeting of the Illinois Archaeological Survey at Champaign. Anderson was there as well and he asked Iseminger was he was doing.

"Looking for a job," Bill replied.

"I've got one for you," said Anderson, who had just been hired as curator of anthropology for the Cahokia Mounds State Park. "You can come on as my assistant." Iseminger did and he has been at Cahokia ever since.

Displays were still confined to one small room because the rest of the former ranger's house was occupied by Charles Bareis, who used it as a headquarters for the University of Illinois field school. After the 1971 season, Bareis moved into another house on the site and the entire building became the museum. Though Anderson and Iseminger now had a building, they had almost no budget for displays or interpretive programs. Iseminger acquired a desk and office equipment from state surplus and began putting together a slide show for visitors. When he saw a school group wandering about the site, he would approach the students and offer to give brief explanatory comments. He launched an educational program by sending letters to area school superintendents announcing his availability for presentations on Cahokia.

It soon became apparent to both men that if the museum was to be at all functional, it would have to be remodeled. Anderson and Iseminger took on the job, knocking out walls, enlarging doorways, and creating passageways. Jim Hauser, a curator at the huge St. Louis Museum of Science and Natural History, became interested in the project and notified the two men whenever his museum was getting rid of old displays. Anderson and Iseminger would drive over and pick up dismantled displays and cases and put them back together for use in the Cahokia Museum.

Because they were continually short of money, they decided to open a small gift shop through the Illinois State Museum Society to help fund operations. The shop was an immediate success. The State Museum Society built a counter for the new shop at the fabrication facilities in Springfield and trucked it down to Cahokia—only to find that the 14-foot case could not navigate the turns in the museum building. They finally got it in by taking out a window and all the attached woodwork and shoving the case through the hole in the wall.

Several times during the 1970s the Illinois Department of Conservation, the Illinois State Museum, and the Illinois Archaeological Survey appointed committees to recommend plans for the development of Cahokia Mounds State Park. Most of these committees were chaired by Melvin Fowler and no plan was too grandiose to be considered. Nelson Reed wanted to build a 40-foot-high replica of the building for which he had found foundations on the fourth terrace of Monks Mound. He believed that this construction would be highly visible from the highway and thus would attract people to Cahokia. Several development plans were submitted that dealt both with an interpretation of the site for the public and the need to buy more land to expand the park. Though no agreement was reached on an interpretive structure, the state did begin to buy more land.

Joseph Caldwell in the 1960s, and later Nelson Reed, had provided the impetus and gradually acres were added in a piecemeal fashion. The Rattlesnake Mound tract to the south was added to the park on November 29, 1980, after lengthy negotiations and court hearings with the railroad. Among those who testified on behalf of the state were Nelson Reed and Melvin Fowler. After the hearing the attorney for the state told Fowler what an excellent witness Reed had been. He obviously thought that Fowler had been too dry and technical in his presentation. Fowler was chagrined because he had interrupted his research in Mexico and returned, at his own expense, to testify on behalf of Cahokia Mounds. During the discussions one railroad representative had asked if it would be possible to move the mounds.

In 1981 the Kreider Truck Company building east of Monks Mound was bought with the assistance of the National Trust for Historic Preservation. This was the first purchase by the Trust of an archaeological site, and the money was later repaid by the Illinois Department of Conservation. To Iseminger's great relief, in 1983 the nearby X-rated Falcon Drive-In Theater was purchased and demolished.

In October 1984, through condemnation proceedings, 376 acres were purchased from Harriet Bunselmeyer for $733,240. Bunselmeyer had been growing corn and horseradish on the land and the agreement with her stipulated that she was to leave the crops in place. When the state took possession, however, officials discovered she had removed the crop, worth about $90,000, and left the land in such poor condition the state had to spend an additional $55,000 for reseeding and repair.

A major acquisition was the Mounds Subdivision of East St. Louis, a tract of 67 houses valued at $2,117,000. The houses were bordered by U.S. 40 on the north, Major Street on the south, and Park and Ramey Streets on the east and west. Beginning in the early 1980s, officials from the state negotiated with each owner and eventually every house was purchased and moved to a new location, the last house departing in 1989.

The system of dividing the administration of Cahokia Mounds State Park between the state conservation department and the Illinois State Museum had never been entirely satisfactory. In 1976 a reorganization had taken place. The Illinois State Museum withdrew and the Department of Conservation took over complete control of the park. This was a time of great uncertainty for the staff. Both Anderson and Iseminger had had job titles as curators when they worked for the State Museum. The Department of Conservation had no classifications equivalent to their positions. For a time the future of the Cahokia Museum itself and of the archaeology being done at the site was in doubt. To protect what had already been done at Cahokia, Anderson and Iseminger shipped off all their archaeological materials and field equipment to the Illinois State Museum for safekeeping.

Though Anderson and Iseminger were promised that they would be offered new jobs at comparable pay under the new organizational structure, they heard nothing definite from the conservation department until June 30, 1976, the last day of the fiscal year. Then Anderson and Iseminger were offered positions as site interpretive specialists, at substantially lower pay. Nevertheless, both stayed on. The status of the site was changed from that of a state park to a state historic site. Management priorities shifted to emphasize the cultural aspects of the site and to underplay the recreational. Playground equipment was removed and trees were cut down.

With the Illinois State Museum no longer managing the Museum Store, which had funded Cahokia's educational programs and newsletter, Anderson organized the Cahokia Mounds Museum Society in 1976 to take its place. With a museum building that was clearly inadequate for an education program, Iseminger and members of the Museum Society turned to the outdoors and the idea of experimental archaeology. Nelson Reed was the first to get involved. In the 1960s he had built a large Mississippian-style house just south of Monks Mound. The building collapsed after a few years but Reed and students from Washington University persisted. In 1972 they built a replica of a small pit house near Monks Mound. Unfortunately, the snow fence they put up to protect it was not sufficient to prevent its destruction by vandals.

During the summers of 1974 and 1975, Reed and his students put up eight houses; covered the roofs with cattail mats and prairie grass thatch; planted gardens of corn, beans, squash, pumpkin, tobacco, and sunflowers; and cultivated the crops with flint and mussel-shell hoes. Around the houses they constructed a replica of the palisade. For much of the summer the students lived in the houses, making cordage from bark fibers, cooking traditional foods, and explaining Mississippian life to visitors.

The program ended with the summer when the students returned to school. When the students left, vandals moved in, partied in the houses at night, and sat on the roofs to watch the pornographic movies at the Falcon Drive-In. Finally one of the houses was set on fire, destroying the large cattail mats Reed had acquired from the Kickapoo Indians in Mexico and Oklahoma.

Because public interest in the structures was high, Anderson and Iseminger decided to try their hand at building a Mississippian house behind the museum building. They got it mostly completed in 1977 but had to wait until the fall of 1978 for another crop of prairie grass to finish the roof. They mixed clay, grass, and a little cement to make the daub for the walls, but they soon found they had to add more and more cement to protect the structure from the ever-present vandals. Despite the problems, the house was popular with school groups and other legitimate visitors.

The last pit house project was started in the fall of 1982 by Dr. Errett Callahan, a purist in experimental archaeology. Callahan made all the stone axes, hoes, knives, scrapers, and other tools. Only authentic materials, such as deerhide lashings, were used. Callahan documented each minute that volunteers spent working on the pit-house project. By the time the house was finished in February 1983, a total of 1,500 hours, contributed mostly by museum volunteers, had been spent on the popular project.

By 1978, membership in the Cahokia Mounds Museum Society had grown to 200 and the organization was funding the archaeological field school, the experimental archaeology, some staff salaries, the printing of the newsletter, and the reprinting of a Time-Life booklet on Cahokia. A public event in 1978, sponsored by the society, drew 3,500 people. Cahokia was finally being discovered. Among the groups that discovered it was the United Nations.

When Melvin Fowler was still at Southern Illinois University at Carbondale, in the 1960s, he had become acquainted with John Corbett and John Cotter, archaeologists with the National Park Service, which was responsible for all salvage archaeology on federal construction projects. The three were working together on a salvage archaeology project in advance of reservoir construction on the Kaskaskia River when Fowler talked to them about Cahokia.

"That place should really be a national park, a federal thing," he told them. At the time, Corbett and Cotter were influential archaeologists in the National Park Service and they agreed to meet with Fowler to discuss it. A few weeks later the three met for lunch at the University Club in St. Louis. The archaeologists had already toured Cahokia and their report was discouraging.

They told Fowler that the site had been too compromised for a national park. They had seen the subdivision with the 60 houses, the bars, and the drive-in theater next to the mounds on the site. They were sorry, they said, but the National Park Service would not be interested. For a brief time, Illinois Senator Everett Dirksen had tried to change the park service's decision, but even he was unsuccessful.

One person at the Park Service did support aspirations for Cahokia, however, and that was Larry Aten. Instead of lobbying for it to become a national park, Aten promoted its nomination to the World Heritage list maintained by UNESCO, the United Nations Educational, Scientific, and Cultural Organization. Aten met with Anderson and Iseminger to develop their site management plan and prepare their application. On the first round, in 1976, Cahokia lost out to Mesa Verde, a national park in Colorado with a new museum and an established development plan. But on the second round, in December 1982, Cahokia Mounds Historic Site was named a World Heritage Site, taking its place beside natural and cultural wonders such as the Pyramids of Egypt, the Taj Mahal, Stonehenge, Yellowstone National Park, and the Grand Canyon as one of the great attractions of the world.

The big brass World Heritage Site plaque lay propped against the wall in a museum building that was slowly disintegrating. There were cracks in the walls that would open in the dry season and close up when the weather turned wet. The roof leaked, the walls were full of mice, and birds nested in the ceilings. The exterior had gone through many changes of paint, from white to chocolate brown to yellow and finally to a three-tone beige and brown combination applied by the vice-president of the Museum Society. The original steam-heat boiler had been converted from coal to oil and the pipes were held together by encrustations and rust. Cahokia's museum did not look at all appropriate for a World Heritage Site.

To be fair, the State of Illinois had been trying, albeit halfheartedly, to appropriate money for a new museum, to be called the Interpretive Center, since 1975. Governor Dan Walker had included $6 million for a new Cahokia museum in his public works budget, and Representative Monroe Flinn, of Cahokia, had sponsored a bill to release $100,000 for planning. In 1976 an architectural firm had been hired to prepare preliminary plans, and archaeological testing began on the proposed new Interpretive Center site on the Dunham Tract, south of 15A.

Testing of the Dunham Tract, called the ICT (Interpretive Center Tract), was divided into two parts. Part 1 was under the direction of Bob Hall from the University of Illinois, Chicago, who conducted a remote sensing project using an instrument that would measure changes in magnetism below the surface of the ground, thus indicating the presence of features. This technique had been used successfully in several archaeological sites around the world and at the Angel Mound sites in southern Indiana. Despite its success elsewhere, the method failed at Cahokia, perhaps because of the presence of numerous overhead power lines.

Part 2 of the investigation was carried out by Elizabeth Benchley for the University of Wisconsin, Milwaukee. Her plan was to pull a number of soil cores from the site and test the levels in the cores for phosphate content. It had been known for years that human occupation increases the phosphate level at a site. People walking around barefoot increase the phosphate level as does the accumulation of refuse that they throw away. A rapid field method for measuring the phosphate content of soil samples had been developed by Robert Eidt, a geographer at the University of Wisconsin, Milwaukee.

Benchley pulled her core samples and analyzed them. Though the data was never published, enough information was accumulated from her efforts and from earlier work by Charles Bareis to show that there was too much archaeology—house basins, possible burials, pits, and hundreds of other features—at the Dunham Tract for it to be a reasonable site for the new Interpretive Center to be built. The new building, the archaeologists decided, could not be erected at this location.

Other sites were proposed within the park. While one archaeologist might agree with the new proposed location, others would not. For three years the archaeologists and state officials argued over where to put the new Interpretive Center, without ever reaching an agreement. One proposed location was a site at the south end of the Mounds Subdivision. This site was called the ICT-I site. In 1979 Fowler and Benchley received a grant to test for significant archaeological remains that might be adversely affected by construction of the new facility. Everyone hoped that the new museum project was finally getting started.

The proposed Interpretive Center tract was a T-shaped piece of land covering about 10 acres, 6 acres of which would be required for the museum building and associated parking lots. Two-thirds of the site was a low-lying field that had been used by local farmers for agriculture. The other third was covered with large trees, almost impenetrable shrubbery, and monstrous poison ivy. From its appearance in the early photographs and from the size of the trees, Fowler and Benchley concluded that the wooded area had never been plowed in historic times.

Determined to do this investigation properly, they settled on four techniques: controlled surface collection; aerial photography, using different kinds of film and with pictures taken at different times of the year; shovel probing; and soil corings. To conduct the surface collection they first had the field plowed and disked to expose artifacts within the plow zone. Fortunately, it rained just after the field was plowed, making it easier to see cultural debris on the surface. The field was marked off into 2.5-meter squares and the student workers were given a time limit—just five minutes—to collect everything they could find in a single square. The collections were placed in numbered bags so that later the students could plot the distribution of the cultural debris. A crew of seven workers collected in 4,246 2.5-meter squares in less than four weeks.

The aerial photographs of the tract were taken from a lower altitude than had been the pictures taken to map Cahokia. When Fowler examined the black-and-white and infrared aerial photographs back in his laboratory he found a series of parallel lines on the pictures, running from the northeast to the southwest at an azimuth of approximately 30 degrees and covering almost the entire field. The lines, he determined, were crop marks spaced about four meters apart.

Since the local farmers had always plowed in rows running north and south, and fertilized their crops in the same directions, Fowler concluded that the diagonal lines were remnants of aboriginal ridged fields. The ridged fields were apparently used to reclaim low-lying wetlands. The soil in low-lying areas was heaped up into ridges, sometimes as high as three feet, and crops such as corn were planted along the summits of the ridges, which elevated the roots above the water line. The ridged fields appeared to have been maintained and rebuilt for many years, creating the soil differences that were reflected in plant growth hundreds of years later. These ridged fields were the first to have been discovered within the confines of Cahokia.

Shovel testing was used in the wooded area. Students forced shovels into the ground at regular intervals and pulled up chunks of earth to examine for potsherds or artifacts. Fowler was amazed that the distribution of materials determined by shovel testing was very close to that revealed by controlled surface collection. While there was a light scattering of material over most of the area, they found a large concentration in the northwest and northeast corners of the tract.

Through the soil coring another discovery was made. The Patrick map showed a causeway connecting Mounds 61 and 62, directly east of the Interpretive Center Tract. Later investigators had been unable to find Patrick's causeway and its existence was questioned until the new soil corings confirmed its presence. Patrick's map also showed a complex of inundated borrow pits east of the two mounds and a low swampy area southwest of the Interpretive Center Tract. Those features were still visible to Fowler and Benchley as they superimposed their tract map over the Patrick map and studied the land around them.

As they summarized their findings, Fowler and Benchley concluded that the entire tract had been utilized to some degree during prehistoric times. They determined that six locations on higher ground had a higher concentration of residences while the lower areas had been used primarily for agriculture. They recommended that two areas of the tract be preserved from any kind of development. First was the causeway between the two mounds. Remnants of the causeway, a unique feature at Cahokia, could actually be seen in an unplowed section of hedgerow on the east side of the tract. The second area was the woods, which, because it had never been plowed in historic times, undoubtedly contained significant archaeological remains in an undisturbed context. The shovel testing had located one large borrow pit and several Mississippian habitation areas on the ridge summits and slopes within the woods.[1]

---

1. Fowler et al. 1980.

The testing continued through another year, called phase 2.[2] In phase 2 Benchley tested to confirm what workers had found in the surface collections from the year before. Benchley and her team used a backhoe to dig trenches across the area where they had not found much material. When they did this they found, buried a meter or more below the surface, what is called an old A horizon—where the ground level had been at that elevation at some time in the past. Associated with the old A horizon were Archaic period artifacts. The level dated to about 1500 B.C., indicating that the land in that area had built up at least three feet or more since Archaic times. On the basis of the phase 2 testing, Fowler and Benchley recommended that a phase 3 test be done, which would be a more complete excavation of the area.

The Illinois Department of Conservation, which had been funding the testing, agreed but this time it gave the contract to archaeologists from Southern Illinois University at Carbondale. Archaeologists from SIU did more extensive tests and found more of the buried A horizon as well as some confirmation in sediments that there was some basis for what Fowler had interpreted as cornfields, or ridged field systems.[3]

Everyone agreed that the testing had gone well. While there were evidences of prehistoric habitation, they were not nearly as numerous and extensive as they had been at the Dunham site. In 1981 the archaeologists gave their approval, with the exclusions recommended by Fowler and Benchley, of the Mounds Subdivision location for the new Interpretive Center.

The archaeologists had no sooner agreed on the location for the new museum when the Illinois Department of Conservation announced that it had run out of money. While the archaeologists and government bureaucrats had debated for three years, the department had spent the capital funds it had reserved for building the museum on other projects. Nonetheless, it continued its land acquisition program in the Mounds Subdivision. The one point on which most people agreed was that ICT-I was where the new Interpretive Center would eventually be built.

When, in 1982, Cahokia was named a World Heritage Site, a collective sense of embarrassment settled over officials of the State of Illinois. Theirs was the only state in the Union with a state-owned park that had been named a World Heritage Site by UNESCO in which the museum building was a 1930s relic that was falling down around its visitors.

James Anderson left his position as site superintendent in December 1983 and was replaced in February 1984 by Dr. Margaret Brown. Brown spent the

2. Benchley and DePuydt 1982.
3. Nassaney et al. 1983.

early years of her tenure coping with a decaying physical plant. She lived in a house on the site and one night the museum alarm went off five times. When it went off the sixth time she turned it off and went back to bed. Mice in the walls, she learned later, were coming out at night and running over the sensors. Crime was a continual problem as well. Brown dealt with shootings, suicides, burglaries, and car chases. The pit toilets in the picnic area were continually vandalized or used as places of assignation.

Mound 72 was near a picnic area with pit toilets and while Fowler and the students were excavating, Fowler saw that men appeared to be using the remote location of the toilets as a place to meet. Other men sat in their cars and on the picnic tables and watched the able-bodied youth with their shirts off working at the dig. Fowler also noticed cars cruising the park. Drivers would circle around and, if they saw a parked car, they would stop. The driver of the cruising car would flash his car headlights and if the second auto contained a willing partner, lights would flash back in reply. Two men would then get out and go into the outhouse together. Occasionally they would post a guard outside as a lookout.

Fowler had observed the pattern for some time when he decided to test it out. "After all," he said to himself, "I am a trained social scientist as well as an archaeologist and this behavior is a cultural phenomenon." One evening he drove around the site and flashed his car headlights. Suddenly he realized there was a car following him. Annoyed with himself for doing such a risky thing and a little frightened, Fowler drove off at a high rate of speed down U.S. 40 with the car following him. In a short distance he managed to lose it.

Chagrined that a significant archaeological site was operating under such conditions, Governor James Thompson, in 1984, announced the immediate release of $6 million for the Interpretive Center at Cahokia. The money would come from a newly levied tax on soda pop.

When the state architects returned to Cahokia and looked out over the site the archaeologists had chosen for the new museum, they shook their heads. The site was under water and had been for much of the time during the previous three years. Anderson had dubbed it "Lake Fowler." Though it was true that the three years had been unusually wet ones at Cahokia, it was also obvious that the site was subject to frequent flooding. Patrick's map had shown that part of the area was a swamp, and Fowler's and Benchley's work had indicated that the Indians had wisely selected higher ground for their homes.

In 1984, control of work at Cahokia was transferred from the Department of Conservation to the newly created Illinois Historic Preservation Agency (IHPA). As part of this process, Tom Emerson, who had gone to work for the Department of Conservation, moved to the new agency and became chief archaeologist for the IHPA with responsibility for managing the state's archaeological resources.

Emerson's first task in his new job was to get consensus on the location for the new Interpretive Center at Cahokia. The issue came down to two considerations. Should money be spent to raise the level of the site so the center could be built where it had been originally planned, or should the center be built on higher ground and the money spent on doing archaeological work at the new location? Many archaeologists opposed building the center at the new higher location because of the sites they feared would be destroyed.

A decision had to be made, and quickly. Emerson favored building the center at the higher location, and at a meeting in Springfield the IHPA director agreed. The two went to the Cahokia Planning Committee with their recommendation and, despite opposition from some of the archaeologists on the committee, convinced the majority to agree. A location one block to the north of the Interpretive Center site was selected and archaeologists from Southern Illinois University at Edwardsville were called in to do archaeological testing. This tract, dubbed ICT-II, was on distinctly higher ground and contained the remains of dwellings. Cahokia had been so densely populated that there was no place where an interpretive center could be built without disturbing some features. From 1984 through 1986, William Woods and other archaeologists from Southern Illinois University at Edwardsville did surface collecting, stripped off the plow zone, and identified and excavated features in the 5,830-square-meter area to be affected by the center. Within that area, about 466 features were identified and excavated.

Woods and his staff found that the initial occupation of the ICT-II site had occurred during Lohmann times, between A.D. 1050 and 1100. This was an unusual discovery as most other excavated areas of Cahokia had shown evidence of earlier Emergent Mississippian occupation. It appeared that during early Lohmann times there had been an expansion of the Cahokia population into new areas of the site. This new information on the expanding population in early Lohmann times had implications for the population size and early organization of Cahokia.[4]

The analysis showed that Lohmann-phase structures were well spaced out and were oriented along the cardinal directions, much as Fowler had suggested they would be in his proposal of a north-south center line. ICT-II had obviously been the site of a planned residential neighborhood, in contrast to the more haphazard placement of residences in Tract 15A. Fowler theorized that since Tract 15A had already been established as a residential area by previous genera-

4. Collins 1990, 1997; DeMott et al. 1993; Gums 1993; Holley 1989; Woods 1993.

tions before ICT-II was occupied, perhaps residents of that "old town" were allowed to keep their neighborhood layout while new construction was required to follow the established city plan.

A large borrow pit located to the west of the ICT-II neighborhood had actually been filled in during this phase. Toward the end of the early Stirling phase the community appeared to have been reorganized and the houses relocated around a central plaza. Two mounds were discovered, one that had been visible as a slight rise in early photographs and another that had not previously been identified.

While Woods and his crew were working on the ICT-II project, Bill Iseminger and others decided this would be a good time to convene another Cahokia ceramic conference, similar to the one held in 1971. Many of the same people were in attendance, along with a new group of archaeologists from the I-270 and ICT-II projects (fig. 22). The conference was an opportunity for the new archaeologists to see ceramics from the previous projects as well as to discuss the newer finds.

Figure 22. Participants of a 1986 ceramic conference at Cahokia, held to update the results of the 1971 meeting. Many were the original conferees. Left to right: James Collins, Mark Mehrer, Robert Hall, Dale McElrath, Douglas Jackson, Brad Kolderhoff, Patricia O'Brien, John Kelly, Harriet Smith, William Woods, Timothy Pauketat, Nelson Reed, Warren Wittry, Elizabeth Benchley, Melvin Fowler, Sid Denny, George Holley, and James Griffin. Used with permission of the Cahokia Mounds State Historic Site.

William Woods discovered that by the Moorehead phase the number of structures declined markedly, although each individual building was significantly larger and had been built on higher ground. The Indians had also built square houses, rather than the rectangular ones of the earlier period. The houses were built in shallower basins with smaller wall trenches, which may have indicated a scarcity of wood in the area.

In a creative compromise with the concerns of the archaeologists, the newly discovered house sites were incorporated into the center's design. Some sites are outside the building, their locations outlined on a concrete plaza, and others form one of the exhibits within the Interpretive Center itself.

When Emerson, Brown, Iseminger, and the rest of the committee sat down with the architects to discuss the design requirements of the new Interpretive Center, security was a prime consideration. They wanted a building that would be vandal-proof and that would complement the mounds, not compete with them. They also determined that the new center would be site-specific, focusing on the Cahokia phenomenon rather than on Native American cultures in general. The architectural firm of Architectural Associates, Inc., was chosen. The design firm was Gerard Hilferty and Associates.

In their meetings with the design firm, committee members decided to make no small plans and asked the firm to design a center that would cost more than had been budgeted for building costs. Although Cahokia had finally gotten the attention of the governor of Illinois and other public officials, the committee knew that the true scope and significance of the site was not generally understood. Only a first-quality center would convey the amazing story of Cahokia. The committee gambled that, once public officials saw the proposed design for the center, they would appropriate additional funds.

The gamble paid off and after an additional $2.2 million were appropriated for the exhibits, the new Interpretive Center opened on September 23, 1989, to acclaim from both museum critics and the general public. The 33,000-square-foot building has 17,000 square feet of exhibit space, including a small theater.

Of special interest was the spectacular set of bronze doors created by Illinois artist Preston Jackson. Public reaction to the doors was so enthusiastic that Jackson was commissioned to prepare a complementary work for the interior lobby doorway. A fundraising campaign was organized to raise the $45,000 cost and a single donor, Miranda Acardo Matthews, of Collinsville, Illinois, donated the total amount for the project in memory of her husband, Jerome.

FOURTEEN

The Slumping of Monks Mound and Discovery of the Grand Plaza

After Southern Illinois University at Edwardsville withdrew from its contract on the FAI-270 project, the university administration established an archaeological salvage program called the "Cultural Resource Management Program," with an emphasis on the archaeology of Cahokia. The program did not gain much headway until it was taken over by William Woods, who, at the time, was an assistant in the SIUE anthropology department.

Bill Woods put together an eclectic staff. One member was Christy Wells, who had worked on the FAI-270 project even though her major was English literature, a field she abandoned just before completing her dissertation. George Holley had recently completed his Ph.D. at Southern Illinois University, Carbondale, in Mayan ceramic studies. Wells and Holley were soon joined by Rinita Dalan, who was to complete her Ph.D. at the University of Minnesota in geology, and Mikeles Skele, who had a M.S. degree in linguistic anthropology from Purdue University and had several years' experience as a surveyor. Within a short time Woods and his staff became major players on the Cahokia stage. They began by developing new theoretical approaches to data that had been previously recovered. One of the first of these new approaches was utilized in a 1985–1986 examination of slumps on Monks Mound.[1]

In February 1984, following periods of heavy rain, a segment of soil had begun slumping away from the east side of Monks Mound. Minor slope failures had taken place in the mid-1950s and again in the late 1960s, but these had been readily patched and were not thought to endanger the mound as an architectural monument. The 1984 slump was more serious and called into question the future stability of the giant mound. The Illinois State Museum was called in to do some archaeological testing in the slump area and the Illinois Depart-

---

1. Skele 1988.

ment of Conservation contracted with an engineering firm to perform a geo-
technical study of slope failures and suggest methods of stabilization.

In 1985 another major slump occurred, this time on the western side of
Monks Mound. Great portions of the second terrace moved down the slope,
leaving behind crevasses and a small escarpment. At the bottom of the slope the
moving mass of earth scooped up the sod and earth in front of it, forming ridges.
This was an additional warning that all was not well with Monks Mound. The
largest example of prehistoric architecture in North America appeared to be in
imminent danger of collapse.

The slumping of Monks Mound raised a critical question for the Illinois Historic Preservation Agency, which managed the site. The slumping had elicited
an immediate public outcry to take action to save the mounds. Emerson coun-
seled caution. He would later recall that one of his hardest jobs as chief archaeologist for the IHPA at that time had been to convince his superiors not to take
expedient action that would have pleased the public but could have had detri-
mental effects on the mound. Before the IHPA took action, he argued, it needed
to collect more information. Emerson called for an engineering study of Monks
Mound and for Bill Woods to compile all the known archaeological information
on the mound and to map and do test excavations on the western slump.

The engineers drilled holes and tried to measure the liquid content of the
mound. Archaeologists from the Illinois State Museum conducted tests to provide an archaeological interpretation of several stratigraphic profiles in the
slump area. While this work was in progress the rains continued and in April
yet another massive slope failure took place on the western face of the mound.
This was the largest known slump, and over the next few months it showed no
signs of stabilizing naturally as the earlier slumps had done.

Emerson called a conference to consider the slumping of Monks Mound. Most
of the archaeologists who had done major work at Cahokia, including Fowler,
Griffin, Benchley, Bareis, and Hall, attended. A debate soon arose between those
who wanted to preserve the mound as a monument and those who thought the
mound was principally important for the information it could provide. Emerson
and the staff from the Illinois Historic Preservation Agency listened to the debate and eventually decided on a conservative treatment that was essentially a
"hands-off" approach to the slumping mound. Excavation, they decided, was too
costly and dangerous. The proposed engineering plans, they feared, would be too
destructive to the archaeology and would drastically change the mound's shape
and profile. In the end everyone stood back and watched and waited as the great
mound settled and, for the time being at least, slowly stabilized itself.

From his studies of the mound Woods hypothesized that original construction had begun during the late Emergent Mississippian period, about A.D. 950,

and that the mound was essentially completed by A.D. 1050, the end of the initial phase of the Mississippian period. Additions of a sequence of caps on the third and fourth terraces, the completion of the first terrace, and the construction of smaller mounds on the southeastern corner of the third terrace and the western end of the first terrace, as well as the erection of wooden buildings and fences, continued for 200 more years.

Critical insights into the internal construction of Monks Mound had been provided by Bareis's earlier work on the interface of the first and third terraces. Bareis found that the earthen zones he encountered in his excavations were constructed as buttresses or retaining walls and that the plateaus were actually a veneer or cap on top of the buttresses. By offsetting a number of these clay retaining walls it was possible to attain a great height and achieve a steep-slope or flat-topped mound. When the desired height of the highest platform or flat surface was attained, the steep slope was prevented from crumbling or slumping by the resistant retaining wall erected laterally around the side of the mound. Interfill areas composed of different soils provided good drainage and stability, which would have been lacking in one solid mass of clay erected from the top to the bottom of the mound.

The Cahokia builders' biggest problem was in the usable materials they had at hand. A significant portion of the mound is built of smectite clays, which have a high shrink-swell capacity and a low hydraulic conductivity. When the clays are wet they swell and when they are dry they contract. Repeated episodes of drying and wetting produce instability. The internal evidence from the mound indicates that the builders of Monks Mound understood very well these characteristics of their building material.

Bareis had pointed out that the different earth requirements for the buttresses and the overlying plateaus imply that soils of different compositions were stockpiled. It was evident to him that the builders of Monks Mound used detailed planning and constructed the mound with mechanical and engineering considerations in mind. Areas of massive silty clay were covered with coarser materials that functioned as internal drains to remove water before it could infiltrate the core sediments. Puddled-clay facings, which facilitated run-off, were also present. Retaining buttresses, incorporated into the internal structure of the mound, had also been placed externally along the southern and western sides.

It is clear that a specialized class of the ancient Cahokians understood the problems inherent in building massive earthen constructions in humid, wet latitudes. These individuals had worked from an original mound design and had incorporated an internal system of buttresses and drainage planes as well as external buttresses. Their success can be measured by the long-term stability of the mound. For more than a thousand years no major failures occurred despite the instability of the materials and the enormous mass and surface area of the mound. Why was it failing now?

The sequence of recent slope failures may be associated with modern changes in ground-water levels. From the 1940s to the early 1960s, the use of water by local industries lowered the ground water table in the northern portion of the American Bottom to the point where many wells went dry. By the late 1960s, water tables began to rise again due to industrial closings and by 1970 they were back to pre-industrial levels. When the water level dropped in the 1950s and 60s, the inner core of the mound, which had previously been kept wet up to a height of about 10 meters, dried out for the first time. When it dried it contracted and developed cracks.

This shrinking of the core would have disrupted the integrity of higher parts of the construction, including the drains and massive fill units. The expansion of the core when it got wet again only compounded the problem. With the internal drains no longer functioning efficiently and with cracks developing in the clay core, the retention of water increased dramatically. As a result of this instability, slumping occurred. The prehistoric planning that had proved successful for centuries had not anticipated modern changes in the water table.

In light of the slumping, Kenneth Williams, who had conducted the 1971 study on the east lobes of Monks Mound, decided to take another look at his data. He noted that the two slope failures differed from each other in several details. On the east side of Monks Mound, a mass of fill fell away from the side of the mound, leaving a crescent-shaped scar. The slumping mass of soil descended nearly intact, coming to rest directly over the northernmost of the two east lobes. The leading edge of the slumping fill dug into the modern humus where the angle of the slope decreased at the base of the mound.

On the west side a large portion of the mound, a section that Titterington had once thought might be the eroded remnant of a second terrace, began to pull away from the side. At the base of the mound a subsurface ridge, similar to the one Williams had observed on the east side in 1971, was formed running parallel to the side of the mound. Much of the slumping appeared to be occurring underneath the present soil surface, like muscles moving under skin.

As Williams studied the slumps on the mound, he speculated that the entire west segment of Monks Mound might have been originally created to shore up old slumpage originating from the upper portion of the mound, near the juncture of the third and fourth terraces. If this was true, the sheer planes of the mound would have already existed and the recent movement would merely represent some additional settling.

The earth movements also strongly suggested that the east lobes of Monks Mound were not the ramps Williams had once supposed them to be but were the result of similar slumpage episodes. If so, this would refute several of the major conclusions in his 1975 report on the east lobes. The origin of the lobes had to be reinterpreted. Williams looked at his 1971 data and concluded that it not only supported but better explained the conclusion that the lobes represented prehistoric slumpage episodes rather than ramp constructions.

Williams noted the nearly four meters of accumulated midden that was discovered in the north and south ends of his trench just east of the tip of the lobe. Siltation and then slumpage from Monks Mound had sealed off 500 years worth of occupation surfaces. The earliest midden, about one meter thick, was attributable to the Patrick and Jarrot phase and consisted primarily of house basin fill and one large pit containing stumpware and quantities of limestone.

At the end of this episode there appeared a large wall trench containing squared posts, indicating that the Indians were shifting to a more specialized use of the area. Several limestone-tempered red-slipped sherds dated the end of the early midden deposit to around A.D. 900–950. On top of this was almost two meters of very fine silt layers, which represented an extended period of rapid sheet erosion from the side of the newly constructed Monks Mound, followed by a foot or two of midden containing Moorehead and Sand Prairie ceramics.

Slumpage can explain the peculiar arm-twisted burial and the fact that the birdman tablet had been found at a distance from the body. Williams suggests that the mass of moving earth from the side of Monks Mound slid over the small platform mound and the residence or charnel house that had been on top of it, dragging the entire mass to the east. As it did so the small mound and building became embedded in the creeping mass of earth. As the tip of the slump crossed over the platform mound and began its descent off the eastern edge of Monks Mound, it pushed a concentration of roots and vegetal material ahead of it and gouged away the ground surface, creating both the ridge and what Williams had previously described as a burial pit. The birdman tablet would have become separated from the burial and the other contents of the building and the arm of the skeleton twisted in its descent down the side of Monks Mound.

If Williams's new interpretation is correct, the east lobe may present a unique opportunity to recover a relatively complete inventory of the contents of the dwelling or temple that was on top of the platform mound. The birdman tablet may be only a sample of what is still to be found. It was in such a location, "in the shade of Monks Mound," that William McAdams had made his 1882 discovery of a cache of ceramic vessels, including human and animal effigy forms.

A similar sealed area may exist under the second east lobe of Monks Mound. Williams concluded that these areas undoubtedly represent some of the most sacred and administratively important areas of Cahokia. Depending on the time period of the other slumpage episodes and the extent to which the mixing at these locations hampers interpretation, the other lobes of Monks Mound might contain many keys to the understanding of Late Mississippian culture, especially during the poorly understood Sand Prairie phase.

While studying the slumps, Woods and the SIUE archaeologists mapped the escarpments, did topographic mapping, and made test excavations on Monks Mound. They found three distinct strata within 80 centimeters of the surface; two of them represented culturally derived fill while the surface stratum consisted of postoccupation redeposition of soils and sediments.

The uppermost cultural zone represents a late addition to the mound, perhaps in late Stirling or Moorehead times. The lower cultural zone exhibited basket loading and formed a domical feature—not the same as had been found in the east lobes, but a structure that may have been built as a buttress during the Lohmann or early Stirling times. This suggests that even in the early development of Cahokia the inhabitants faced the problem of slumping and built buttresses in an attempt to contain the movement of the soil.

In 1987 and 1988, through summer field schools, Woods undertook to find the southern end of the palisade using a new technique for geological prospecting called "electromagnetic conductivity" (EMC). The graduate student in charge of the work, Rinita Dalan, had a degree in geology and was working toward an advanced degree in geophysics. Geophysical surveys offer a solution to the problem of how to gather archaeological information about a site without destroying it through excavations. Large excavations are costly and time consuming while the use of EMC is not only less expensive and quicker but noninvasive and nondestructive. A geophysical survey requires only minimal test excavations to confirm results and provides a cost-effective way to explore large areas.[2]

Using two small instruments called the Geonics EM38 and EM31-D ground conductivity meters, Dalan put electricity into the ground and measured how the soil conducted the current. Conductivity is a measure of the ability of the sediments to conduct electrical current. The more conductivity of the sediments, the higher the reading. Conductivity depends largely on porosity, water content, water quality, and the permeability of the soil. The effective penetration depth for the EM31-D was approximately six meters and that of the EM38 about a meter and a half.

The digging of post pits or trenches by Cahokians and the subsequent refilling of them by a combination of natural and anthropogenic processes

---

2. Dalan 1989a, 1989b, 1991, 1994, 1997; Dalan et al. 1993; Dalan and Ollendorf 1991; Dalan and Watters 1994; Holley, Dalan, Lopinot, and Smith 1990; Holley, Lopinot, Dalan, and Woods 1990; Holley et al. 1992, 1995; Watters et al. 1997.

would produce differences in conductivity. In clayey substrate, where the pit fill was coarser-grained or less compact than the surrounding sediments, a low conductivity signature would be observed over a disturbed location. Where the fill is finer-grained, more compact, or otherwise more capable of holding moisture than the surrounding sediments, a higher conductivity anomaly would be expected.

Dalan used data from the excavations of the central and southern palisade to project a set of expectations regarding the general nature of the conductivity anomaly over the buried palisade trenches. The trenches had apparently been backfilled immediately with the same excavated material. The soils were the same, but because they had been dug up and then replaced, they were more porous and well drained than the surrounding soils. This fact would be indicated by a low conductivity over the length of the palisade.

To locate the palisade trenches, both meters were used and both detected the remains of the southern portion of the central palisade as well as the locations of bastions. When trenches representing rebuilding episodes of the palisade were separated by a horizontal distance of more than one meter, the EM38 instrument registered double conductivity lows. Test excavations confirmed the EMC readings. They also confirmed that the southern portion of the palisade had been constructed during the Stirling and Moorehead phases, which was consistent with the dating of the eastern palisade excavations of the 1960s and 1970s.

Dalan and her fellow investigators confirmed more than the southern terminus of the central palisade. Their survey revealed the existence of a previously unknown mound that had been destroyed, and two borrow pits south and west of Mound 56. One pit was excavated by field school students and found to be 2.5 meters deep, its bottom surface pockmarked with gouges from prehistoric excavating tools.

The area where Dalan and her colleagues were working was directly south of Monks Mound at the foot of two huge twin mounds, numbers 59 and 60, called, respectively, Round Top and Fox. As Dalan and Woods studied the results of her geophysical survey and of their test excavations, they found they had stumbled into a complex situation of construction and fill in the area.

From studying the contours on the 1967 maps, Fowler had noted that the big mounds of Fox and Round Top had been built, not on the ground, as everyone had previously supposed, but on a massive clay platform. The area of the south palisade had been filled in to raise it a meter or more above the original surface of the ground. If the south palisade area had been covered with more than three feet of fill, what about the remainder of the open space? Had that been filled as well? The thought was staggering.

Dalan and Woods walked around the twin mounds and stared across the field at Monks Mound, the length of seven football fields to the north. In contrast to the ridge-and-swale topography of the surrounding area, the land before them was as level as a playing field. For 100 years archaeologists, believing that the plazas would yield little archaeological data, had focused their attention on the mounds—ignoring the plazas that lay between them. Could the fill that modern-day investigators had discovered be the southern terminus of built-up land relating to the plaza? Was it possible the Cahokians had filled and leveled this great expanse? If they had, what came to be known as the Grand Plaza (fig. 23) would rank as one of the largest artificial land forms in North America.

Woods promptly organized another field school and coordinated research program for the summer of 1989 to explore the Grand Plaza area. Field investigators would be Rinita Dalan, George Holley, and Philip Smith. The Grand Plaza fronts the massive Monks Mound, continues south in a vast rectangle to Fox and Round Top Mounds, and is bordered by a string of mounds along its east and west flanks. The total plaza area encompasses approximately 40 acres. The Mounds Subdivision had been built on the east side of the plaza and U.S. 40 ran along its northern edge, cutting Monks Mound off from the main body of the plaza. The western portion of the plaza had been cultivated in historic times and has been planted in grass since the 1920s.

Dalan and her associates determined on a three-part plan of action. First they would conduct a systematic, large-scale remote sensing program over a 324-by-450-meter section of the western half of the plaza area to discover the major geomorphologic trends. This would be followed by push-tube probing in se-

Figure 23. Mural from the Cahokia Mounds Interpretive Center showing the Grand Plaza as viewed from the south. Fox (right) and Round Top (left) Mounds are shown in the foreground; Monks Mound is in the background. The painting by L. K. Townsend is used here with permission of the Cahokia Mounds State Historic Site.

lected areas followed in turn by hand excavation of five blocks along a single electromagnet transect to "ground-truth"—corroborate by digging—the remote sensing data. Dalan used her Geonics EM31-D meter with its effective penetration depth of approximately six meters.

The largest feature the investigators encountered was a large buried sand ridge and its accompanying swale running northwest-southeast through the survey area and under Mounds 48 and 56. The ridge had been stripped of an unknown amount of soil by the Cahokians and then the area had been covered with about two and a half feet of soil to attain the present elevation of the plaza. The earliest use of the plaza area had been as a place to dig borrow pits to get sediments for mound building. The base of Monks Mound is a black organic clay, probably the material that Moorehead referred to as "black buckshot gumbo," similar to the silty-clay sediment that covered the original surface of the plaza.

At some point the Indians stopped digging pits and began to fill the plaza area. The first fill activity looked to be a haphazard dumping of domestic debris. This called to mind the practice of later southeastern Indians in which they used household sweepings and debris to demarcate an area as part of a purification ritual. The ritual was believed to seal off the underworld spirits and to have ritually cleansed an area for the building of important monuments such as platform mounds. Could the dumping of domestic refuse at Cahokia, the archaeologists wondered, have been a ritual process involved in the beginning stage of construction of the Grand Plaza? The debris layer was followed by deposits of massive, mottled silty clays that contained relatively few artifacts, indicating that the final stages of construction were aimed at elevating and leveling the plaza surface.

The building of the Grand Plaza began near the end of the Emergent Mississippian period, or before A.D. 1000. This suggests that mound construction at Cahokia also began at this early time as well. Radiocarbon dates from Monks Mound support this conclusion. The exploration of the Grand Plaza revealed that the Cahokians' earth-moving activities far exceeded previous expectations and called for a reevaluation of their level of planning and political organization. Before the first millennium had ended, Cahokia had become a burgeoning mound center that, in the words of Woods, "was initiated relatively early and was far from a humble beginning."

FIFTEEN

Woodhenges Revisited

Warren Wittry's discovery of the woodhenges and all that they implied about the Cahokians' science had been among the most significant findings at Cahokia (fig. 24).[1] In an attempt to delineate the full extent of one of the woodhenge circles and to locate additional posts for several others, Wittry returned to Cahokia in 1977 and 1978 under the auspices of his old friend Bob Hall from the University of Illinois, Chicago.

Wittry had originally found five woodhenges, four of which were overlapping. The eastern edge of two of the circles had been inadvertently destroyed when the highway department dug for fill dirt. Woodhenge III (also known as Circle 2) was the most complete so it became the focus of the project. The circle contained 48 posts and had a diameter of 410 feet.

A reanalysis of the context of the radiocarbon dates by Hall suggests that all of the circles found by Wittry probably postdate A.D. 1050 and relate to the early Stirling phase.[2] Though this was contrary to the statements made at the 1971 Cahokia ceramic conference, it was supported by Tim Pauketat's analysis of all the Tract 15A data. Pauketat noted that many of the post pits had been superimposed on Lohmann phase structures.

Eventually, Wittry and Hall were able to find all but three of the remaining post pits (nine had been lost to the highway borrow pit) and Iseminger later found the missing three in 1985. Several posts had apparently been replaced, as they had two or more insertion ramps. A red-cedar post was found in one pit where it had broken off when the Indians had tried to remove it.

While doing their earlier work with the woodhenges, Wittry and Hall had found that the builders of Woodhenge III had erected an observation post, not

---

1. Hall 1964; Iseminger 1985, 1986; Wittry 1969, 1980, 1996.
2. See Wittry 1996:28, table 3.1.

Figure 24. A mural from the Cahokia Mounds Interpretive Center showing the wood-henge. The painting by L. K. Townsend is used here with permission of the Cahokia Mounds State Historic Site.

in the geometric center of the circle, as the archaeologists had expected, but 5.56 feet to the east, giving an angle greater than 30 degrees or a viewing angle to the solstice posts of 30.8 degrees north and south of east. At the end of the 1977 season Wittry went to see Owen Masterson, superintendent of distribution and service for the Union Electric Company. Masterson was also a volunteer at Cahokia Mounds State Park.

"I want to test these alignments at Woodhenge III," Wittry told Masterson. "Do you have any used power poles?"

"Sure," replied Masterson. "I can let you have a couple."

"How about four?" asked Wittry.

Wittry placed his four poles in the ground, one at the off-center observer's site, and the other three in the eastern segment of the circle, in the post pits lining up with the positions of the sunrises of the equinoxes (directly to the east), of the summer solstice (northeast), and the winter solstice (southeast). Though there is no way to know the heights of the original posts, Wittry guessed that they were tall enough to permit an observer to climb above the level of the roofs of surrounding houses and other buildings that had been there in Cahokian times.

On September 22, 1977, the autumnal equinox occurred at 22 hours, 30 minutes, Central Daylight Saving Time. Sunrise that day in Cahokia was to be at 6:48 A.M. On the morning of the twenty-second a small group gathered around the observer's post at Woodhenge III. The night before, a small platform had been fastened to the post, about 21 feet above ground level.

Just before sunrise, Wittry climbed a ladder and positioned himself on the platform. The morning was clear. When the sun came up, the interface between the first and third terraces of Monks Mound provided an artificial horizon that allowed for a due-east alignment at the first sighting of the sun. Photographs Wittry took the next morning, September 23, show the sun to have moved about its own diameter to the south. Since this first test, Woodhenge III has been reconstructed with 48 posts (except for the missing nine on the west) around its perimeter, thanks to generous donations by George and Mildred Arnold of Edwardsville, Illinois.

Fowler observed Wittry's woodhenge test with interest. Wasn't it possible, he wondered, for there to be other woodhenges at the Cahokia site? If so, where would they be?

Fowler had been working at ICT-I in 1979 when the Illinois Department of Conservation flew one of its officers in a helicopter to Cahokia to confer with Anderson and Iseminger. While the men were meeting, Fowler commandeered the pilot and his helicopter to go up and take more aerial photographs of Cahokia. He found taking photographs from a helicopter to be far superior to his former experiences with small planes. With the helicopter, his field of view was unobstructed and he could hover over the location where he wanted to take his pictures.

Fowler took pictures of the reconstructed Mound 72 and when he later examined his prints, he saw that he had also taken a picture of the small mound that his workers had commented on when they had been excavating Mound 72. Viewed from the air, the mound looked to be far more interesting than it had appeared on the ground. Fowler told his field assistant that when their work on ICT-I was finished, they would stay in Cahokia for a few extra days to do some mapping of the little mound.

The first step in mapping the mound was to tie the mound into the existing grid in a precise manner. This involves a process called "traversing." The surveyor starts from a known point with his surveying instrument and charts a loop that ties into the point he is interested in. Then he comes back to his starting point and hopefully ends up with the same elevation and grid controls with which he started.

Fowler started out with a known grid station that had been put in the ground near Fox Mound, continued all the way down to the little mound, and then went over to the location of Post Pit 1 on Mound 72. Then it was time to turn the instrument and move back north to the original starting point. The area had not been mowed for some time and was a thick tangle of brambles and brush. One of the employees of the park happened to be mowing in a nearby area and Fowler asked him if he would cut a swath straight through the brush so he could get a straight line shot with his transit. Fowler would still have to set up his instrument halfway in between to do the final stage of the traverse, but mowing would help.

The mower plowed through the brush, cutting down small trees and brambles as he went, clearing a path for Fowler, who was following close behind. Halfway through, Fowler stopped to set up his instrument. Suddenly he was attacked by hundreds of bumblebees that came swarming out of the ground at his feet. The mower had mowed over their nest and Fowler had chosen that exact spot to set up his transit. Abandoning his instrument, Fowler ran, swatting at the bees in his hair. The stings he received left him weak and sick and it was several hours before they could recover the transit.

As a result of the encounter with the bees, the traverse was unsuccessful and Fowler had to go back and do it all over again the next day. When he again reached the little mound he took dozens of shots so he could make a contour map of it. The map that resulted tied it in to the permanent grid and also showed him something of the shape of the mound. It was a T-shaped mound with an oval shape oriented north and south and what appeared to be a ramp running directly to the east. The mapping proved that this was truly a mound and not a natural little bump rising from the ground. The surveying indicated that the mound was about a meter high. Fowler estimated from the numerous observations he made that a 50-centimeter contour interval was about as accurate as the map could be. Fowler assigned the mound the number 96.

What could have been the relationship of Mound 96 to Mound 72, Fowler asked himself. Could Mound 96 have been a charnel house where bodies were kept before they were buried in Mound 72? Could there have been a kind of sociology-of-the-dead relationship between the two mounds? He studied his maps, drawing lines and circles as he had done when he had been studying Mound 72. Nothing seemed to make any sense. Then Fowler decided to measure the distance from the location of Post Pit 1 on Mound 72 to the center point that he had used for mapping Mound 96.

He discovered that it was 125 meters, the same distance as the diameter of Woodhenge III that Wittry had discovered. Now that was interesting. Fowler checked the line between Mound 96 and Post Pit 1 and found that it was on a 30-degree axis and lined up with the summer solstice sunrise and the winter solstice sunset.

Fowler continued drawing circles and found that if he picked a point halfway between Post Pit 1 on Mound 72 and the center of Mound 96 and used that as the center of a circle, he could draw a circle that had Post Pit 1 and Post Pit 2 on the perimeter, and that they were about 30 degrees apart. That was four times the spacing that Wittry had found between his post pits, though the circle was similar to Wittry's Woodhenge III. If Wittry had 7.5 degrees of arc and Fowler had two posts with 30 degrees, Fowler proposed that there might be other posts that had been placed with the same spacing that Wittry had found.[3]

Fowler drew his circle on his map and went around its circumference, putting in dots every 7.5 degrees where he thought the posts should be. He found that one post would be at true north from the center point he had projected and another would be at true south. This was the same phenomenon Wittry had found. Fowler realized that he was creating a hypothesis based on very little data: only three basic points that he could define, Post Pit 1, Post Pit 2, and the center of Mound 96, which is where his surveying point was. One can make a circle out of any three points, he reminded himself. People had every reason to be skeptical. Fowler's colleagues looked at his maps and thought his idea was sort of crazy. But on the other hand, they knew that Fowler had predicted where Post Pit 1 would be and had hit it right on the head.

When he had reached this stage in his investigation, Fowler was convinced he was on to something. He wrote a proposal to the National Geographic Research Committee, laid out all the data that he had, and asked for 10,000 dollars to test the locations where he had predicted the post pits would be.[4] The review committee was interested but cut back his proposal by 2,000 dollars. Fowler had put money in the budget for housing for his student workers. He could not pay them a salary but he wanted to provide lodging and a modest per diem so they could buy food. The review committee asked why the students could not pitch tents and camp at the site.

What they did not understand was that Cahokia was now a historic site, not a park, and camping was no longer permitted. Other than Cahokia itself, there was literally no safe place where students could camp in the area. Bill Woods solved the problem by arranging to have the students live in graduate student apartments at Southern Illinois University, Edwardsville.

Testing began in the summer of 1991. The operating proposition was that anthropogenic disturbances should be found at the predicted loci. A corollary of this proposition was that indications of post pit disturbance should *not* be found outside a two- to three-meter radius of the posited loci. Therefore, an area of five by ten meters, centering on the proposed pit, was chosen for examination. This would include feature disturbance as well as undisturbed sediments.

---

3. Fowler 1991.
4. Fowler et al. 1992.

Previously recovered data from Circle 2 and Post Pit 1 indicated that these features could be over two meters in depth and about one meter in diameter and would be most clearly defined in the clay sediments about one meter below the present surface of the ground. A wider area of disturbance could be expected in the upper levels resulting from insertion and extraction ramps, tunnel erosion, and the flowing of the natural strata.

Fowler proposed to test his hypothesis of the location of the posts by using three different methods. One method was Dalan's use of electromagnetic conductivity (EMC). Readings over an area of 5 by 10 meters around the proposed pit and at a depth of 1 meter were recorded at 50-centimeter intervals.

Here, thought Fowler, was a noninvasive way to check for the locations of the posts. The Indians would have dug these deep holes to put the posts in and even though the holes had since filled back in through various processes, the ground had still been disturbed and would conduct electricity differently from soil that had not been disturbed.

A second technique he used was soil coring. A rig drives a steel tube down in the ground and extracts a core. A second tube length, from a deeper level, can also be obtained and the two cores laid end to end to get a stratigraphic sequence. The third technique was the digging of some traditional archaeological test pits in locations that the first two testing methods indicated would be promising.

Eleven locations were tested with electromagnetic conductivity surveys, eight with soil corings, and three with archaeological test excavations. Fowler concentrated the electromagnetic testing on post locations that might be affiliated with astronomical observations and mound alignments, those designated III Northeast (III-NE), I East (I-E), and V Southeast (V-SE). Evidence of anthropogenic disturbances were found by all three of the methods when they were applied to the locations.

As Fowler studied his maps he saw that Mound 72 was located just inside the perimeter of the circle he had proposed. When he had excavated the beaded burial and mapped its location he had noted that it was not oriented in a north-south or east-west direction; in fact it had not been intentionally oriented in any direction that he could tell. Now, when he plotted this burial, he noted that it was oriented head-to-toe pointing directly at the location of the post at III Northeast, the third post north of the east direction. When he saw that, he began looking at the orientation of the other burials in Mound 72. He found that several other burials and mound orientations were pointing at post III Northeast, the post that was halfway between the east post and the summer solstice sunrise post.

Why would the burials and mound construction be oriented toward this post location? It bore no relationship to the cardinal or intercardinal directions nor to the solstice alignment, located halfway between the equinox and summer solstice. If the woodhenges were used to observe the points on the horizon where the sun came up, the sunrise over this position would occur twice a year. One time would be around May 15, as the sun moves rapidly northward toward the summer solstice. The other would be about August 15, or after the summer solstice. A conversation with his colleague Robert Hall may have given Fowler the answer.

A major ceremony among the southeastern Indians, as observed by many of the eighteenth-century explorers, was the Green Corn ceremony. This important ceremony was a "first fruits" ritual and the ripening corn could not be eaten until the ceremony was completed. Included as part of the Green Corn, or Busk, celebration was the rekindling of the sacred fire in the temple. (See chapter 17 for further discussion of the Green Corn ceremony.) This ceremony usually took place about a month after the solstice, which, in the latitude of Cahokia, was when the corn was ripening. Was it possible that this post location was so important because, when the sun appeared over it, it signaled the time when ceremonies significant to the community and its rulers were to begin?

Dalan had gotten the best electromagnetic indicator of disturbance at the area of post III Northeast in precisely the location where Fowler had predicted the post should be. There was also a shallow depression in that same location. On that basis Fowler had his workers dig test pits measuring two meters by two meters, down to one meter in depth, to test for indications of disturbance in the soil. They also tested the locations of the east post (I East) and the post that would be the winter solstice sunrise post (V Southeast) if one were looking from the center of the circle in that direction. All of the test pits revealed soil disturbance.

Before they could do more testing, the season ended. Most of the funds spent that first summer had gone for Dalan to do her electromagnetic conductivity testing and to Woods for the soil coring rigs and his work in sediment analysis. Volunteers helped with the digging.

Despite the reduced size of Fowler's National Geographic Society grant, he had managed to save some funds for work in 1992 and the society agreed he could continue. He then applied for a National Science Foundation grant and a small grant from the Cahokia Mounds Museum Society. The NSF turned him down but the Museum Society agreed to support the work for another year. With those funds and with his cadre of enthusiastic students, Fowler set out to find and uncover what he called the Mound 72 woodhenge post pits.

The preliminary "black-box" testing (EMC) and the archaeological testing had been done in 1991. In 1992 the group would dig the pits all the way to the bottom and determine conclusively if there had been a woodhenge associated with Mound 72. Working with Fowler were two graduate students, Rob Watson, in anthropology, and Bill Gartner, who had his M.A. degree in geography but was also a soil scientist. They were joined by Andy Martignioni, a volunteer from the Cahokia Mounds Museum Society. The four were assisted by groups of volunteers who would come to work for a few days or a week at a time.

Fowler decided to reopen post pit III Northeast, the first one they had tested the year before, because it had looked the most promising. He began by clearing out the excavation with a backhoe. Then he set up a cross-trench procedure in which they approached the location of the post pit from four directions, north, south, east, and west, so they could define the extent of the pit and reach the deepest part at the end of their excavation.

They worked for three weeks, keeping the side walls of the trenches straight and going deeper and deeper. The east-west trenches were showing evidence of disturbance but the excavators were not getting much from the north side. Fowler told Watson, "Get on the north side and dig a big hole down there until you get to the sand and see if you can find the north side of the post pit."

Watson started digging. In the meantime Gartner was finding good solid evidence of disturbance on the south side in his trench. Watson was now down eight feet in his hole, had hit a little water, and had to use a ladder to climb in and out of the pit. He was not finding soil disturbance so Fowler suspected that the post pit had not extended quite that far north. Gartner was getting close to the deepest part of the post pit. It was a beautiful, classic excavation that was exceeding their expectations. The three were busy digging and drawing profiles when Fowler looked up and saw the biggest, blackest cloud he had ever seen coming in from the west.

They left the ladder in the pit and scrambled out. Rob said, "Where's my tool bag?" "Leave it on the ledge," replied Fowler. "It will be all right. We'll cover the whole thing with the black plastic and seal if off from the direct downpour of the rain." The crew covered the excavation, weighted down the edges of the plastic with sandbags, and raced for Collinsville Road, 800 yards away. By the time they reached it three inches of water was running over the highway. Fowler knew they were in deep trouble.

More than six inches of rain fell that night and when Fowler and his companions returned to the excavation the next morning they found that the rainfall had caved in the plastic tarps. The long cross trenches they had dug so carefully were completely filled with water. Plastic sheets had ripped away in the wind. Walls had collapsed. When they removed what plastic they could, rented a pump, and pumped out the water, they found that not only had the walls collapsed but the clays underneath had gotten wet when rain seeped through the soil and flowed into the excavation. The place where they had left the ladder was filled with clay and the ladder itself was completely covered over. Rob's tool kit had washed away from the main trenches and was buried somewhere in the mud and flowing clay. The site was ruined.

As Fowler stood at the site of his flooded excavation he realized how fortunate he had been in 1967 when they had dug out Post Pit 1. That season had been dry and they had been able to get to the bottom of the pit and draw a complete profile. This time he had only a partial profile and though he could reconstruct that there was a pit there, he did not have the data he wanted that would take the pit all the way down.

The ladder had been borrowed from Al Meyers, an artist who had worked with Fowler at Cahokia for years doing many of his drawings of excavations. The least we can do, they said, is to salvage Al's ladder. The three men dug into the clays that had flowed in and filled the deep hole. When they had uncovered the top of the ladder they put a cable around it and pulled, but the suction power of the clay was so great that the ladder only bent and did not come out. They had to leave it there, where Meyer's ladder is to this day. There was nothing to do but close down the excavation and call it a summer. They backfilled the trenches and brought in a bulldozer to push all the dirt back in the hole and smooth out and level the site.

Despite the untimely arrival of the rainstorm, Fowler felt that he had learned a great deal from the 1992 summer's work. The confirmation of his prediction of the post pit at III Northeast was very important. They had been able to photograph the profiles and also get them drawn up very close to the center before the rain came.

Equally important was what Fowler learned about soils from Woods of the geography department at Southern Illinois University, Edwardsville, and from Gartner, the soil scientist from the University of Wisconsin, Madison. Both men were skilled at understanding sediment disposition and the process of change through time. They pointed out to Fowler that in a clay area such as the one they were digging in, the normal processes of soil formation were modified because of the peculiar characteristics of these particular sediments.

Beneath Cahokia lies a complex series of meander loops and fluvial landforms such as point bars and ridge-swale topography related to late Pleistocene and Holocene movements of the Mississippi River channel. The flooding of the river results in ponding and slackwater sedimentation along tributary, wetland, and low-elevation areas across the American Bottom. This creates the gumbo clays that underlie much of the region. Archaeological features located in these clay-rich, low-lying areas are more difficult to define than elsewhere because of the physical behavior of gumbo clay. The deposits may expand to twice their size when saturated, only to return to their original configuration when dry. Shrinking and swelling produces slickensides along pressure surfaces, disrupting the pre-existing stratigraphy. The area around Mound 72 was a low-elevation swale, rich in gumbo clay because of an accumulation of slackwater sediments.

The top soil over the clay is what geologists and archaeologists call the A horizon. In the Mound 72 area, below the A horizon, is a horizon the soil scientists call the E horizon rather than the normal B horizon. This E horizon is created by water percolating through the soil through hundreds of years. The moisture moving through the sediment leaches out the iron and other minerals as well as the fine clay particles and deposits them at the bottom in what is called a BT horizon. In the case of Cahokia, this BT horizon was just above the ancient A horizon where Benchley, in her phase 2 testing of the first Interpretive Center Tract, had found Archaic-type artifacts. In the area around Mound 72, the BT horizon was just a little over a meter below the present-day ground surface.

The effect of this formation of the E horizon tends to make the sediments look uniform in color because all the minerals and organic materials and fine clay particles have been leached out. Upon first examination one cannot see outlines of features in the profile. With careful observation and by knowing what to look for, an investigator can see some very subtle texture differences where the features were. Once down to the BT and buried A horizons, the features become apparent. Visitors to Fowler's excavation in its early stages had trouble seeing the features. "Look how uniform that is," they said. "There's nothing in there. It is natural."

If it had not been for the contributions of Woods and Gartner, Fowler would not have understood this peculiarity of clay soils. He credits their advice with giving him the information that allowed him to persevere and make his later discoveries. As he thought about it, he wished he could have had the insights of soil scientists much earlier.

He remembered his puzzlement in 1967 when his crew had been doing the original excavation for the palisade. That first year they had to dig down at least a meter before they could find the bottom of the trenches. Little was apparent in the soil until they reached the bottom, where they could easily see the post positions. Later they learned how to see these features by carefully studying the profiles for textural differences.

What Fowler learned from his quick education in soil science was that though the color differences—which is what most archaeologists rely on to see soil disturbances—were so slight as to be almost invisible, the disturbed sediments still retained their structure, which was different from that of the surrounding materials. The size of the chunks of disturbed earth and the graininess of the filled-in soil were still discernible. A close examination of the sediment structure could help to determine seemingly invisible features. It was these structural differences that were most significant to the soil scientists.

With his new insight into soils, Fowler began to think about Reed's work on the top of Monks Mound. Reed had claimed there had been a sterile cap of clay without any features on the top of the mound and he had removed it with a backhoe. Fowler now conjectured that Reed's sterile clay cap may have been the same sediment-formation process Fowler was dealing with, only in a different context. It is probable that there was evidence of structures in the material bulldozed off the mound that would pertain to the later Mississippian occupations of Monks Mound. That is a question that can never be answered because much of the fourth terrace was scooped away to get down to the features that Reed found.

As he thought about the implications of the insights of soil scientists to archaeology, Fowler realized he had had hints of this information as early as the 1950s. He had given a lecture in Madison, Wisconsin, on a Hopewell burial mound he had excavated near the Ohio River in southern Illinois. It had been traditional at that time to say that there were two stages to these mounds, the primary mound where one could see the basket loading, and a secondary mound that capped the earlier primary mound where, in many cases, one could not see evidence of basket loading.

A soil scientist in the audience had raised his hand and had begun to explain the process of soil formation as an explanation for the different character of the secondary mound. Fowler, whose ideas at the time came from reading the handed-down wisdom of previous archaeologists, had insisted that there was a distinct line between the two mounds. He now thought that if he had not been so quick to respond to the man and, instead, had listened to him, he might have learned, at a much earlier date, about the processes of soil formation and their implications for an archaeological site.

Finding three post pits in locations where he had previously predicted them (Post Pits 1, 2, and III Northeast) caused Fowler to reassess the earlier excavation of Mound 72. Though 25 years had now passed, he pulled the profile drawings from his file and laid out the sketches from the east half of Mound 72. The workers had dug just north of the Beaded Birdman Burial along a profile wall that Fowler had called the south 859 line on his grid. This was the south wall of the northeast area of the mound, the portion that was never excavated.

As Fowler had always insisted they do, his students had recorded this profile very carefully at the time. They had dug through what Fowler had considered to be mound fill to what he then believed was the base of the mound. He had not had them do any further investigations at that location because the students were finding all of the burials in the center and on the west side of the mound, which had immediately absorbed their attention.

As he now studied the profile drawings at the center of the south 859 trench, he saw lines indicating a depression or a dip in the deposits. The dip went right down to the premound level of the ground and into the old topsoil that had been there a thousand years ago. It was obvious to Fowler that there was some disturbance below the mound in that area that had caused the dipping lines where the mound fill was depressed. When he checked this location out with his predicted locations of the post pits, they corresponded exactly. The dipping lines were precisely where he had predicted there would be another post pit (VI Northeast) just northwest of Post Pit 1.

Fowler is a man who is not easily excited, but he was excited now. Mound 72, he was now convinced, was part of another woodhenge. There were Post Pits 1 and 2, which the archaeologists had found while excavating Mound 72; there was the clear indication of the post pit in the profiles of the south 859 line at Mound 72; and there was the post pit at the III Northeast location, the complete excavation of which had been flooded out. This made a total of four post pits in the northeast quadrant and every one of them was located at points Fowler had predicted they should be.

Fowler paced around his laboratory. The existence of another woodhenge would have enormous implications for an understanding of the organization and complexity of Cahokia. Woodhenges appeared to Fowler to be more than calendrical observatories. He began to think of them as monuments that enclosed sacred space. In a complex chiefdom, which is an early stage of civilization, leaders needed to find ways to legitimate their dominant position in society. One way they did this was to manipulate the ideological base of society so as to solidify and justify their own position. This was probably done in a variety of ways but one that is significant to archaeologists is the creation of sacred landscapes where ceremonies are carried out.

Sacred landscapes are created by building monumental constructions within a community. These sacred landscapes are the focal points of ceremonies in the ritual calendar at which chiefs played the roles of gods on earth to connect themselves to cosmic forces, not unlike manifestations of Europe's medieval belief in the divine right of kings. Mounds and woodhenges express in monumental fashion the importance of a particular site and affect human consciousness through the creation of a new sense of place and time. Because monuments commemorate and endure, they are tangible reminders of the past, connecting people to events that span many generations.

Monuments anchor the present to a chain of historic events that are responsible for the current structure of reality. If the design of the monument has cosmological referents it can alter human perceptions to tie a people to a timeless past, represented by the endless movement of heavenly bodies in a cycle that transcends time. By linking monuments to the unchanging world of nature, their builders were putting the significance of these edifices beyond challenge. Fowler began to think that Cahokia's leaders built their great mounds and woodhenges to link their society to the timeless, orderly universe and, in doing so, reaffirmed the eternal nature of their own social order.

Fowler was intrigued by the fact that Mound 72 and little Mound 96 were both within the circumference of what he proposed as Woodhenge 72. The relationship of burials in Mound 72 to the woodhenge was complex. Besides the proximity of the two status individuals to post pits 1 and 2, all of the burials were inside the circumference of the circle. Submounds were oriented toward specific woodhenge post locations. Mound 72Sub1 points due west toward the summer solstice sunset position (V Northwest), mound 72Sub2 points toward the north position (XIII North), Mound 96 faces to the east or toward the winter solstice sunrise (V Southeast) position, and the foot-to-head axis of the beaded burial was aligned with post III Northeast. Later reorientations of primary mound axis and burial pits included in the final construction of Mound 72 also were aimed at post pit III Northeast.

Fowler and his associates came to the conclusion that Woodhenge 72 had come before the mounds and had dictated the location and orientation of Mound 72 as well as the location and orientation of burials and other features within it. The fact that Mound 72 was confined within the northeast quadrant of Woodhenge 72 indicated to them that the primary personages buried there were tied to that segment of the community—or in the Cahokians' view of cosmology, to that quarter of the world.[5]

Fowler had always believed that Wittry's discovery of the woodhenges had been significant. Now it was assuming even more importance. At this point Fowler believed that he had enough information about Woodhenge 72 to move beyond the small grants and cadres of volunteers that had supported his work for the past two years. It was time to launch a major investigation. He wrote a grant proposal and submitted it to the National Science Foundation. The proposal was turned down.

Fowler believed there were two reasons his request was rejected. In the first place, he conceded that his proposal had not been as well written as it could have been. The second reason was that there was a great deal of resistance from other archaeologists to the concept of another woodhenge—though Fowler had published an article outlining his ideas. Peer reviewers wrote that they doubted there was a woodhenge there. Some had made brief visits to Fowler's excavation and, not understanding the E horizon, found it very hard to see any features, particularly in the glaring sunlight. Some declared there was nothing there so no further money should be invested in the project.

---

5. Fowler 1996.

Fowler had come too far to give up at this point. He went back to the Cahokia Mounds Museum Society and they gave him a small grant, enough to pay the lodging and per diem for Rob Watson, Bill Gartner, and two other students. In the summer of 1993 the five of them went to Cahokia and began to dig. Soon they were joined by a group of volunteers who believed in the project. One was Martignioni, of the Cahokia Mounds Museum Society, who had worked with the crew the previous summer. None of the volunteers received any reimbursement. They worked in the mud and hot sun for the excitement of the project.

The investigators decided to work on three locations. One was the III Northeast location that had been partially excavated before. The second was the due-east location (I East) and the third was the V Southeast location, the winter solstice sunrise location. These sites in the east section of the woodhenge had been tested in 1991 and found to have reasonably good electromagnetic anomalies as well as indications of soil disturbances in the original test excavations.

Fowler tried to clean out the cross trenches at the III Northeast location to get the full cross section of the post pit rather than just the beginnings of it as they had the year before. But he found it hard going. The trenches had retained moisture and the fill was a minor swamp. Cattails and other moisture-loving plants had started growing in the filled-in pit. The project had created a miniature wetland. Every time the crew members got the pit partially cleaned out it would rain, making it even messier than it had been the year before. They tried building a big tent out of black plastic to protect the site but there was no way, in that saturated soil, to keep the pit from filling in with mud and water. Finally, and with great reluctance, Fowler gave up on getting any further information that year on III Northeast and he closed the excavation down.

The I East and V Southeast locations were new excavations and they were drier. Borrowing a technique from the FAI-270 and ICT-II excavations, the workers began by bringing in a backhoe to take off the first meter of soil in an area measuring five meters by five meters. Fowler proposed that the post pit would be more or less in the center of that excavation. When they trimmed off the south walls of the big square excavation they noticed they were getting dipping soil strata, indicating disturbance. Though they worked and worked on those, they could not get the kind of definition they were looking for.

Fowler finally decided they should go back and dig trenches from the south into the center of the square where they thought, from Dalan's EMC data and the earlier test excavations, that the deepest portion of the post pit could be found. When they did they found good definition and a plan view of the post pit. There was the familiar circular discoloration in the soil just above the buried A or Archaic horizon.

When they found this at the I East location, Fowler decided to dig a deep trench to get a profile and, this time, to get to the bottom of it. Rob Watson was in charge. When Watson determined to dig a deep hole he would make a nice square excavation, and he would dig fast. Watson dug down like a frantic badger, but no one had reckoned with the fact that the floods of the past two years had saturated the soil and caused the water table to rise. Water began seeping into the hole. Fowler rented pumps and pumped out the water. Watson continued digging while volunteers hauled the dirt away in wheelbarrows.

The men were down in the trench, examining the profile where it went straight down into the ground, when Fowler again looked up and saw another huge black cloud coming. While his crew raced to cover and seal everything as best they could before the storm broke, Fowler stayed down in the hole a little longer, taking photographs and making drawings of the profile.

When they returned the next morning they found that the walls had been undercut by the flowing of the sediments and had collapsed. Though they were able to dig out the excavation and even make Watson's hole deeper, in a short time they hit a major vein of water that was impossible to pump out. As a result they were not able to get to the bottom of that post pit either.

In the V Southeast excavation a similar procedure was followed with similar results. They found dipping strata in the south wall and dug a trench north toward the center. The difference with the east pit was that, although some indication of a deep pit was found, it was not as clearly defined as had been the others. However, the data were sufficient to indicate there had once been a post pit at that location. With the dipping strata in the south walls of each of these excavations and separate features near the EMC anomalies and predicted locations, Fowler and Watson began to wonder if perhaps they were not finding evidence of more than one post pit in each location and perhaps more than one circle. Despite the rains that had almost defeated Fowler and his crew, he had found evidence to support his hypothesis.

Although Fowler should have been discouraged, he was not. He had discovered evidence of two more post pits. The evidence was not as complete as he had wanted, but it was enough to be convincing. The posts had been found within one or, at most, two meters of where he had predicted they would be. That was very close, considering he had made the predictions by plotting the known information, Post Pit 1 and the center of Mound 96, on a big map, then drawing a circle and spacing in where he thought the post pits should be. He had extrapolated, from the information plotted on a large sheet of graph paper, the necessary coordinates.

Fowler reminded himself that there was no reason to believe that the Cahokian engineers, though highly skilled in designing and constructing these monuments, had the ability to match modern surveying techniques or even simple plotting on graph paper. He had to be careful not to force his own standards of precision, made possible by finely machined instruments, on people of the past.

Wittry had pointed out that his woodhenge, while it first looked like a circle, was found not to be a perfect circle. The line around the perimeter was more of a zig-zag line than a smooth circle because of the problems the Indians themselves had faced in measuring distances, digging the holes, having the holes collapse on them, and having to dig new ones.

Everything about the woodhenge project had been a challenge. There had been the challenge of trying to find features in those particular kinds of sediments, made more complicated by the heavy rains that had plagued Watson, Gartner, and Fowler for two summers. There was the challenge of making a prediction based upon limited data, of having gone into the field and tested it, and the excitement of finding the features right where they had predicted they would be. Finally, there was the challenge of finding information that would convince Fowler's skeptical colleagues, some of whom did not think he was achieving anything.

As Watson, Gartner, and Fowler reviewed their summer's work, they decided that, if they could get funding, they would move over to the west side of their proposed woodhenge, to the Mound 96 area, and see how it fit into the whole situation. They had found enough to convince themselves, if not others, that the east side of the woodhenge was where they had said it would be. They knew that Mound 96 was at the winter sunset solstice position on their circle but they had no evidence on the west side of any post pits. They had predicted that the post pits would be there, but they had not excavated or found any of them. Rinita Dalan had tested the area and found some EMC anomalies at proposed postpit locations but the soil coring had not been conclusive. Dalan had also done a more extensive survey of the area and found that a sand ridge, rather than a swale, ran through the western half of the proposed Woodhenge 72, which would make it much easier for the archaeologists to define post pits.

How could Watson, Gartner, and Fowler solve this problem and get the additional data they needed? To them, Woodhenge 72 was real. But they needed more information to convince their colleagues and to understand, themselves, the nature of these post circle monuments and the role they played in Cahokia's life and development. Watson and Gartner urged Fowler to make one more attempt to get a National Science Foundation grant.

Fowler was not optimistic. He had been turned down by the National Science Foundation in 1992, 1993, and 1994. He would be retiring at the first of the year in 1995 and he began to question whether it was worth the effort to send in one more proposal. Then he looked across his laboratory at Watson and Gartner, young men whose careers were still ahead of them. Fowler sat down at his desk and, with Watson's help, wrote another grant request to the National Science Foundation.

The National Science Foundation archaeological program was under the direction of Dr. John Yellin. It had been started in the 1950s and was one of the first in the United States to fund archaeology. The program works on a system of peer review. Applicants submit proposals to the NSF, which sends them out to a select group of peers for evaluation. Fowler felt that one of his previous proposals had been reviewed by an individual who had been unfair and even flippant in his review, so this time he requested that the anonymous reviewer not be selected to comment on his 1995 request. Dr. Yellin agreed.

The thrust of Fowler's proposal was that the proposed Woodhenge 72 was more than an astronomical observatory. It was also a monument that enclosed sacred space, a locality built to symbolize the royal lineage of a chieftain who, in the minds of his subjects, could control both the physical world and the esoteric data of the community.

As 1995 ended and 1996 began, Fowler resisted the impulse to call the National Science Foundation to check on the status of his grant request. Though he was retired, his professor emeritus status allowed him to apply for further NSF grants through the university. He had decided in his own mind that there was no chance they would be funded by the NSF that year and he advised Watson, who was hoping to use the information for his Ph.D. thesis, to give up and turn his mind to other projects. As the winter turned to spring in Milwaukee and the time grew closer for fieldwork, students came into Fowler's office to ask when he would know if he would be able to use them in his summer's project. He told them that it did not look feasible that he would be doing fieldwork that summer or even the following year.

This was the year of the budget crisis between the president and Congress and of the temporary shutdown of the federal government. When this happened Fowler became convinced that the NSF would be unable to fund the proposal. He advised the students that if they had any other opportunities to participate in research or fieldwork, they should take them. The NSF proposal had gone completely out of Fowler's mind when he walked into his office one day to find a message for him from Dr. Yellin.

When he called back, Yellin told him, "I have good news. Your project has been included on the list for funding for this year." Fowler was dumbfounded, and Yellin may have been as well. It was now almost summer, too late in the season to begin fieldwork as the students had already taken positions elsewhere. Fowler explained the problem and Yellin agreed to extend the financing of the project for another year so the fieldwork could be done during the summer of 1997. When he hung up the telephone, Fowler was in a state of utter disbelief.

It took him a few minutes to comprehend the fact that his proposal had been approved.

Fowler immediately contacted the Cahokia Mounds Museum Society. The society had agreed to provide a supplemental grant to the NSF project conditioned on his NSF approval, and it agreed to the new schedule. Fowler then arranged to combine the 1997 University of Wisconsin, Milwaukee, archaeological field school training program with the NSF grant to give him additional staff to do the work he had outlined.

This was his big opportunity to define Woodhenge 72 and Fowler wanted to do as much preparation as he could before he moved his workers into the field for the short season of excavation. He and Watson decided they needed better mapping detail on the west half of the woodhenge area. During the summer they drove to Cahokia and asked the grounds crew to mow down the poison ivy and brush that had grown up.

To do the basic control surveying they brought in an archaeological surveyor, Harold Waters, who worked for Bill Woods at Southern Illinois University at Edwardsville. Waters used an electronic surveying instrument called a "Total Station" that provides a much greater degree of accuracy over long distances than does an older-style surveying transit. He was able to tie in the grid in a couple of hours, a task that had taken Fowler, not counting the bee stings, two days to do previously.

Using a regular old-style transit, Fowler and Watson took hundreds of elevation shots over the area, collecting horizontal and vertical data on each of their survey points so Fowler would be able to plot a contour map.

The difference in elevation between the contour lines is called the "contour interval." On the big aerial maps of Cahokia, the contour interval was one meter. Fowler believed that with the hundreds of precise shots that had been taken of the area he could plot a map with about 4-inch intervals. Though there are computer programs that, once the data has been fed into them, can produce contour maps, Fowler decided to draw the map himself. The computer program available to him drew the lines in angular connections, connecting the dots with straight lines. True contour lines are curves, not straight lines, and contour plotting by hand is as much an art as it is a science. Fowler painstakingly drew curved lines between the points and produced a very fine map.

When Fowler finished drawing the contour map he found that Mound 96 was basically a square mound with an east-west, north-south orientation with a small ramp, which might have been a stairway, on the east side. It was very similar to Mound 72Sub1, though it was not quite as high and was more spread out. Fowler believed the difference between them occurred because Mound 72Sub1 had been protected from erosion by the construction of the mound over the top of it while Mound 96 had been exposed to the weather for 900 years, allowing erosion and slope wash to spread out the contours.

As the archaeologists studied their new map they noted that scattered about the area were numerous shallow, circular, smooth depressions in the ground that were located almost exactly where Fowler had predicted post pits would be. The same sort of depressions had been noticed in post pit areas on the east side of the circle. The depressions had been created over the past thousand years, as the post pits filled in and the sediments settled.

As Fowler studied the depressions he remembered that he had an example of this process in his own backyard in a Milwaukee suburb. When his house had been built in the 1950s a septic tank had been buried in the yard. Later the tank had been removed and the hole filled. Despite the filling of the hole, the area continued to sink, and each year Fowler had a slightly deeper depression in his backyard.

With support from the Cahokia Mounds Museum Society, Watson and some student volunteers went back to Cahokia that fall and dug three test pits, measuring one by two meters, down to what they considered sterile soil along the west half of the proposed woodhenge. The locations were carefully chosen to be outside where the crew thought any ancient construction might have taken place.

One of the test pits was placed outside of the proposed woodhenge circle, to the west, because part of the archaeologists' hypothesis was that the circle enclosed sacred space. Sacred space, they speculated, would be free of debris, compared to the area outside the circle. They found confirmation of this hypothesis in the presence of fragments of galena (lead ore) in the test pit outside the circle but none on the inside. Galena was used by Mississippian peoples for various purposes and was one of those special resources likely to be controlled by the elite of the society. Altogether the investigators found nearly twenty times as many prehistoric artifacts in the test pit outside the circle as were recovered from the test pits inside the circle, confirming their hypothesis that the area inside of the circle was being kept clear for special functions.

The pits also showed what the natural stratigraphy was like before it was disturbed. Watson was successful in that he recovered good stratigraphic data, some of it showing a buried sand ridge at a high level. He also confirmed that there had been no disturbance in the area caused by the prehistoric digging of pits. Watson and Fowler spent much of the summer and fall of 1996 getting their controls in place to set them up for the big push that would take place the following summer.

An announcement of the 1997 Cahokia field school and the research project sponsored by the National Science Foundation was put on the Internet and appeared on fliers that went up on university bulletin boards throughout the country. The response from qualified applicants was so great that Fowler and Watson were able to hire people with a broad range of experience in archaeology. Eventually 25 men and women were chosen for the summer's work. Fowler was principal investigator. Under him was Watson, the field director, assisted by two teaching assistants. Gartner was to serve as a consultant on the sediments and stratigraphy.

Bill Woods arranged to house the students in graduate student housing units at Southern Illinois University, Edwardsville. Margaret Brown had advised them that they would not be able to leave their tools overnight in a locked toolbox at the site—it would be broken into—so Fowler arranged to have an equipment trailer built that could be towed back and forth from the site to a secure area near the museum. Work was scheduled to begin on June 16 and when the students arrived that day, Bill Iseminger took them on a tour of the site. For many of them it was their first visit to Cahokia.

Their initial project was to test the concept that the interior of the woodhenge circle was sacred space to the ancient Cahokians. If the woodhenges enclosed sacred space, as was suggested by the presence of the elaborate Mound 72 burials, it was probable that they were not used for secular purposes. There would not have been houses built within the circle, or debris scattered there. Fowler's hypothesis was that the area inside the woodhenge circle would yield very few artifacts, while the area outside the circle would contain many more. This hypothesis had been partly tested by Watson's test excavations the summer before.[6]

Further testing of this hypothesis came by shovel testing. A grid was staked out and at every five-meter interval a small pit, measuring 50 by 50 centimeters and 50 centimeters deep, was dug. All of the material from the pits was screened and recorded as to the location of its recovery. The results of the shovel testing were that many more Precolumbian artifacts were found outside than inside the circle. Ethnographic information collected among southeastern Indian groups notes that plazas and other public spaces were swept clean of debris as part of the special use of these areas. If neatness was a criterion of sacredness, then inside the woodhenge was indeed sacred space.

The next step was to test areas where Fowler believed post pits of the western segment of Woodhenge 72 should be found. He selected five areas on the post circle monument for detailed testing: the north location, the center of the circle, the west or equinox sunset location, the summer solstice sunset location, and Mound 96, which was at the winter solstice sunset.

---

6. Fowler and Watson 1998.

One of the many problems attendant to excavating large post pits was the size and complexity of the features. The various insertion and extraction ramps and the central pit of Post Pit 1 in Mound 72 had covered an area of 12 square meters and reached a depth of three meters. That feature had at least three episodes of insertion and extraction of large posts. Fowler would have to devise a strategy that would determine both the extent of the features and the sequence of aboriginal excavations.

Because of his unfortunate experience in former years with rainstorms, Fowler decided to excavate in a five-by-five-meter area, going down a level at a time. He would not dig any more deep holes that could collapse on him or fill with water. If the investigators found a feature, they could recreate its dimensions by drawing the details on what they called floor plans, level by level. The levels went down in no more than 20-centimeter increments.

One of the first areas to be opened up was the central area, where Fowler hoped to find a post pit near the geometric center of the circle. This location was very near the old road of the park. Rinita Dalan's electromagnetic conductivity work there had shown some low reading but nothing as definitive as the east post they had worked on two years before. The workers dug and dug and found nothing. Fowler expanded the size of the pit beyond the five by five meters and still nothing. The students dug deeper but found no indication of a post pit.

Confirming the shovel testing data, almost no artifacts were found in the center of the circle, leaving few clues to go on. Fowler thought the sediments looked different from those in other areas and considered the possibility that the area might have been built up—either as a result of park road construction or the building up of the area by Precolumbian people. Though the crew continued working on the area while other work was going on, eventually he had to call it off. It was a discouraging beginning.

A second significant area to examine was the post pit location called I West, the due-west or equinox sunset position in the proposed Woodhenge 72. This was relatively close to the test pit that Watson had dug outside the circle, in which he had found pottery and galena fragments. When the workers measured to set up their five-by-five-meter test pit, they found they were up against a tree in the park so they opened up a trench measuring four by five meters. The first 20 centimeters of ground were hard and full of roots—and most of the roots were poison ivy. Even though the students wore gloves, many of them got cases of poison ivy and had to be sent off to the Southern Illinois University health center for treatment.

When the first 20 centimeters were removed and the floor cleaned, it appeared to Fowler and Watson that they were not quite below the A horizon as they had a very mixed surface. A few centimeters more were cleaned off. Using flat shovels with sharpened blades, the students trimmed off the floor in such a way as to show the fresh sediments on a smooth surface. On his hands and knees, Watson finished off the surface with a sharp-edged trowel that didn't smear but cut cleanly through the thin layer of sediments to expose a clear picture. When he had finished and the floor was perfectly smooth, Watson called Fowler over to take a look. The students stood in silence around the edges of the excavation, watching as Fowler bent over and peered through his bifocals at the ground. There at his feet, less than two feet northeast of where he had predicted the west post would be located, standing out in sharp contrast to the lighter-colored sediments surrounding it, was a large circular stain in the ground, a meter in diameter.

That evening, as the students crowded around the trailer, putting away the tools and enjoying the cold beer provided for the occasion, Fowler told them that this had been one of the most satisfying days of his entire archaeological experience. He had found another feature exactly where he had predicted it would be. It was akin to his finding Post Pit 1 in the original excavation of Mound 72.

A few days later a group of archaeologists came to visit. It was a good time for them to have come. The students had the feature cleaned off, the area gridded with strings, and it had been extensively photographed. The leader of the visiting group was particularly impressed with the finding. Some of his colleagues were among those who had previously been skeptical of Fowler's claims. Most now agreed that he had, indeed, found a new post pit that fit into the pattern of a Woodhenge 72.

Fowler had not been surprised to find that digging on the west side of the woodhenge was different from his earlier experience on the east, but he had been unprepared for how clearly the features showed up. On the east side, workers had to dig down over a meter below the surface to find evidence of a post pit, while here on the west they had found the west post under just 25 centimeters of soil. The sediments on the west side were different from those on the east and showed up the features much more clearly. On the west side, particularly in the location of I West, the sand ridge mapped by Dalan was very close to the modern surface. On the east side the excavations had been in the deepest part of the swale and the sandy sediments were much deeper.

At this point, Fowler had three well-confirmed points on the Woodhenge 72 circle—the east post, Post Pit 1, and now the west post. There were also four others confirmed but not so well defined. They were Post Pit 2, VI Northeast, II Northeast, V Southeast. Assuming these posts were all from one circle, he could draw an east-west line and calculate the diameter. When he drew this on a piece of graph paper, with the graph paper oriented toward the grid, he found that the line from the east post to the west post was exactly on the true east-west line and that the circle was 412 feet in diameter. Wittry's Woodhenge III had measured 410 feet.

This detailed evidence confirming his hypothesis was a strong indication to Fowler that his research was on the right track. However, finding the top of the post pit was not enough for him. He wanted to follow the staining in the soil down to the bottom, as he had been able to do during that dry summer 25 years before, when he had excavated Post Pit 1 in Mound 72. Fowler had the students continue taking the pit down by levels, but after two more strippings of levels he decided that procedure was not going to yield the information he needed. He and Watson studied the sky. They remember only too well the previous two years when torrential rains had destroyed the evidence in their excavations. By contrast, this spring had been a dry one. The ground was brittle and hard to work. They had had only one heavy rain so far this season and when it came the pit had been shallow and no great damage had been done. They had simply bailed out the water and continued.

Fowler decided to gamble on the weather. The west post pit was divided into quadrants with the center of the four sections in the center of the post pit. The students dug two of the quadrants, the northeast one and the southwest one, so they could get continuous profiles into the pit from two different directions. Fowler decided to leave the other two quadrants standing so that if they did have a problem with rain they could take those quadrants down in horizontal excavations.

The pit went down and the students drew profiles as the pit got deeper and deeper. They could see a quarter of the circle in each of the quadrants. A meter below the surface they hit sand. From the staining in the sand, it looked as if the post pit kept on going. They followed the post pit down until they were two meters below the surface. Post Pit I West had the best definition of any post pit they had yet found and closely resembled, in diameter and depth, Post Pit 1 from Mound 72.

As they dug they encountered evidence of disturbances outside the central core of the pit, which may well have been ramps. It will take future analysis of the profiles as well as an examination of the unexcavated quadrants before archaeologists will be able to define the insertion and extraction ramps of Post Pit I West.

Critical to Woodhenge 72 was an understanding of Mound 96. Though greatly eroded and deflated through time, Mound 96 was nearly identical in form to Mound 72Sub1. Both were nearly square mounds with ramps. Mound 96 faced due east, toward V Southeast, or the winter solstice sunrise, and Mound 72Sub1 faced west, to V Northwest, or the summer solstice sunset. In 72Sub1 the post pit was found to the east of the center of the mound. Fowler proposed that, on Mound 96, a post pit would be found to the west of the center of the mound.

The two mounds were, in effect, mirror images of each other. According to Fowler's projections and maps, the winter solstice sunset post, which he called V Southwest, would be located at the west end of Mound 96. He proposed that Mound 96 was associated with the winter solstice sunset position and the southwest quadrant of Woodhenge 72, while Mound 72Sub1 was at the summer solstice sunrise position and was associated with the northeast quadrant of the woodhenge.

Fowler made this association because he knew that many cultures divide their perceived world into quadrants based upon the cardinal points of the compass. Mississippian peoples, along with many other cultures of the Americas, symbolized this by a circle with a cross in the center. Woodhenges can be viewed as icons implanted in the ground—as architectural manifestations of the world view—as well as a place for noting the sun's annual pilgrimage. Woodhenges were public architecture incorporating many social and sacred values.

As Fowler studied his detailed contour map of Mound 96 he decided that it was a large square platform on which a smaller mound had been built in the center. Two or three of the proposed post pits should be within this square platform and one, at least, should be associated with the low mound. Just south of the highest contour of the mound and on top of the rectangular platform was a shallow depression, approximately 10 to 15 centimeters in depth. The depression was very close to one of the proposed post pits.

Fowler faced two problems in his approach to Mound 96. The first was that it was under undisturbed mound fill and very probably contained burials. Unlike conditions in the 1960s when Mound 72 was excavated, it was now the policy of the Illinois Historic Preservation Agency that no areas could be excavated where burials were likely to be encountered. Because all of the burials in Mound 72 were found inside the circumference of Woodhenge 72, Fowler decided to approach from outside the circumference and work in toward the post pit locations.

The second problem was a tree growing very close to the proposed post pit location. Fowler decided to excavate this area by running a trench from the south to the center and then approach the post pit location from the east. The trench would run through the depression to see if a post pit was associated with it and on into the small upper mound that had been built on top of the larger platform.

He began the excavation with a long trench parallel to the edge of the platform base. In the middle of that he opened a two-meter-wide trench running in toward the center. It was very difficult to distinguish the dark soils, one from the other, and to locate what was probably the original ground level. After they had gone in a few meters with the two-meter-wide trench, Fowler and Watson decided that it would take too long to get to the feature area and narrowed the excavation trench down to one meter in width and continued pressing on toward the center.

When they reached the area of the depression they found what looked like a mixing of the soils, but Fowler could not define a post pit either in the profile or in any other feature that would account for what appeared to be the disturbance in the surrounding sediments. There were some indications in the north profiles of the excavation that the disturbance was tipping toward the north but when they followed it up it disappeared.

In examining the profiles of the east and west walls of the trenches, they found there was a depression of the disturbed sediments in the west wall and an even deeper one in the east wall. The entire disturbed area coincided with the dip in the ground soil, the shallow basin Fowler had noticed from his contour map. Fowler finally decided that what they were seeing in the profiles was a ramp that was getting deeper as they dug toward the east, where the proposed post pit location would be. The ramp was one that had been used for the sliding of the post into the post pit. If his hypothesis was correct, then the ramp had been excavated through the mound fill, after the mound had been constructed, and the hole had been refilled with sediments very similar to the black fill of the mound.

A little further north, close to the upper elevation of the mound, the students came upon what appeared to have been a post pit that had been cut through the mound fill. After the post was removed, the gap in the mound had again been filled with materials almost identical to those from which the mound had been built. When they excavated into the sediments below to get to the base of the pit, they found that the post pit had extended into the sand area below the mound and they could see evidence of the original top soil that had been there before the mound had been built. This new post pit fit closely to the circumference of the proposed circle and the predicted location of post VI Southwest.

Again, the similarity to Post Pit 1 from Mound 72 was striking. Post Pit 1 had originally been constructed before Mound 72Sub1 had been built. But the post continued in place after the mound was constructed. In the post's final episode, it had been removed via an extraction ramp dug through Mound 72Sub1 and the pit had been filled with sediments almost identical to those out of which the mound had been constructed. In the case of Mound 72Sub1 it was easier to see the mixture of black and lighter-colored soils than it was in Mound 96. In Mound 72Sub1 the archaeologists had been able to identify the layers and even the basket loads of soil where they had been carefully placed to match the mound fill around them.

As Fowler and his crew of students continued northward in their excavation of Mound 96, just beyond the post pit they began to notice, in the north wall of their excavation and in the corners of the east and west walls, a brownish sand line showing up quite distinctly from the fill around it. Just above the sandy line was a dark black sediment. As they slowly dug northward they found this sand line expanding and in the north wall there were distinct layers of different colors of sand. Some were brown, some light brown, and some very dark in color. The top of the sand levels sloped up gradually to the north but the bottom of the basin of sand fill was level.

What they had discovered was a well-defined basin that had been cut into the black mound fill and through the black mound cap, as had been the post pit just to the south. The basin had then been carefully filled with selected sandy sediments. It was probably at this time that the post had been removed and the pit filled in. Both of these features had been capped over with a heavy layer of black clay. Fowler did not know what to make of it. He had never encountered anything like it before. It was some kind of feature that had been carefully dug to give it a level floor and curving sides. Since Fowler had only a one-meter cut through the basin, he had the east-west and north profiles but nothing to indicate the dimension of the total feature. The south edge of the feature coincided almost exactly with the elevation above sea level—127.5 meters—of the highest contour of the mound.

Could the sand basin with the black clay cap be the same dimension as that contour line? Even though there have been a thousand years of erosion and weathering of the mound, Fowler believes that, because of the hard clay cap that had been placed over the sandy fill, the contour approximates the original outline of the mound.

The summer season was passing rapidly and Fowler still had other post pit areas to excavate. With his crews working on several sites simultaneously, Fowler brought a group back to continue work on the central post location. Fowler had been worrying about that location since the beginning of the summer. There had to be something there.

As he talked about it with his students, who had now had a summer's experience with these sediments, it seemed more and more likely to him that the sediments in the center of the circle were different from those elsewhere in the area. The sediments in the central location were a hard, tacky clay, almost like a modeling clay. They did not look like an E horizon or some other natural horizon, which would have had a different color. When he consulted his map from the 1966 aerial survey, he noted a one-meter contour line that extended roughly from Mound 96 out toward the center location.

Fowler's original interpretation of this line was that it was the result of modern grading of the area to prepare it for use as a state park. The contour line ended just before the spot Fowler had projected to be the geometric center of the circle. The more he studied his map the more Fowler wondered if that 127-meter contour projection had been made by human hands and might be an extension of a platform from Mound 96 out toward the center of the circle. When Mound 96 was mapped in great detail the mapping did not extend as far as the 1966 127-meter contour. Fowler speculated that the 1966 contour might represent a sort of causeway from Mound 96 up to the center of the circle. This could account for the different nature of the sediments found in the central area excavations. The idea occurred to Fowler late in the summer and there was no time to investigate it further.

Another crew was at work trying to pin down the location of the north post of Woodhenge 72. This proved to be one of the more complicated locations because a borrow pit had been dug at some time after the construction of the woodhenge. The students dug down until they reached the natural sand and could see the stepped nature of the original borrow pit. Fowler decided to dig a deeper trench on the north half of the excavation where one of the EMC anomalies was located. When the students cut through the borrow pit fill into the sandy strata underneath, almost directly under the EMC indication, they found the remains of a post pit running into the ground. It had been dug prior to the construction of the borrow pit.

The students called this location the pit from hell because it was out in the open, away from any shade. Many days they could work only during the morning hours before having to close the dig down because of the intense heat.

To the west of the west post pit was another depression that had also shown a relatively large EMC disturbance. They decided to put a trench into that area to see if they could find the cause of the slight depression and the EMC anomaly. They cut the trench at an angle rather than on the east-west, north-south grid lines so that it would cut through the longest axis of the EMC anomaly. This excavation was called I West B (IWB).

At the beginning of the excavation very little was noted in the stratigraphy of the walls of the trench. It seemed to be very similar to the basic stratigraphy the excavators had found from their test trenches. As they expanded the trench to the southwest they found the appearance of a sandy layer in the profile. They cut through this and found the corner of another sand-filled basin—very similar to what they had found on top of Mound 96. Fowler decided to expand the excavation on the surface so he could determine the size of this feature, rather than cross-sectioning it halfway through as they had in Mound 96. They were able to follow the sand around and get the dimensions of the pit. It measured 2.5 by 4 meters. There was not enough time to cross-section the feature to see if it too had been built with layers of different-colored sand, but every characteristic confirmed that it was the same sort of structure as had been found on top of Mound 96.

One more basin was found before the season ended. Students working to locate post pit IV Southwest found a corner of what is probably another of the sand basins. There wasn't enough time to cross-section it or clear off the surface to find its surface dimension as they had been able to do with the others.

The summer of 1997 drew to a close with as many questions raised as questions answered. The best-defined post pit was the I West location but several other indications of post pits were found where Fowler had predicted they would be. Mound 96 turned out to be a highly complex operation with post pits close to where they had been predicted, although the workers were not able to excavate the winter solstice sunset post (V Southwest) in Mound 96, which had been an original target. They also found indications of ramps in the post pits in the VI Southwest locations in Mound 96, confirming that there had been posts there, probably related to Woodhenge 72.

The great surprise of the season were the sand-filled basins, both in Mound 96 and in two other locations, one inside and one outside the woodhenge circle. The summer's excavation fully confirmed the hypothesis of the Woodhenge 72 monument. The work also affirmed, by the discovery of the sand basins, that this area of Cahokia was, in some unknown way, special to its ancient inhabitants and may indeed have represented sacred ground.

SIXTEEN

The Physical Landscape of Cahokia

When Fowler first set about determining the population centers at Cahokia during the ICT-I work in 1979, he used a controlled surface collection procedure in the area around the Ramey farmhouse and over the field on the east side of Monks Mound. The Ramey family home, a large, square, two-story farmhouse, had originally stood on the west side of Monks Mound. This was the portion of the Ramey farm that was originally purchased by the state in 1923 for the Cahokia Mounds State Park. After the sale, the family moved the house to the east side of the mound, near the center of its farming operation just outside the eastern boundary of the park, and continued living in it.

Fowler had had the area plowed to remove surface cover and marked off in a grid of 2.5-meter squares. A student was assigned to each square and told to put everything in that square into a numbered bag. The collecting went right over the tops of mounds and up to the palisade excavations.

With a grant from the Illinois Department of Conservation he hired Barbara Vander Leest to do the analysis. A computer coding system was set up in which all of the artifacts were entered into a computer so that the distribution of flint chips, types of pottery, and other artifacts could be known within the 2.5-meter limit of refinement. Nelson Reed lent Vander Leest the materials from a controlled collection he had made at a small mound near Wittry's woodhenge and she gained access to another collection that had been made on the Dunham Tract across the highway from Tract 15A.[1]

The plotting of the data turned up some interesting information. The earliest occupation of the Cahokia area had been on the east-west ridge to the north that ran along the banks of Cahokia Creek. While there was a scattered distribution of Patrick phase (the earliest) materials in Tracts 15A and 15B and on

---

1. Benchley 1981; Vander Leest 1980.

the Powell Tract, the larger amounts were at the northern limits near the bank along the creek. It appeared as if there had once been a series of scattered villages there.

During the next phase, called the Jarrot phase by the researchers, there appeared to have been a major consolidation of these small villages into a larger community. This was a major insight because at the time, it was thought that the big population growth at Cahokia had taken place in the later Stirling and Moorehead phases. Vander Leest's analysis showed that this tremendous growth and expansion had taken place much earlier.

Another peculiarity noted in the distribution was that there were spaces scattered throughout the area where the students had found nothing, no chips, no pottery or artifacts of any sort. These were open spaces within the built-up area of Cahokia, areas that may have been plazas with specific purposes in the community organization. Fowler noted that one large plaza was where the old Ramey farmstead had stood.

Fowler, Porter, and others had used the Ramey house as a headquarters building until 1968 when the state decided that it was blocking the view of Monks Mound and decided to tear it down. Fowler was working with his crews in the field at Cahokia when he became aware that a bulldozer had moved into the park and the operator had started to dig a big hole in the ground right next to the Ramey house.

Fowler raced to the site. "Wait a minute," he shouted. "What are you doing? This is an archaeological site. You can't dig there."

The operator climbed down from his bulldozer. "We have to have some place to put the debris from knocking down the house," he explained.

"For crying out loud," Fowler exclaimed. "There is a basement under this house. Why don't you put the debris in the basement, pack it down and cover it over?"

No one had thought of that. The bulldozer operator was merely following his instructions, which had been to dig a trench in which to bury the debris of the house. The incident illustrated how little even the state officials in charge knew about how to manage an archaeological site. After much discussion Fowler's suggestion was followed. He took pictures of the Ramey house as the bulldozer buried it in its own basement. If people ever want to excavate an old farmhouse, Fowler can show them where to dig.

What did Cahokia look like when its residents lived there? Is there some significance to the various groupings of mounds and their different shapes? What was the nature of the society that organized the hundreds of work crews required to construct the giant earthworks, palisades, and woodhenges?

Much of what is known of Cahokia comes from a careful examination of sur-

face features. Only a small fraction of one percent of the Cahokia site has been
excavated and these excavations have dealt with very specific problems. It is the
data that exists above ground, mounds, borrow pits, plazas, and surface debris—
the works of human energy—that reveal the pattern of community organization.

Most of the areas of Cahokia that have been investigated thus far were occupied by Native Americans throughout the total time range of Cahokia's development, particularly the earlier periods. Nearly everywhere that archaeological excavations have been conducted there is evidence for occupation during
Emergent and Early Mississippian times.

The first early evidence of this long period of occupation came from Harriet
Smith's 1941 excavation of Mound 55, the Murdock Mound.[2] As described earlier, Murdock Mound was built over what had previously been a residential area
that contained unusual structures, including a round building with a deep cy-
lindrical clay-walled fireplace and a cross-shaped construction. These buildings
had been preceded by simpler wall-trench buildings, possibly arranged around
a courtyard. These structures, in turn, had been built over the site of pit houses
designed with single-post construction. Altogether, Smith noted five different
stages of habitation construction before the mound was built over the area.

Smith interpreted this as indicating that the area was originally one of elite
residences that was later covered over with an even more prestigious residential mound. Data from the four levels of structures and the mound indicate an
occupation of the area from at least Emergent Mississippian to Late Mississippian times. Although no detailed ceramic analysis was ever done on the materials Smith excavated, she did recognize "periods" within her stratigraphic sequence, such as Late Woodland, Developmental Mississippian, Mississippian,
and Late Mississippian. A casual inspection of the ceramics she recovered indicates that this sequence undoubtedly spans Emergent Mississippian and Lohmann as well as later Mississippian phases.

When Caldwell conducted his test excavations in Mound 31, archaeologists
were just beginning to suspect that the Cahokia ceramic sequence might be more
complicated than the Old Village–Trappist dichotomy with which they had been
working. Because of the press of his other duties, Caldwell had not had time to
analyze the materials he had excavated. Years later Fowler borrowed the artifacts
and notes from the Mound 31 excavation for his class in archaeological analysis. A team of students, headed by Lynne Sullivan, a Ph.D. student who later went
on to the New York State Museum, undertook the analysis of the materials.

Sullivan's analysis showed that the deposits under Mound 31 span the Emergent Mississippian and Lohmann periods (A.D. 900–1100). The sequence of

_____

2. Smith 1969.

single-post-pit structures to wall-trench houses found under the mound fits this appraisal, and the first eight stages of the mound built over these structures match the early part of the Stirling phase, approximately A.D. 1100–1200.

There was a gap in the sequence of this mound construction in that no late Stirling material was found. The last two stages of mound construction were added during the Moorehead phase. A small number of ceramics of the Late Mississippian Sand Prairie phase (A.D. 1275–1350) were found on the summit of the mound. Caldwell's excavations provided evidence that the Mound 31 area had been utilized throughout the entire span of Mississippian occupation in the American Bottom with only a slight lapse in use in the Middle to Late Stirling phases.

The Emergent and Early Mississippian use of the area was for residential purposes whereas the later Mississippian use was for mound construction. Although no remains were found of structures that might have been placed on top of the 10 mound stages, such structures may well have been elite residences. The occupation sequence that Caldwell discovered on Mound 31 was similar to that which Smith found at Mound 55.

Additional evidence for the widespread early use of the Cahokia site comes from the excavations in the borrow pit under Mound 51. The earliest premound fill of this borrow pit is contemporary with or earlier than Mound 72. This suggests that the Persimmon Mound (Mound 51) borrow pit had been dug, abandoned, and the filling of it begun in Early Mississippian times. This borrow pit was probably the source for the clay used in the early stages of the building of Monks Mound. After the pit was filled in with refuse, Mound 51 was built over it, probably in Stirling times. It is obvious that a great deal of activity was going on in the central part of Cahokia before and during the tenth century A.D.

Other examples of this activity come from the Powell Mound area, Tracts 15A and 15B, and several smaller mound groups that have been recently tested.[3] All show utilization from Emergent Mississippian to Late Mississippian times, or approximately A.D. 850 to at least A.D. 1300. The ICT-II tract was first intensively occupied in the Lohmann phase. The primary utilization of Mound 72 was largely a Lohmann phenomenon, with later burials placed in pits that were dug into the completed mound.

Another theme that runs through Cahokia is the changing of land-use patterns through time. Tract 15A was first used, during Emergent and Early Mississippian times, for housing. Then, during the later Stirling times, the houses were removed and the tract became the location for a series of woodhenge constructions. Still later, the area reverted to residential use.

---

3. Holley et al. 1992, 1995; Watters et al. 1997.

What is missing from the archaeological record is evidence of occupation during the later periods. This suggests that early in its history, from A.D. 900 to 1100, Cahokia already had grown to the full extent of the mounds that are now visible. During later periods less of the site may have been occupied as influence and population declined. This drop in population is indicated by the paucity of Sand Prairie–phase materials at Cahokia. Those artifacts that are found tend to be in the center of the site, such as on Monks Mound and the nearby Mound 31.

Can Cahokia's original plan of organization be determined from the current distribution of mounds and other features? Though the site is extraordinarily complicated, Fowler believes that it can. Cahokia's city plan was laid out in the earlier periods of its occupancy. Fowler's discovery of a north-south axis in the Lohmann phase is evidence of this, as is the data suggesting that the Grand Plaza and Monks Mound were begun at this time. Lohmann-phase houses in ICT-II also followed the original plan and were oriented with their north-south axes paralleling Monks Mound.[4]

Fowler[5] has named the central portion of the Cahokia site Downtown Cahokia (fig. 25). The focus of this area is the imposing Monks Mound. Monks Mound was built in this location and to its towering height precisely for the purpose of centering attention on it. The giant mound and the area around it was the center of the community and the seat of control. Surrounding this seat of control were points of lesser focus in the community, the residences of lower level officials and the satellite communities they controlled.

The palisade enclosed an area of about 200 acres, which included Monks Mound as well as 17 other mounds. While the watchtowers constructed on the palisade clearly indicate that it was built for defensive purposes, the great wall also defined the central area of the Cahokia community. The area within the palisade was not only the seat of power but also the residential area for Cahokia's elite.

The 17 mounds, in addition to Monks Mound, that are located inside the palisade are arranged in rows along the east and west walls. There are two exceptions to this: Mound 49, called Red Mound, and Mound 56, called the Jesse Ramey Mound.[6] Red Mound is a ridge-top mound located on the north-south center line of the site. Mound 56 is either a conical or ridge-top mound and is centered between the two walls of the palisade.

Facing the north side of the plaza is Monks Mound. The ramp on the first

---

4. Collins 1990, 1997; Mehrer 1995.
5. For one version of how the Cahokia site may have been organized, see Fowler 1997:193 ff., chap. 10.
6. Dalan et al. 1993; Holley, Dalan, Lopinot, and Smith 1990.

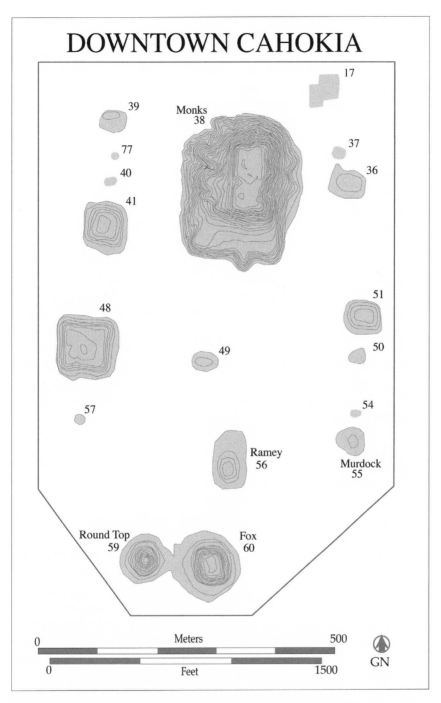

Figure 25. Downtown Cahokia, showing the locations and numbers of the mounds within the palisade (indicated by six-sided outline). Used with permission of M. L. Fowler.

terrace more or less centers on the Grand Plaza. If this ramp was the stairway leading to the upper levels of Monks Mound, this would have been the principal access from the plaza to the most important structure at Cahokia. The Jesse Ramey Mound (56) is centered on the southern edge of the plaza. A north-south line through the center of the upper terraces of Monks Mound and the south ramp intersects the center of Mound 56. The Jesse Ramey Mound was aligned with its long axis north to south. The orientation of this mound and the foundation upon which it was built was toward Monks Mound. These two great mounds face each other across the Grand Plaza at Cahokia.

The east side of the plaza is defined by four mounds just inside the palisade. The mound at the northeast corner is the Persimmon Mound (51), a platform mound whose upper levels were hauled away for fill dirt before detailed study of it could be made. At the southeast corner of the plaza area is Murdock Mound (55), excavated in 1941 by Smith. This mound has been reconstructed as a double-terrace mound facing to the west. Between 51 and 55 were two small mounds, 50 and 54, which may be conical dedicatory mounds.

The west side of the plaza is dominated by a large, square, platform mound, number 48, the second-largest mound inside the palisade after Monks Mound. From the refuse found at the base it appears to have been an elite residential area. A line through its center and the long axis of Red Mound would bisect the plaza. About 100 meters south of Mound 48 is Mound 57. Since this mound was cultivated for many years, little is known of its original form. A 128-meter contour line surrounds both of these mounds, which may indicate that they were built on a platform.

Electromagnetic surveys[7] indicate there may have been another small mound to the south of Mounds 48 and 57. If so, this would give a line of three mounds on the west paralleling the line of Mounds 51 to 55 on the east side of the plaza area. The quadrangle of space that the mounds surround was the Grand Plaza of Cahokia, a major focal point of the greater Cahokia community.

Throughout the Cahokia site there are at least nine examples of conical mounds that have been paired with platform mounds. The largest and best preserved pair are Round Top (59) and Fox (60) located just inside the southern point of the palisade and to the south of Mound 56. Round Top and Fox were never cultivated and look very much as they did in Patrick's or Brackenridge's time. Both were built on an earthen platform and they are clearly associated with each other. Fowler believes that Fox Mound was a charnel-house mound and Round Top its affiliated burial mound. He proposes that the two mounds represent the mortuary precinct for the leaders of Cahokia who lived on the platform mounds within the palisaded area.

---

7. Dalan 1989a, 1991; Dalan and Watters 1994.

Seven mounds lie within the palisade in the vicinity of Monks Mound. Along the west side of Monks Mound, ranging north to south, are Mounds 39 (Sawmill), 77, 40, and 41. Mounds 39 and 41 are platform mounds whereas 77 and 40 are small conical mounds. Mounds 77 and 39 are connected by a platform. The pattern of these four mounds and their relationships to each other are nearly identical to those of the row of mounds, 51, 50, 54, and 55, on the east side of the Grand Plaza.

Located approximately in the center of the area between the east side of Monks Mound and the northeast section of the palisade is Mound 36, a platform mound. The 1922 Goddard aerial photos clearly indicate that 36 was a terraced mound with the higher terrace on the south and a narrower lower terrace along the entire northern edge of the mound. Connected to the northwest corner of Mound 36 was a small conical mound, Mound 37. The location of these two mounds in the area east of Monks Mound is similar to the positioning of Mounds 48 and 57 on the west side of the Grand Plaza.

Mound 17, near the northeast corner of Monks Mound, is the only other mound within the palisade. The Patrick map illustrates it as if it were comprised of two abutting but slightly offset platforms. Later maps show it as an oval mound with its long axis east to west. No excavations were ever made into this mound and it has long since been plowed away.

The palisaded area of Downtown Cahokia can be subdivided into three precincts. The Monks Mound precinct takes up the northern third of Downtown Cahokia and is centered on Monks Mound. On the east side is a platform mound and its associated conical mound. On the west side is the row of four mounds: two platforms and two conicals.

Covering the central third of the palisaded area is the Grand Plaza precinct. Its focal point is the Grand Plaza itself, with a ridge-top mound close to its center. On the west side of the plaza is a large platform mound. Fronting the east side of the plaza is a group of four mounds, two platforms and two conicals.

The mortuary precinct occupies the southern third of the central city of Cahokia and is composed of Fox and Round Top, a platform mound and a conical mound built upon a large support platform. Because no other paired mounds, either within or outside the palisade, are as large and as close to Monks Mound—the central focus of Cahokia—as are these two mounds, they may be the burial sites of the highest-ranking persons of Cahokia.

Outside the palisaded area of Downtown Cahokia are the suburbs, or "neighborhoods," of the city, consisting of 86 numbered mounds scattered over nearly five square miles (fig. 26). Most of these mounds are within a radius of three-fifths of a mile of Monks Mound. The mounds are grouped in clusters of platform and conical mounds (sometimes with a ridge-top mound) and many are arranged around open spaces that are interpreted to be plazas. Eleven clus-

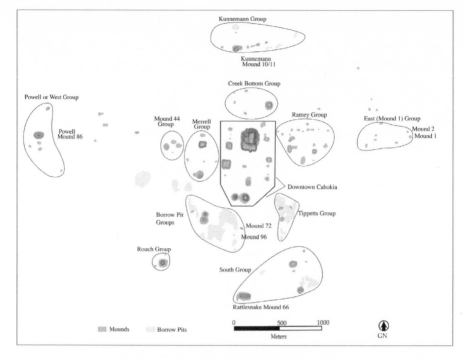

Figure 26. Map of Cahokia site showing groupings of mounds and borrow pits forming the subcommunities of Greater Cahokia. Used with permission of M. L. Fowler.

ters of mounds have been identified as representing separate subcommunities of suburbs. All of the groupings of mounds that are oriented around plazas are within a radius of three-fifths of a mile of Downtown Cahokia. The clusters in which mounds are more loosely grouped are at the margins of the site, well beyond the three-fifths of a mile range.

The mound clusters form two concentric rings around the central city. The inner ring of six communities tightly encircles central Cahokia, while the communities in the outer ring are more scattered.

The northernmost of the outer-ring communities is called the Kunnemann, or North, Group. It is composed of seven mounds (6, 7, 8, 9, 10/11, 12, and 89) located on the north bank of Cahokia Creek. The largest mound of this group is Mound 10/11, which Patrick numbered as two mounds but is more likely a two-terraced mound with the lower terrace (10) facing east. To the east of this large mound are two sets of paired mounds, each set consisting of a platform mound and a conical mound connected by a causeway. About 280 meters north of Mound 10/11 is a small mound (89) by a borrow pit. This mound, which was not mentioned by either Patrick or Moorehead, has been cultivated and its form is indistinct. Mound 12, about 200 meters west of Mound 10/11, was probably a conical mound but it has been cut down by plowing. Titterington reported that a group of unfinished stone celts were found in Mound 12.

The Kunnemann Group is lined up along the banks of Cahokia Creek, an arrangement that is unusual for Cahokia. The surface evidence of widespread habitation debris suggests that the Kunnemann suburb was much more extensive than just the area of the mounds and that it was the site where specialized shell-bead and other craft manufacturing was carried out.

Moving clockwise around the outer ring of suburbs, one encounters the East Group. Mound 1, a platform mound on the west bank of Canteen Creek, just below its juncture with Cahokia Creek, is at the eastern limit of the greater Cahokia area. Mound 1 lies just south of a small ridge mound (2) and 500 meters from a group of mounds (97 to 104). Only traces of these mounds still exist and their forms are not known. Mound 3, which was to the northwest of the East Group, has totally disappeared and there is no data as to its form or function.

At the south end of the Cahokia site is the Rattlesnake, or South, Group. Rattlesnake Mound (66) is the largest of the ridge-top mounds. At the western edge of Mound 66 are two very small conical small mounds (82 and 83), which may have been dedicatory mounds. Aerial photographs of Rattlesnake Mound show it is encircled by individual soil marks similar in configuration to the shapes of these little mounds, indicating that it may once have been surrounded by small dedicatory mounds similar to those found inside the palisade.

Near Mound 66, to the east, are two other large mounds, a ridge-top (64) and a platform (65), located near a borrow pit. Moorehead's map shows three other mounds (63, 80, and 81) in this vicinity but details are lacking as to the form of these mounds. Because Rattlesnake Mound and its associated dedicatory mounds comprise such an unusual feature of the South Group, due to their shape and positioning, that group can be considered a special-function area—such as a marker mound for the north-to-south axis of Cahokia.

The fourth group of mounds on the outer ring is the Rouch Group, composed of three mounds (69, 70, and 71) that are located about a mile northwest of their nearest neighbors. Mound 70, a platform mound, is one of the largest in Cahokia and so must have been the foundation for an imposing structure.

The fifth and last group of mounds that form the outer ring of suburbs is the Powell, or West, Group. The focus of this group is the Powell Mound (86), a large ridge-top mound that is the marker mound for the western limit of Cahokia. Associated with it are two mounds of indistinguishable form (84 and 87) just south of Powell; another mound, Mound 88, to the west; and, 350 meters to the north, another large ridge-top mound, Mound 85. About 500 meters southeast of the Powell Mound is the Jondro Mound (78).[8]

The northern group of the inner circle of communities is the Creek Bottom Group, composed of five mounds (5, 13, 14, 15, and 16) that enclose an area that probably was a plaza. These mounds are located about 984 feet north of Monks Mound in the bottoms of Cahokia Creek. Mound 5 is clearly distinguishable today due to its height of 20 feet but the other mounds have been cultivated and buried under sediments from extensive flooding. The surface on which the mounds were built is buried a meter or two below the present surface of the ground.

Just east of the palisade is the largest cluster of mounds at the Cahokia site. Known as the Ramey Group, it is made up of 21 mounds surrounding an open area of about 10 acres, probably a plaza. Some of the mounds in this group, including the James Ramey Mound and Mound 34, were excavated by Moorehead, Spaulding, and Perino. If this grouping of mounds is indeed a discrete community, then it is larger than many other Mississippian sites in the Midwest and is certainly the largest of the subcommunities of greater Cahokia.

The most unusual mound grouping in the inner ring of suburbs is the Tippetts Group,[9] just to the southeast of Murdock Mound (55) and the southeast section of the palisade. This group is made up of Mounds 61, 62, and 95, all located on the banks of a borrow pit. The mounds include a platform (61), a conical (62), and a ridge-top (95), forming an inverted L, with 61 and 62 in a north-south alignment and 95 due east of 61. Patrick's map shows a causeway connecting 61 and 62. Mound 95 was numbered by Fowler and included as a mound in his *Cahokia Atlas* even though it had not previously been tested. Subsequent testing by Holley and Dalan demonstrated that it was indeed a mound.

A peninsula extends northeastward from Mound 62 into the borrow pit. This tongue of higher ground ends in a square area with the sides oriented to the cardinal points. The square is 35 meters on a side, with the center of the square at the geometric center of the mound distribution. The peninsula is a deliberately constructed feature that served as the plaza for the Tippetts Group. Woods and Fowler proposed that there should have been a large post in the center of this square area but testing by Holley and Dalan did not locate it. Both Moorehead's work and recent surveys suggest that there was extensive habitation to the north of the Tippetts Group.

Five mounds, called the Borrow Pit Group, are located near the banks of the

8. See Moorehead 1929:51–52 and Fowler 1997:250–251.
9. See Holley et al. 1995 and Fowler 1997:198.

largest borrow pit at Cahokia. There is no pattern to the placement of these mounds that would suggest they represent a subcommunity. This could well have been a special-use area such as the mortuary precinct inside the palisade. Ideally the mounds should not be lumped under one heading since field research has shown that they are distinct in form and probably in function. The only factor linking the Borrow Pit Group of mounds together is their proximity to the largest borrow pit at Cahokia.

One such distinct group of mounds includes Mound 72 and Mound 96. Mound 72 is a marker mound containing commemorative burials, and Mounds 72 and 96 are both associated with an early woodhenge at Cahokia. The ceramic data as well as radiocarbon dates indicate that Mound 72 was utilized for a short period of time around A.D. 1000.

Another small mound, Mound 94, about 250 meters north of Mounds 72 and 96, is built on a promontory extending into the northeast edge of the large borrow pit and may not be related to Mounds 72 and 96. Its relationship to the other mounds at Cahokia is not discernible.[10]

A cluster of three mounds, referred to as the West Borrow Pit Group, is located, as the name implies, to the west of the large borrow pit. The two major mounds in this area are a conical mound (67) and an associated platform mound (68). These two mounds are on a north-south axis and were built on a connecting platform. They are nearly identical to, but smaller than, Fox (60) and Round Top (59) and are assumed to be a charnel house and burial mound complex.

Two hundred meters west of Mound 67 is Mound 93. The contours defining this mound are irregular but they suggest that this mound may have been oriented with its long axis in a northeast-southwest direction.

The relationship of Mound 93 to Mounds 67 and 68 and the borrow pit is very similar to the arrangements of mounds and borrow pits in the Tippetts Group. Indeed, these two groups appear to be mirror images of each other. These two groups of mounds, the Tippetts Group and the West Borrow Pit Group, were begun early in the history of Cahokia and may have been part of the original master plan of the site during the Lohmann phase. Fowler's original mapping of Mound 72 and its relationship to other mounds showed distinct alignments with Post Pit 1 and with mounds in these two groups, all of which date to the Lohmann phase.

The mounds at the southern end of the palisaded area are thought to be the charnel group associated with Downtown Cahokia. If Mound 56 is considered to be part of that group, the mounds form an L-shaped pattern similar to that of the Tippetts and West Borrow Pit groups. These three groups, together with

10. Watters et al. 1997.

the Mound 72 complex, may signify a special precinct of Cahokia that was set apart by its special architecture and location.

The Mound 44 Group, another part of the inner ring of suburbs, is composed of four mounds (43, 44, 91, and 92) around a small plaza. This is the smallest but best-defined of the satellite communities. Mound 44 was a large rectangular platform mound. The other three mounds are small and, due to continuous cultivation for more than 150 years, are not well enough defined to be classified by shape. They surround a small open area about 70 meters square. A controlled surface collection of the area around the Mound 44 Group was made and the amount of material found between the mounds was much less than that found outside, indicating that this open area was indeed a plaza and had not been used for habitation. Moorehead marked this area as a "village," meaning habitation, presumably based on surface materials that he observed on the ground. The woodhenges discovered by Wittry are just to the west of, and most probably related to, the Mound 44 Group.

The last of the groups in the inner ring of communities is the Merrell Group. The largest mound of this grouping is the Merrell Mound (42), a large, rectangular, platform mound. It is oriented with its long axis east to west and its platform is higher on its southwest corner. About 150 meters south of the Merrell Mound was a large conical mound (58) and associated with it is a smaller mound (74) that is either a small conical mound or a west platform extension of 58. Moorehead called Mound 58 one of the "very large mounds of the group." The mound was totally destroyed sometime after Moorehead's time and was only a slight rise in the field when it was mapped in 1967.

Bisecting a line between Mounds 42 and 58 is an east-west axis defined by Mound 75 and 47. Both of these mounds have been cultivated extensively so their exact form is not known. At the center of the area defined by Mounds 42, 47, 58–74, and 75 is Mound 73. The formal arrangement of these five mounds and their alignments define them as a group. One other small mound to the north of Merrell Mound, Mound 76, should also be considered part of this group.

Several mounds at Cahokia cannot be directly associated with any of the defined groups. These mounds are located on the south bluff of Cahokia Creek between Downtown Cahokia and the Powell Group. Two of these mounds, 45 and 46, were destroyed or buried under highway construction though they are shown on the Patrick map on the banks of Cahokia Creek overlooking swampy bottomlands and meander channels. A recently discovered and numbered mound (90) is also on the creek bank.

The location of these mounds at regular intervals on the south bank of Cahokia Creek, the highest ridge of ground in the region, is similar to that of the forty or more mounds reported by Brackenridge in East St. Louis. This ridge, extending all the way from the East St. Louis group to Downtown Cahokia, was undoubtedly the major pedestrian traffic route, and these isolated mounds may have served as way stations or monitoring points along the avenues leading to Downtown Cahokia.

Many archaeologists, looking at this group of mounds connecting the Cahokia site with the East St. Louis group, have asked if these discrete groups may not have functioned as a large single community. Trying to understand the intricacies of an archaeological zone of six square miles and 120 mounds is a sufficiently complex problem that most archaeologists have filed this question in the backs of their minds and worked from the traditional interpretation of the Cahokia site.

This layout of Cahokia has deep roots in time going back to the Lohmann phase nearly a thousand years ago. Many changes took place in the city plan during the three centuries Cahokia was densely occupied. The difficulty of separating those changes into the time periods when they occurred is illustrated by the differences in the opinions held by Kelly and Fowler concerning the location of plazas around Monks Mound.

Both Fowler and Kelly[11] propose a series of four plazas and related mounds surrounding Monks Mound in a cross-shaped configuration. The largest of the plazas is the Grand Plaza, extending south of Monks Mound. Kelly believes that the Grand Plaza was rectangular in shape and extended down to Mounds 59 and 60. Fowler proposes a similar plaza but believes it extended southward only to Mound 56 since he considers that Mounds 56, 59, and 60 constitute a separate precinct of Downtown Cahokia within the palisade region.

Kelly places the East Plaza just to the east of Monks Mound and bases this location on the Vander Leest controlled surface survey of the Ramey field. The problem with Kelly's placement, for Fowler, is that the palisade runs right through the middle of the East Plaza. Fowler bases his East Plaza on the arrangement of mounds in the Ramey Group, which locates the plaza outside the palisade.

Kelly's West Plaza is located to the northeast of the Merrell Group, a placement based upon excavations in the Merrell Group and data from Tract 15B. This plaza is also nearly bisected by the proposed west palisade wall. Fowler therefore places the West Plaza in the open space between the mounds in the Merrell Group. Both archaeologists agree about the location of a possible North Plaza.

The disagreement in regard to the locations of the East, South, and West Plazas may relate to the temporal sequence of the building of Downtown Ca-

---

11. Fowler 1997; Kelly 1996.

hokia. There is no disagreement that there were four plazas and that they were in a cruciform pattern (a configuration important for cosmological reasons) around Monks Mound. Fowler's plazas lie outside the palisade walls whereas Kelly's are cut by the palisade. Since the palisade was built in Stirling times, Kelly's plazas may represent the earlier Lohmann-phase site organization while Fowler's plazas may represent a later site plan. In earlier times, elite residential complexes were built closer to Monks Mound. As the community grew, rebuilding of the expanding city became necessary.

Four large areas have been excavated at Cahokia where the remains of houses or residential areas have been uncovered. The areas are Tracts 15A and 15B, the Merrell Tract, the Powell Tract, and the Interpretive Center Tract (ICT-II). All four excavations were undertaken as a result of highway construction or the building of the Interpretive Center. None of the large-area excavations were within Downtown Cahokia but they were associated with groupings outside the center.

Tract 15A is the housing area associated with the Mound 44 Group. Tracts 15B and Merrell are associated with the Merrell Group. The Powell Tract residential area is in some way connected to the Powell or West Group and the ICT-II Tract is closest to the Tippetts Group. Despite its proximity, the ICT-II area may not be related to the Tippetts Group since evidence of mounds related to housing compounds was found within the ICT-II Tract itself. The Tippetts Group of mounds may represent a separate precinct or "neighborhood."

While all these excavated areas of Cahokia show evidence of use throughout the entire sequence from Lohmann through Moorehead (A.D. 1050 to 1275), not all of the area was filled with houses all of the time. There were periods when reorganization occurred and residential areas were demolished to make room for other structures or functions.

Around A.D. 800, possibly due to the beginnings of productive maize cultivation, people began to settle in the Cahokia area. They lived in single-post-pit houses clustered around an open space marked with a large central post. In some cases there were four special pits around the post, which may represent the storage of communal property from four segments of the community. In still other cases a large structure provided the community focus.

These house clusters were separated from each other by empty space, suggesting that they represented household or kinship groups. Mound construction and borrow pits were probably already underway during the Emergent Mississippian time. Though Downtown Cahokia was developing with its central focus on the Monks Mound area, most of the community still consisted of a series of small farming villages scattered along the east-west ridge of ground next to the south bank of Cahokia Creek.

Beginning with the Lohmann phase of the Early Mississippian period (A.D.

1050–1100), the first fully Mississippian culture can be seen at Cahokia. People were using shell-tempered pottery and living in wall-trench rectangular houses surrounded by storage buildings and pits. The population was expanding rapidly and more emphasis was being placed on public works and the Monks Mound precinct of the community.

A cluster of buildings called cluster 1, excavated at the ICT-II site, gives a picture of Lohmann-phase household organization. The focal point of the household was a courtyard or work area that was used for cooking and food processing. To the north and east of the courtyard were five houses built in deep pits of wall-trench construction. A smaller and less well constructed building, which may have been a detached kitchen, was located just northwest of the courtyard. To the west of the courtyard was a series of large pits or "root cellars" for the preservation of grains and other products. Another type of storage facility was a *barbacoa,* a term used by members of the De Soto expedition to describe an above-ground granary. One of these was found at cluster 1. Also nearby was a butchering area, a pit oven, a dump heap, and a semicircular structure with a well-used fire pit in its center—probably a sweat lodge or sauna.

This cluster pattern is defined as the living area of related individuals in an extended family. The five houses may have been the sleeping areas, and the group probably shared in the preparation of food as well as the use of the storage facilities and other one-of-a-kind features such as the pit oven and sweat house.

These extended family clusters were integrated into a larger society or subcommunity as evidenced by a communal plaza and a large T-shaped structure that may have been a public building. The community plaza was at the northeast end of the ICT-II tract. Two very large post pits, two meters deep and a meter in diameter, were found, as were the remains of a community granary. The T-shaped structure was located between two household clusters and its size, unusual form, and location argue for its interhousehold integrating functions. Associated with the structure were two post pits that, along with the posts in the plaza, were the location of household and clan standards.

The Lohmann phase households and the larger units of which they were a part were also related to the greater Cahokia community. All of the Lohmann structures were oriented either parallel with or perpendicular to the Cahokia axis. Evidence from several areas of Cahokia indicate that this was a broad pattern. The woodhenges are along these same axes, and controlled surface collections from the Ramey Tract indicate the possibility of rows of features with a similar alignment. The overall plan for the organization of greater Cahokia was probably in place by A.D. 1000. When the first occupants moved into the ICT-II area they did so as kin groups with a clear understanding of the direction their houses had to face to fit into the community plan.

Sometime around A.D. 1100, at the beginning of the Stirling phase, there was a change in household patterns and the way these smaller units were integrated into the larger Cahokia community. Households were made up of fewer but larger structures than had been the case in the earlier Lohmann households. One or two houses per household were typical, occasionally with an open porch attached to a structure. Firepits were located inside the houses along with large indoor storage pits for the caching of family resources and equipment. Some houses had outdoor hearths and storage pits as well as barbacoas or menstrual huts. Each household cluster had a pole in the center of the courtyard area that may have served as a standard for the unit.

There were more clusters during the Stirling phase than during the Lohmann but since the structures are larger and the clusters smaller, they may well represent the same number of kinship groups. Once a household was established, houses were built and rebuilt in the same location many times over the 100 years of this period. A few of these houses were destroyed by burning and were covered with earth, which preserved their contents. One of these burned houses was found in the excavation of the palisade area. The house had not only been burned, it had been cut in two by palisade construction. Since the structure was found with 20 crushed ceramic vessels in the ruins, it has been called Pottery House. More mundanely, it is also known as House 4.[12]

Pottery House was a Mississippian wall-trench structure about 30 square meters in overall area with 26 square meters of usable floor space. The house was oriented to the cardinal directions with the long axis running east to west. The walls, interior screens, and platforms had been built of hickory, oak, red cedar, bald cypress, and cottonwood.

The remains of four burned posts, which may represent the location of a platform, were found in the northwest corner. Three other smaller posts were near the eastern wall and probably also supported a platform. It appears that the eastern quarter of the house was for sleeping and for the storage of blankets and other organic goods, which would have been destroyed in the fire.

Along the north-central area were six large ceramic vessels—jars and jugs with a capacity ranging from 17 liters to 110 liters. Vessels with narrow necks had an average capacity of 23 liters while open-mouth jars had a much larger capacity—one of 55 liters and another of 109 liters. The forms and large size of the jars indicate that this was a storage facility for dry foodstuffs in jars and liquids in jugs. The liquid storage was at the west end and the jars were placed to the east. Since these vessels have no loop handles for suspension, they were probably stored sitting upright on the floor.

---

12. Pauketat 1987a.

In the northwest area was a series of post holes, which may indicate the presence of a small storage shelf. Found in this area were several limestone and sandstone slabs with indications of grinding on one or both sides. These were milling stones used for the processing of seed foods into meal. At least one of these had been broken and a fragment then used as an anvil. Other utilitarian items in this region included small stones used as hammers, a mussel-shell hoe, ceramic pots, a turtle carapace, and fragments of conch shell. Just to the east of the post holes was a concentration of persimmon seeds, broken marine-shell columns (the tightly curled part of the shell), a battered and reused celt, and other trash.

Along the south wall were several items including a galena cube, a clay ball, a mussel shell, a bowl, and a fragmentary corncob. Nearby was a storage pit that contained a complete marine whelk shell, unfinished marine-shell beads, a sandstone abrader, and the wing elements of a swan. The top half of the pit was taken up with a 20-liter jug that had been placed in the pit and the neck broken off so that the remaining portion of the vessel was more or less even with the surface of the floor. Other miscellaneous items found in the house were a complete flint (Mill Creek) hoe, a projectile point, a bone pin, and a juice press.

One other burned house has been found at Cahokia and the contents of the two houses are strikingly similar. Both contained Ramey Incised pottery, but the most unusual ceramic pieces are stepped bowls (bowls with vertical sides but of two different diameters, with a horizontal platform joining the smaller to the larger), found in both houses. The decorations on the dishes are different, though the vessels from each structure have a consistent set of motifs. The variation in decoration may indicate different sources for the ceramics or a difference in social distinctions. The two structures are nearly 1,200 meters apart and are associated with separate subcommunities.

The households of the Stirling phase were organized into larger social units than those of the Lohmann. The households surround an open plaza in the center of which is a large post, probably carved and painted with symbols, representing the corporate identity. The plaza with its post is centered directly over the T-shaped structure that was the integrating feature of the earlier Lohmann group. Further evidence for the interhousehold integration comes in the form of a mound at the south end of the plaza-residential complex. There was at least one large late Stirling structure on its surface. North of the mound were two single-structure households facing the plaza. The mound was possibly the residence of the lineage group "Big Man" and the two associated structures represented the power of the leaders of this group.

During the Moorehead phase (A.D. 1200–1275), structures are larger, tending more to a square floor plan than to a rectangular one, and are organized into clusters. Many fewer Moorehead phase structures have been found than Lohmann and Stirling. Nearly 80 percent of the ICT-II tract is devoid of Moorehead data. This may indicate that the Cahokians of the late twelfth century were moving their households to higher ground to the east. In Tract 15B the Moorehead buildings are built over what had been a large walled compound and a cleared plaza area to the east. Thus what had been public and ceremonial ground in Stirling times now became the site of residences.

The palisade was built sometime around A.D. 1150, or in late Stirling times, bringing about many changes in land use, such as the destruction of the Pottery House when the palisade was built. If the Cahokians wanted to have a cleared area outside the palisade wall and removed houses from the area, it would explain the vacant portions of the ICT-II Tract at this time.

The shift from Stirling to Moorehead was a time of reordering the community. The area enclosed by the palisade was enlarged. Though the enlarged Downtown Cahokia remained the focus of the community, the plaza-and-mound neighborhoods outside the wall increased in population and may have become as rigidly delineated and nucleated as the community inside.

The Late Mississippian Sand Prairie phase (A.D. 1275–1350) at Cahokia is the period with the least amount of data. One of the few locations where Sand Prairie–related materials, such as the birdman tablet, were encountered in stratigraphic context was under the east lobes of Monks Mound, where they had been effectively sealed from later destruction by the slumping of the mound. Nineteenth-century investigators found a large burial complex with many ceramic vessels north and east of the lobes but they unfortunately left few detailed written records. None of the areas that have been excavated have yielded the type of detailed information that would permit a description of the layout and organization of a Sand Prairie household and community.

While some archaeologists have interpreted this lack of data as an indication of Cahokia's decline and depopulation, Fowler is not so sure. Brackenridge, who saw Cahokia in the first decades of the nineteenth century, before modern agriculture and settlement had changed the land, described a major prehistoric presence:

> As the sward had been burnt, the earth was perfectly naked, and I could trace with ease any unevenness of surface, so as to discover whether it was artificial or accidental. I everywhere observed a great number of small elevations of earth, to the height of a few feet, at regular distances from each other, and which appeared to observe some order; near them I also observed pieces of flint and fragments of earthen vessels. I concluded that a populous town had once existed

here, similar to those of Mexico, described by the first conquerors. The mounds were the sites of temples, or monuments to the great men.[13]

The "small elevations" were residential platforms, which Brackenridge distinguishes from the mounds where "temples" were located. In 1811 the locations of the dwellings of the last inhabitants were clearly visible to him as were fragments of tools and utensils. Collections made by nineteenth-century visitors to Cahokia are mostly of Late Mississippian character, with very few items representing earlier times. These were the items that littered the ground in Brackenridge's time. This extensive evidence for the Late Mississippian occupation at Cahokia was largely picked over by nineteenth-century collectors, and the few pieces that were missed were later destroyed by plows and urban sprawl.

Through five hundred years, from A.D. 800 to 1300, Cahokia functioned as the central community of the American heartland. During that time several trends in civic organization took place. These were a general increase in the size and complexity of household units, the development of ritual space as the overall community focus, and the increasing formalization of the subcommunities related to the civic and ritual center.

Even before A.D. 950, Downtown Cahokia was becoming the dominant communal area, as is shown by the land-leveling and borrow pit excavation that was going on in the Grand Plaza area at the time. Household clusters became integrated into larger units, and subcommunities fused together into the greater Cahokia community. Communitywide integration is represented by the building of public works and monuments that had significant meaning for the entire population. Woodhenges were built in Tract 15A and in the Mound 72 area and became the solar calendars, surveying instruments, and markers of the boundaries of the planned core of the city. Thousands of individual decisions, guided by powerful leaders, melded the small villages, clan leaders, and chieftains of subcommunities into a single organic entity in the American Bottom, a Native American city that, even after it was abandoned, inspired awe in the hearts of its nineteenth-century visitors.

---

13. Brackenridge 1814:188.

SEVENTEEN

The Spiritual Landscape of Cahokia

In Mississippian society the leaders legitimated their power over the commoners through the careful manipulation of culturally meaningful symbols. Just as the illiterate peasants of the Middle Ages in Europe could read their own creation story in the stone carving and stained glass windows of the cathedrals to which they had contributed their labor, the residents of the American Bottom drew their life's meaning from the physical arrangement of their community and the rituals they observed.

The world is known through emotional states as well as by rational constructs. The beliefs of the ancient Cahokians were demonstrably powerful for they commanded the allegiance and labor of multitudes and could be codified by the priests for export throughout the heart of North America. A comparison of the physical layout of Cahokia and the features found in Mound 72 with the ethnographic literature gives researchers of the late twentieth century some insight into the thinking of their counterparts of a millennium ago.

An understanding of the ideological basis of Cahokia begins with Monks Mound and the four plazas that surround it, one at each of the cardinal directions. Monks Mound and its plazas form a cross, making it the central icon around which the landscape was organized and oriented (fig. 27). The mound with its four plazas embodies the concept of quadrilateralness, of the four-cornered world, and reflects the profound significance of directional symbolism to early Native Americans. Monks Mound and its four plazas formed the cross axis of power at Cahokia. The layout of the mounds and plazas according to the

The ideas presented in this chapter are based upon Fowler's interpretations of many sources. Among these are: Bradley 1993; Earle 1978, 1987, 1990, 1991; Earle ed. 1991; Emerson 1997a, 1997b, 1997c, 1997d; Hudson 1976; Knight 1981, 1986, 1990, 1997; Milner 1984d, 1985, 1986, 1990, 1991a, 1996; Pauketat 1992, 1993, 1995; Pauketat and Emerson 1991, 1997a, 1997b; Wright 1978, 1984, 1986, 1987.

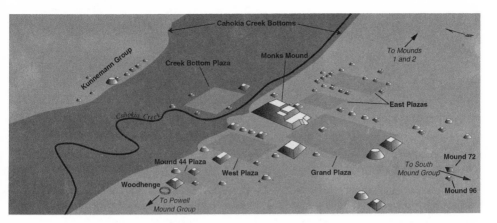

Figure 27. Map of Cahokia showing locations and forms of mounds, plazas, and the lower-lying bottomland of Cahokia Creek. Used and revised with permission of the Illinois Transportation Archaeological Research Program, University of Illinois.

four cardinal directions, one of the basic organizing principles of Native American society, was not happenstance. It was a powerful religious and political symbol that communicated the essence of Cahokian beliefs.

This concern with the quantity of four can be seen at the Range site.[1] At Range the northern courtyard centers contained a set of four pits in the ground grouped around a center post. The northern plaza had the largest residential house and at its center was a pit with a limestone slab floor. At the west side of the central plaza was a large structure with the four-part pit pattern at the opposite end.

During the Emergent Mississippian period at the Range site there were two other central features besides the post and pits. One was a single post without surrounding pits and the other was a large central building on the plaza that was larger than any of the surrounding dwellings. The building could have been a council house the Indians had built to hold token amounts of sacred corn, rather than storing it as seed corn in cache pits in the plaza.

The Native American belief in dualism holds that there is a division between the world above and the world below. Dualism represents balanced reciprocity between the parts, a system that may have helped reduce conflict. The chief is the man in the middle, the negotiator who mediates between discordant sides and between the forces from above the earth and the forces below. Much energy was expended on maintaining the separation of the upper and lower worlds and avoiding the resulting chaos if they should become mixed.

1. Kelly 1990a, 1990b, 1996.

The writings of Francis LaFlesche, a member of the Omaha, about his neighboring people, the Osage, provide insight into what first appears to be a confusing scene. The Osage village, according to LaFlesche, was a recreation of the world and the cosmos. Each community saw itself as a map of the universe, divided into clans, which were themselves divided into two parts, moieties headed by two hereditary chiefs.

> Just as the cosmos was divided between sky and earth, so the clans were divided into groups. . . . The nine clans of the Sky People symbolically represented all of the forces of the sky, whereas the fifteen Earth clans symbolically represented all of the forces of the earth. . . . Osage villages . . . were organized as mirror images of the cosmos. They were divided in half by an east-west street that symbolized the surface of the earth . . . and the path of the sun on its daily journey. Each clan had its own section of the village. Families of the Sky People were arranged by clan groupings in precise locations along the north side of the street. Similarly, families of the Earth People were arranged in clan order along the south side.[2]

Each half of the Osage town had a leader. The houses of the leaders were situated near the central divide on an east-west alignment with the Sky Chief to the north and the Earth Chief to the south. The leaders had equal power and were considered the ultimate authorities. One subclan was called "House in the Middle," a provocative reference when one considers Monks Mound with its large palace on the mound summit.

The cosmos, like the villages of the Osage, was also divided into an upper Sky World and a lower Earth World by an east-west axis that represented the passage of the sun. At sunrise the sun was reborn in a daily resurrection and light and life returned. At sunset the sun descended into the lower world and, in effect, died. It was this constant cycle that guided much of Native American life.

In Osage cosmology the upper or Sky World represented life and the lower Earth World represented death, with the east-west axis standing for, among other things, the mitigation between the two powerful forces. The birdman tablet found by Ken Williams under the east lobe of Monks Mound may illustrate both worlds. On one side of the tablet is the representation of a avian-human figure with a beaked nose and wings, suggesting the Sky World. On the reverse side is a crosshatched design that may represent either a serpent or an alligator—both symbolic of the Earth (and water) World.

Fowler believes that the Cahokia woodhenges may be a monumental representation of this same cosmology. The line from equinox sunrise to equinox

---

2. Quoted in Bailey 1995:40–41.

sunset divides the circle into an upper (north) half, representing the Sky World, and a lower (south) half, representing the Earth World. The persons buried in the submounds of Mound 72 may have been from the northern or Sky World division of Cahokia since they are buried north of the east-west line. Fowler's interpretation is strengthened by the symbolism inherent in the burial of the Beaded Birdman, who rests on a falcon-shaped bead platform. Raptors are powerful symbols of the Sky World.

Several burials in Mound 72 convey this same theme of duality. The Beaded Birdman, who was buried face up, was placed on top of another male individual who was buried face down and turned 180 degrees from the body above him. The upper burial can be interpreted as a Sky World Chief and the face down burial underneath as the Earth World leader. When Moorehead excavated the Jondro Mound he found a similar burial with one body placed on top of another.

There are other paired burials in Mound 72, along with sets of arrowhead caches and chunky stone piles, which may reflect this dual leadership and cosmological division as well. If the burial group is divided by a line between the two chunky-stone piles, two burial sets are definable, each having chunky stones and projectile point caches. In historic times chunky stones were the property of and symbols of corporate groups.

Even the two primary mounds, 72Sub1 and 72Sub2, may reflect this dual pattern. Although they have different burial programs, both contained paired and attendant burials. The artifacts from 72Sub1 are mostly from outside the Cahokia area whereas those from 72Sub2 are from sources within or close to Cahokia.

It is Robert Hall who has provided the closest links between the ethnographic literature and the Mississippian society of Cahokia and the American Bottom.[3] To explain the four pits in the plazas, as well as the cross-shaped houses found by both Harriet Smith and Joseph Caldwell (for which both were ridiculed by their fellow archaeologists, who were sure they had missed a wall trench or superimposition), Hall refers to work done by the ethnologist Frank Cushing. A century ago Cushing lived with the Zuni of New Mexico and described what he called the "mythosociologic organization" of their pueblo.

The Zuni of today number scarcely 1,700 people and inhabit only a single large pueblo. The pueblo is divided into seven parts, Hall writes, in a way that is not always clear to an outsider but is very clear to the people themselves. The seven parts correspond, not in topographical arrangement but in sequence, to Zuni subdivisions of the "worlds" or world-quarters of this world. One divi-

---

3. Hall 1996, 1997, 1998, 1999.

sion of the town is related to the north and is centered in its kiva, or *estufa,* which may or may not, however, be in its center; another division represents the west, another the south, another the east, another the upper world, and another the lower world, while a final division represents the middle, or mother, and synthetic combination of them all.

The Zuni conception of the world was mirrored not only in the organization of the pueblo, but also in a small shrine constructed by Zuni men at the center of their cornfields. Hall reports that when a Zuni man goes into his cornfield he goes to a well-known spot near the center. Here he digs in the soft sandy soil by pushing his prod down with his foot and turning it around and around. Using this method, he digs four deep holes equidistant from a central place. The first hole is to the north, the second to the west, the third to the south, and the fourth to the east. By the left side of the northern hole he digs another to represent the sky regions, and by the right side of the southern hole another hole relating it to the lower regions. In the central space he kneels facing the east and, drawing forth a plumed prayer-wand, sprinkles prayer-meal to form a cross on the ground—symbolizing not only the four cardinal points but also the stars, which shall watch over his field by night. Then, with prayer, he plants the plumed prayer-wand at the intersection of the cross, sprinkles it with more cornmeal, and departs.

When he is ready to plant, the Zuni man drops four grains of yellow corn in the northern hole, four grains of blue corn in the western hole, four grains of red corn in the southern hole, four grains of white corn in the eastern hole, four kernels of speckled corn in the hole for the upper world, and four kernels of black corn in the hole for the lower world. He covers these seeds carefully with earth and then plants rows of corn extending outward in four directions, like paths. This planting creates what Hall has called a "ritual center," a kind of heart for the field and a world center shrine.

Hall compares the Zuni ritual with that of the Hopi. The Hopi construct an altar with fine sand and white cornmeal so that six lines radiate out pointing northwest, southwest, southeast, southwest, north, and south. Ears of corn of the colors corresponding to each direction are placed on the lines. At the center of the Hopi six-direction altar is a bowl containing springwater.

Among the Tewa pueblos in New Mexico and northeastern Arizona, where the language is different from that of the Zuni and Hopi, a world center shrine is located on the summit of Chicomo Mountain. There is a central shallow, wet depression symbolic of water, similar to the bowl of water in the Hopi shrine. There is also a pole held up by rocks and, as in the Hopi and Zuni shrines, paths leading in various directions outlined by field stones. The paths are "rain roads" to direct the rain to the pueblos.

Hall compares these shrines with the pattern of large posts erected in the center of the plazas at Range. The posts were set up within a quadrangle defined by four pits. He suspects that each pit could have contained seed corn of a different color corresponding to the color-directional symbolism of the greater Cahokia area. While there is no way to know what those colors were, it is known that for the Pawnees who lived to the west of Cahokia, black corn was for the northeast, yellow for northwest, white for southwest, and red for southeast.

Hall speculates that the cross-shaped houses found by Smith and Caldwell also carried cosmological significance related to the points of the compass and whatever colors of corn the ancient Cahokians associated with those directions.

Hall has also suggested a connection between the Green Corn ceremony and the four headless and handless men found in Mound 72. The Green Corn ceremony, or Busk, was the most important social and religious event of the year for Indians of the southeastern United States. The ceremony included a New Fire ritual and a World Renewal ceremony in which the sacred fire would be relit and the world order reestablished. The word "Busk" comes from a corruption of a Creek Indian word meaning "to fast." At the time of the Busk, household fires were put out to be relit with fire from the Sacred Hearth; plazas were swept clean, houses cleaned, and old clothing and furnishings destroyed.

Among the Cherokees, corn was believed to have originated from the body of a corn maiden called Selu, whose husband was Kanati, or Lucky Hunter. The Cherokee believed that one must not blow on an ear of corn to cool it because that would be disrespectful of Selu, whose husband and twin sons were thunder spirits and would cause thunderstorms. It was also believed that the cobs of green corn must be kept in the house for four days after the kernels were eaten because Selu's body remained on the ground for four days after she was killed by her sons.

"Selu" is the word for maize in the Cherokee language but it has no cognates in either Cherokee or any other language of the Iroquoian family. Selu cannot be a survival from the earlier Proto-Iroquoian language because corn was unknown when the northern and southern Iroquoian languages split apart around 2000 B.C. However, Hall points out that the word "selu" is strikingly similar to "silo" or "xilo," the root word of the Nahuatl word for "tender ear of green maize" and the name of the Mexican goddess Xilonen, who personified ears of green corn—that is, corn whose kernels have not yet hardened.

In the Mexican state of Puebla, where Fowler believes corn may first have been domesticated, a surrogate of the goddess Xilonen was sacrificed on a platform formed from the bodies of four men laid together. In preparation for the Mexican sacrifice a roaring fire was built of oak wood and allowed to burn continuously for four days, until a large bed of glowing coals, called the divine hearth, had accumulated.

An hour before dawn on the day of the sacrifice, Hall reports, the priests of the goddess gathered together the four male captives who were to become the sacrificial platform of the goddess. Taking one man at a time, the priests held each by the hands and feet, swung him four times toward the bed of hot coals, and with the fourth swing—four being a sacred number—let the captive plunge alive into the burning embers. Each victim was allowed to remain on the coals a fearful few moments before he was retrieved, still alive. The priests immediately placed him upon a sacrificial stone, opened his chest with a flint knife, and swiftly ended his misery by plucking the heart from his body. Thus prepared, the bodies of the four men were laid close together and on them the young girl representing Xilonen, the young corn goddess, was placed, her throat cut, and her heart extracted.

Both the American Indians and the Aztecs had stern prohibitions against eating any corn until the completion of the Green Corn festival. The Caddoan Indians of East Texas took the prohibition so seriously that, before their Green Corn ceremony, they tied their dogs' mouths shut and a hind leg to their necks so even they would be unable to violate the taboo.

The sacrifice of the Xilonen Green Corn maiden over the bodies of four men resonates at Cahokia, where the four headless and handless men were found in Mound 72, as well as at the Dickson Mounds Site in Fulton County, Illinois. One of the first burials the Indians placed in the Dickson cemetery was a deep mat-lined pit burial with four men who were laid on their backs, side by side. The four men were missing their heads, and four pots had been placed near where their heads would have been. Over the years the pit was opened numerous times and eight other individuals, male and female, were buried in a semiflexed position along with two additional bundle burials. Finally the long bones of eight adolescent and young adult males were added to the grave.

Hall suggests the four men in each of the two graves (Cahokia and Dickson Mounds) had significance not as individuals but as groups of four, a number universally significant to Indians of North America. Four represented the four cardinal directions or world quarters. A fifth direction, the center, was often added, which was the pattern of sacrifice of Xilonen, as represented by four men and one young woman.

Any one of the bodies superimposed over the four men in the Dickson Mounds burial, Hall suggests, could have represented the missing fifth element to complete the pattern of four plus one. Similarly, at Mound 72, while there was no maiden buried above the four headless and handless men, the burial episode belonged to the same construction as the adjacent grave of 53 young women believed by some to have been sacrificial victims.

In his analysis of the two sets of headless burials, Fowler speculates on their possible relationship to the political world. He notes that the four pots found with the men in the Dickson Mounds were of four distinct types and may represent the four parts of the world as perceived by the Indians of that section of the Illinois River Valley. The heads and hands from the Mound 72 burial may have been retained by the political unit of their origin as symbols of their ties to their home. Skulls often received deferential burial treatment in the Southeast. At the Jondro Mound a skull was found at the bottom of a six-foot-deep pit. The pit may have been a post pit and the skull a dedicatory offering, suggesting that heads may have been saved for burial during some ritual in their community of origin.

If the Green Corn ceremony did indeed come from Mexico, it would have to have come from the Toltecs and not the Aztecs. The Dickson Mounds and Mound 72 burials date no later than the early eleventh century A.D., 300 or more years before the Aztecs' reign. Aztec rituals were, in many cases, derived from the Toltecs, whose civilization dates from A.D. 900 to 1200 and so was contemporary with that of the Mississippian people of the North American Midwest.

During the decade of the 1990s a group of American Bottom scholars sought to construct a new synthesis of Cahokia archaeology through the use of social theory to explain the growth, life, and eventual decline of that impressive archaeological site. Earlier approaches had emphasized ecological and environmental causes. The new approach, while not totally discounting the effects of environmental degradation and climatic change, focuses much more closely on the role of political and religious organizations and leaders. Where, the scholars ask, did the power at Cahokia come from? How did the leadership maintain its control? Why did thousands of people, who appeared to be living well and relatively autonomously, agree to be governed by a central authority?

One investigator who has both raised and answered some of these questions is Timothy R. Pauketat, now a professor of anthropology at the University of Illinois at Urbana-Champaign.

Pauketat attended Belleville (Illinois) Township High School West, the same high school Perino had attended a generation earlier. Later, as a graduate student at Southern Illinois University at Edwardsville, Pauketat worked on the ICT-II excavation at Cahokia.

While a Ph.D. student at the University of Michigan, Pauketat undertook the analysis of Holder's notes and artifacts from the Kunnemann Mound excavation, which Holder's widow had given to the university. That work further refined his ideas about the sociology of Cahokia and led him to draw some assumptions about how politics and belief may have played a central role in the growth and decline of Cahokia.

It was obvious to Pauketat, as it had been to others, that sedentary communities of Native American farmers had lived in the floodplain of the Mississippi River for centuries. There was nothing extraordinary about that. What *was* extraordinary was the sudden social change that took place. Pauketat suggests that some of the local lords of Cahokia created their great city by managing the symbols of belief and getting enough people to give credence to those symbols that they could dominate the region. Ideology explained and made sense of their social and natural world.

In Pauketat's view, a group of Cahokia chiefs developed an ideology; expressed it though the production of craft items, ritual, exotic goods, and monumental architecture; and succeeded in dazzling the commoners of the region who flocked to the city to share in this new world order. These ascendant lords of Cahokia were not invaders. They had been in the American Bottom all along. But the ideology they developed, while it had roots in the Archaic past, was elaborated rapidly, and by 1050 it was fully defined and in place.

Major icons of the new belief system were the temples and their contents, symbols of the political and religious authority of the priests. The temples tied the populace to their ancestors and to the power of the natural world. The temple represented a dual order of being, in that events in this world reflected events in the world of supernatural forces. Priests of the temple stood at the frontier between the security of the new civilization and the monstrous destructive power of the underworld.

Sacred fires were kept burning in the temples day and night and annual rituals renewed and maintained the mounds. Members of the elite were continually reinforcing and expanding their princely authority by importing exotic goods through long-distance trade, by directing production of local craft goods, and by controlling esoteric knowledge such as the kind required for the building of a woodhenge.

The production center at Kunnemann Mound, which made a wide variety of craft goods, may have been under the control of the elite, who would have needed the craft output to exchange for foreign goods. Near Kunnemann Mound is where Perino discovered a high concentration of microdrills, used for drilling holes in shell beads. When that piece of land later came into the possession of the state, Southern Illinois University at Edwardsville conducted a massive surface collection. More than 1,500 20-by-20-meter blocks, covering approximately 148 acres, were marked off and collected. Blades, resharpening flakes, and the actual cores from the manufacturing of the drills were abundant in an area of about 3.7 acres, concentrated primarily near Mound 12, suggesting that the shell-bead manufacturing industry was confined to this particular Kunnemann area. Emerson suggests that Cahokia may have been a central production facility for fertility cult figures that were then distributed to centers in the American Bottom.

Most of the goods imported into Cahokia were, in fact, raw materials that were then transformed into products at Cahokia's workshops. Red flint clay, galena, hematite, Burlington and Mill Creek chert, diabase, and salt from the Missouri Ozarks were all transported to Cahokia and made into statuettes, pigments, tools, and ritual paraphernalia. People who lived at Kunnemann and other Downtown Cahokia precincts led favored lives. The faunal remains show that the residents were provisioned with choice cuts of meat that had been butchered elsewhere and brought into the central city.

The 17 or more buildings excavated on the top of the Kunnemann Mound had floor areas of 40 to 90 square meters each, far larger than any buildings in the rural areas or in the Lohmann- and Stirling-phase houses at the ICT-II or 15B tracts. The floors of the Kunnemann Mound houses were specially prepared with a black gumbo and then plastered with a red paintlike substance. Some floors had red, black, and yellow plaster. Every house had well-maintained hearths, some of which were lined with the same red plaster found on the floors. The sweat lodge on the Kunnemann Mound had four sequential hearths and may have had an earth-covered roof for heat retention.

In Pauketat's estimation, it was political and religious order that mediated the social order and social change at Cahokia. The sacred temples and mounds were shrines to the authority of the elite class. The commoners felt honored to perform work on the mounds and temples, directed, as they believed they were, by the emissaries of the gods. Mound building and renewal, ritual burials, even the distribution of exotic goods from far-off places, all contributed to the maintenance of social order. Pauketat noted that what was sacred to a commoner was the focus of competition to another aristocrat. Nobles competed to control the prestige goods, which were potent symbols of political power and tangible proof of their contacts outside the community. Much of Cahokia's power came from the simple fact that it was the first large population center in North America. That fact alone allowed it to set the pattern for later cultures in southeastern North America. While Pauketat does not believe Cahokia controlled an economic empire—as some have postulated, particularly in the northern hinterlands—Cahokia was so large that economic control was not necessary for it to have had a cultural impact far beyond its domain. What, he wonders, must have been the effect on outsiders of a metropolis with 10,000 to 20,000 people within the city proper and with thousands more in living in satellite communities throughout the American Bottom? Cahokia was North America's Rome, the center to which awe-struck pilgrims traveled miles to worship at the sacred eternal fires burning on the hilltops of the gods.

EIGHTEEN

Cahokia's Engineers and Builders

Whether Cahokia's core community had 15,000 or 20,000 residents may be relatively immaterial; its size and organization indicates that it was a very large and complex chiefdom—one well on its way to becoming a state.[1] One of the characteristics of a chiefdom is that the ruling chief and his associates gain control of the products created by people with special abilities, such as the potters and the skilled workers in stone, shell, and copper. Much like the Medici, who controlled the artistic output of Italy's great Renaissance painters and sculptors as a manifestation of their power, the chiefs of Cahokia ordained for themselves the work of the area's most skilled craftspeople.

Among the fine-art goods were the items of Ramey Incised pottery, which may have been used in special ceremonies and belonged only to the elite—analogous to the gold-rimmed china used by heads of state.[2] Other special goods were the beads, gorgets, and stone statuary manufactured in specialized workshops, such as the one in the Kunnemann Mound area.[3] One of the most striking examples of luxury goods produced for the elite are the projectile points found in large caches in Mound 72. These are far more finely made than any other points discovered at Cahokia. While some came from stone quarried in far-distant places, most were crafted from a kind of chert available from a quarry close to St. Louis and were probably produced at Cahokia. These points are so precisely and beautifully made that George Milner believes they were done by one master craftsperson, working under the patronage of a chief of Cahokia.

Many other skilled specialists, besides potters, beadmakers, and flint-knappers, were required to build the planned community of Cahokia. The

1. Brackenridge 1813; Gregg 1975; Milner 1986; Pauketat and Lopinot 1997.
2. Griffith 1981; Pauketat and Emerson 1991.
3. Holley 1990; Mason and Perino 1961.

massive constructions required the specialized services of people who today would be called engineers, astronomers, master builders, and city planners. At Cahokia their skills were intertwined with the belief system, the practical conjoined with the magical. As with all of Cahokia life, it is impossible to separate the occult from the everyday, the pottery making, engineering, and designing of the city from the principles of the cosmos as they were interpreted for the people by the priests and ancient watchers of the sky.

At the time of the first European contact with Native American societies, some were still maintaining many of their ancient practices, including reliance on an official known as a sky watcher, one of the most important officials of the community. Among the Hopi and Zuni of the Southwest, this official had the responsibility to observe the sunrise every day from a fixed location.[4] All the irregularities on the distant horizon were known to this priest and those geographical features that related to the passage of the sun were given names. Through daily observations of the position of the sunrise in relation to these named points, the Sun Priest would forewarn the people of significant dates in the passage of the year, such as the approaching solstices, so that the appropriate religious societies could prepare the necessary ceremonies.

Among the Natchez, of Louisiana, the principal chief was known as "The Sun" because he was believed to be a direct descendant of the sun.[5] He had the task of greeting the sun every morning at sunrise, making an offering of tobacco smoke to the four directions, and then, with a wave of his arm, showing the sun its path across the sky.

Neither the historic southwestern Hopi and Zuni nor the Natchez cultures were as complexly organized as Cahokia appears to have been. It seems likely that at Cahokia there was a class of sky specialists, priests of the sun, who used the post circle monuments, with the distant horizon as a fore sight, to measure the passage of time and alert the chiefs when special ceremonial activities should take place.

The Crab Nebula of A.D. 1054, a spectacular astronomical display that lasted for weeks, was recorded in ancient records of China and the Arab world and would have been observable from Cahokia. Although there is no evidence in the archaeological record of Cahokia that the phenomenon was noted, there are some petroglyphs in the southwestern U.S. that may refer to this event.[6] The appearance of Halley's comet in A.D. 1066 would have been noted by the sky

---

4. Forde 1934.
5. See the citation by Swanton (1911:174) of the French writer LePetit of the presence and actions of a Sun Chief among the Natchez.
6. Brandt et al. 1975.

watchers of Cahokia, perhaps with alarm, and may be the source of the forked-eye motif common in later Mississippian phases. Both of these uncommon celestial occurrences took place in the early formative years of Cahokia, when priests were preoccupied with the sky and when shrines were being built that codified cosmological concepts. Despite the lack of archaeological evidence it seems probable that these events would have had a major impact on the thinking of the leaders of that time.

Among the structures that illustrate the engineering skills of the early Cahokians were the post circle monuments, or woodhenges. The builders of these monuments showed a knowledge of practical geometry, units of measurement, and astronomy based on observations of the sun. One circle of large posts was constructed in the swampy area of the Cahokia site in relationship to Mound 72 sometime around A.D. 1000. A nearly identical woodhenge was built to the west of Monks Mound in Tract 15A a few decades later. When completed, these woodhenges measured 410 feet in diameter with 48 posts spaced at even intervals on the circumference of the circle. The posts were a little less than a meter in diameter and were set into the ground about two meters below the surface. There is no way to know if they were painted (there is some evidence that they may have been painted with red ocher) and carved, or otherwise ornamented. In none of the excavated post loci is there evidence that the woodhenge posts were left in place; instead, they were apparently removed and replaced several times.

Whether the posts were decorated or not, Woodhenge 72 and Woodhenge III must have been impressive monuments. The precisely spaced posts set off a circular area of over 40,223 square feet—or slightly over three acres—creating a dramatic visual effect that would have engendered the belief that this enclosed space was sacred, a monument of human workmanship setting aside special ground. A woodhenge surrounding sacred space would have created awe in the viewer, not only for the structure itself, but for the individual or group in Cahokian society that had garnered the resources and organized the work force to build such a monument.

While it is relatively easy to calculate the person hours needed to construct a woodhenge (each log weighed in the neighborhood of half a ton), there is no way to calculate the symbolic, ceremonial, and emotional investment in such an undertaking. How were the woodhenges planned, laid out, and constructed in the early eleventh century? There are some things Fowler can postulate from the archaeological data and others that he must guess at.

Drawing a circle on such a large scale could have been accomplished with a long rope pinned down to a center point. To do this, trees, shrubs, and other impediments would have to have been removed. While drawing the circle would have presented no problem to the ancient Cahokians, it was the plotting of the locations of the posts around the circumference that presented the real challenge. Since Woodhenge 72 and Woodhenge III are the same diameter, it is apparent that some concept of metrical units was utilized by early Cahokian engineers.

One suggestion is that a basic module of 47.5 meters was used by Cahokian and other Mississippian peoples of the Southeast.[7] This unit was worked out based on data from the Toltec archaeological site in Arkansas and was apparently used, in combination with astronomical sightings of the sun, in laying out the location of mounds and other important locations within the community. (This Toltec site should not be confused with the Toltec culture of Mexico. The Arkansas site, like Aztalan in Wisconsin, was given its name by early visitors to the American heartland who misunderstood the relationship of the Mesoamerican cultures with the midcontinent region.) If one assumes that the Toltec module was involved in the laying out of woodhenges at Cahokia, the radii of both 72 and III would be 1 ⅓ (1.33) times the 47.5-meter module.

It is reasonable to assume that, in actual practice, this module was divided into smaller, more manageable subunits. Based upon distances between mounds, sizes of woodhenges, and other factors, Wittry proposed a unit he called the "Cahokia yard" of 1.044 meters (3.42 feet) in length.[8]

Archaeologists and engineers at Teotihuacán in central Mexico have proposed a unit of 57 meters that was used in the laying out of that metropolis.[9] Fowler found that, based on multiples of three, both the Toltec and Teotihuacán modules could be reduced to a standard of 1.055 meters (3.46 feet) in length. This is very close to Wittry's Cahokia yard. If the two are averaged, they come out to a standard of 1.05 meters (3.44 feet). Thus, if the 47.5-meter Toltec module is divided by the modified Cahokia yard it comes out to very close to 45 units. If the Teotihuacán unit is divided by the same number it comes out to about 54 units. The common denominator of these two large units is closer to 1.055 meters than to Wittry's Cahokia yard.

None of this speculation can prove what the unit of measurement actually was in Cahokia times but it gets close to some sort of approximation. Present-day researchers must be cautious in applying contemporary standards of precision to ancient constructions. Nonetheless, one thing does seem certain: the woodhenge monuments were laid out with great precision and care. To build them, a detailed system of measurement would have been necessary, the measurement module would have to have been subdividable into more manageable

---

7. Rolingson 1996; Sherrod and Rolingson 1987.
8. Norrish 1978b.
9. Drewitt 1969; Millon 1973; Millon et al. 1965; Tompkins and Harleston 1978.

units for precision in measurement, and an understanding of ratios and proportions was required.

Another facet of Woodhenges 72 and III is the precise spacing of the poles around their circumferences. One of the first steps of the Cahokian planners in plotting the post locations would have been to establish the north-south and east-west axes that divide the circle into quadrants. Sighting Polaris from the established center point would establish the north orientation. The North Star makes a circular migration in the northern sky every 24 hours and the center of the circle is true north. Many Native American sky watchers knew the polar star pattern and used it for orientation and cosmological purposes. It is probable that the Cahokians also had this knowledge though they may have solved the problem of locating north by utilizing solar observations.

The annual movement of the sun across the horizon at sunrise is a phenomenon that has been recognized by peoples for countless centuries. Through the use of marker points on the eastern horizon and daily observations, groups such as the Hopi established a seasonal calendar. The most useful points are the sunrise points on and about the winter and summer solstices. At these times of the year, about June 21 and December 21, the sun comes up at nearly the same point on the horizon for several days in a row. Thus, two fixed points on the eastern horizon, indicating the outside limits of the solar movement, can be marked with fair accuracy. In the latitude of Cahokia, this is very close to an azimuth of 60 and 120 degrees. The horizon markers for each of these solstice points would have to be observed from each observation point.

As in modern surveying, a person standing at the center point of the proposed woodhenge would align a "rodman" standing on the circle's circumference with the horizon mark. Once on line, the rod person could mark a point at the measured radius. In this way three points in the circle would be established; the center; the summer solstice position, which in the latitude of Cahokia is slightly more than 30 degrees north of east; and the winter solstice position, 30 degrees south of east.

How accurate were the astronomical sightings in early Cahokia times? The 30-degree angle is actually accurate a little further south in Illinois. At Cahokia the precise angle is 30.8 degrees. However, we do not know what the Cahokians considered to be the sunrise. Was it when the first light of the sun appeared? Or was it when the full solar orb could be seen touching the horizon? The sun rises at an angle to the horizon in northern latitudes so that the position noted on the horizon would be different if the full orb, rather than the rays, was being observed. There is also the question of defraction of the sun's rays by the atmosphere.

It appears that the ancient astronomers had anticipated some of these problems. When Wittry discovered the center observation post of Woodhenge III he found that it was not at the geometric center, as he had expected, but was offset to the east just the right amount to observe the summer solstices at exactly 30.8 degrees.

In the latitude of Cahokia the two solstice sunrise points and the geometric center point form a nearly perfect equilateral triangle, the sides of which are the same as the radius. The east-west alignment at Cahokia could be obtained by utilizing the two solstice points established on the circumference of the circle. A line connecting these points would be a true north-south line. Marking a point halfway between the solstice points would define a point that, in conjunction with the center point, would define an east-west line. If Cahokia had been located a few degrees north or south, the triangle would not have been an equilateral one since the solstice alignments would not be near 30 degrees. This would not affect this method since half the distance between the solstice sunrise points would still define the east alignment. This east-west line could be pegged down at the radius by the surveyor's sighting along the point established and marking the point of intersection of that line and the circumference. The western counterparts of these three points on the circumference could be established by line-of-sight observations and measurements of the radius from the center point. The north-south line through the center could be quickly established by measuring half the distance between the summer solstice sunrise and sunset positions. This point would be on a true-north line with the center location. Another way of determining the north-south line would have been by noting that the winter solstice and summer solstice sunrise positions are on a true north-south line. By drawing a line parallel to the solstice north-south line through the established center point, the central north-south line could have been established.

By these simple geometric methods, points on the circumference and the center point of a woodhenge could have been established. The remaining number of points could have been marked by using methods based upon triangles or, once the circumference and the base points had been established, they could have been placed by simple measurement. Wittry thought that the intermediate points were not so carefully laid out and may just have been "eye-balled" as these are the posts that vary the most from the exact circumference and angular spacing. The solstice posts are the most precisely located. Any even number of posts could have been placed in circular patterns using these approaches, as was the case with the several woodhenges in the vicinity of Woodhenge III, all with even numbers of posts divisible by units of twelve.

Once the positions for the posts were marked, the next step would have been the excavation of the post pits and the installation of the posts. It could be said simply that the posts were placed in the ground by digging a deep hole wide enough to fit the post. But the hole into which a post was to be placed was actually a long trench with a shallow end and a deep end. In Post Pit 1, cribbing logs had been placed in the deep part of the pit to provide a solid base for the post as it slid down the ramp. The cribbing also provided a firm block for pivoting the post upright. After standing a post upright, workers packed earth around it to hold it in place. At Woodhenge III the original insertion ramps were all oriented in the same direction, along the radii of the circle, as if this were part of the planning and meaning of these pits.

At post pit 1 of Woodhenge 72, the only one of the five pits in that monument to have been excavated in detail, the original insertion ramp was oriented with its shallow end to the northwest of the deep post location. This orientation is parallel to the Beaded Birdman Burial, which was placed near the post pit sometime after the original construction of Woodhenge 72. At some later time, extraction ramps, which were about 90 degrees, or perpendicular, to the original insertion pit, were dug to remove the post. The process was repeated at least three times, two before the mound was built and at least once afterward.

The soil at Cahokia is incredibly difficult to work. Today's archaeologists, who find the sediments hard to excavate using steel-bladed implements, marvel at the deep holes dug by the Cahokians, who used deer scapulas and chipped stone hoes made of Mill Creek flint. The compact, dense, and tacky composition of the gumbo clays and the wetland nature of the area create major excavation problems. When there are heavy rains the excavations fill with water and undercut the walls of the pit. When the sediments are saturated they tend to flow en masse into the open pit. Water also tends to flow along the unconformities of the different sediments, tunneling out the seams and causing large blocks of intact sediments to collapse into open pits.

These problems must have also plagued the Cahokians a thousand years ago and created problems in the construction of their monuments. There is evidence of such calamities in the section views of their excavations. When the walls of the pits collapsed and the holes filled with flowing sediments, the Cahokians had no option but to dig new holes. These kinds of incidents probably account for the slight irregularities of post placement noted by Wittry.

Woodhenges were not built in a piecemeal fashion. Once conceived and designed, they were probably built as rapidly as possible. Key posts, such as the solstice and directional markers, may have had special significance and were built first. There was a dedicatory offering of a seed jar and some fabric and seeds near the base of Post Pit 1 in Woodhenge III, which is in the location of the summer solstice sunrise line. So far, none of the other pits has been excavated in sufficient detail to determine if this offering is an isolated or common practice.

Why did the ancient Cahokians build woodhenges and why was one built in the swampy Mound 72 area of greater Cahokia? The first interpretations of woodhenges at Cahokia suggested that they were astronomical or calendrical. By observing the sunrise along the posts and the distant bluff, Cahokian sky watchers could have predicted the coming of the solstices fairly accurately, as did the Hopi. By observing the turning points of the sun, they could control the sequence of community rituals and develop a sort of calendar, but not in the sense of determining and marking the exact number of days in the year.

They may also have used the shadows cast by the poles at sunrise and through the day as a way of measuring the progress of time seasonally, if not daily. The shadows cast at the summer solstice sunrise, all pointing to the southwest, would have been dramatic. The shadow from the summer solstice sunrise post would point directly at the center location and any post at the center would have cast a long shadow toward the winter solstice sunset position. Likewise, the shadow cast by the east post at the time of the equinox would have pointed directly at the center post. In this way the progression of shadows at sunrise could have served as a calendar marking the progression of the year.

The basic astronomical concepts implicit in woodhenges had been known for generations before woodhenges were built at Cahokia. It is probable that woodhenges were built at Cahokia as symbols of this information rather than as a means of determining it. The solar alignments that appear in the organization of woodhenges embodied important cosmological concepts of Native American religions and community organization. It is these symbolic aspects of astronomical phenomenon that were incorporated into woodhenge architecture.

So far, woodhenges have been found only at Cahokia. There may be several reasons for their absence from other Mississippian sites. Cahokia is unique in its size and the presence of large mounds. This one-of-a-kind nature of Cahokia may also extend to woodhenges. Another factor in the unique presence of woodhenges at Cahokia may be the coincidence of the solstice alignment at 30 degrees north or south of the east-west or equinox alignment. It is this solstice angle that allows the use of an equilateral triangle in the planning of a woodhenge. To the architect of a monument dedicated to the sun and its annual movement, such a coincidence could have had powerful and mystical significance. Only near the latitude of Cahokia does this particular combination of solar movement and geometry take place.

Post circle monuments may have had a role in the layout of the entire Cahokia site. Martha Rolingson, of the University of Arkansas and the Toltec Mounds State Monument, has proposed that Woodhenge III, the most completely excavated of the woodhenges, was an aligner—an instrument used for laying out the site and positioning the mounds. Rolingson was also responsible for the study that suggested a basic measurement module of 47.5 meters. She predicted that there would be a woodhenge near Mound 72 long before Fowler and his associates actually began to visualize one. The excavations at Woodhenge 72 have demonstrated the sagacity of her prediction. Rolingson also predicted another woodhenge aligner to the east near Mound 27, a prediction that probably can never be tested as this area is presently a housing subdivision.

Fowler's original north-south centerline of the Cahokia site runs through the sunrise solstice position of Woodhenge 72. In 1984, however, Wittry suggested that the actual north-south center line of Cahokia was probably to the west of Fowler's original proposal. Wittry's remark sent Fowler back to drawing lines.

The geometric center of Woodhenge 72 has been defined although no marker post has yet been found at that location. If the north-south center line ran true north from this geometric center spot it would intersect at a 90-degree angle a line running east from the geometric center of Woodhenge III. Both geometric centers are 974 meters from this point of intersection. If the east line from Woodhenge III were continued the same distance from the intersection point, it would fall right in the middle of the Mound 27 group, very near to the point Rolingson predicted. If the north line were extended the same distance from the intersection point, Fowler would propose a fourth post circle monument located just south of the Kunnemann Mound 10/11.

Could the planners of Cahokia have had in mind such a grand scheme—the creation of four woodhenges at the cardinal points with the center of this arrangement just to the southwest of Monks Mound?[10] As suggested in chapter 17, the Cahokian cosmos was envisioned as a great circle with an east-west axis representing the pathway of the sun. The north half of the circle represented the Sky World and the southern half represented the Earth World. This proposed location of post circle monuments encircling Downtown Cahokia could suggest that the master plan of Cahokia was a mirror of the cosmos. The mound groups near these four circle monuments could represent subchiefdoms tied into the cardinal directions.

In an analysis of Pawnee community organization, William Gartner[11] has pointed out that the placement of Pawnee villages in relation to each other was based upon the locations of significant stars in the heavens. Each village was named after a star or constellation. The location of the seat that the ritual leader from each village took in the ceremonial lodge was based upon replicating the stellar name and geographic position of his village. The concept of Monks

---

10. A similar cruciform pattern for Teotihuacán has been discussed by Rene Millon (1973:42–44).
11. Gartner 1996.

Mound as "the house in the center," proposed by Kelly[12] and based on Osage community organization and cosmology, thus takes on an even more potent meaning.

Fowler's proposal requires that Woodhenge 72 and Wittry's woodhenges existed at the same time. Present data indicates that Woodhenge III was built later than Woodhenge 72, the former in early Stirling times and the latter in the early Lohmann phase. However, data is accumulating that Woodhenge 72 was rebuilt two or three times, so it could have been contemporary with Woodhenge III.

The large circle defined by the known woodhenges and the proposed east and north locations encompasses not only Downtown Cahokia with the palisade but also the proposed inner ring of subcommunities. This concept of four post circle monuments placed equidistant from a center point near Monks Mound is similar to the concept of the four plazas surrounding Monks Mound. Both represent the idea that the community organization reflected the cosmos. Whether any of these hypotheses will ever be "proven" is a question. From the present data it is known that the Cahokians had the knowledge, the technology, and the ability to have accomplished this.

Dirt, a substance immediately at hand and extensively utilized, was the ubiquitous building material at Cahokia. All of the mounds and plazas were built from earth. These were not haphazard constructions but were planned with care. Huge areas were leveled by grading and filling to produce large flat plazas. Proper sediments were selected for specific purposes by construction specialists who had a clear understanding of the characteristics of their building materials. While wood was extensively used, it has not been preserved, and there is only scant evidence at the present time that stone was utilized in mound construction or to face the structures.

Dirt to build the mounds and plazas came from the huge borrow pits visible today at Cahokia and from many more that had been used earlier and then filled in. The soil was excavated with stone tools and carried by basket loads to the site of the building project. Where these basket loads are preserved they show up as oval concentrations of sediments of different colors—some dark, some light, some clayey, and some sandy. Early assumptions held that this was a hit-or-miss process and that the early workers had filled their baskets with whatever dirt was most easily available.

The process of mound building was in fact deliberate and planned. If a mound was made of black fill, the builders, for social and sacred reasons, intended it to be black. At the Mitchell site Porter found that what he thought was a mound turned out to be a stockpile of carefully graded clay. It is apparent that

---

12. Kelly 1996.

when it came to building with dirt, the Cahokians knew their material and how to work with it.

The platform mounds were built to provide a base for public and elite buildings. The higher the platform the more outstanding and visible would be the building on its summit. The trouble with piling up earth to make the platforms is the "angle of repose." In building a vertical side to a platform, one can go only so high before the side will slide and collapse into a sloped surface. This is the angle of repose. The ancient Cahokians understood the principal of the angle of repose and developed strategies to cope with it. They discovered that the angle was different for different mound shapes and for different sediments and built their mounds accordingly.

Conical mounds retain their shape better than platform mounds. The Cahokia builders preserved their mounds by covering them with a material that resists slumpage. Some of the smaller mounds, such as Mound 72Sub1, were covered with specially prepared mixtures of clay and sand to make an erosion-resistant surface. Mound 72Sub1 had such a covering, which was then painted with a white clay wash to give it a uniform white surface. The durability of the clay cap was demonstrated during the excavations of Mound 72Sub1 when it was left exposed for weeks. Fowler was surprised to see that even torrential downpours did not affect the surface.

Caldwell had found similarly prepared surfaces in Mound 31, as did Fowler in 1997 when his students cut into Mound 96. They encountered a specially prepared black clay surface that was highly resistant to excavation with pick axes and sharpened steel shovels. The hard black cap of this low mound was so durable that it had resisted erosion, the natural soil formation process, and the footsteps of humans for a thousand years and was recognizable from the contours of the mound's surface, which had the same shape as the clay cap below.

The large mounds were probably once plastered with the same clay substances, but those surfaces would have been less resistant to the pressures of gravity and water accumulation within the mound itself. On Monks Mound, however, the Cahokia engineers recognized these problems and designed ways of coping with them.

Monks Mound was built early in the history of Cahokia as a series of platforms, each larger than and covering its predecessor, reaching nearly to the height observable today.[13] It was probably a high, steep-sided structure. Woods's investigations have revealed that, internally, the base of the mound is composed

---

13. Much of the following discussion of Monks Mound and the Grand Plaza is based upon fieldwork conducted by archaeological crews from Southern Illinois University at Edwardsville under the direction of William I. Woods. Interpretations are also based upon interviews and discussions with Woods. However, Woods is not responsible for any errors of interpretation that may have occurred in our writing.

of a clay platform six to seven meters high. Water was pulled up into the mound by capillary action to a height of up to ten meters, which kept the smectite clays in the core in a perennially expanded condition providing excellent support for the enormous weight above it. Above the core, massive fill units were constructed with their upper surfaces sloping to the exterior. Woods is convinced that the building of the main body of Monks Mound was directed by a single engineer who had a remarkable understanding of materials and how to work with them. The internal drains this unknown builder constructed into the mound are still functioning, as Woods discovered in 1998 when he drilled into one and water, under pressure from the weight of the mound, shot out as from an artesian well. Woods believes the later additions to the mound lacked the skilled direction demonstrated by its original builder.

The early builders may have had angle-of-repose problems as a second terrace was soon added, and, thereafter, the first terrace. While the terraces may have been added for architectural reasons, they also served as buttresses to prevent the slumping of the original mound. In Bareis's 1970s excavation on the first terrace, he found that it was built with a series of hard clay ridges that served as the main buttressing structure for the south side of the mound. The deep ditches between the ridges were partially filled with coarse, gravely material before being fully filled and the surface leveled. The ditches served as drains to siphon off the buildup of water inside the mound. This cleverly designed portion of the mound both reinforced the sloping side and also relieved the hydrostatic pressure that could lead to collapse. Today, using modern technology, engineers are using the same approach to protect the mound from further collapse.

In March 1998, engineers drilling drainage holes into the side of Monks Mound made a startling discovery. They hit a layer of rock at least 32 feet long inside the mound. The layer of rock lies about 40 feet beneath the surface of the second terrace and nearly 140 feet into the mound. The size of the rock layer is unknown and even the 32-foot dimension is an estimate based on the fact that a $5,000 "smart drill" passed through 32 feet of stone before the drill bit broke off and was lost. Woods and Iseminger speculate that the rock structure may be made of slabs of limestone. The find was totally unexpected as stone was not believed to have been used for a construction material by the Cahokians. The nearest source of limestone is approximately 10 miles south of the site.

In late July 1998, geologists from Southern Illinois University, Edwardsville, using a magnetometer, discovered two additional anomalies in the second terrace. These may be buried walls attached to the stone layer 20 to 30 feet below them or possibly part of yet another structure. One of the anomalies is 6.5 feet south of the stone layer and the other ranges from 65 to 82 feet further south. Woods hopes to use hand coring with an auger on the northern "wall" in an attempt to determine what it is. Working with an auger at a depth of 25 feet (15 feet above the layer of stone), Woods hit a layer of coarse material, presumably one of the groundwater drains of sandy loam alternating with layers of clay that the architect of the mound had incorporated into the original construction.

Because excavation of the find could lead to structural problems in the mound, seismic waves and electromagnetic impulses will be used to learn the size and shape of the rock construction. Robert Hall noted that James Porter had encountered a layer of hard blue-black clay at the same 40-foot depth on Monks Mound when he had been coring the mound in 1964.

Another major building project at Cahokia was the construction of the Grand Plaza in conjunction with the building of Monks Mound. This was probably the most massive undertaking of all, requiring techniques of insuring a level surface as well as calculations of grading and filling. It also required that the builders have a grand overall vision of what Cahokia, the city, should be like.

All of these projects indicate that early Cahokia contained specialists who were involved in the planning of the community. They had knowledge of geometry, mensuration, and building materials and an overall community vision. The principles guiding their work were cosmological. The resulting city, built by these engineers, was a reflection of the universe as they knew and understood it.

NINETEEN

The Outposts of Cahokia

By the end of the first millennium Cahokia had become an immense presence in the valley of the Mississippi. Like a boulder falling into a lake, Cahokia sent shock waves throughout the heart of a continent already populated with diverse groups of people. Responses to the growing power of Cahokia and its expanding needs and influence differed from group to group as each came to terms in its own way with the startling phenomenon on the American Bottom.

One of the major regions of Cahokian influence was in the culturally complex northern area that extended from an east-west line connecting the cities of Kansas City, St. Louis, and Cincinnati all the way north to the Straits of Mackinac. Residents of this broad area, which included parts of present-day Iowa, Minnesota, Wisconsin, and Michigan, were practicing a way of life known as Woodland—a successor culture of the earlier Hopewell. The Woodland culture extended over a large section of northeastern United States, all the way to the Atlantic.

The differences between the Woodland peoples and the Mississippians were significant. The Mississippians were farmers who grew corn on fertile alluvial plains near rivers.[1] They established planned communities of different types, including regional centers, ceremonial locations, hamlets, and farms. They traded with peoples who lived outside their region and, as their population increased, they developed a complex religious-political governance system.

The Woodland peoples to the north of Cahokia lived on the periphery of the Mississippians' sphere of influence. Though they grew a few food items, they were principally hunters and gatherers, people who were highly mobile and who relied, in their lifestyle, on being able to move freely over long distances. Their

---

1. Smith 1975, 1978, 1985.

success depended upon the free flow of information regarding the seasonal availability of foods, the locations and activities of other Woodland groups, and the timing and locations of ceremonial gatherings. They were involved in the movement of finished goods as well as raw materials such as copper and special stone for tools, and they also may have traded foodstuffs and animal skins. The Woodland people were a sophisticated group who, overall, developed one of the more successful prehistoric adaptations in North America.

Woodland culture was far from monolithic. Regional variations abounded as groups adopted innovations from their neighbors, adjusted to the peculiarities of their local geography and climate, and constantly moved across a five-state region.

The Woodland people who occupied the territory north of Cahokia in what is now northeast Iowa, southeast Minnesota, southern Wisconsin, and northern Illinois were members of the Woodland Effigy Mound tradition,[2] who left more than 10,000 effigy mounds shaped like animals, birds, and geometric figures scattered over the landscape. The mound sites marked places where the Effigy Mound people periodically gathered together to look for spouses, to feast, to renew ties, and to exchange goods and information.

Besides their effigy mounds, these Woodland people left behind a distinctive pottery, called "collared ware," named for the distinctive collars on the pots. The pottery was tempered with grit and the surface was marked with cords in a distinctive and easily recognizable style. This Effigy Mound Woodland pottery has been found in northern sites dating from A.D. 300 to approximately A.D. 1000.

Around the beginning of the second millennium, a new kind of pottery appeared in the Woodland sites, pottery that looked very much like Mississippian. The collared Woodland pottery was still present, but this new material had arrived and it bore a startling resemblance to pottery from Cahokia. How could this be explained?

All societies that are in contact with each other eventually exchange materials, items, and ideas. If two societies are in long-term contact and are at different economic and technological levels, modifications will be introduced into the material culture of the less-developed society. It was obvious to archaeologists that a new development was taking place in the northern hinterland. Almost by accident, they gave this new development the name "Oneota." A geologic formation in Iowa is called the "Oneota formation," and the upper Iowa River in northeast Iowa was, for a time, also called the Oneota. When an archae-

---

2. For one point of view regarding the relationships of Mississippian to Effigy Mound culture, see discussion by Hurley (1974).

ologist first collected from sites in the area he called them "Oneota" sites and the name stuck—later to be applied to the entire cultural development.[3]

It was hard to define the Oneota people. They seemed to share characteristics with both the Effigy Mound Woodland and the Emergent Mississippian peoples. No one was quite sure who they were or just where they had come from. While they were hunter-gatherers like the Effigy Mound people, they were more focused on growing maize than were the Woodland people and they made a different kind of pottery—a smooth-surfaced grit- or shell-tempered ware. While their early pottery was quite plain, as time went on it became heavily decorated with motifs that were clearly related to those of the Mississippians. The Oneota were also more territorial than the Woodland Effigy Mound people had been and they established palisaded villages from Iowa to the Upper Peninsula of Michigan and up the south shore of Lake Superior.

Where did the Mississippian traits come from? James Griffin was among the first to suggest migration as an explanation. He gave a paper in 1960 stating that the Oneota developed as a result of Mississippians from Cahokia migrating north around A.D. 1000. He suggested that the Lohmann and Stirling phases at Cahokia were the source of disaffected social groups that either moved north on their own or splintered off from other large migrating entities.[4]

Griffin based his migration hypothesis on the widespread distribution in Minnesota and Wisconsin of Powell Plain and Ramey Incised pottery, the latter an elite Cahokia product. He took these pottery forms as markers of the culture that had crystallized within the American Bottom by A.D. 1000, the elements of which were maize agriculture, platform-mound construction, wall-trench houses, social stratification, tri-notched triangular projectile points, and shell-tempered pottery.

Griffin's view was later challenged and largely dismissed when radiocarbon dates appeared to place the beginning of Oneota earlier, around A.D. 900, which meant that the Oneota would have developed on a parallel track with Cahokia and could not be derived from it, as Griffin had argued.

That is where matters stood, with most archaeologists in agreement with the early Oneota development theory, until James Stoltman of the University of Wisconsin, Madison, challenged it. Stoltman was working on a midden site in the Mississippi Valley when a local collector approached and asked him to look

---

3. There is a great deal of discussion of the origins, development, and historic affiliation of the Oneota culture. Among these are: Brown 1982; Dobbs 1983; Dobbs and Shane 1983; Gallagher 1985; Gallagher and Stevenson 1983; Gibbon 1970, 1972, 1995; Griffin 1995; Henning 1971; Hurley 1974; Milner and Emerson 1984; Overstreet 1978; Peske 1966; Rodell 1999; Tiffany 1983; Wedel 1959.
4. Griffin 1960.

at an Oneota site he had found. They were in Grant County in southwest Wisconsin and Stoltman did not believe there were any Oneota sites in that area.[5]

Stoltman told the collector he would come when he had a chance, but he was in no rush to visit the site and eventually forgot about it. However, the collector did not forget. When Stoltman failed to respond to his invitation, the collector brought a potsherd to him and put it in his hand. When Stoltman looked at the piece the man had given him, he saw he was holding a rim of a piece of shell-tempered Ramey Incised pottery.

"Whoops," he said. "Let's go see this Oneota site." The collector took him to what was to become known as the Fred Edwards site in southwestern Wisconsin, about ten miles up the Grant River. The site was not Oneota, as the collector had supposed, but a Woodland site with major Mississippian elements in it. Everything about the site was nonlocal. There was no Oneota or Effigy Mound pottery there. Instead, what stood out were Stirling-period Mississippian sherds mixed in with non–Effigy Mound Late Woodland. The Fred Edwards site had no mounds but the village had a palisade. Radiocarbon dates for the village clustered around the period A.D. 1050–1150.

For a symposium in Red Wing, Minnesota, in the 1970s, Stoltman looked at all the radiocarbon dates at all the Mississippian and Oneota sites in the upper Mississippi Valley and found that, while there were a few dates in the A.D. 900 range, almost all the dates clustered around A.D. 1000 or younger. Arguing that the margin for error in radiocarbon dating is wide, Stoltman basically threw out the few A.D. 900 Oneota dates, believing them to be suspect, and came to the conclusion that there were no Oneota in existence anywhere before A.D. 1000. Not everyone was in agreement, but if Stoltman was right, the implications would be dramatic.

To buttress his argument Stoltman pointed out that the appearance of the Oneota at A.D. 1000 coincides with the disappearance of the Woodland Effigy Mound Builders, who depart from the archaeological scene at the very same time. There is nothing after A.D. 1100 that is Late Woodland. Where did the Effigy Mound people go? The answer Stoltman suggests is that the Effigy Mound people transformed themselves into the Oneota. What inspired that epic cultural change? Cahokia.

There was no single mechanism for this transformation along the northern frontier of Cahokia. It happened in a multitude of ways and with varying results. The most dramatic of these transformations occurred at a site called Aztalan in south-central Wisconsin. Aztalan got its name from the first Europeans who came to the area in the 1830s. The settlers had read Alexander von

---

5. Stoltman 1991, 1999; Stoltman ed. 1991.

Humboldt's account of the Aztecs and when they saw the pyramid-shaped mounds at the site they erroneously assumed these had been built by Aztecs who had somehow wandered up to Wisconsin from Mexico.

Aztalan was settled by Woodland people.[6] Some archaeologists believe they came from northern Illinois while others say they were already in Wisconsin.[7] Wherever they came from, the founders of Aztalan were Woodland makers of collared pottery, were semimigratory, and had probably made their way up the Mississippi River to the Rock River in Wisconsin and from the Rock to the Crawfish. An ideal settlement site on the Rock River would have been on the shores of Lake Koshkonong. Despite its attraction as a village location, the bands of migrating Woodland people did not stop there but continued on up the Rock River to the mouth of the Crawfish and followed that stream 20 miles northwest to what became their town site.[8]

The village of Aztalan was located just to the south of the boundary between the northern hardwood region and the southern prairie-forest floristic area. To the north it is relatively cool and moist and to the south it is warmer and drier. The southern zone averages 160 frost-free days a year and the soil is fertile. Between the Crawfish and the Rock River is an oak, maple, and basswood forest and to the west is oak with marshes throughout the region.

Archaeologists have long speculated on why the Woodland founders of Aztalan passed up Lake Koshkonong as a settlement site. John Richards, of the University of Wisconsin, Milwaukee, believes Koshkonong was bypassed because the area was already occupied by the Effigy Mound Builders, whose dense clusters of mounds ring the lake. When the incoming Woodlanders saw the Effigy Mound Builders in possession of the lake shores, Richards believes, they simply moved on.

The Woodland people of Aztalan and their Mississippian neighbors to the south had a symbiotic relationship. Since farming and seminomadic hunting occupy different niches in the ecological system, the two groups were not in competition with each other and could afford to be cooperative. The Mississippians benefited from the exchange of goods and information with the northern Woodland people and may even have depended on them as a source of valuable raw materials from the north.

Richards speculates that it was easier for Mississippians to rely on Woodland wanderers who were already moving through the countryside to bring copper down from the Lake Superior region than it was for them to make the

---

6. McKern 1946; Goldstein 1991.
7. Goldstein and Richards 1991; Richards 1992.
8. Goldstein 1991; Kelly 1991a, 1991b.

long trek up there themselves. There is evidence that the Mississippians took full advantage of this ready-made Woodland network of trade and information exchange. Richards believes that the initial northern spread of Mississippian goods, ideas, and even people was conducted over the previously established Late Woodland channels.

By A.D. 1000, two Woodland groups, the Effigy Mound Woodlanders at Lake Koshkonong and the Woodland community on the Crawfish River, were living in close proximity in central Wisconsin. There is strong evidence that the two groups did not get along. The Aztalan people's requirement for freedom of movement and communication with other groups may have conflicted with the more settled agricultural lifestyle of the Effigy Mound people, who were culturally changing into the territorially minded Oneota. Or the Effigy Mound–Oneota community may have threatened the sophisticated exchange and trade network the Woodlanders had developed with the Mississippians. Whatever the source of the conflict, it was there.

Richards suggests that communication went back and forth between Aztalan and Cahokia, causing the leadership at Cahokia to believe that their northern network of information and goods was being threatened. As a result they took steps to protect it. Cahokia's response to the Effigy Mound–Oneota threat was to send a group of Cahokians up to Aztalan to support and, in the process, reorganize the community. Within a brief period of time, the Cahokians transformed the existing Woodland village on the banks of the Crawfish River into a typical American Bottom temple town in every detail, including a Cahokia-style high log palisade with bastions.

Richards bases this scenario on his excavations of a large midden or garbage dump on the Aztalan site. At the bottom of the dump he uncovered layers of grit-tempered, collared Woodland pottery along with the ashes from cooking fires and other domestic refuse. The earliest radiocarbon date from the bottom of the midden pile was A.D. 850. As Richards worked his way up through the pile he suddenly encountered, without any kind of transformative stage, full-blown, mature, shell-tempered Cahokia ceramics. Some of the Cahokia pottery was what is called "signature ware"—a kind found only at Cahokia. Moreover, he did not find just a few pieces of Cahokia-style pottery. He found the full range of Cahokia ceramic production, more than has been found at any other site outside of Cahokia itself.

After about A.D. 1050, the garbage dump was converted into a house site and a Cahokia-style wall-trench house was built over the dump. Richards asked himself what would cause people to build a house over what, for decades, had been a large trash heap. He decided that it was because people were moving closer together, into the center of town, and becoming more formally organized.

Houses that had earlier been scattered about the site, located at long distances from each other, were moved closer together into tight little neighborhoods. Large mounds and public plazas were constructed and less space was available for scattered housing. Then the log palisade with bastions similar to those at Cahokia was erected around the town. Starting at the beginning of the Stirling phase, newcomers from Cahokia brought about a quick and massive transformation at Aztalan. It was to last about one hundred years, until around A.D. 1120.

In Richards's opinion, the changes made in Aztalan were an implicit but determined political declaration to the Effigy Mound–Oneota people from the lords of Cahokia that they would defend their frontier. He does not believe that those who journeyed up from Cahokia were a military garrison as such. It may have been a kinship group. Chiefdoms, even those as complex as the one at Cahokia, could not muster the manpower to launch a major offensive.

The newcomers from Cahokia probably came to Aztalan as permanent colonists. Whatever their guise, it is evident that a group came to Aztalan from Cahokia with the express purpose of taking Aztalan's side against their enemies at Lake Koshkonong. Their efforts quickly transformed the Woodland community into a fortified Cahokian temple town.

For whatever reason, there were now two distinct warring camps, the Effigy Mound–Oneota and the Woodland-Cahokia alliance that had been forged at Aztalan. As evidence that these two neighboring groups were not interacting in a friendly way, Richards notes the complete absence of Oneota-style pottery within Aztalan and the corresponding absence of any Middle Mississippian pottery in the Oneota settlements at Lake Koshkonong or at nearby Carcajou Point. The two groups were obviously not sharing neighborly hot dishes. The stage was set for war.

There is ample evidence of conflict. The palisade at Aztalan was burned down at least twice and curious fragments of human bones have been found in nonburial contexts, suggesting the torture of captives. While there is no way to deduce from the archaeological record the flow of battle, it is apparent that, over the short term, the Mississippians at Aztalan were the victors. As evidence of this, Richards refers to some startling radiocarbon dates for the Oneota settlements in southeast Wisconsin.

The early dates range from A.D. 900 to 1020. There are no more radiocarbon dates at the Oneota sites until A.D. 1140. For a little over a hundred years the Oneota left no evidence of any occupation of southeast Wisconsin. Richards believes the Oneota were defeated by the people from Aztalan and, as a result, left the Lake Koshkonong area to move up the Fox River passage, where they formed other strong settlements.

The corresponding radiocarbon dates for the occupation of Aztalan by its

Cahokia allies are from A.D. 1050 to 1130—the same period of time when the Oneota are absent. After 1150 the Mississippian presence at Aztalan abruptly declines and the Oneota reappear at their old town locations. By A.D. 1250 Aztalan had been abandoned, its demise coming at the same time a sharp decline takes place at Cahokia. In Richards's opinion, with the political and economic changes at Cahokia and the decline of the Cahokian exchange network, Aztalan lost its reason for being and rapidly disappeared.

Not all archaeologists agree with Richards. While he sees the Aztalan-Mississippian relationship as one involved with an exchange of information, others place more emphasis on the exchange of goods. Many believe that the location of Mississippian sites on the northern frontier was neither sporadic nor random but was intentional, providing immediate access to major routes of communication and exchange. Fowler suggests that the Crawfish River site of Aztalan may have been chosen because, with only a short portage, there is access to the Lake Superior region where copper could be obtained.

Aztalan and the Fred Edwards site are the only genuine Cahokia outposts to have been identified as yet on the northern frontier. The sites of Diamond Bluff (also called Moro), Wisconsin, and Red Wing, Minnesota,[9] across the Mississippi River from each other, show extensive Mississippian influence but not enough, in the mind of University of Minnesota archaeologist Clark Dobbs, to suggest actual colonization from the south.

The Red Wing area contains more than 2,000 mounds and earthworks, the largest concentration of mounds in the upper Mississippi Valley. The mounds range from six to forty feet in diameter with heights of from three to ten feet. Some were effigy mounds, built in the shape of birds, wolves, or lizards; others have the familiar cone shape.

The locations of the Red Wing–area mounds, and hundreds more that have since disappeared, were mapped in the 1880s due to the extraordinary efforts of two bachelors living in St. Paul, Minnesota. Alfred Hill had been born in London in 1823. He came to the United States in 1854 and settled for a brief time in Red Wing before moving to St. Paul. A civil engineer who worked in the land office in St. Paul, Hill became fascinated by the mounds he saw about him and used his land office contacts to systematically gather information about them. When, in 1881, he met a young surveyor, Theodore Hayes Lewis, Hill began his project to survey and map all of the mounds in an eleven-state area north of Cahokia.

For the next fourteen years, until Hill's sudden death of typhoid in 1895, Lewis surveyed mounds and earthworks in what became the most extensive

---

9. Dobbs 1983; Dobbs and Shane 1983; Gibbon 1995; Rodell 1991, 1999.

archaeological activity privately initiated and supported in the entire United States. Hill paid Lewis three dollars a day and his expenses to find and survey mounds. Lewis found 2,000 village sites containing 17,000 mounds. More than 7,700 were in Minnesota alone. Lewis traveled more than 54,000 miles, 10,000 of them on foot. Among Lewis's records are 40 leather-bound books of field notes, 100 plots of mound groups, 800 plots of effigy mounds, 50 plots of village sites, more than 100 tissues of petroglyph rubbings, as well as bound record books and 1,000 letters from Lewis to Hill.

Red Wing was an environmentally rich area. The Cannon River and a number of small streams empty into the Mississippi at this location, replenishing the soil with nutrients and creating habitat for water fowl. Wild rice once grew in abundance.

There is another geographic distinction to the Red Wing area. Like Cahokia, it is located on a major delta of the Mississippi River. The rich bottomland at Red Wing, created by the receding shoreline of Lake Pepin (a widening of the Mississippi River created by the delta of the Chippewa River), extends over several square miles and is ideal soil for growing corn, the signature crop of the Mississippians.

The Red Wing mound area was an early regional gathering place for family-based clans that would congregate at certain times of the year for feasting, rituals, and the exchange of goods. Many of the mounds contain burials, and the bones of those who died elsewhere were probably carried in for burial in the sacred mounds. Over time the mounds grew larger and larger, suggesting that this was a major site where extended family groups and clans would gather for potlatch-type observances. The number and density of the mounds suggest that there had to have been a great deal of political activity going on. Archaeologist Roland Rodell suggests that some of the mounds could have been built to commemorate gatherings and to serve as territorial markers. In the absence of writing, they would have been graphic statements that everyone could interpret. The mounds may also have been adorned with sticks and feathers.

The dramatic changes ushered in at the beginning of the second millennium strongly affected the area around Red Wing, Diamond Bluff, and Lake Pepin. New people—traders, hunters, or migrant families—began to move in from the south. These new people established relationships with the northerners and brought with them new ideas and technologies, making Red Wing a major conduit for the transmission of Mississippian influences up the Mississippi Valley. The Effigy Mound people, who had been coming to Red Wing to enact their ceremonies for centuries, now came to learn about the new magic, to be taught new ways of making pottery, and to learn new ways to grow food. They gravitated to Red Wing, Silvernail, and Diamond Bluff and once they arrived found that they did not have to leave again. The new technologies they had learned allowed them to stay. Rodell believes change came rapidly, perhaps even within an individual's lifetime.

Though the Effigy Mound peoples had grown small plots of corn as early as A.D. 400 as a ritual grain, similar to the use of tobacco, under the tutelage of the Cahokians they now intensified their maize horticulture, planting vast fields on the bottomland and leaving traces of it in carbon 13 in their bones. They adopted new styles of pottery, tempering it with mussel shells from the river. The new pottery incorporated themes from Mississippian ideology, in particular the curvilinear falcon image, which is associated with aggression and warrior cults. The new larger, rounder, thinner-walled pots could take more heat and stress and did not break up as readily when used over a cooking fire. Many of the new ceramic items look very much like the pottery from Cahokia. As Dobbs put it, "You could throw some of the [Red Wing] pottery down in Cahokia and the people would say, 'Boy, that is kind of odd, but it's still Cahokia.' The pottery would fit. It has the rolled rim, the sharp shoulders." At the Energy Park site near Red Wing, Minnesota, Dobbs's crews found a projectile point whose form was similar to that of points found in Mound 72.

In Dobbs's view the Red Wing region is unique in the upper Mississippi Valley. "If you want to look for Mississippian stuff in the upper valley, you go to Red Wing and there it is," he says. "There are 400 sites, eight major villages and a whole constellation of smaller ones." While everyone agrees that the Mississippian influence is present, they are not in agreement on how it got there. Was there an infusion of colonists from Cahokia, as took place at Aztalan and Fred Edwards? Or was the influence indirect?

Both Dobbs and Guy Gibbon, of the University of Minnesota, argue against the concept of a substantial Middle Mississippian migration into the Red Wing locality while Tom Emerson argues just as forcefully in favor of it. What is certain is that there *was* contact between the Red Wing area and Cahokia. A group of projectile points made from Hixton silicified sandstone from near Red Wing was found in Mound 72. As Griffin wrote in a postcard to Rodell, "I still think the Mississippians were moving up there and interacting with the local yokels."

Dobbs has the view that Mississippian culture as a whole developed as an adaptation to a specific environmental condition—namely, the floodplain valleys of the Mississippi River and some of its tributaries. These locations were ideal for growing massive amounts of corn. It was this intensification of corn agriculture that led to other ideological and technological changes, changes that moved upriver from Cahokia to the delta corn growers around Red Wing. The rivers had been the Indians' highways for hundreds of years. While Dobbs questions the idea of trade, in the sense of the capitalist model that the word implies, he agrees there had to have been some sort of exchange of goods between Cahokia and the villages around Red Wing.

Though the northerners adopted many traits of the people from Cahokia, in significant ways they maintained their differences. Contrasting lifeways existed simultaneously. Some villages, such as Bryan and Diamond Bluff, were palisaded and obviously occupied year round, while others remained seasonal camps. The mounds were not built around plazas, as they were at Cahokia, but were arranged in semicircles, like doughnut halves, and located outside and on the landward side of the villages. While the Red Wing ceramics echoed the styles of Cahokia, suggesting that Cahokia's symbols of power and authority had been adopted by Red Wing chiefs, many elements differed markedly from those at Cahokia. Oneota and Late Woodland ceramics are mixed with Cahokia-style pottery, and Ramey designs show up on Woodland pots.

It is Stoltman, who began his career as a geologist, who has brought the most precision to the study of Cahokian ceramics.[10] He has revived the technique of thin-sectioning ceramics to determine their mineral content, not as a means of physically describing them so much as to use the information to resolve cultural problems of interaction. The study of Cahokia and its relationship with its hinterland was a natural application for the thin-section technique.

In this process, a thin slice of a potsherd is mounted on a glass slide and put on a special stage of a microscope, where light is passed through it. The minerals present, the characteristics of the clay, and the kind of temper used can all be identified. This has allowed Stoltman to distinguish locally made pottery from imports and to identify pottery made in Cahokia from imitations produced elsewhere. When he examined the Cahokia-style pottery at the Fred Edwards site, he found that though the shape conformed to the Powell Ramey vessel forms, the pottery had been tempered with grit. When he took samples of the local soils and local pottery, he found the same grit tempering, indicating that most of the Cahokia-style pots were locally made imitations. Nevertheless there were also some genuine Cahokia pots at Fred Edwards. The Stoltman tests in the Red Wing and Diamond Bluff areas revealed that almost all the pottery found there had been locally made but the shapes were imitations of the Powell and Ramey forms. Stoltman found that while the local pottery contained from 15 percent to 20 percent silt, the imported pottery from Cahokia had almost no silt and was shell tempered.

When Stoltman studied the pottery at Aztalan he found a complicated pic-

---

10. Stoltman 1989, 1991.

ture. Side by side there were examples of locally made Woodland pottery, imitations of Mississippian pottery with a grit temper, Mississippian imitations made with shell temper, and genuine Cahokia imported pots.

While he was working on the thin sections of pottery Stoltman decided to compare his microscopically derived analysis with pottery that had been analyzed by the legendary Griffin. He had once asked Griffin how he could determine locally made pottery from that made in Cahokia and Griffin had replied, "By the amount of shell temper." When Stoltman tested pottery Griffin had identified, he found that James Griffin, just by eyeballing the pot sherds, had been almost 100 percent accurate in his analysis.

As the pottery indicated, life in the North was a kind of blend. The people were not as bound by class and hierarchy as were those in Cahokia. In Cahokia the residents conformed to their proscribed social positions, defined as they were by their relationships to the chiefs and nobles. Red Wing, by contrast, was on the frontier and the people had all the freedom that frontiers afford their residents. The pottery shows more variety of decoration and the people demonstrated greater elasticity in their evolving uses of the landscape and its resources.

Whatever the process for the exchange of goods and ideas that took place between Cahokia and villages in the northern river valleys, it is probable that Cahokia instigated the interaction and dictated the terms of the trade. Among the northern sites that may have experienced direct contact with Cahokia were Eveland and Mills in central and northwest Illinois, Steed Kisker in western Missouri, Red Wing and Lake Pepin in Minnesota, and Aztalan and Trempealeau in Wisconsin. Other sites may have exchanged more objects and influence than people.

About 80 miles south of Red Wing is the city of La Crosse, Wisconsin, and the archaeological site of Trempealeau. Unlike so many archaeological sites that were lost to farming operations, this site still exists because it is on a narrow bluff not suitable for building or farming. It also survived because its owner, George Squire, whose family had the property from 1860 to 1920, was interested in geology and natural history. Squire went to Harvard in the late 1870s and came back to farm and study the mound on his property. He mapped it three times (it is a Middle Mississippian three-tiered platform mound), corresponded with the state historical societies in Wisconsin and Minnesota, and collected the pottery shards he found. Unfortunately, Squire's son later destroyed his father's correspondence and threw out his artifact collection but not before many of the pottery pieces had been identified as Monks Mound Red, a distinctive Cahokia ceramic type. There could be little doubt about Cahokia's connection to Trempealeau.[11]

---

11. Green and Rodell 1994.

Rodell believes that a Mississippian presence at Trempealeau is indicated by a well-documented platform mound, a possible second platform mound, and diagnostic Mississippian ceramics. To him, the ceramics are unequivocally from Cahokia, either made by people from Cahokia or copied by someone who had been there. He believes there had to have been direct influence but it is hard to say how close that influence was.

If direct influence had taken place, Trempealeau would have served as a point of early contact between Cahokia and peoples of the upper Mississippi Valley. Trempealeau is on the Trempealeau River, which flows into the Mississippi, and up the river is the site where Hixton silicified sandstone comes from. No Ramey Incised pottery has been found at Trempealeau, which indicates the site was occupied during the Lohmann and not the Stirling phase.

In 1990 Rodell drove to the location of the Squire farm and garden, where Squire had found the Monks Mound Red shards. The area is now the front yard of a church parsonage, and part of Squire's garden has been cut into by the Great River Road running along the Mississippi River. Rodell got permission to dig in the church yard, and in four test pits he found four pieces of red-slipped pottery, one with a rim. A local collector gave him two pieces of red-slipped pottery that came from a location less than a quarter mile from the church.

When he searched the local records Rodell turned up a reference to a second flat-topped mound that had once been in the area. With the existence of the two platform mounds from Trempealeau, a sampling of Monks Mound red pottery, and the distinctive rim, all dating from the Lohmann-phase Mound 72 period, Rodell believes he now has compelling evidence of the direct influence of Cahokia on the peoples of the North.

The leaders at the American Bottom were locked into some kind of exchange network that was functioning on the northern frontier. The distance is not too far. The Huron traveled great distances to avoid the Iroquois, and the Inuit regularly covered up to 1,000 miles overland to rendezvous. Traveling on the Mississippi would have been comparatively easy. The big question is, How were the northerners locked into the network?

However it was done—whether Native Americans physically journeyed from Cahokia to the Red Wing area, went from Red Wing to Cahokia as pilgrims for ceremonies, or passed goods from band to band—connections were made. Cahokia-style pottery appeared very quickly in the Wisconsin-Minnesota border area, suggesting it may have served some kind of social or ritual purpose. Whether it represented gifts, tribute, or a connection with religion or cosmology will probably never be known. What can be stated is that the reach of Cahokia stretched far beyond the American Bottom and extended along the river routes hundreds of miles to the north.

Guy Gibbon believes the Mississippian influence also may be seen in settlements along the banks of the Minnesota River, a short portage from the Cannon River, all the way north to the Dakotas. Called the Cambria Focus, these settlements had Cahokia-like pottery and platform mounds that were diamond-shaped, rather than square.

One of the most intriguing mysteries of the northern frontier of Cahokia is the distribution of the Long Nose God symbol.[12] The Long Nose God is one of the Mississippian motifs that has been found throughout the watersheds of the Ohio and Mississippi Rivers, from the North to the deep South. The god is shown with a human face and a very long, Pinocchio-like nose. Depictions of the Long Nose God have been etched into clay, carved in shell, and hammered out of copper. A pipe from Spiro, Oklahoma, has a cross-legged male carved on the pipe bowl. On his ears are earrings of Long Nose God masks.

Many of the Long Nose God masks that have been found in the North, in Minnesota, are made of shell from the Gulf of Mexico, while the masks that have been found in the deep South have predominantly been made of copper, which comes from the Lake Superior–Minnesota region. Rodell believes the masks were part of an extensive exchange network devoted to the distribution of elite goods that, once obtained, conferred prestige upon their owners.

It seems probable that "Big Men" or chiefs in the Red Wing–Wisconsin areas were manipulating the exchange with Cahokia for their own benefit and that of their followers. The exchange network and the Cahokia belief system were tightly joined. The pieces of galena and chunky stones found in the Red Wing area and the Long Nose God masks and pottery found through central and southern Wisconsin were all part of an elaborate system of belief and symbols that the priests of Cahokia dispatched to the hinterlands. It was this symbolism and the game of chunky that brought together the far-flung communities. Not unlike the Dominican and Franciscan friars who followed Cortez into Mexico, the priests of Cahokia forged a realm of belief and practice that extended far beyond the American Bottom's political boundaries.

As had happened at Aztalan, by the end of the Stirling period the strength of the northern communities began to wane. From the great central chiefdom at Cahokia to the most remote northern Minnesota site, something was happening to break down the system. The trading mechanism may have become so elaborate that it could not be sustained and, when stressed, it simply broke down. In some areas the climate changed, becoming cooler, and the length of the growing season for successful maize production fell below the minimally

---

12. For the most recent discussion of the Long Nose God and its symbolic importance see Hall 1997.

required 140 days. This may have affected corn crop surpluses and the numbers of people who could attend regional ceremonies and feasts. Warfare, common among tribal societies, may have broken out. Human skeletal remains exhibiting evidence of trauma have been found in both the Red Wing-Lake Pepin areas and at La Crosse-Trempealeau.

Other northern towns show signs of warfare. Skeletons have been found in refuse pits, skulls show marks of having been scalped, jaw bones and teeth have cut marks. Both Aztalan and Fred Edwards were abandoned, never again to be inhabited. After A.D. 1200, Mississippian influence declined, along with the shrinking of Cahokia, and, as though poised at the opposite end of a teeter-totter, the Oneota culture in the North began its ascendancy.

The exchange that existed between Cahokia and the northern villages operated under the umbrella of magico-religious sanctions and guarantees. The presence of Ramey symbolism and the artifacts of Cahokia imply that the Oneota people had adopted the ideology identified with these ritual objects. As the Cahokian exchange system began to unravel, internal strife may have arisen, making it more and more difficult to maintain the beliefs that sustained the network.

Two of the better-understood cultures that developed between the Red Wing-Aztalan area and the Cahokia heartland were the Spoon River culture of the central Illinois River Valley[13] and the Apple River culture of northwestern Illinois.[14] Both were Woodland cultures that were dramatically changed by their contact with Cahokia. From a study of the ceramics in the area, Robert Hall and Lynne Goldstein propose that the Aztalan Mississippian culture may have originated somewhere in north-central Illinois.

Emerson points out that of all the northern sites, the one that bears the closest relationship to the Apple River culture is Aztalan. The similarity between the two goes beyond that of ceramic forms to include temple mounds and the full Mississippian social and religious paraphernalia.

Excavations at the Eveland site and its nearby cemetery, Dickson Mounds, show that in the latter part of the eleventh century distinctive elements of Cahokia Mississippian culture (mounds, fortifications, status burials, and exotic items) abruptly appeared in the area, which was already populated by three different groups of Woodland peoples.

The interaction of Cahokia with the three resident Woodland cultures may be dramatically represented by the group of four headless skeletons buried in a pit at Dickson with pots in place of the heads. Fowler notes that the pots are of

---

13. Harn 1971, 1991.
14. Emerson 1991b.

four different types—one is Mississippian and the other three are from each of the three Woodland groups in the area. The burial can be interpreted to represent the melding of one society out of four. The bodies of the four leaders of the communities were buried together to indicate their unity and the central authority of the Dickson community.

Opinions vary as to how the interaction with Cahokia took place. The abruptness of the appearance of Cahokia-related traits suggests an actual movement of people at the time when Cahokia and the American Bottom were rapidly expanding. However, there is no indication of warfare in the Spoon River area or of new people forcibly imposing themselves on a resisting indigenous population there.

Al Harn suggests that Spoon River was an agricultural area that raised foodstuffs such as maize for the burgeoning population at Cahokia. In the resulting exchange, which probably included animals from the hunt as well, Cahokian status goods and the supporting belief systems, with all their elaborate iconography, moved north.

After A.D. 1200 the Illinois River Valley was occupied with fortified towns spaced at regular intervals along the river. They represent independent chiefdoms, and fewer elite goods have been found there. The Cahokian influence was waning. Later burials excavated at the Norris Farms site, near Dickson Mounds, show indications of trauma and malnutrition, scalping and bone fractures. When the peace of Cahokia ended, new people—the Oneota—moved into the area and the Cahokian period in American prehistory gradually came to a close.

The dominance of Cahokia as a political entity was largely limited to the central and northern portions of the American Bottom. South of this Cahokia heartland were Mississippian cultures that had developed out of the local Woodland base. Each of these areas showed evidence of interaction with Cahokia, largely through the presence of limited amounts of Powell and Ramey ceramics, which may indicate contact at an elite level.

Immediately to the south of the Cahokia-dominated American Bottom is a series of distinctive Mississippian cultures in discrete regions centered on the Mississippi River Valley, extending southeast all the way to the mouth of the Ohio River (fig. 28).[15] Around the mouth of the Ohio is the Cairo Lowlands Mississippian culture.[16] A short distance up the Ohio River were two fortified Mississippian towns, Kincaid in Illinois and Angel in Indiana, that were dominant communities in their areas.[17]

---

15. Schroeder 1997.
16. Williams 1954.
17. Cole et al. 1951; Muller 1978, 1986, 1987; Muller and Stephens 1991.

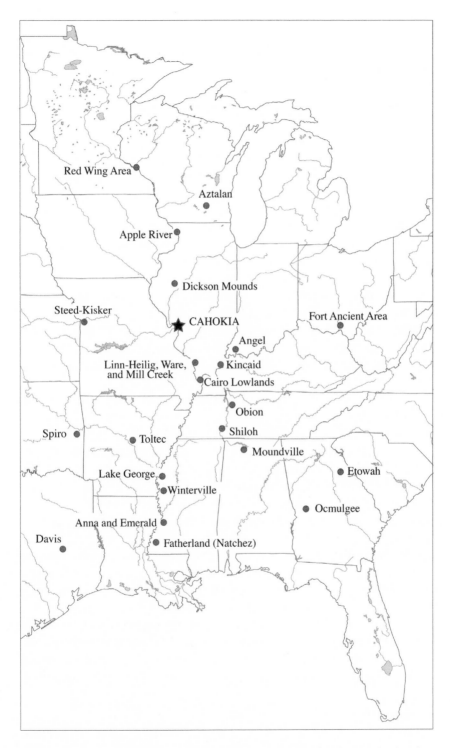

Figure 28. Map showing the location of Cahokia (star) and related Mississippian sites. Used with permission of M. L. Fowler.

The settlement systems of the "near Cahokia" Mississippian variants were dominated by central, sometimes fortified, mound communities. Around each regional center were smaller communities that were tied by their political and economic dependence to the larger central temple towns. Some of these communities were linked to specialized resources. Ware and Linn-Heilig, two towns in the general vicinity of the Mill Creek chert quarries in southern Illinois, may have been located where they were in order to control the mining of this valuable commodity and channel it into the economic exchange system dominated by Cahokia. Mill Creek chert is the stone that was utilized almost exclusively for hoes by Cahokia agriculturists.[18]

Cahokia's interaction with Mississippian cultures further to the south was qualitatively different from its influence in the North. "Mississippian" is a broad umbrella that includes a variety of peoples. In the lower Mississippi Valley and near the river's tributaries were several cultural patterns, many of which had temple mounds, palisaded towns, and communities that were probably organized on a chiefdom basis. They can be recognized as being different from each other through the stylistic differences of their ceramics and other works of art. Though these groups never achieved the size and complexity of Cahokia, many were substantial chiefdoms whose rulers lived in the familiar fortified towns with platform mounds and rectangular wall-trench houses.

One of the major Mississippian developments in the Southeast was in west-central Alabama, around the Moundville site.[19] Many times smaller than Cahokia, Moundville is the second-largest site of the Mississippian tradition (fig. 29) and is one of the major archaeological sites of the late period in eastern North American prehistory. Located on the banks of the Black Warrior River in central Alabama, Moundville is at the northern edge of the Gulf Coastal Plain and the southern edge of the ridge and valley sections of the Interior Plateau region. The natural resources of three major zones—the agricultural lands of the riverine bluffs and terraces, the pine forests of the Gulf Coastal Plain, and the oak-hickory forests of the north—were available to the Moundville inhabitants.

The Moundville site encompasses about 400 acres—less than one-tenth the size of Cahokia. Within this area are 20 flat-topped platform mounds arranged in a nearly circular pattern around what has been interpreted as a plaza area. Roughly in the center of the plaza is the largest of the mounds. This large mound is oriented in a north-to-northeasterly direction. The mounds on the margins of the plaza are paired; there are flat-topped mounds with no burials and smaller mounds with abundant burials, suggestive of a charnel house mound with an

---

18. Brown et al. 1990.
19. Knight 1997; McKenzie 1966; Moore 1907; Peebles 1983, 1971, 1987.

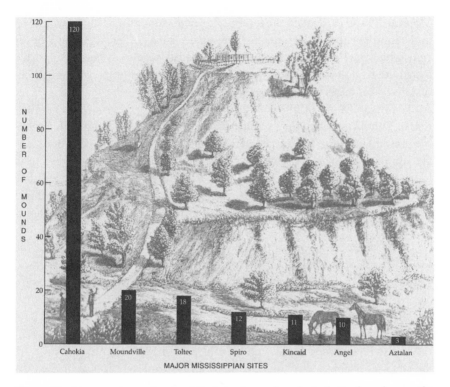

Figure 29. A comparison of major Mississippian archaeological sites based upon the number of mounds. Cahokia has six times as many mounds as Moundville, the second-largest Mississippian site. If a comparison is made on the basis of area, the positions of Spiro and Moundville would be reversed. By any measure, Cahokia is several orders of magnitude larger than any other known Mississippian site. William McAdams first published the background picture of Monks Mound in *History of Madison County, Illinois* (1882). Graph by M. L. Fowler; photo by James Anderson.

associated burial mound. Around these mounds and peripheral to the plaza was a residential area.

In the Black Warrior River bottoms north and south of Moundville were smaller sites that were related to Moundville and with it formed a sociopolitical unit. Some of them had mounds and others did not. Moundville, by far the largest and most complex site, was undoubtedly the major center. Smaller sites with single mounds were minor centers and the moundless sites were residential villages. The political control of the area was centered in Moundville with the smaller communities functioning as regional administrative centers.

Moundville and its related sites suggest a ranked society or chiefdom level of sociopolitical organization. The paramount chief undoubtedly lived in

Moundville and controlled the territory through subordinate chiefs who lived in the minor centers and controlled the smaller villages. The upper rank of society, which may have included the craft specialists, would have been supported by tribute paid during harvest, planting, and burial and other ceremonial occasions by residents of the outlying villages.

The organization of Moundville and its subsidiary communities parallels that of Cahokia, though on a smaller scale. Moundville was located in a riverine bottomland very similar to the American Bottom. It developed about A.D. 900 out of a Woodland base of village farming communities, reached its peak in the thirteenth century, declined during the fourteenth, and was abandoned by the fifteenth century. Though its trajectory was similar, Moundville shows little relationship with Cahokia and developed, for the most part, independently of it.[20]

There were other strong, independent chiefdoms, besides Moundville, in the lower Mississippi Valley. Among them were the Toltec site[21] near Little Rock, Arkansas, which may be earlier than both Cahokia and Moundville; the Spiro site[22] in Oklahoma, representative of the Caddo Mississippian; the Etowah site[23] in eastern Georgia, on the eastern edge of Mississippian development; and later sites such as Winterville and Lake George,[24] in western Mississippi, which represent the Plaquemine Mississippian subtradition. These communities were already well established at the time of Cahokia's explosive appearance on the scene, a factor that may have made Cahokia's interaction with its neighbors to the south so different from that of the north.

The earliest interactions between the American Bottom and the lower Mississippi Valley may have been initiated from the south. Temple-mound building began earlier in the lower valley. Monks Mound Red, a globular vessel form, usually grog or limestone tempered, is common in Emergent and Early Mississippian phases in the American Bottom but there are no clear-cut antecedents for this vessel style in Cahokia. Fowler once raised this issue with James Griffin.

"Where did this type of vessel originate?" he asked. Without hesitation Griffin replied, "The red-slipped, grog-tempered seed jar is earlier in the lower valley than at Cahokia. It came to Cahokia from the south." A group of artifacts supports this early Cahokia connection with the south. Some of the projectile points from Mound 72 are of a material and form directly linked to the Caddo Mississippian. Examples of pottery that looks like Caddoan and Coles

20. Knight 1997.
21. Rolingson 1982a, 1982b, 1990.
22. Brown 1971, 1973; Brown et al. 1978; Moorehead 1923.
23. Blakely 1977; Larson 1971, 1989; Moorehead 1923.
24. Brain 1978, 1989; Williams and Brain 1983.

Creek have been found at Cahokia, including a crushed vessel from Mound 72Sub2. When Griffin examined the ceramics he could not decide whether the vessels had actually been made in one of the southern communities or if their style had been copied by a potter in Cahokia. Stoltman has not yet examined the ceramics with his thin-section process but there is little doubt that, stylistically, the items represent some sort of connection of the lower Mississippi Valley with the Emergent and Early Mississippian peoples of Cahokia.

This does not suggest that Cahokia was settled by a migration of people from the lower valley. There is no question that Cahokia was developing along the same lines as hundreds of other chiefdoms in the Southeast as one consequence of the success of maize agriculture. Between A.D. 700 and 900, Cahokia and other Mississippian societies participated in a group of innovations that included the development of hierarchical political and religious systems emphasizing the relationship between the society and the cosmos. Cahokia suddenly burst on the scene with rapid growth and became, by several orders of magnitude, the largest, most complex, and dominant Mississippian complex. Cahokia's impressive development exerted a strong drawing power on the people of its day.

Why did Cahokia develop where it did? Fowler suggests the answer lies in Cahokia's geography.[25] The American Bottom, one of the largest expanses of fertile bottomland in the Mississippi Valley, sits astride the confluence of the major drainage systems of the midcontinent, giving it access to sources of elite and practical goods from a tremendous area of North America. Cahokia functioned as a gateway city. Gateway cities developed on the margins between major cultural and resource areas and served as ports through which ideas and physical and human resources could be channeled. The chiefdom that gained control of such a situation also gained power and prestige. Moundville may have been such a gateway city between the Gulf Coastal Plain and the rich mountains and river valleys of Tennessee to the north. The settlement at Aztalan may have been an attempt to establish a gateway city.

Sometime after A.D. 1200 a set of iconographic concepts developed in artifacts of the lower Mississippi Valley that reflected what came to be called the Southern Cult.[26] Since one of the motifs in these pieces of artwork is the severed head, it has also been called the Death Cult. As understanding of this work grew, it has been designated the Southeastern Ceremonial Complex (SECC). The original pieces were copper repoussé plates, shell gorgets, carved stone figures of animals and humans, and symbols painted or engraved on pottery that had been found at Etowah, Moundville, and Spiro. It has been noted that SECC items

---

25. Fowler 1974; Peregrine 1991.
26. Brown 1976, 1989; Brown and Kelly 1999; Waring 1968.

were not common at Cahokia. Analysis of the materials has revealed several different styles, one of which was so distinctive that it could be the work of a single artist, or at least artists from a single locality.

One of these styles is what James Brown, who has examined the SECC materials in great detail, refers to as "Braden A." Working with John Kelly on materials from the Cahokia area, Brown has discovered artifacts that tie Cahokia to the SECC. Looking at some of Perino's pottery from Mound 34 (the pottery that earlier had baffled Fowler), Brown and Kelly saw motifs that they tie in with the Braden A style. The materials probably date to the Moorehead phase and could predate the SECC items.

Tom Emerson's interest in Cahokian art styles dates to his finding of the Birger figure in a village site. Emerson has proposed the existence of a fertility cult that was one of the ways the Cahokia elite exercised their control over the surrounding countryside. The Birger figure compares in many details to SECC figurines found at Spiro. Both are Braden A style. Other motifs present in the SECC materials are bird-and-human combinations and the cross in the circle.

Pauketat and Emerson feel that these motifs, although probably widely used in earlier times, were brought together in a "package" of elite ideology during the Lohmann and early Stirling phases at Cahokia. The Mississippian culture may have consisted of this package of elite ideology that was formulated at Cahokia and adopted and adapted by chiefdoms to the south, eventually to become known to archaeologists as the Southeastern Ceremonial Complex. Brown believes the Braden A style was formulated at Cahokia, perhaps in Stirling times, and that it spread outward from Cahokia toward the end of the Moorehead phase.

Fowler, whose interest has focused on large monuments rather than on motifs and patterns employed in ceramics and other artifacts, speculates that some of the motifs common in SECC art may be represented at Cahokia in the monumental constructions of the Lohmann and early Stirling phases. The cross-in-circle motif may be a representation of the woodhenge monuments. The cruciform layout of Cahokia, dating to early times, is an architectural representation of the cross motif. Another common SECC theme, the bird-man combination, was first noted at Cahokia in the Beaded Birdman Burial in Mound 72Sub1. These are all part of a system of ideas that may have spread southward from Cahokia and was appropriated by southern chiefdoms as part of their legitimation process, much as the Aztecs appropriated ideas and sacred places from the earlier Toltecs.

There are some artifactual indications of Cahokia's interaction with the South. Stoltman's three best candidates for sites that absorbed pottery influences directly from Cahokia are Winterville in western Mississippi and Obion and

Shiloh in central Tennessee. Jeffrey Brain, of the Peabody Museum at Harvard University, has made much of the Cahokia-related materials at Winterville and has argued for an actual influx of Cahokians who inspired a transformation of local Coles Creek/Plaquemine culture into a Mississippian culture on the Yazoo.

Stoltman thin-sectioned some of the relevant pottery and the Powell look-alikes turned out to be of local manufacture. He found the same to be true when he thin-sectioned pottery from Obion. In the case of Shiloh, both Griffin and Bruce Smith reported that Powell pottery occurs at Shiloh, but Stoltman has not seen the materials or had the opportunity to thin-section any of them. There appear to have been Cahokia contacts with the communities to the south, but it is doubtful that they brought about major local transformations.

While Cahokia absolutely made its presence felt with its neighbors to the south, it was a different sort of presence than to the north. In the North there is evidence of actual migrations and certainly direct contact. The interaction with the South was probably more on the ideational level.[27] Cahokia was the largest chiefdom ever developed in North America and the smaller chiefdoms to the south had to have taken notice of the potent gateway city. It was the powerful, established ideological base of the Cahokia leaders and its iconographic representations that were accepted by the chiefdoms of the South and that tied them into the power of Cahokia.

---

27. Anderson 1997.

TWENTY

The Abandonment of Cahokia

Why was Cahokia abandoned? Theories to explain its decline and eventual abandonment center on factors ranging from disease, change of climate, and external warfare to a failure of the internal governance system. Most theories, however, focus on climatic change and a modification in cultural agency. Bill Woods is one of those who believes Cahokia declined because of human alterations to the environment.

Cahokia's burgeoning population and the fact that the population utilized large quantities of wood for fuel, houses, and other construction led, over time, to a general degradation of the environment.[1] The decline of Cahokia, in Woods's view, did not involve a single catastrophic event. Instead, it was gradual, taking place over 50 to 100 years. The crisis began during the Stirling phase (A.D. 1100–1200) and gradually mounted, reaching a climax during the Moorehead phase (A.D. 1200–1275). By the end of the Sand Prairie phase (A.D. 1275–1350) Cahokia had been virtually abandoned.

Woods arrived at his hypothesis for the decline by looking at three factors: the size of Cahokia's population during the Stirling phase, the availability of wood in the American Bottom, and the effects of erosion on the farmers' ability to grow crops, particularly corn.

One estimate of Cahokia's population that is based on rigorous calculations rather than impressions is that made by Michael Gregg,[2] who, in 1975, came up with the figure of 25,500 individuals. While many consider that number to be inflated and criticize Gregg's procedures,[3] Woods believes that more recent in-

---

1. Holley et al. 1989; Lopinot 1997; Lopinot and Woods 1993; Pauketat and Lopinot 1997; Woods and Holley 1991.
2. Gregg 1975.
3. Ford 1974; Milner 1986; Pauketat and Lopinot 1997.

vestigations may support a population figure not too different from Gregg's. Within the ICT-II tract, Woods notes, occupation was intense and continuous during the Lohmann and Stirling phases. The area excavated at the ICT-II site measured about 1.5 acres. Within that 1.5 acres, sixty wall-trench structures were uncovered that represented both Lohmann and Stirling period occupations.

Woods estimates that from five to seven households in the ICT-II tract were continuously occupied during the Stirling phase. If the ICT-II occupation represented the typical household density of Cahokia, and if residences covered half of the six and a half square miles of the Cahokia site, given four households with four persons per household, the population would have been around 22,069. Other recent estimates of Cahokia's population are smaller, ranging from 10,000 to 15,000 inhabitants at any one time.

Mississippian wall-trench buildings used an average of 80 posts per structure. Assuming that a household of five individuals utilized two structures, 800,000 wall posts alone would be needed to house 25,000 people. While a single tree could have supplied more than one post, wood was also needed for roof frames, household furniture, and watercraft as well as the building and rebuilding of the palisade. Wood was also used for fuel (5,000 cooking fires burning daily) and trees were cut to clear fields for crops.

Wood was not plentiful at Cahokia. The terrain of the American Bottom is a mixture of floodplain prairies, lakes, sloughs, ponds, creeks, and savanna-like habitats. Between the American Bottom and the bluffline, prairies occupied about 50 percent of the land. Trees were largely restricted by the ridge-and-swale topography to the north and northwest areas of the site. Oak and hickory trees dominated the upland forest to the east while cottonwoods and willows grew adjacent to the river. Between these two zones, at a slightly higher elevation, grew oak, elm, and ash, along with sycamore, mulberry, black walnut, persimmon, and honey locust. Bill Woods estimates the total number of trees within six miles in all directions around Monks Mound at 628,000.

An examination of 1,863 charcoal fragments found at the ICT-II excavation revealed extensive use of nonlocal woods such as white oak and hickory from the uplands (located about 15 miles from Cahokia) and red cedar and bald cypress, which came from as far south as the mouth of the Ohio River. During Lohmann and early Stirling times as much as 60 percent of the identified wood came from outside Cahokia. The importation of wood symbolized the wealth and power of the ruling class and the sacredness of the Cahokia community.

The best fuel and construction woods in the immediate Cahokia vicinity were largely used up by the Lohmann and early Stirling occupants of ICT-II. By later Stirling times a greater variety of woods was being used, leading Woods to suggest that local wood was becoming scarce and the ruling elite used its authoritarian power to bring wood into Cahokia from ever longer distances, either as tribute or by instituting some kind of forced labor. When the power of the rulers declined, the supply of imported wood also went down, putting greater pressure on the local supply. By the Moorehead phase less-desirable floodplain woods such as maple, birch, hackberry, elm, cottonwood, and willow, which have a lower fuel efficiency, were being widely used.

The exploitation of the local wood resources, within 15 miles of Cahokia, would have led to the deforestation of the American Bottom and extensive cutting of trees on the bluffs above the river. The result would have been erosion from the rapid runoff after each heavy midsummer rainfall and the filling up with silt of the existing drainage channels. This, in turn, would have caused major flooding of the maize fields below the bluffs, a catastrophic event for a large population dependent on corn for its subsistence. Forest clearance and the subsequent flooding would also have eliminated many wildlife habitats.

Amy Ollendorf[4] has compared the evidence of changing climatic conditions with the agricultural practices and the decline of Native American communities in the Southwest and Mesoamerica. When the Spaniards arrived in the New World, they did not encounter a pristine environment. Through agriculture and construction, Native Americans had altered the natural landscape to create the cultural landscape. Land had been cleared for agriculture in Mesoamerica for more than four thousand years.

The population of the central Mayan lowlands in A.D. 850 has been variously estimated at from 3 million to 14 million people. Yet by the ninth century A.D. classic Mayan civilization had collapsed, followed by a sudden dislocation and reorganization of populations. Social malfunction alone cannot account for the enormous population loss that took place between A.D. 900 and 1000. Significantly, before their decline, the Mayans had shifted their agriculture from dependence on a variety of crops to the monoculture of maize.

Paleolimnological data from lakes in the Petén, in northern Guatemala, show that the sediments are composed of redeposited soils from erosion. The erosion was the result of deforestation, cultivation, and urban construction. When the organic surface soils were depleted, the sediments became increasingly inorganic and unable to support food crops. The tremendous loads of silt deposited in the lakes of the Petén removed a large source of nutrients that had formerly been available for agricultural crops.

In the American Southwest, between A.D. 900 and 1100, early villages were growing into towns, and systems of regional integration were developing. Chaco Canyon developed into a major regional center with connections to widely dis-

---

4. Dalan and Ollendorf 1991.

persed communities. After A.D. 1050, however, construction at Chacoan towns ended and their abandonment began. By A.D. 1300 the last sedentary people had either migrated out or adopted a nomadic lifestyle. What happened?

An analysis of tree rings in the region shows a series of droughts, one after another, from A.D. 1090 to 1101, with another severe drought in the area that lasted from A.D. 1276 to 1299. A tree-ring analysis in southwestern Colorado revealed a drought period between A.D. 1130 and 1180 that was greater than any historic occurrence of drought. A second drought lasting about ten years, from A.D. 1280 to 1290, also took place.

While drought was not a problem at Cahokia, flooding may well have been. Woods finds it significant that during the Moorehead phase, the time when problems of erosion, silting, and flooding would have become most acute, there is evidence of the moving of houses to higher ground and a migration of residents back into interior upland settings. Individuals had more autonomy, as evidenced by the greatly increased number of interior storage pits—hidden household reserves—that appear at this time.

During the Sand Prairie phase, burial practices changed. Instead of burying their dead in large mortuary complexes, as had been the former practice, people utilized stone box graves in small local cemeteries, suggesting that each community may have functioned as a quasi-autonomous social unit. The central control once exerted by Cahokia was largely gone. The economic and social consequences of crop failure and declining food production would have been disastrous to a ruling elite.

Ollendorf suggests that the large-scale abandonment of the American Bottom by Mississippian peoples may be attributed to a combination of factors, of which the change in the environmental condition was among the most crucial. Repeated years of poor harvests would have strained the political structures, particularly the ability of the leaders to mobilize tribute and to maintain their aura of sanctity and supremacy. Unfortunately, the effects of human alterations of the environment—the cutting down of thousands of trees with the resultant flooding—would have been so gradual that neither the commoners or the leadership would have realized what was happening until it was too late to make meaningful changes.

The interpretations of Woods and Ollendorf regarding the decline of Cahokia are largely ecological in their theoretical base. Others, such as Pauketat and Emerson, see sociological and political explanations as more useful. A chiefdom, even a complex one such as Cahokia, is a fragile political consolidation where the power of a chief is based upon his ability to produce benefits for the people. Much of the chief's power was legitimated by the mitigation of the uncertainties of the real world through belief systems and the monuments that represented these beliefs. The chief enhanced his control by representing himself as living close to the center of natural power—the sun in the case of the Mississippian culture—and had little need for military force to legitimate or usurp further control.

Pauketat believes that the decline of Cahokia came about from some of the same forces that created it originally. He notes that by the Moorehead phase, craft goods that earlier had been owned only by the elite were now available to everyone. Signs of violence appear: people were beheaded. During the Moorehead phase the massive palisade around Cahokia's central mound and plaza appears, not only as a defense measure but, in Pauketat's view, as an offensive tactic as well. With a wall in place, fewer armed men would have been needed to protect the heart of the capital.

Pauketat questions the argument put forth by Woods and Ollendorf, that Cahokia failed because of the felling of trees in the uplands and the subsequent erosion, silting, and flooding of the cornfields. The depopulation of Cahokia came about in large part, he believes, because of a political failure and the resultant drifting away of the population. The chiefs of Cahokia ignored the practical matters of political reality, engaged in disputes among themselves, and neglected the business of governing. In Pauketat's estimation, it was the failure of the gods of Cahokia, not of the crops, that led to the decline and abandonment of the city. Deforestation and its results would certainly have aggravated the discontent and disputes among the chiefs of Cahokia. Like the soil, the power of the paramount chief was seriously eroded.

In the rural areas, the break with the complex Stirling bureaucratic phase came during the Moorehead period. Within a short time all of the specialized facilities and elites disappeared and leadership reverted to a simpler system of local autonomy without the services of obvious political or religious specialists. The final Cahokia decline, when it came during the early Sand Prairie phase, was complete.

When political rivalries arose, as they surely must have, one response was for a dissenting segment of the community to leave and establish its own independent society. Many current interpretations posit the life of Cahokia as an ebb and flow of populations into and out of the Cahokia center, as minor chiefdoms vacillated in their loyalty to the paramount chief. The conclusion of this view is that eventually the size of the Cahokia chiefdom became too large for one elite group to control. The society fragmented into smaller groups that either drifted away or, if they stayed in nearby areas such as the Illinois River Valley, disavowed the Cahokia power.

These political, charismatic, and individual-agency models for Cahokia's decline are provocative and each one contains part of the truth. To make their point, proponents of these models tend to minimize the ecological explanations that for many years were popular in archaeological theory. However, stresses on the ecological system would have put a tremendous burden on the political system. Lowered food productivity, caused by deforestation and the consequent siltation and flooding, would have raised serious questions in the minds of the Cahokians about the power of their chief. The decline and subsequent dispersal of Cahokia's population have many explanations, all of which are intertwined. After the Mississippians departed, the American Bottom remained largely empty of human habitation until the arrival, in the seventeenth century, of the Europeans.

TWENTY-ONE

Cahokia's Place in the Pre-Conquest World

Despite the hundreds of acres that have been added to the site and the countless hours of archaeological excavation that have taken place, Cahokia still remains an enigma that, for the most part, defies understanding. Robert Hall once remarked that the study of Cahokia is like the fable of the blind men and the elephant. Each scholar, blinded by his or her own limited perspective, develops a different interpretation of Cahokia.

Within the past decade a method of trying to understand the whole by consolidating the bits and pieces has come to the fore, made possible by increased cooperation among archaeologists and by the broadening of the theoretical base for archaeological inquiries—asking how to look at prehistoric cultures and infer their beliefs, organization, activities, and relationships with others.

The overwhelming size of Cahokia has raised many questions. One of these regards the size of the population. Estimates have fluctuated over the years but the present consensus puts it at between 10,000 and 20,000 at about A.D. 1100, with several thousand more in the American Bottom outside of Cahokia who were under the influence of the central community. This puts Cahokia in the upper ranks of preindustrial communities in the world for that time period. Moorehead referred to Cahokia as a "village," obviously a misnomer. To refer to it as a "city" may be a slight overstatement on the other end of the scale.

Archaeologists have also debated over whether Cahokia was a chiefdom or a state-level society. A chiefdom is a society based upon inherited leadership. Everyone in the society is graded in the hierarchy by his real or imagined kinship with the chief. The chief has no police power to force his will on the populace. Instead he governs by his control of esoteric knowledge, ceremonies, displays of wealth, and the force of his personality.

By contrast, a state-level society has distinct social classes, with the ruler coming from the upper classes. There is a state religion, market economies, and a coercive police force that the state uses to gain control of resources and expand the size of the territory. The boundaries between these two organizational levels of society are blurred and the issue for anthropologists is how to tell the difference between these levels of social, political organization based on the archaeological record.

Patricia O'Brien, at Kansas State University, on the basis of criteria formulated by V. Gordon Child, argues that Cahokia was a state. Guy Gibbon also speculates about a possible "Ramey State." Emerson is not so sure.

"Cahokia is unique," Emerson says. "I have changed my thinking through the years. In 1991 I was writing that if we want to understand Cahokia we need to look at chiefdom-level societies in the United States. I thought Fowler was using the wrong models from Mexico. But with more and more work, I still can't say it is a state but it sure as hell is a different kind of chiefdom. Cahokia was much more complexly organized than we ever had any idea." Emerson points out, "They had a form of bureaucracy; they exported their philosophy; they exerted authority over the American Bottom. That is not what you typically read about chiefdoms. Cahokia was in some sort of intermediate stage. Clearly, hundreds of thousands of chiefdoms died without reaching statehood. Cahokia never made the jump but it was really close to making it." Bob Hall would concur: "Cahokia was a chiefdom on its way to becoming a state." Both would agree that while Cahokia almost made it to statehood, it never quite got there.

The key distinction between a chiefdom and a state is the presence of a police or military force. If warfare and conquest were used as means of control and to acquire new territory, the society had probably achieved the level of a state.

When this test is applied to Cahokia, it indicates that Cahokia was a chiefdom. There is no evidence that Cahokia dominated any territory outside the north and central American Bottom. This is not to say there wasn't conflict and even warfare. The distinction is whether warfare was used to establish and maintain hegemony. Some suggest that the Cahokians' use of severed heads in their artwork was an indication of warfare. Heads are sometimes shown in the hands of people doing a dance. While these might be the heads of captives, there is also evidence of a cult of reverence for ancestors, particularly among the ruling lineages. The severed heads could be a public display of relics from revered ancestors.

The palisade built around Cahokia in late Stirling and Moorehead times is sometimes cited as an indication of the presence of warfare. There is little doubt that the palisade, with its evenly spaced watch towers, was constructed for military purposes. But the palisade was built to keep people out rather than to expand territory. It surrounded the central core of the community and protected the elite and their riches. Undoubtedly defensive, the palisade set apart the most impressive and influential part of the community.

A common motif in Cahokian and other Mississippian iconography is the combined raptor and human figure. Such figures are often shown as ceremonial dancers with maces or other stylized weapons in their hands. This suggests to many people that the dancers are warriors. The stylized "weapons" that these dancers sometimes carry may not be weapons at all but *bâtons de commandement,* similar in concept to the *fasces,* or bundles of rods, carried by lictors before Roman emperors as symbols of their authority. Very finely made artifacts such as celts (or what collectors call "spuds") have been found in Mississippian sites. These are too fine to have been used for chopping down trees and may have been specially manufactured emblems of power. Copper repoussé representations of these were also made. Fowler believes that the celts are meant to represent power and that the dancers carrying them are conducting a ceremony commemorating the power of ancestors or intermediating between the "real" or earthly world and the forces of the spiritual world in the sky.

Of the hundreds of skeletons found in Mound 72 there were some from individuals who had not been buried in the flesh but had died elsewhere and the remains stored until the proper time for burial. It is tempting to think of these as unwilling sacrifices taken from among war captives. Only one group shows signs of the kind of violent deaths that could have resulted from such a situation. The rest, though they may have been killed to attend the primary persons in the mound, all show signs of having been carefully kept for varying lengths of time. This suggests that they were not antagonists of the chief of Cahokia but rather displays of wealth and human surplus reinforcing the perception of his power and position.

There is no evidence in either the North or the South that Cahokians engaged in a war of conquest. Because of this lack of evidence of organized warfare, Fowler believes the concept of chiefdom best describes what was happening in the American Bottom. Cahokia was one of the most elaborate chiefdoms ever known and it was located in the heartland of American, where no one believed such an enterprise could have been possible.

It has been difficult for both anthropologists and the public to grasp the size and complexity of Cahokia and to admit to the significance of the new archaeological data. One reason for this is that our information on Native American cultures has come from the written records of the past three hundred years. These describe Native American life long after the tremendous destruction wrought by European diseases had taken place. This catastrophe, along with the imposed economic system of the conquerors, brought about a tremendous reorganization of the indigenous societies.

Another factor was the intellectual climate of the late eighteenth and early nineteenth centuries. American Indians, and other indigenous peoples around the world, were looked on as Noble Savages, people who lived a simpler, purer life. This attitude led to a patronizing view of native peoples. The religiously engendered prejudice against all non-European peoples fostered the belief that "white" populations were people favored by God and that all others were at a lower level, at best candidates for forced conversion. While not subscribing to these views, anthropologists were influenced by them and, until recent decades, these attitudes limited their interpretations.

One of the earliest interpretations of Cahokia was that its development was influenced by the high civilizations of Mexico. In the early 1940s a special archaeological team (MacNeish and Griffin were members) was organized to look into this possibility in an area in northeastern Mexico called the Huasteca. The Huasteca includes portions of the Mexican states of Tamaulipas and San Luis Potosí and contains some large archaeological sites not too far from the Caddo Mississippian cultures of Texas, Oklahoma and Arkansas. The team found tobacco pipes and some pottery types that were tantalizingly similar to those made by the Mississippians. But when they looked out over the arid desert that separated the Huastecans from the Mississippians, they abandoned the idea of contact, deciding that the inhospitable terrain made it unlikely the two cultures had had any relationship with each other.

The two most obvious Mesoamerican connections are the cultivation of Indian corn, the basis on which the Mississippian culture developed, and the presence of pyramidal mounds in both cultures. There is no question that maize was first domesticated in central Mexico and spread northward into the area of the United States. However, it literally took a thousand years for this tropical plant to become adapted to the northern climes. Its movement northward was a long process and cannot be related to a migration of Mexican people into the Mississippi Valley to give rise to Cahokia.

The building of platform mounds around plazas, at first, seems very Mexican. The form and function of these constructions are very similar. This type of structure was also built earlier in Mexico than in the American Bottom so the ideas could have diffused northward. There is one major difference. The pyramids of Mexico are, for the most part, built and faced with stone. There is no evidence that stone was used in the construction of major mounds in the Mississippi River Valley and none were faced with stone.[1] This has been attrib-

---

1. This point of view has been recently jolted by the findings of William Woods and his crew from Southern Illinois University at Edwardsville, who have been working with construction crews on Monks Mound. The main work of these construction crews has been the building of a new and more durable stairway on Monks Mound and the installation of a drainage system that might help avoid the massive slumpages that have occurred in the past. In drilling for these drainage tubes, rocks were encountered. Nothing is known of the extent of these rocks and what they represent. Research on this is continuing and until more data are presented the statement about the lack of use of stone by Mississippians must be accepted.

uted to the fact that stone for building is scarce in the Mississippi River Valley area. However, there are limestone bluffs near Cahokia so the stone was available if the builders had chosen to use it.

Platform mounds similar to those at Cahokia are almost worldwide in their distribution. Temples in Japan were often built on a platform. The biblical Tower of Babel was probably a ziggurat or ancient Near Eastern tower platform. People everywhere had the concept of placing important buildings on platforms to emphasize their significance. In Fowler's view, the concept of a platform mound and a plaza is too general to qualify as evidence for Mexico's being the source of these architectural ideas at Cahokia.

James Porter, basing his idea on years of experience at Cahokia and the Mitchell site, believes there *were* direct contacts between Cahokia and Mexico. Those contacts, he postulates, came about through the work of the Pochteca, who were merchant-traders well known from the time of the Aztecs. It is probable that the earlier Toltecs had a similar group.

The Pochteca ranged far from their capital cities with large caravans of human carriers bearing manufactured goods to exchange for slaves and produce from far-off regions. The Pochteca merchants ranged as far south as the Mayan area in Central America and north into modern Arizona and New Mexico, where they traded macaw feathers for turquoise. Along with their trade goods they undoubtedly brought with them ideas about the Mexican gods and the cosmos.

Porter suggests that the Pochteca also came to Cahokia but he has not been able to find any evidence of their visits, such as exotic bird skeletons or artifacts, that could indicate a direct Mexican contact. Fowler is skeptical, joking that "unless an artifact is stamped 'Made in Mexico'" he will not accept Mesoamerican contact as having occurred. Even if an artifact were to be found, Fowler would have to be shown how it had influenced the development of Cahokia.

Fowler may now have to rethink his position. The question of a Huasteca connection has recently been revisited by two Mexican archaeologists, Patricio Dávila Cabrera and Diana Zaragoza de Dávila, who, as students, worked near Fowler's Amalucán site. From an examination of artifacts in storage and their own fieldwork, they noted that the pipes found at Huasteca are not like any others in Mexico but are similar to those found in the Caddo area. The shell gorgets found at Huasteca were very like those found in the Mississippi Valley. The Dávilas found triangular arrowheads whose closest analogs are those at Cahokia and they examined disk-shaped stones very like the chunky stones found at Mississippian sites.

There are other exciting parallels. The Huasteca site of Tantoc contains over a dozen mounds constructed of earth instead of stone, as was more common in pre-Hispanic Mexico. The mounds are located around plazas in a roughly north-to-south and east-to-west orientation and are surrounded by small lakes, similar to the borrow pits of Cahokia.

If these "foreign" ideas did come south to the Huastecans from the Mississippians, how did they get there? Diana Dávila notes that the site of Tantoc is located along the Pánuco River, which empties into the Gulf of Mexico at the modern city of Tampico. In the past, the river must have been a major avenue of communication. The Gulf Coast from Tampico north to Corpus Christi, Texas, is protected by barrier islands that would have allowed large canoes to traverse the coastal waterways and move into the Mississippi River.

Diana Dávila refers to the De Soto expedition as evidence of this possibility. When the expedition fell into chaos following the death of Hernando De Soto and the loss of many men and horses to the attacking Indians, the survivors built boats and fled down the Mississippi, ending up in Tampico, which by then was a Spanish settlement. The idea that the Huastecans also would have made use of the rivers and coastal waters resolves the problem of how they could have crossed the inhospitable land of northeastern Mexico and southern Texas.

Much of the data presented by the Dávilas has been known and basically rejected by most archaeologists for more than fifty years. Their review of the older data supplemented with new investigations emphasizing community organization, mound construction methods, and distinctive artifacts is an appropriate approach to the nagging question of Mesoamerican and Mississippian interactions. If the Dávilas are correct, the interaction between Mexico and Cahokia looks more like a north-to-south, Mississippian influence on Huasteca rather than a Mexican influence on the Mississippians.

Robert Hall has come the closest to providing some evidence of the interrelationship of the pre-European cultures of the present United States and Mesoamerica. These data are not in the form of artifacts or architectural constructions but lie in the ideological realm—creation or origin stories, motifs on artifacts, and ethnohistorical descriptions of ceremonies conducted by the Aztecs and Mayans as well as by such North American peoples as the Choctaw, Pawnee, Osage, and Winnebago.

There is a surprising specificity to these comparisons. The details of the adventure of the twins in the Mayan Popul Vuh are strikingly similar to the Winnebego story of Red Horn. The rituals of the Green Corn ceremony are similar whether performed by the Mississippians or the people of Mexico.

In explaining these similarities, Hall borrows a term from James Griffin. Griffin suggested that there was a "seepage" of ideas and mythology from Mexico that extended back into the Archaic, before 1000 B.C. This undercurrent of creation concepts and stories about the natural world may have been adopted and adapted by North American cultures to become a common New World heritage.

If there was a Mexican connection to Cahokia, from which culture did it come? Not the Aztecs; they were too late in time. The Olmecs were too early and the Mayans were too far away. The cultures to look at would be the Teotihuacán civilization of central Mexico, which dominated the area before A.D. 600, and the Toltec culture, which was precisely contemporary with the rise and decline of Cahokia.

Though the main influence of Teotihuacán was to the south, when it disintegrated as an empire and the city was burned, repercussions must have been felt over great distances. Though there is no evidence of this, the ripples of the calamity could have been felt as far away as the Mississippi River Valley. The Toltec empire began to rise from the ashes of Teotihuacán and by A.D. 1000 it was the dominating political, military, and economic force over much of Mexico and into the American Southwest. It was Toltec Pochteca who traded in the north for the *chalchihuitl,* or turquoise.

Both the Toltec culture and Cahokia went through their cycles of rise and fall at the same time. Strangely, the ascent and decline of the northernmost southwestern U.S. culture, the Anasazi, occurred in this period as well. The Toltec influence, moving on a carpet of corn, may have expanded far to the northwest to help bring about these phenomena. Centered on Chaco Canyon in New Mexico, the Anasazi built great multiroomed stone pueblos and large ceremonial buildings called *kivas.* Their constructions show a detailed familiarity with the annual sun cycle that their descendants, the Hopi and Zuni, used for calendrical and ritual purposes. Roadways were built radiating out from Chaco Canyon to distant communities. Because the buildings were made of stone, they appear more sophisticated than those at Cahokia. They are not. The Cahokia phenomenon was much larger.

The almost identical timing of the rise and fall of these three cultures raises questions that cannot as yet be answered. The Toltecs were preceded by a complex civilization while Cahokia and the Anasazi were not. Yet the course of their trajectories was the same. Future research, combining a variety of disciplines, should examine more fully the periods just before the sudden expansion of Cahokia and the Anasazi to check for patterns and explanations. To fully understand Cahokia the entire complex of Precolumbian civilizations, like pieces of a hemispheric three-dimensional puzzle, must be judiciously fitted together.

Cahokia's unique place in the prehistory of North America has at last been firmly fixed. There are few places in the world where such a complex level of social organization evolved independent of outside conquest or diffusion. The ancient Zimbabwe culture of Africa, the early Egyptian cultures, Mesopotamia, the Indus Valley, the Yalu River area of China, Mesoamerica, and the Andean region of South America are examples of areas in which humans adapted and tried to control the complexities of population expansion, the need for additional resources, and the capricious nature of the cosmos. Cahokia appeared later in time and may give us a more detailed understanding of this great transformation.

There is no longer any question that Cahokia was the work of ancestors of contemporary Native Americans, though we may never know which groups participated since a thousand years have elapsed since that great experiment took place. That may not matter for, as one Native American recently stated, we are all a part of humanity and should emphasize our unity rather than focus on our differences. Cahokia does that. It shows Native Americans facing the same problems as other societies, solving them in much the same way, and making many of the same mistakes, such as the overexploitation of the environment. Cahokia reminds us that the indigenous North Americans had a past of complexity and great achievement. Their urban center of Cahokia was a presence on the world stage. It was a place where complex societies were formed, engineers planned large communities, and a view of humanity's relationship to the spirit world was formulated. After centuries of neglect, Cahokia has emerged from the shadows, no longer forgotten, to add its saga to the ongoing human story.

THE archaeology laboratory of the University of Wisconsin, Milwaukee, is located a few blocks from the shore of Lake Michigan, in a structure that formerly housed a Model A Ford assembly plant, a warehouse, and a missile guidance systems manufacturing plant. There are no signs on the building or around the door stating that this is an outpost of the university or announcing the kind of work that goes on inside. Heavy wire mesh covers the opaque glass of the windows. The archaeologists and their graduate students let themselves in with keys and once they are inside, the exterior door closes and locks behind them.

The building is as large as a city block and has labyrinthine corridors and halls. Inside, the archaeology department has partitioned off its own section of the building with offices, areas of laboratory tables, storage, a kitchen of sorts, and specialized analysis space. Fowler's office occupies a corner on the street side of the building but because of the opaque glass and the heavy mesh over the windows, he cannot see out and only pale light filters in. The office is sectioned off from the larger room by a partition, file cabinets, and book shelves. Maps, papers, and books cover his desk and spill off tables. Across the open space from his office is the computer room where earnest young students sit in front of screens and coax multicolored slides of stratigraphy from the graphics programs.

Occupying the open space between the offices are long, wide tables salvaged from the sewing classes of the university's home economics department. Instead of fabrics and patterns, the tables are covered with potsherds, carefully laid out on a grid drawn on brown butcher paper. Each potsherd has a small white square painted on it and, on that white space, in tiny black letters, is meticulously inked an identifying number. Bending over the tables are students and volunteers who study each half-dollar-sized piece of clay, trying to match it with another that came from the same object. It is a jig-saw puzzle of antiquity—bits and pieces put together to present a semblance of the whole.

As Fowler walks by the tables he nods encouragingly to the students and glances down at the potsherds. He knows them well and can identify their typology at a glance. Discarded remnants of pots for cooking and storage—evidence of craftsmanship, of households and families—are the primary markers of a people and a culture. Broken pots, left on the ground, betray a people's migrations and activities as if they were footprints. It was not the high priests, declaiming their dogmas to the multitudes from the heights of Cahokia's mounds, who projected knowledge of their people, like arrows, through the centuries. It is skilled makers of pots, incorporating changing ideas into their designs and leaving them for distant generations to find, whose voices speak from out of the dust to the archaeologists.

Potsherds are highly personal artifacts. Looking at them, it is not hard to imagine the ancient potter at work. Could a forebear of Fowler's own Native American ancestor have dug the clay and shaped it into the pot that now lies in fragments on the tables in his laboratory? Fowler often wonders if an ancestor could have lived at Cahokia. Until DNA testing can be done, no one will know for certain which Native American groups are descended from the lords of Cahokia. But it is certain that a great many people in North America are. The handwork of their ancestors, holding elusive clues to their lives, lies spread out on tables like codices waiting to be read.

Though he is now retired and a professor emeritus, Fowler pushes ahead on his work at Cahokia. Graduate students crowd around as he applies for yet another grant to do summer work at the American Bottom. Rob Watson will soon finish his Ph.D. and join the line of idiosyncratic archaeologists, from Moorehead to Griffin to Fowler, who have invested their careers in Cahokia. Jim Anderson, whose excavations at Cahokia were always cleaner and had straighter walls than anyone else's, died of a massive stroke at the end of June 1998. James Griffin, who also died as this volume was being written, was remembered by Fowler. "All things considered, I had a good relationship with Griffin," he said. "Though he was arrogant and condescending he was never aloof or distant. He often said to others in my presence, 'I've let Fowler get by with a lot because he had to work for Deuel for so many years,' adding, 'and that was after Deuel had mellowed.' Griffin would always send me any information I asked for about Cahokia from his files and he attended every conference that I ever called, except at Modoc."

With each generation of archaeologists the picture of Cahokia comes into clearer focus. It is now known that at the time the Saxons were first settling into Bristol, when Leif Eriksson was blown off course from Greenland and encountered the Western Hemisphere, and when England's King Ethelred II was demanding that merchants in London pay their taxes in peppercorns, the Indians of Cahokia were constructing a city near the banks of the Mississippi—the first expression of urbanism in North America. For more than three hundred years that mighty city influenced life over half of the continent. Yet when the first Europeans came down the river, Cahokia did not exist in a single living memory. America's first metropolis had truly been forgotten.

At least once during his summer excavations at Cahokia, Fowler leaves the dig and climbs to the top of Monks Mound. It takes him longer now to get to the summit than it did on that first visit in 1951. The trees have been cut down and when he looks west, across the Mississippi River, he can see the great Saarinen arch at St. Louis. This is a place of monuments, he thinks, arches and mounds and a millennium of time. The sun is setting behind the arch and casting shadows on the first terrace of Monks Mound. Though it is time to go, Fowler decides to stay on the summit a few minutes longer to enjoy the view.

anthropogenic: Of human origin.

artifact: Any objects made by human beings, such as pottery, flint tools, axes, celts, scraping tools, are called artifacts. In archaeology an entire object is seldom found, but fragments—for example, broken pieces of ceramics, called "sherds"—are considered artifacts as well. In a broad sense, earthworks such as mounds or the engineering layout of a community could be considered artifacts.

attribute analysis: The study and classification of artifacts on the basis of physical characteristics that can be precisely defined.

basket loading: The soil to build a mound at Cahokia was carried from the borrow pit in baskets and dumped in the construction area. As different basket loads came from different areas of the borrow pit, they contained sediments of different colors. These separate loads are often visible in the excavations of mounds.

borrow pit: In an earthen construction, such as mounds, but also in modern dams and highways, the material to be used has to be excavated somewhere and brought to the construction site. The earth is "borrowed" from one locality to be used at another. The depressions left in the ground are called "borrow pits." These are common at Cahokia, where many were left as open pits, which filled with water. These were probably sources of food, such as fish, for the Cahokian population. Others were filled in with refuse to level the land for later construction of mounds and plazas.

bundle burial: A bundle or group of disarticulated human bones buried in a mound. It is assumed that these individuals were stored in a charnel house and their remains were "bundled" together, perhaps wrapped in a blanket or kept in a wooden chest and buried.

ceramic sequence: A ceramic sequence results when clay artifacts, usually pottery, are sorted into time periods based upon stylistic changes such as those affecting vessel form, decoration, and tempering.

ceramic type: A lumping together of pottery fragments (sherds) into a single group having shared traits such as tempering, form, and decoration.

charnel house: This was a special structure where the remains of the dead, especially those of higher status in a society, were prepared and stored until a propitious time for their interment.

chert: One of several types of silica rock materials. Chert, flint, and chalcedony are all rocks of this type, with chert having more impurities and chalcedony having fewer. Because these types of rock fracture along even and predictable planes, they were used for the manufacture of stone-cutting tools and spear and arrow points.

contour line and contour interval: In making three-dimensional maps the vertical dimension is often shown by *contour lines.* These lines connect all the points in the area that have the same elevation. The *contour interval* (C.I.) is the uniform difference in elevation between contour lines.

coprolites: Desiccated and sometimes fossilized feces.

cord-marked: In making a pot, the craftsperson often smoothed and formed the surface by beating it with a wooden paddle. Sometimes the paddle was wrapped with cords. This gave the clay surface a roughened texture. The actual marks of the individual cords can be seen on the pot's surface.

discoidals: Also called *chunky stones,* these finely made disc-shaped stone objects were used in a ceremonial and sporting game.

effigy-headed bowl: A bowl-shaped vessel with an animal or human head modeled on or attached to the rim.

equinox: The times of year, around September 21 and March 21, when there are equal amounts of daylight and darkness all over the world. These are the days when the sun is exactly halfway between the summer and winter solstices (see *solstice*) and the sun comes up due east.

ethnography: A branch of anthropology that studies living peoples and their cultures. Ethnography is a descriptive discipline. *Ethnology* utilizes the data of ethnography to formulate scientific generalizations about human societies and cultures.

experimental archaeology: The attempt to reconstruct how houses were built, tools made, and mounds constructed, and to determine the time it took to build them, by actually doing the work.

feature: A feature, in archaeological terms, is any concentration of artifacts, evidence of sediment disturbance such as storage pits, construction such as mounds, and other items that indicate past human activity in an area.

gorget: A pendant, usually made of shell or stone, and often engraved with symbolic designs. It was worn as part of a necklace of cords or strung shell beads.

house basin: A shallow rectangular pit excavated into the ground as a basin for the construction of a semisubterranean building.

incising: A method of decorating a clay pot by dragging a blunt-tipped object, such as the tip of a deer antler, over the surface to produce geometric or curvilinear designs. This is done before the vessel is fired.

isotope: An isotope is a variant of a chemical element. For example, Carbon 14 is the radioactive isotope of regular carbon, or Carbon 12.

kinship: Kinship is the biological relationship in groups of people or societies.

loess: Loess is a fine-grained, calcareous sediment, usually yellowish in color. It is the pulverized and finely ground rock left behind when the glaciers retreated. It was then picked up by the winds and deposited along the bluff lines of the Mississippi River and other areas.

maize: The word "maize" is derived from the Precolumbian word *maiz,* meaning "corn" in the United States. To avoid confusion, archaeologists use the word "maize" to describe corn because in British English the word "corn" is used to mean any cereal grain, such as wheat or oats.

Mesoamerica: A cultural area of Mexico and the northern part of Central America. This included the cultures of the Olmecs, Aztecs, Mayans, Toltecs, and others. It is the area of North America where true state-level societies, forms of writing, and great artwork developed.

microdrill: Microdrills are very small (about one inch in length) tools with sharpened points on both ends. This tool, usually made of chert, was used to drill holes in shell beads.

mound: A term used to describe any structure made by humans by piling up earth. Mounds have been constructed in a variety of forms including cones, platforms, ridge-tops, rectangles, and animal shapes.

North America: Geographically, North America is a continent that covers the area of Canada, the United States, Mexico, Guatemala, and the northern portions of Central America. In popular usage this term is limited to the United States and Canada. In archaeological studies this term is used as a vast culture area north of Mesoamerica (see above). It is this latter definition that is used in this book.

ossuary: An area, usually a deep pit, where large numbers of dead bodies and bundle burials were interred.

osteologist: A person who studies bones.

ox-bow lake: A remnant of an ancient river channel. The lakes are usually horseshoe shaped as they were formed when river channels cut through a sharp bend in a river and left the remnants of the old U-shaped channel.

paleopathology: The study of ancient diseases, principally through the examination of bones and teeth.

radiocarbon dating: When radiocarbon dating was first developed by Willard Libby, a basic part of his hypothesis was that there was a stable amount of the radioactive carbon isotope in the atmosphere through time. Dates based on this presumption of stability are called "uncalibrated" dates. It was later discovered that this stability did not occur and that the amount of radioactive carbon had fluctuated through time. This was tested by making assays of the radiocarbon in individual growth rings of long-living trees such as pinion trees of the Southwest. From these studies, charts were made of the variation of atmospheric radiocarbon. Using these charts (or formulas derived from them), one could calibrate the raw, or uncalibrated, dates. Thus, in publishing dates, it is important to distinguish between uncalibrated (raw) and calibrated dates. In this book, unless otherwise noted, we have used calibrated dates, particularly in discussing the time span of the phases at Cahokia.

ridge and swale: Ridges and swales are remnants of ancient river channels. The ridges are sandy and represent areas where sediments were carried by rapidly moving water. The swales are the old river channels where fine-grained sediments, such as clays, were deposited by standing or slow-moving water. Swales are in-filled ox-bow lakes.

salvage archaeology: Archaeological excavations conducted in localities that will be destroyed by construction such as highways, pipelines, housing developments, and reservoirs.

shovel testing: A method of testing an unexcavated archaeological site to determine the presence and distribution of artifacts. This is done by excavating at regular intervals to a depth of about one foot. The artifacts recovered are then plotted on a distribution map to note any concentrations or overall distribution. This procedure is usually carried out in advance of more detailed archaeological work to appraise the archaeological significance of the area and where specific buried features might be.

slickensides: Slickensides are much like the word sounds. They are polished and grooved surfaces that are produced when one mass of sediment moves against another. They are common in mineral soils containing more than 30 percent clay and are distinguished by deep, wide cracks when the sediments are dry.

slope wash: Over time, rainfall on a mound or hill gently erodes the surface, depositing layers of sediment downslope. This slope wash adds additional layers to the lower levels of the mound, smoothes its contours, and widens its apparent basal outline.

smectite: A group of fine-grained, multilayered clay sediments, particularly silicates.

solstice: The solstice occurs two times a year, around June 21 and December 21, when the sun is at its greatest distance—either north or south—from the equator. Over a period of 365.25 days, starting about December 21, the sun appears to move northward for six months, until it reaches its northernmost limit about June 21. Then it slowly begins its movement south, returning to its December 21 location. Knowledge of the solstices allowed early peoples to predict the changing seasons.

solsticial: Pertaining to the solstice or solstices.

stratigraphy: This term is borrowed from geology and pertains to layers of rock and soils found in the earth. The deepest sediments are usually the earliest deposited. However, in archaeology as in geology, there are factors that disturb this rule. Later people may have dug in the ground and brought to the surface materials from an earlier time. The sediments must be examined carefully to note any possible disturbance.

stumpware: Stumpware is a very thick form of pottery, tempered with coarse material. It is usually in a conical form with projections extending from the base to lend support. For this reason, it is sometimes referred to as "Cahokia Boot." It is thought by some to have been manufactured as supports for pottery cooking vessels.

tempering: To eliminate the problems of the shrinking and swelling of pure clays when they are used in making pottery, an aplastic material has to be mixed in with the clay. This is called "tempering." In the Cahokia area this tempering material is of different types. Crushed rock is called *grit temper.* Crushed sherds is called *grog temper.* Limestone and mussel shells are also common tempering materials.

wattle and daub: A method of construction of houses that involves placing upright poles in the ground. These poles are then interwoven with vines and smaller saplings. This is the *wattle.* A mixture of clay and straw is then "daubed" on the wattle and poles to form a plastered wall.

woodhenge: A circle of large wooden posts thought to have been used for calendrical purposes as well as to enclose sacred ceremonial space.

Ahler, S. R., and P. J. DePuydt. 1987. *A Report on the 1931 Powell Mound Excavations, Madison County, Illinois.* Reports of Investigations, vol. 43. Illinois State Museum, Springfield.

Anderson, D. G. 1997. The Role of Cahokia in the Evolution of Southeastern Mississippian Society. In *Cahokia: Domination and Ideology in the Mississippian World,* edited by T. R. Pauketat and T. E. Emerson, pp. 248–268. University of Nebraska Press, Lincoln.

Anderson, J. P. 1969. A Cahokia Palisade Sequence. In *Explorations into Cahokia Archaeology,* edited by M. L. Fowler, pp. 89–99. Illinois Archaeological Survey Bulletin, no. 7. Urbana.

Bailey, G. A. (editor). 1995. *The Osage and the Invisible World from the Works of Francis La Flesche.* University of Oklahoma Press, Norman.

Baldwin, J. 1872. *Ancient America.* Harper, New York.

Bareis, C. J. 1964. University of Illinois Project. In *Third Annual Report: American Bottoms Archaeology, July 1, 1963–June 30, 1964,* edited by M. L. Fowler, pp. 4–10. Illinois Archaeological Survey, Urbana.

Bareis, C. J., and J. W. Porter (editors). 1984. *American Bottom Archaeology.* University of Illinois Press, Urbana.

Benchley, E. D. 1974. *Middle Mississippian Secondary Mound Loci: A Comparative Functional Analysis in a Time-Space Perspective.* Ph.D. dissertation, Department of Anthropology, University of Wisconsin–Milwaukee.

———. 1975. Summary Field Report of Excavations on the Southwest Corner of the First Terrace of Monks Mound: 1968, 1969, 1971. In *Cahokia Archaeology: Field Reports,* vol. 3, edited by M. L. Fowler, pp. 16–20. Illinois State Museum, Springfield. Forthcoming.

———. 1981. *Summary Report on Controlled Surface Collection of the Ramey Field, Cahokia Mounds Historic Site, Madison County, Illinois.* Report of Investigations, no. 61. University of Wisconsin–Milwaukee Archaeological Research Laboratory, Milwaukee.

Benchley, E. D., and P. DePuydt. 1982. *Final Report of Excavations at the Interpretive Center Tract, Cahokia Mounds Historic Site.* Report of Investigations, no. 61. University of Wisconsin–Milwaukee Archaeological Research Laboratory, Milwaukee.

Binford, L. R. 1964. A Consideration of Archaeological Research Design. *American Antiquity* 29:425–441.

Blakely, R. L. 1977. Sociocultural Implications of Demographic Data from Etowah, Georgia. In *Biocultural Adaptation in Prehistoric America,* pp. 45–66. Southern Anthropological Society Proceedings, vol. 11. University of Georgia Press, Athens.

Brackenridge, H. M. 1813. On the Population and Tumuli of the Aborigines of North America: A Letter from H. M. Brackenridge, Esq. to Thomas Jefferson. Read Oct. 1, 1813. *Transactions of the American Philosophical Society* 1:151–159.

———. 1814. *Views of Louisiana Together with a Journal of a Voyage up the Missouri River, in 1811.* Modern Edition, 1962. Quadrangle Books, Chicago, Pittsburgh.

———. 1818. Brief Report on the Cahokia Mounds. *Analectic Magazine,* p. 328.

Bradley, R. 1993. *Altering the Earth: The Origins of Monuments in Britain and Continental Europe.* Society of Antiquities of Scotland Monograph Series Number 8, Edinburgh.

Brain, J. 1978. Late Prehistoric Settlement Patterning in the Yazoo Basin and Natchez Bluffs Regions of the Lower Mississippi Valley. In *Mississippian Settlement Patterns,* edited by B. D. Smith, pp. 331–368. Academic Press, New York.

———. 1989. *Winterville: Late Prehistoric Culture Contact in the Lower Mississippi Valley.* Archaeological Report 23. Mississippi Department of Archives and History, Jackson.

Brandt, J. C., S. P. Maran, R. Williamson, R. S. Huntington, C. Cochrane, M. Kennedy, W. J. Kennedy, and V. D. Chamberlain. 1975. Possible Rock Art Records of the Crab Nebula Supernova in the Western United States. In *Archaeoastronomy in Pre-Columbian America,* edited by A. F. Aveni, pp. 45–58. University of Texas Press, Austin.

Brown, J., and J. Kelly. 1999. Cahokia and the Southeastern Ceremonial Complex. In *Mounds, Modoc, and Mesoamerica: Papers in Honor of Melvin L. Fowler,* edited by S. A. Ahler. Illinois State Museum Scientific Papers, vol. 48. Springfield. Forthcoming.

Brown, J. A. 1971. The Dimensions of Status in the Burials at Spiro. In *Approaches to the Social Dimensions of Mortuary Practices,* edited by J. A. Brown, pp. 92–112. Memoir 25. Society for American Archaeology, Washington, D.C.

———. 1976. The Southern Cult Reconsidered. *Midcontinental Journal of Archaeology* 1:115–135.

———. 1982. What Kind of Economy Did the Oneota Have? In *Oneota Studies,* edited by G. Gibbon, pp. 107–112. Publications in Anthropology 1. University of Minnesota, Minneapolis.

———. 1989. On Style Divisions of the Southeastern Ceremonial Complex. In *The Southeastern Ceremonial Complex: Artifacts and Analysis,* edited by P. Galloway, pp. 183–204. University of Nebraska Press, Lincoln.

Brown, J. A. (editor). 1971. *Mississippian Site Archaeology in Illinois.* Illinois Archaeological Survey, University of Illinois, Urbana.

————. 1973. *Spiro Art and Its Mortuary Contexts.* Trustees for Harvard University, Washington, D.C.

Brown, J. A., R. E. Bell, and D. G. Wyckoff. 1978. Caddoan Settlement Patterns in the Arkansas River Drainage. In *Mississippian Settlement Patterns,* edited by B. D. Smith, pp. 169–200. Academic Press, New York.

Brown, J. A., R. A. Kerber, and H. D. Winters. 1990. Trade and Evolution of Exchange Relations at the Beginning of the Mississippian Period. In *The Mississippian Emergence,* edited by B. D. Smith, pp. 251–280. Smithsonian Institution Press, Washington, D.C.

Bushnell, D. I. 1904. The Cahokia Site and Surrounding Mound Groups. *Papers of the Peabody Museum of American Archaeology and Ethnology* 3(1):3–20.

————. 1922. Archaeological Reconnaissance of the Cahokia and Related Mound Groups. *Smithsonian Miscellaneous Collections* 72(15):92–105.

Caldwell, J. R. 1958. *Trend and Tradition in the Prehistory of the Eastern United States.* Illinois State Museum Scientific Papers, no. 10. Springfield.

————. 1964. Interaction Spheres in Prehistory. In *Hopewellian Studies,* edited by J. R. Caldwell and R. L. Hall, pp. 133–143. Illinois State Museum Scientific Papers, no. 12. Springfield.

Caldwell, J. R., and R. L. Hall (editors). 1964. *Hopewellian Studies.* Illinois State Museum Scientific Papers, no. 12. Springfield.

Chmurny, W. 1973. *The Ecology of the Middle Mississippian Occupation of the American Bottom.* Ph.D. dissertation, University of Illinois, Department of Anthropology, University Microfilms, Ann Arbor, Mich.

Cole, F.-C., R. Bell, J. Bennett, J. Caldwell, N. Emerson, R. MacNeish, K. Orr, and R. Willis. 1951. *Kincaid: A Prehistoric Illinois Metropolis.* University of Chicago Press, Chicago.

Collins, J. M. 1990. *The Archaeology of the Cahokia Mounds ICT-II: Site Structure.* Illinois Cultural Resources Study 10. Illinois Historic Preservation Agency, Springfield.

————. 1997. Cahokia Settlement and Social Structures As Viewed from the ICT-II. In *Cahokia: Domination and Ideology in the Mississippian World,* edited by T. R. Pauketat and T. E. Emerson, pp. 124–140. University of Nebraska Press, Lincoln.

Crook, A. R. 1915. Origin of Monks Mound. *Bulletin of the Geological Society of America* 26:74–75.

————. 1916. The Composition and Origin of Monks Mound. *Transactions of the Illinois Academy of Science* 9:82–84.

————. 1922. The Origins of Monks Mound. *Bulletin of the Illinois State Museum* (May).

Dalan, R. A. 1989a. Electromagnetic Reconnaissance of the Central Palisade at the Cahokia Mounds State Historic Site. *Wisconsin Archeologist* 70(5):309–332.

————. 1989b. *Geophysical Investigations of the Prehistoric Cahokia Palisade Sequence.* Illinois Cultural Resources Study, no. 8. Illinois Historic Preservation Agency, Springfield.

————. 1991. Defining Archaeological Features with Electromagnetic Surveys at the Cahokia Mounds State Historic Site. *Geophysics* 56(8):1280–1287.

————. 1994. SIUE–Cahokia Mounds Field School Summary. *Cahokian* (Summer):10–11.

————. 1997. The Construction of Mississippian Cahokia. In *Cahokia: Domination and Ideology in the Mississippian World,* edited by T. R. Pauketat and T. E. Emerson, pp. 89–102. University of Nebraska Press, Lincoln.

Dalan, R. A., G. R. Holley, and H. W. Watters. 1993. *An Assessment of Moorehead's Investigations at Mound 56, Cahokia Mounds State Historic Site.* Office of Contract Archaeology, Southern Illinois University at Edwardsville.

Dalan, R. A., and A. L. Ollendorf. 1991. *Report of the SIUE-Cahokia Mounds Field School in Geoarchaeology.* Office of Contract Archaeology, Southern Illinois University at Edwardsville.

Dalan, R. A., and H. W. Watters. 1994. *Determining the Original Form of Mississippian Mounds.* Office of Contract Archaeology, Southern Illinois University at Edwardsville.

DeHass, W. 1869. Archaeology of the Mississippi Valley. In *Proceedings of the American Association for the Advancement of Science. 17th Annual Meeting held at Chicago, Illinois, August, 1868,* pp. 288–302. Joseph Lovering, Cambridge.

De la Vega, G. 1962. *The Florida of the Inca.* Translated by Varner and Varner. Reprinted. University of Texas Press, Austin. Originally published 1605.

DeMott, R. C., D. J. Marcucci, and J. A. Williams. 1993. Chipped Lithic Materials. In *The Archaeology of the Cahokia Mounds ICT-II: Testing and Lithics,* edited by T. E. Emerson, pp. 1–135. Illinois Cultural Resources Study, vol. 9, T. E. Emerson, general editor. Illinois Historic Preservation Agency, Springfield.

Deuel, T. (editor). 1952. *Hopewellian Communities in Illinois.* Illinois State Museum, Springfield.

Dobbs, C. A. 1983. Oneota Origins and Development: The Radiocarbon Evidence. In *Oneota Studies,* edited by G. E. Gibbon, pp. 91–106. Publications in Anthropology 1. University of Minnesota, Minneapolis.

Dobbs, C. A., and O. C. Shane III. 1983. Oneota Settlement Patterns in the Blue Earth River Valley, Minnesota. In *Oneota Studies,* edited by G. E. Gibbon, pp. 55–68. Publications in Anthropology 1. University of Minnesota, Minneapolis.

Dobyns, H. F. 1983. *Their Numbers Became Thinned: Native American Population Dynamics in Eastern North America.* University of Tennessee Press, Knoxville.

Drewitt, B. 1969. Data Bearing on Planning at Teotihuacán. Paper presented at the Meeting of the American Anthropological Association, Toronto.

Earle, T. K. 1978. *Economic and Social Organization of a Complex Chiefdom.* Anthropological Papers 11, Museum of Anthropology, University of Michigan.

————. 1987. Chiefdoms in Archaeological and Ethnohistorical Perspective. *Annual Review of Anthropology* 16:279–308.

————. 1990. Style and Iconography as Legitimization in Complex Chiefdoms. In *The Uses of Style in Archaeology,* edited by M. Conkey and C. Hastorf, pp. 73–81. Cambridge University Press, Cambridge.

————. 1991. The Evolution of Chiefdoms. In *Chiefdoms: Power, Economy, and Ideology,* edited by T. K. Earle, pp. 1–16. Cambridge University Press, Cambridge.

Earle, T. K. (editor). 1991. *Chiefdoms: Power, Economy, and Ideology.* Cambridge University Press, Cambridge.

Emerson, T. E. 1989. Water, Serpents, and the Underworld: An Exploration into Cahokian Symbolism. In *The Southeastern Ceremonial Complex: Artifacts and Analysis: The Cottonlandia Conference,* edited by P. Galloway, pp. 45–92. University of Nebraska Press, Lincoln.

———. 1991a. The Apple River Mississippian Culture of Northwestern Illinois. In *Cahokia and the Hinterlands: Middle Mississippian Cultures of the Midwest,* edited by T. E. Emerson and R. B. Lewis, pp. 164–182. University of Illinois Press, Urbana.

———. 1991b. Some Perspectives on Cahokia and the Northern Mississippian Expansion. In *Cahokia and the Hinterlands: Middle Mississippian Cultures of the Midwest,* edited by T. E. Emerson and R. B. Lewis, pp. 221–236. University of Illinois Press, Urbana.

———. 1992. The Mississippian Dispersed Village as a Social and Environmental Strategy. In *Late Prehistoric Agriculture: Observations from the Midwest,* edited by W. I. Woods, pp. 198–216. Studies in Illinois Archaeology, no. 8. Illinois Historic Preservation Agency, Springfield.

———. 1997a. *Cahokia and the Archaeology of Power.* The University of Alabama Press, Tuscaloosa.

———. 1997b. Cahokian Elite Ideology and the Mississippian Cosmos. In *Cahokia: Domination and Ideology in the Mississippian World,* edited by T. R. Pauketat and T. E. Emerson, pp. 190–228. University of Nebraska Press, Lincoln.

———. 1997c. Reflections from the Countryside on Cahokian Hegemony. In *Cahokia: Domination and Ideology in the Mississippian World,* edited by T. R. Pauketat and T. E. Emerson, pp. 167–189. University of Nebraska Press, Lincoln.

Emerson, T. E., B. Koldehoff, and T. R. Pauketat. 1999. Serpents, Female Deities, and Fertility Symbolism in the Early Cahokian Countryside. In *Mounds, Modoc, and Mesoamerica: Papers in Honor of Melvin L. Fowler,* edited by S. A. Ahler. Illinois State Museum Scientific Papers, vol. 48. Springfield. Forthcoming.

Emerson, T. E., G. R. Milner, and D. K. Jackson. 1983. *The Florence Street Site.* American Bottom Archaeology FAI-270 Site Reports, vol. 2. University of Illinois Press, Urbana.

Emerson, T. E., and W. I. Woods. 1990. The Slumping of the Great Knob: An Archaeological and Geotechnic Case Study of the Stability of a Great Earthen Mound. In *Adobe 90 Preprints of the 6th International Conference on the Construction of Earthen Architecture,* edited by N. Agnew, M. Taylor, A. Balderama, and H. Houben, pp. 219–224. Getty Conservation Institute, Los Angeles.

Emerson, T. E., and R. B. Lewis (editors). 1991. *Cahokia and the Hinterlands: Middle Mississippian Cultures of the Midwest.* University of Illinois Press, Urbana.

Finney, F. A., and A. C. Fortier. 1985. *The Carbon Dioxide Site and the Robert Schneider Site.* American Bottom Archaeology FAI-270 Site Reports, vol. 11. University of Illinois Press, Urbana.

Flagg, E. 1838. *The Far West: or, A Tour beyond the Mountains,* vol. 1. Harper and Brothers, New York.

Ford, J. A., and C. H. Webb. 1956. Poverty Point, a Late Archaic Site in Louisiana. *American Museum Anthropological Papers* 46(1). American Museum of Natural History, New York.

Ford, R. I. 1974. Northeastern Archaeology: Past and Future Directions. *Annual Review of Anthropology* 3:385–413.

Forde, C. D. 1934. *Habitat Society and Economy*. E. P. Dutton, New York.

Fortier, A. C. 1985. *Selected Sites in the Hill Lake Locality*. American Bottom Archaeology FAI-270 Reports, vol. 13. University of Illinois Press, Urbana.

Foster, J. W. 1873. *Pre-Historic Races of the United States*. S. C. Griggs, Chicago.

Fowler, M. L. 1952. Ware Groupings and Decorations of Woodland Ceramics in Illinois. *American Antiquity* 20:213–225.

———. 1959a. Modoc Rock Shelter, an Early Archaic Site in Southern Illinois. *American Antiquity* 24(3):289–298.

———. 1959b. *Summary Report of Modoc Rockshelter 1952, 1953, 1955, 1956*. Reports of Investigations, vol. 8. Illinois State Museum, Springfield.

———. 1962. John Francis Snyder: Pioneer Illinois Archaeologist. In *John Francis Snyder: Selected Writings*, edited by C. C. Walton, pp. 181–273. Illinois State Historical Society, Springfield.

———. 1969. The Cahokia Site. In *Explorations into Cahokia Archaeology*, edited by M. L. Fowler, pp. 1–30. Illinois Archaeological Survey Bulletin, no. 7. Urbana.

———. 1971. The Origin of Plant Cultivation in the Central Mississippi Valley: A Hypothesis. In *Prehistoric Agriculture*, edited by S. Struever. American Museum Sourcebooks in Anthropology. Natural History Press, Garden City, New York.

———. 1974. *Cahokia: Ancient Capital of the Midwest*. Modules in Anthropology 48. Addison-Wesley, Reading, Pa.

———. 1978. Cahokia and the American Bottom: Settlement Archaeology. In *Mississippian Settlement Patterns*, edited by B. D. Smith, pp. 455–478. Academic Press, New York.

———. 1988. *Las Sociedades No Nucleares de Norteamérica: Llanuras, Praderas y El Este*. Historia General de America Periodo Indigena 8. Universidad de Simon Bolivar, Caracas, Venezuela.

———. 1991. Mound 72 and Early Mississippian at Cahokia. In *New Perspectives on Cahokia: Views from the Periphery*, edited by J. B. Stoltman, pp. 1–28. Monographs in World Prehistory, no. 2. Prehistory Press, Madison, Wis.

———. 1992. The Eastern Horticulture Complex and Mississippian Agricultural Fields: Studies and Hypotheses. In *Late Prehistoric Agriculture: Observations from the Midwest*, edited by W. I. Woods, pp. 1–18. Studies in Illinois Archaeology, no. 8. Illinois Historic Preservation Agency, Springfield.

———. 1996. The Mound 72 and Woodhenge 72 Area of Cahokia. In *The Ancient Skies and Sky Watchers of Cahokia: Woodhenges, Eclipses, and Cahokian Cosmology*, edited by M. L. Fowler, pp. 36–59. *Wisconsin Archeologist* 77(3, 4). D. Overstreet, general editor. Wisconsin Archeological Society, Milwaukee.

———. 1997. *The Cahokia Atlas: A Historical Atlas of Cahokia Archaeology*. Rev. ed. Studies in Archaeology, no. 2. University of Illinois at Urbana-Champaign.

Fowler, M. L. (editor). 1969. *Explorations into Cahokia Archaeology*. Illinois Archaeological Survey Bulletin, no. 7. Urbana.

―――. 1996. *The Ancient Skies and Sky Watchers of Cahokia: Woodhenges, Eclipses, and Cahokian Cosmology. Wisconsin Archeologist* 77(3, 4). D. Overstreet, general editor. Wisconsin Archeological Society, Milwaukee.

Fowler, M. L., and J. P. Anderson. 1975. Report on 1971 Excavations at Mound 72, Cahokia Mounds State Park. In *Cahokia Archaeology: Field Reports,* edited by M. L. Fowler, pp. 25–27. Illinois State Museum Research Series, Papers in Anthropology, no. 3. Springfield.

Fowler, M. L., E. D. Benchley, and P. DePuydt. 1980. *Final Report of the 1979 Archaeological Investigations at the Interpretive Center Tract at Cahokia.* Report of Investigations, no. 40. Archaeological Research Laboratory, University of Wisconsin–Milwaukee.

Fowler, M. L., and R. L. Hall. 1972. *Archaeological Phases at Cahokia.* Illinois State Museum Research Series, Papers in Anthropology, no. 1. Springfield.

―――. 1978. Late Prehistory of the Illinois Area. In *Handbook of North American Indians: Northeast,* edited by B. G. Trigger, pp. 560–568. Vol. 15. Smithsonian Institution, Washington, D.C.

Fowler, M. L., and E. C. Krupp. 1996. Sky Watchers, Sacred Space, Cosmology and Community Organization at Ancient Cahokia. In *The Ancient Skies and Sky Watchers of Cahokia: Woodhenges, Eclipses, and Cahokian Cosmology,* edited by M. L. Fowler, pp. 151–158. *Wisconsin Archeologist* 77(3, 4). D. Overstreet, general editor. Wisconsin Archeological Society, Milwaukee.

Fowler, M. L., J. Rose, B. Vander Leest, and S. R. Ahler. 1998. *The Mound 72 Area: Dedicated and Sacred Space in Early Cahokia.* Reports of Investigations, vol. 54. Illinois State Museum, Springfield.

Fowler, M. L., and R. J. Watson. 1997. *The Woodhenge 72 Project: 1996 Survey and Testing.* University of Wisconsin–Milwaukee Archaeological Research Laboratory.

―――. 1998. *The Woodhenge 72 Project Cahokia Mounds State Historic Site: 1996–1997 Survey, Testing, and Excavation.* University of Wisconsin–Milwaukee Archaeological Research Laboratory.

Fowler, M. L., H. D. Winters, and P. W. Parmalee. 1956. *The Modoc Rock Shelter Preliminary Report.* Reports of Investigations, vol. 4. Illinois State Museum, Springfield.

Fowler, M. L., W. I. Woods, and R. A. Dalan. 1992. *Mound 72, Woodhenge 72, Archaeoastronomy and Public Monuments at Cahokia.* Report Submitted to the Committee on Research and Exploration of the National Geographic Society (Grant #4577–91).

Gallagher, J. P. 1985. Oneota Ridged Field Agriculture in Southwestern Wisconsin. *American Antiquity* 50:605–612.

Gallagher, J. P., and K. Stevenson. 1983. Oneota Subsistence and Settlement in Southwestern Wisconsin. In *Oneota Studies,* edited by G. E. Gibbon, pp. 15–27. Publications in Anthropology 1. University of Minnesota, Minneapolis.

Gartner, W. G. 1996. Archaeoastronomy as Sacred Geography. In *The Ancient Skies and Sky Watchers of Cahokia: Woodhenges, Eclipses, and Cahokian Cosmology,* edited by M. L. Fowler, pp. 128–150. *Wisconsin Archeologist* 77(3, 4). D. Overstreet, general editor. Wisconsin Archeological Society, Milwaukee.

———. 1999. The Geoarchaeology and Earthen Architecture of the Woodhenge–Mound 72 Complex, Cahokia. In *Mounds, Modoc, and Mesoamerica: Papers in Honor of Melvin L. Fowler,* edited by S. A. Ahler. Illinois State Museum Scientific Papers, vol. 48. Springfield. Forthcoming.

Gibbon, G. 1970. A Brief History of Oneota Research in Wisconsin. *Wisconsin Magazine of History* 53:278–293.

———. 1972. Cultural Dynamics and the Development of the Oneota Life-way in Wisconsin. *American Antiquity* 37:166–185.

———. 1995. Oneota at the Periphery: Trade, Political Power, and Ethnicity in Northern Minnesota and on the Northeastern Plains in the Late Prehistoric Period. In *Oneota Archaeology: Past, Present, and Future,* edited by W. Green, pp. 175–199. Vol. 20. Office of the State Archaeologist, University of Iowa, Iowa City.

Gibson, J. 1974. Aboriginal Warfare in the Protohistoric Southeast: An Alternative Perspective. *American Antiquity* 39:130–133.

Goddard, G. 1969. *Overview: A Life-long Adventure in Aerial Photography.* Doubleday, New York.

Goldstein, L. G. 1991. The Implications of Aztalan's Location. In *New Perspectives on Cahokia: Views from the Periphery,* edited by J. B. Stoltman, pp. 209–228. Monographs in World Prehistory, no. 2. Prehistory Press, Madison, Wis.

Goldstein, L. G., and J. D. Richards. 1991. Ancient Aztalan: The Cultural and Ecological Context of a Late Prehistoric Site in the Midwest. In *Cahokia and the Hinterlands: Middle Mississippian Cultures of the Midwest,* edited by T. E. Emerson and R. B. Lewis, pp. 193–206. University of Illinois Press, Urbana.

Graham, R. W., C. V. Haynes, D. L. Johnson, and M. Kay. 1981. Kimmswick: A Clovis-Mastodon Association in Eastern Missouri. *Science* 213:1115–1117.

Green, W. (editor). 1997. Tribute to James B. Griffin (1905–1997). *Midcontinental Journal of Archaeology* 22(2):125–157.

Green, W. E., and R. L. Rodell. 1994. The Mississippian Presence and Cahokia Interaction at Trempealeau, Wisconsin. *American Antiquity* 59(2):334–359.

Gregg, M. L. 1975. A Population Estimate for Cahokia. In *Perspectives in Cahokia Archaeology,* edited by J. A. Brown, pp. 126–136. Illinois Archaeological Survey Bulletin, no. 10. Urbana.

Griffin, J. B. 1941. Report on Pottery from the St. Louis Area. *Missouri Archaeologist* 7(2):1–17.

———. 1949. The Cahokia Ceramic Complexes. In *Proceedings of the Fifth Plains Conference for Archaeology,* edited by J. L. Champe, pp. 44–58. Laboratory of Anthropology, Notebook no. 1. University of Nebraska, Lincoln.

———. 1957. Review of *Modoc Rockshelter: Preliminary Report. American Antiquity* 23(2):197.

———. 1960. A Hypothesis for the Prehistory of the Winnebago. In *Culture in History: Essays in Honor of Paul Radin,* edited by S. Diamond, pp. 809–868. Columbia University Press, New York.

———. 1977. The University of Michigan Excavations at the Pulcher Site in 1950. *American Antiquity* 42(3):462–490.

————. 1978. The Midlands and Northeast United States. In *Ancient Native Americans,* edited by J. D. Jennings, pp. 220–279. W. H. Freeman, San Francisco.

————. 1984. Observations on the FAI-270 Project. In *American Bottom Archaeology: A Summary of the FAI-270 Project Contribution to the Culture History of the Mississippi River Valley,* edited by C. J. Bareis and J. W. Porter, pp. 253–262. University of Illinois Press, Urbana.

————. 1985. Changing Concepts of the Prehistoric Mississippian Cultures of the Eastern United States. In *Alabama and the Borderlands,* edited by R. R. Badger and L. A. Clayton, pp. 40–63. University of Alabama Press, Tuscaloosa.

————. 1993. Cahokia Interaction with Contemporary Southeastern Societies. *Midcontinental Journal of Archaeology* 18(1):3–17.

————. 1995. The Search for Oneota Cultural Origins: A Personal Retrospective Account. In *Oneota Archaeology: Past, Present, and Future,* edited by W. Green, pp. 9–18. Vol. 20. Office of the State Archaeologist, University of Iowa, Iowa City.

Griffin, J. B., and A. C. Spaulding. 1951. The Central Mississippi Valley Archaeological Survey, Season 1950—A Preliminary Report. *Journal of the Illinois Archaeological Society* n.s. 1(3):74–81.

Griffith, R. J. 1981. *Ramey Incised Pottery.* Circular 5. Illinois Archaeological Survey, Urbana.

Gums, B. L. 1993. Groundstone Tools, Modified Rock, and Exotic Materials. In *The Archaeology of the Cahokia Mounds ICT-II: Testing and Lithics,* pp. 1–121. Illinois Cultural Resources Study, vol. 9. T. E. Emerson, general editor. Illinois Historic Preservation Agency, Springfield.

Hall, R. L. 1964. *Report of Phase 3 Archaeological Salvage Project, FAI Route 70, Section 60-6, Tract 15A, Project I-70-1 (50) 4, Section 0+30 to 8+30 (FAI 255), the Cahokia Site, 3500 feet West of Monks Mound.* Illinois State Museum, Springfield.

————. 1975. Chronology and Phases at Cahokia. In *Perspectives in Cahokia Archaeology,* edited by J. A. Brown, pp. 15–31. Illinois Archaeological Survey Bulletin, no. 10. Urbana.

————. 1996. American Indian Worlds, World Quarters, World Centers, and Their Shrines. In *The Ancient Skies and Sky Watchers of Cahokia: Woodhenges, Eclipses, and Cahokian Cosmology,* edited by M. L. Fowler, pp. 120–127. *Wisconsin Archeologist* 77(3, 4). D. Overstreet, general editor. Wisconsin Archeological Society, Milwaukee.

————. 1997. *An Archaeology of the Soul: North American Indian Belief and Ritual.* University of Illinois Press, Urbana.

————. 1998. A Comparison of Some North American and Mesoamerican Cosmologies and Their Ritual Expressions. In *Explorations in American Archaeology: Essays in Honor of Wesley R. Hurt,* edited by M. G. Plew, pp. 57–89. University Press of America, Lanham, Md.

————. 1999. Sacrificed Foursomes and Green Corn Ceremonialism. In *Mounds, Modoc, and Mesoamerica: Papers in Honor of Melvin L. Fowler,* edited by S. A. Ahler. Illinois State Museum Scientific Papers, vol. 48. Springfield. Forthcoming.

Harn, A. 1971. *The Prehistory of Dickson Mounds: A Preliminary Report.* Dickson Mounds Museum Anthropological Studies, no. 1. Illinois State Museum, Springfield.

————. 1980. *The Prehistory of Dickson Mounds: The Dickson Excavation.* Reports of Investigations, vol. 35. Illinois State Museum, Springfield.

————. 1991. Comments on Subsistence, Seasonality and Site Function at Upland Subsidiaries in the Spoon River Area: Mississippianization at Work on the Northern Frontier. In *Cahokia and the Hinterlands: Middle Mississippian Cultures of the Midwest,* edited by T. E. Emerson and R. B. Lewis, pp. 157–163. University of Illinois Press, Urbana.

Helms, M. W. 1992. Political Lords and Political Ideology in Southeastern Chiefdoms: Comments and Observations. In *Lords of the Southeast,* edited by A. W. Barker and T. R. Pauketat, pp. 185–197. Archaeological Papers of the American Anthropological Association, vol. 3. Washington, D.C.

Henning, D. 1971. Development and Interrelationships of Oneota Culture in the Lower Missouri River Valley. *Missouri Archaeologist* 32:1–180.

Holley, G. 1989. *The Archaeology of the Cahokia Mounds, ICT-II: Ceramics.* Cultural Resource Study Series 11. Illinois Historic Preservation Agency, Springfield.

————. 1990. *Investigations at the Kunnemann Tract, Cahokia Mounds Historic Site, Madison County, Illinois.* Office of Contract Archaeology, Southern Illinois University at Edwardsville.

Holley, G. R., R. A. Dalan, N. H. Lopinot, and P. A. Smith. 1990. *Investigations in the Grand Plaza, Cahokia Mounds Historic Site, St. Clair County, Illinois.* Office of Contract Archaeology, Southern Illinois University at Edwardsville.

Holley, G. R., R. A. Dalan, and H. W. Watters. 1992. *Archaeological Investigations at the Rouch Mound Group, Cahokia Mounds State Historic Site.* Field School Report Submitted to the Office of Contract Archaeology, Southern Illinois University at Edwardsville.

Holley, G. R., R. A. Dalan, H. W. Watters, and J. N. Harper. 1995. *Investigations at the Tippets Mound Group, Cahokia Mounds State Historic Site.* Office of Contract Archaeology, Southern Illinois University at Edwardsville.

Holley, G. R., N. H. Lopinot, R. A. Dalan, and W. I. Woods. 1990. South Palisade Investigations. In *The Archaeology of the Cahokia Palisade,* edited by T. Emerson. Illinois Cultural Resources Study, vol. 14. T. Emerson, general editor. Illinois Historic Preservation Agency, Springfield.

Holley, G. R., N. H. Lopinot, W. I. Woods, and J. E. Kelly. 1989. *Dynamics of Community organization at Prehistoric Cahokia.* Households and Communities. Proceedings of the 21st Annual Chacmool Conference. Archaeological Association, University of Calgary, Calgary.

Hudson, C. 1976. *The Southeastern Indians.* University of Tennessee Press, Knoxville.

Hurley, W. 1974. Culture Contact: Effigy Mound and Oneota. In *Aspects of Great Lakes Anthropology: Papers in Honor of Lloyd A. Wilford,* edited by E. Johnson, pp. 115–128. Minnesota Historical Society, St. Paul.

Iseminger, W. 1985. *Cahokia Mounds Museum Society Archaeological Field School, 1985 Woodhenge Excavations at Cahokia Mounds State Historic Site, Summary Report.* Cahokia Mounds Museum Society, Cahokia.

————. 1998. SIUE Monks Mound Project: 1997–98. *Cahokian* (Spring):9–10.

Iseminger, W. R., T. Pauketat, B. Kolderhoff, L. Kelly, and L. Blake. 1990. East Palisade Excavations. In *The Archaeology of the Cahokia Palisade*. Illinois Cultural Resources Study. vol. 14. T. Emerson, general editor. Illinois Historic Preservation Agency, Springfield.

Jennings, J. D. 1997. James B. Griffin Tribute. *Midcontinental Journal of Archaeology* 22(2):139–140.

Johannessen, S. 1984. Paleoethnobotany. In *American Bottom Archaeology,* edited by C. J. Bareis and J. W. Porter, pp. 197–214. University of Illinois Press, Urbana.

Kelly, A. R. 1932. Some Problems of Recent Cahokia Archaeology. *Illinois Academy of Science Transactions* 25:4.

Kelly, A. R., and F.-C. Cole. 1931. Rediscovering Illinois. In *Blue Book of the State of Illinois 1931–1932,* pp. 328–344. State of Illinois, Springfield.

Kelly, J. E. 1980. *Formative Developments at Cahokia and the Adjacent American Bottom: A Merrell Tract Perspective.* Ph.D. dissertation, Department of Anthropology, University of Wisconsin–Madison.

———. 1990a. The Emergence of Mississippian Culture in the American Bottom Region. In *The Mississippian Emergence,* edited by B. D. Smith, pp. 113–152. Smithsonian Institution Press, Washington, D.C.

———. 1990b. The Range Site Community Patterns and the Mississippian Emergence. In *The Mississippian Emergence,* edited by B. D. Smith, pp. 67–112. Smithsonian Institution Press, Washington, D.C.

———. 1991a. Cahokia and Its Role as a Gateway Center in Interregional Exchange. In *Cahokia and the Hinterlands: Middle Mississippian Cultures of the Midwest,* edited by T. E. Emerson and R. B. Lewis, pp. 61–80. University of Illinois Press, Urbana.

———. 1991b. The Evidence for Prehistoric Exchange and Its implications for the development of Cahokia. In *New Perspectives on Cahokia: Views from the Periphery,* edited by J. B. Stoltman, pp. 65–92. Monographs in World Prehistory, no. 2. Prehistory Press, Madison, Wis.

———. 1993. The Pulcher Site: An Archaeological and Historical Overview. *Illinois Archaeology* 5(1–2):434–451.

———. 1996a. Redefining Cahokia: Principles and Elements of Community Organization. In *The Ancient Skies and Sky Watchers of Cahokia: Woodhenges, Eclipses, and Cahokian Cosmology,* edited by M. L. Fowler, pp. 97–119. *Wisconsin Archeologist* 77(3, 4). D. Overstreet, general editor. Wisconsin Archeological Society, Milwaukee.

———. 1996b. Study of a Unique Sand Prairie Phase House at the Merrell Tract at Cahokia. *Cahokian* (Spring):3–6.

———. 1997a. Stirling-Phase Sociopolitical Activity at East St. Louis and Cahokia. In *Cahokia: Domination and Ideology in the Mississippian World,* edited by T. R. Pauketat and T. E. Emerson, pp. 141–166. University of Nebraska Press, Lincoln.

———. 1997b. "Western" Cahokia. *Cahokian* (Winter):10–11.

———. 1999. The Grassy Lake Site: An Historical and Archaeological Overview. In *Mounds, Modoc, and Mesoamerica: Papers in Honor of Melvin L. Fowler,* edited by S. A. Ahler. Illinois State Museum Scientific Papers, vol. 48. Springfield. Forthcoming.

Kelly, J. E., S. J. Ozuk, D. K. Jackson, D. L. McElrath, F. A. Finney, and D. Esarey. 1984.

Emergent Mississippian Period. In *American Bottom Archaeology,* edited by C. J. Bareis and J. W. Porter, pp. 128–157. University of Illinois Press, Urbana.

Kelly, L. S. 1997. Patterns of Faunal Exploitation at Cahokia. In *Cahokia: Domination and Ideology in the Mississippian World,* edited by T. R. Pauketat and T. E. Emerson, pp. 69–88. University of Nebraska Press, Lincoln.

Kelly, L. S., and P. G. Cross. 1984. Zooarchaeology. In *American Bottom Archaeology,* edited by C. J. Bareis and J. W. Porter, pp. 215–232. University of Illinois Press, Urbana.

Knight, V. J. 1981. *Mississippian Ritual.* Ph.D. dissertation, Department of Anthropology, University of Florida.

Knight, V. J., Jr. 1986. The Institutional Organization of Mississippian Religion. *American Antiquity* 51:675–687.

———. 1990. Social Organization and the Evolution of Hierarchy in Southeastern Chiefdoms. *Journal of Anthropological Research* 46(1):1–23.

———. 1997. Some Developmental Parallels between Cahokia and Moundville. In *Cahokia: Domination and Ideology in the Mississippian World,* edited by T. R. Pauketat and T. E. Emerson, pp. 229–247. University of Nebraska Press, Lincoln.

Krupp, E. C. 1977. Cahokia: Corn, Commerce and the Cosmos. *Griffith Observer* 4:1–20.

———. 1983. *Echoes of the Ancient Skies.* Harper and Row, New York.

———. 1996a. Eclipse over Cahokia. In *The Ancient Skies and Sky Watchers of Cahokia: Woodhenges, Eclipses, and Cahokian Cosmology,* edited by M. L. Fowler, pp. 12–25. *Wisconsin Archeologist* 77(3, 4). D. Overstreet, general editor. Wisconsin Archeological Society, Milwaukee.

———. 1996b. How Much Sun Can a Woodhenge Catch? In *The Ancient Skies and Sky Watchers of Cahokia: Woodhenges, Eclipses, and Cahokian Cosmology,* edited by M. L. Fowler, pp. 60–72. *Wisconsin Archeologist* 77(3, 4). D. Overstreet, general editor. Wisconsin Archeological Society, Milwaukee.

Larson, L. H., Jr. 1971. Archaeological Implications of Social Stratification at the Etowah Site, Georgia. In *Approaches to the Social Dimensions of Mortuary Practices,* edited by J. A. Brown. Memoir 25. Society for American Archaeology, Washington, D.C.

———. 1972. Functional Considerations of Warfare in the Southeast during the Mississippian Period. *American Antiquity* 37:383–392.

———. 1989. The Etowah Site. In *The Southeastern Ceremonial Complex: Artifacts and Analysis: The Cottonlandia Conference,* edited by P. Galloway, pp. 133–146. University of Nebraska Press, Lincoln.

Lathrap, D. W., and J. Douglas (editors). 1973. *Variation in Anthropology: Essays in Honor of John McGregor.* Illinois Archaeological Survey, Urbana.

Leighton, M. M. 1923a. The Cahokia Mounds: Some Geological Aspects. *University of Illinois Bulletin* 21(6), pt. 2, pp. 108–143.

———. 1923b. The Origin of the Cahokia Mounds. *Transactions of the Illinois State Academy of Science* 16:327.

———. 1928. The Geological Aspects of Some of the Cahokia (Illinois) Mounds. *University of Illinois Bulletin* 26(4), pt. 2:109–143.

Long, S. H. 1903 [1823] An Account of an Expedition from Pittsburgh to the Rocky Mountains Performed in the Years 1819, 1820. Compiled from the Notes of Major Long, Mr. T. Say, and Other Gentlemen of the Party by Edwin James. In *Early Western Travels 1748–1846,* edited by R. G. Thwaites. Vol. 14. Reprint, Arthur H. Clark, Cleveland.

Lopinot, N. H. 1997. Cahokian Food Production Reconsidered. In *Cahokia: Domination and Ideology in the Mississippian World,* edited by T. R. Pauketat and T. E. Emerson, pp. 52–68. University of Nebraska Press, Lincoln.

Lopinot, N. H., and W. I. Woods. 1993. Wood Overexploitation and the Collapse of Cahokia. In *Foraging and Farming in the Eastern Woodlands,* edited by C. M. Scarry, pp. 206–231. University of Florida Press, Gainesville.

Mason, R. J., and G. Perino. 1961. Microblades at Cahokia, Illinois. *American Antiquity* 26(4):553–557.

Matson, F. R. 1955. Charcoal Concentration from Early Sites for Radiocarbon Dating. *American Antiquity* 21(2):162–169.

Mayer-Oakes, W. J. 1960. Review of *Modoc Rock Shelter: A Summary and Analysis of Four Seasons of Excavations* by M. L. Fowler. *American Antiquity* 26:299.

McAdams, W. R. 1881. Ancient Mounds of Illinois. *Proceedings of the American Association for the Advancement of Science.* 29th Meeting Held at Boston, Massachusetts, August, 1880, 710–718.

———. 1882. Antiquities. In *History of Madison County, Illinois,* pp. 58–64. W. R. Brink, Edwardsville, Ill.

———. 1883. *Antiquities of Cahokia on Monk's Mound in Madison County Illinois.* W. R. Brink, Edwardsville, Ill.

———. 1887. *Records of Ancient Races of the Mississippi Valley.* C. R. Barns Publishing Company, St. Louis.

———. 1895. Archaeology. In *Report of the Board of World's Fair Commissioners at the World's Columbian Exposition.* H. W. Rokker, Springfield, Ill.

McKern, W. C. 1946. Aztalan. *Wisconsin Archeologist* 27:41–52.

Mehrer, M. W. 1995. *Cahokia's Countryside: Household Archaeology, Settlement Patterns, and Social Power.* Northern Illinois University Press, DeKalb.

Millon, R. 1973. *The Teotihuacán Map.* Urbanization at Teotihuacán, Mexico. Volume 1, Part 1, Text; Part 2, Maps. University of Texas Press, Austin.

Millon, R., B. R. Drewitt, and J. A. Bennyhoff. 1965. The Pyramid of the Sun at Teotihuacán, 1959 Investigations. *Transactions of the American Philosophical Society* n.s. 55, pt. 6.

Milner, G. R. 1982. *Measuring Prehistoric Levels of Health: A Study of Mississippian Period Skeletal Remains from the American Bottom, Illinois.* Ph.D. dissertation, Department of Anthropology, Northwestern University.

———. 1983a. *The East St. Louis Stone Quarry Site Cemetery.* American Bottom Archaeology FAI-270 Site Reports, vol. 1. University of Illinois Press, Urbana.

———. 1983b. *The Turner and DeMange Sites.* American Bottom Archaeology FAI-270 Reports, vol. 4. University of Illinois Press, Urbana.

———. 1984a. Bioanthropology. In *American Bottom Archaeology,* edited by C. J. Bareis and J. W. Porter, pp. 233–240. University of Illinois Press, Urbana.

————. 1984b. *The Julien Site.* American Bottom Archaeology FAI-270 Reports, vol. 7. University of Illinois Press, Urbana.

————. 1984c. *The Robinson's Lake Site.* American Bottom Archaeology FAI-270 Reports, vol. 10. University of Illinois Press, Urbana.

————. 1984d. Social and Temporal Implications of Variation among American Bottom Cemeteries. *American Antiquity* 49(3):468–488.

————. 1985. Culture in Transition: The Emergent Mississippian and Mississippian Periods in the American Bottom, Illinois. In *The Emergent Mississippian: Proceedings of the Sixth Mid-South Archaeological Conference,* edited by R. A. Marshall, pp. 194–211. Occasional Papers 87-01. Cobb Institute of Archaeology, Mississippi State University, Mississippi State.

————. 1986. Mississippian Period Population Density in a Segment of the Central Mississippi River Valley. *American Antiquity* 51:227–238.

————. 1990. The Late Prehistoric Cahokia Cultural System of the Mississippi River Valley: Foundations, Florescence, and Fragmentation. *Journal of World Prehistory* 4(1):1–43.

————. 1991a. American Bottom Mississippian Culture: Internal Developments and External Relations. In *New Perspectives on Cahokia: Views from the Periphery,* edited by J. B. Stoltman, pp. 29–48. Monographs in World Prehistory, no. 2. Prehistory Press, Madison, Wis.

————. 1991b. Health and Cultural Change in the Late Prehistoric American Bottom, Illinois. In *What Mean These Bones,* edited by M. L. Powell, P. S. Bridges, and A. M. W. Mires, pp. 52–69. University of Alabama Press, Tuscaloosa.

————. 1992. Morbidity, Mortality, and the Adaptive Success of an Oneota Population from West-Central Illinois. In *Late Prehistoric Agriculture: Observations from the Midwest,* edited by W. I. Woods, pp. 136–166. Studies in Illinois Archaeology, no. 8. Illinois Historic Preservation Agency, Springfield.

————. 1996. Development and Dissolution of a Mississippian Society in the American Bottom, Illinois. In *Political Structure and Change in the Prehistoric Southeastern United States,* edited by J. F. Scarry, pp. 27–52. University Press of Florida, Gainesville.

Milner, G. R., Eve Anderson, and Virginia G. Smith. 1981. Warfare in Late Prehistoric West-Central Illinois. *American Antiquity* 56(4):581–603.

Milner, G. R., and T. E. Emerson. 1984. Mississippian and Oneota Period. In *American Bottom Archaeology,* edited by C. J. Bareis and J. W. Porter, pp. 158–186. University of Illinois Press, Urbana.

Moore, C. B. 1907. Moundville Revisited. *Journal of the Academy of Natural Sciences of Philadelphia* 13:594–600.

Moorehead, W. K. 1921. *Help Save Cahokia Mounds.* Phillips Academy, Andover, Mass.

————. 1923. The Cahokia Mounds: A Preliminary Report. *University of Illinois Bulletin* 21(6), pt. 1. University of Illinois, Urbana.

————. 1928. The Cahokia Mounds. *University of Illinois Bulletin* 26(4). University of Illinois, Urbana.

Morand, A. 1990. *Splendors of the American West.* Birmingham Museum of Art, Birmingham, Ala.

Muller, J. 1978. The Kincaid System: Mississippian Settlement in the Environs of a Large Site. In *Mississippian Settlement Patterns,* edited by B. D. Smith, pp. 269–292. Academic Press, New York.

———. 1986. *Archaeology of the Lower Ohio River Valley.* Academic Press, New York.

———. 1987. Salt, Chert, and Shell: Mississippian Exchange and Economy. In *Specialization, Exchange, and Complex Societies,* edited by E. M. Brumfiel and T. K. Earle, pp. 10–21. Cambridge University Press, Cambridge.

Muller, J., and J. E. Stephens. 1991. Mississippian Sociocultural Adaptation. In *Cahokia and the Hinterlands: Middle Mississippian Cultures of the Midwest,* edited by T. E. Emerson and R. B. Lewis, pp. 297–310. University of Illinois Press, Urbana.

Nassaney, M. S., N. Lopinot, B. Butler, and R. W. Jeffries. 1983. *The 1982 Excavations of the Cahokia Interpretive Center Tract, St. Clair County, Illinois.* Archaeological Salvage Report, no. 23. Southern Illinois University, Carbondale.

Norrish, R. 1978a. Woodhenge—Work of a Genius. *Cahokian* (February):2–11.

———. 1978b. Red Cedar Found. *Cahokian* (September):3–10.

O'Brien, P. J. 1969. Some Ceramic Periods and Their Implications at Cahokia. In *Explorations into Cahokia Archaeology,* edited by M. L. Fowler, pp. 100–120. Illinois Archaeological Survey Bulletin, no. 7. Urbana.

———. 1972. *A Formal Analysis of Cahokia Ceramics from the Powell Tract.* Monograph 3. Illinois Archaeological Survey, Urbana.

Overstreet, D. F. 1978. Oneota Settlement Patterns in Eastern Wisconsin: Some Considerations of Time and Space. In *Mississippian Settlement Patterns,* edited by B. D. Smith, pp. 21–52. Academic Press, New York.

Pauketat, T. R. 1987a. A Burned Domestic Building at Cahokia. *Wisconsin Archeologist* 68:212–237.

———. 1987b. A Functional Consideration of a Mississippian Domestic Vessel Assemblage. *Southeastern Archaeology* 6:11–15.

———. 1992. The Reign and Ruin of the Lords of Cahokia. In *Lords of the Southeast,* edited by A. W. Barker and T. R. Pauketat, pp. 31–51. Archaeological Papers of the American Anthropological Association, vol. 3. American Anthropological Association, Washington, D.C.

———. 1993. *Temples for Cahokia Lords.* Memoirs of the Museum of Anthropology, no. 26. University of Michigan, Ann Arbor.

———. 1995. *The Ascent of Chiefs: Cahokia and Mississippian Polities in Native North America.* University of Alabama Press, Tuscaloosa.

———. 1996. The Place of Post-Circle Monuments in Cahokian Political History. In *The Ancient Skies and Sky Watchers of Cahokia: Woodhenges, Eclipses, and Cahokian Cosmology,* edited by M. L. Fowler, pp. 73–83. *Wisconsin Archeologist* 77 (3, 4). D. Overstreet, general editor. Wisconsin Archeological Society, Milwaukee.

———. 1997a. Cahokian Muscle and Might: The 1997 Grand Plaza Waterline Excavation. *Cahokian* (Winter):12–13.

————. 1997b. Cahokia Political Economy. In *Cahokia: Domination and Ideology in the Mississippian World,* edited by T. R. Pauketat and T. E. Emerson, pp. 30–51. University of Nebraska Press, Lincoln.

————. 1997c. Carbon Dating of Early Cahokia. *Cahokian* (Winter):14.

————. 1998. Prefiguring the Archaeology of Greater Cahokia. *Journal of Archaeological Research* 6(1):45–89.

Pauketat, T. R., and A. W. Barker. 1999. Mounds 65 and 66 at Cahokia: Additional Details of the 1927 Excavations. In *Mounds, Modoc, and Mesoamerica: Papers in Honor of Melvin L. Fowler,* edited by S. A. Ahler. Illinois State Museum Scientific Papers, vol. 48. Springfield. Forthcoming.

Pauketat, T. R., and T. E. Emerson. 1991. The Ideology of Authority and the Power of the Pot. *American Anthropologist* 93:919–941.

————. 1997a. Cahokia and the Four Winds. In *Cahokia: Domination and Ideology in the Mississippian World,* edited by T. R. Pauketat and T. E. Emerson, pp. 269–278. University of Nebraska Press, Lincoln.

————. 1997b. Domination and Ideology of Mississippian World. In *Cahokia: Domination and Ideology in the Mississippian World,* edited by T. R. Pauketat and T. E. Emerson, pp. 1–29. University of Nebraska Press, Lincoln.

Pauketat, T. R., and N. H. Lopinot. 1997. Cahokian Population Dynamics. In *Cahokia: Domination and Ideology in the Mississippian World,* edited by T. R. Pauketat and T. E. Emerson, pp. 103–123. University of Nebraska Press, Lincoln.

Pauketat, T. R., and T. E. Emerson (editors). 1997. *Cahokia: Domination and Ideology in the Mississippian World.* University of Nebraska Press, Lincoln.

Peale, T. R. 1862. Ancient Mounds at St. Louis, Missouri. In *Annual Report of the Smithsonian Institution 1861,* pp. 386–391. Washington, D.C.

Peebles, C. S. 1971. Moundville and Surrounding Sites: Some Structural Considerations of Mortuary Practices II. In *Approaches to the Social Dimensions of Mortuary Practices,* edited by J. A. Brown, pp. 68–91. Memoir 25. Society for American Archaeology, Washington, D.C.

————. 1983. Moundville: Late Prehistoric Sociopolitical Organization in the Southeastern United States. In *The Development of Political Organization in Native North America,* edited by E. Tooker and M. Fried, pp. 183–198. American Ethnological Society, Washington, D.C.

————. 1987. Moundville from 1000 to 1500 A.D. as Seen from 1840 to 1985 A.D. In *Chiefdoms in the Americas,* edited by R. D. Drennan and C. Uribe, pp. 21–41. University Press of America, Lanham, Md.

Peet, S. D. 1891a. The Great Cahokia Mound. *American Antiquarian* 12:352–356.

————. 1891b. Note. *American Antiquarian* 13(1):58–59.

Peregrine, P. 1991. A Graph-Theoretic Approach to the Evolution of Cahokia. *American Antiquity* 56(1):66–75.

Perino, G. 1947. Cultural Problems at Cahokia. *Illinois State Archaeological Society Journal* 43(3):14–17.

————. 1957. Cahokia. *Central States Archaeological Journal* 3(3):84–88.

————. 1959. Recent Information from Cahokia and Its Satellites. *Central States Archaeological Journal* 6(4):130–138.

————. 1968. *Guide to the Identification of Certain Native American Indian Projectile Points.* Special Bulletin, no. 3. Oklahoma Anthropological Society, Oklahoma City.

————. 1971a. The Krueger Site, Monroe County, Illinois. In *Mississippian Site Archaeology in Illinois,* edited by J. A. Brown, pp. 142–148. Illinois Archaeological Survey Bulletin, no. 8. Urbana.

————. 1971b. The Mississippian Component at the Schild Site (no. 4), Greene County, Illinois. In *Mississippian Site Archaeology in Illinois,* edited by J. A. Brown, pp. 1–148. Illinois Archaeological Survey Bulletin, no. 8. Urbana.

————. 1971c. The Yokem Site, Pike County, Illinois. In *Mississippian Site Archaeology in Illinois,* edited by J. A. Brown, pp. 149–186. Illinois Archaeological Survey Bulletin, no. 8. Urbana.

Peske, G. R. 1966. Oneota Settlement Patterns and Agricultural Patterns in Winnebago County. *Wisconsin Archeologist* 47:188–195.

Porter, J. W. 1969. The Mitchell Site and Prehistoric Exchange Systems at Cahokia: A.D. 1000 ± 300. In *Explorations into Cahokia Archaeology,* edited by M. L. Fowler, pp. 137–164. Illinois Archaeological Survey Bulletin, no. 7. Urbana.

————. 1974. *Cahokia Archaeology as Viewed from the Mitchell Site: A Satellite Community at A.D. 1150–1200.* Ph.D. dissertation, Department of Anthropology, University of Wisconsin–Madison.

Porubcan, P. J. 1999. Human and Nonhuman Surplus Display at Mound 72, Cahokia. In *Mounds, Modoc, and Mesoamerica: Papers in Honor of Melvin L. Fowler,* edited by S. A. Ahler. Illinois State Museum Scientific Papers, vol. 48. Springfield. Forthcoming.

Putnam, F. W., and J. J. R. Patrick. 1880. *Twelfth Annual Report of the Peabody Museum.* Reports of the Peabody Museum of American Archaeology and Ethnology. Harvard University, Cambridge, Mass.

Rau, C. 1867. Indian Pottery. In *Annual Report of the Smithsonian Institution, 1866,* pp. 346–355. Washington, D.C.

————. 1869. A Deposit of Agricultural Flint Implements in Southern Illinois. *Annual Report of the Smithsonian Institution, 1868,* pp. 401–407. Washington, D.C.

Reed, N. A., J. W. Bennett, and J. W. Porter. 1968. Solid Core Drilling of Monks Mound: Technique and Findings. *American Antiquity* 33:137–148.

Richards, J. D. 1992. *Ceramics and Culture at Aztalan A Large Prehistoric Village in Southeast Wisconsin.* Ph.D. dissertation, Department of Anthropology, University of Wisconsin–Milwaukee.

Rodell, R. L. 1991. The Diamond Bluff Site Complex and Cahokia Influence in the Red Wing Locality. In *New Perspectives on Cahokia: Views from the Periphery,* edited by J. B. Stoltman. Monographs in World Prehistory, no. 2. Prehistory Press, Madison, Wis.

————. 1997. *The Diamond Bluff Site Complex: Time and Tradition in the Northern Mississippi Valley.* Ph.D. dissertation, Department of Anthropology, University of Wisconsin–Milwaukee.

———. 1999. Patterns of Oneota Settlement within the Middle Portion of the Upper Mississippi Valley. In *Mounds, Modoc, and Mesoamerica: Papers in Honor of Melvin L. Fowler,* edited by S. A. Ahler. Illinois State Museum Scientific Papers, vol. 48. Springfield. Forthcoming.

Rolingson, M. A. 1982a. The Concept of the Plum Bayou Culture. In *Emerging Patterns of Plum Bayou Culture,* edited by M. A. Rolingson, pp. 87–93. Research Series, vol. 18. Arkansas Archeological Survey, Fayetteville.

———. 1982b. Emerging Patterns at the Toltec Mounds Site. In *Emerging Patterns of Plum Bayou Culture,* edited by M. A. Rolingson, pp. 60–63. Research Series, vol. 18. Arkansas Archeological Survey, Fayetteville.

———. 1990. The Toltec Mound Site: A Ceremonial Center in the Arkansas River Lowland. In *The Mississippian Emergence,* edited by B. D. Smith, pp. 27–49. Smithsonian Institution Press, Washington, D.C.

———. 1996. Elements of Community Design at Cahokia. In *The Ancient Skies and Sky Watchers of Cahokia: Woodhenges, Eclipses, and Cahokian Cosmology,* edited by M. L. Fowler, pp. 84–96. *Wisconsin Archeologist* 77(3, 4). D. Overstreet, general editor. Wisconsin Archeological Society, Milwaukee.

Rowe, C. 1956. *The Effigy Mound Culture of Wisconsin.* Milwaukee Public Museum Publications in Anthropology, no. 3. Milwaukee.

Schroeder, S. 1997. *Place, Productivity, and Politics: The Evolution of Cultural Complexity in the Cahokia Area.* Ph.D. dissertation, Department of Anthropology, Pennsylvania State University.

Sherrod, P. C., and M. A. Rolingson. 1987. *Surveyors of the Ancient Mississippi Valley.* Research Series, no. 28. Arkansas Archaeological Survey, Fayetteville.

Skele, M. 1988. *The Great Knob.* Studies in Illinois Archaeology, no. 4. Illinois Historic Preservation Agency, Springfield, Illinois.

Smith, B. D. 1975. *Middle Mississippi Exploitation of Animal Populations.* Anthropological Papers 57. Museum of Anthropology, University of Michigan, Ann Arbor.

———. 1978. Variation in Mississippian Settlement Patterns. In *Mississippian Settlement Patterns,* edited by B. D. Smith, pp. 479–503. Academic Press, New York.

———. 1984. Mississippian Expansion: Tracing the Historical Development of an Explanatory Model. *Southeastern Archaeology* 3(1):13–32.

———. 1985. Mississippian Patterns of Subsistence and Settlement. In *Alabama and the Borderlands,* edited by R. R. Badger and L. A. Clayton, pp. 64–79. University of Alabama Press, Tuscaloosa.

———. 1991. Mississippian Elites and Solar Alignments—A Reflection of Managerial Necessity or Levers of Social Inequality? In *Lords of the Southeast: Elites in Archaeological and Ethnohistorical Perspective,* edited by A. Barker and T. Pauketat. Archaeological Paper, no. 3. American Anthropological Society, Washington, D.C.

———. 1992. *Rivers of Change: Essays on Early Agriculture in Eastern North America.* Smithsonian Institution Press, Washington, D.C.

Smith, H. M. 1969. The Murdock Mound: Cahokia Site. In *Explorations into Cahokia Archaeology,* edited by M. L. Fowler, pp. 49–88. Illinois Archaeological Survey Bulletin, no. 7. Urbana.

Smith, M. T. 1994. Aboriginal Depopulation in the Postcontact Southeast. In *The Forgotten Centuries: Indians and Europeans in the American South, 1521–1704,* edited by C. Hudson and C. C. Tesser, pp. 227–253. University of Georgia Press, Athens.

Squier, E. G., and E. H. Davis. 1848. *Ancient Monuments of the Mississippi Valley: Comprising the Results of Extensive Original Surveys and Excavations.* Smithsonian Contributions to Knowledge 1. Reissued, 1998, with an introduction by David Meltzer, Smithsonian Institution Press, Washington, D.C.

Steponaitis, V. 1978. Location Theory and Complex Chiefdoms: A Mississippian Example. In *Mississippian Settlement Patterns,* edited by B. D. Smith, pp. 417–453. Academic Press, New York.

———. 1983. *Ceramics, Chronology, and Community Patterns.* Academic Press, New York.

———. 1986. Prehistoric Archaeology in the Southeastern United States. *Annual Review of Anthropology* 15:363–404.

Stoltman, J. B. 1983. Ancient Peoples of the Upper Mississippi River Valley. In *Historic Lifestyles in the Upper Mississippi River Valley,* edited by J. Wozniak, pp. 197–255. University Press of America, Lanham, Md.

———. 1989. A Quantitative Approach to the Petrographic Analysis of Ceramic Thin Sections. *American Antiquity* 54:147–160.

———. 1991. Ceramic Petrography as a Technique for Documenting Cultural Interaction: An Example from the Upper Mississippi Valley. *American Antiquity* 56(1):103–120.

———. 1999. A Reconsideration of the Cultural Processes Linking Cahokia to Its Northern Hinterlands during the Period A.D. 1000–1200. In *Mounds, Modoc, and Mesoamerica: Papers in Honor of Melvin L. Fowler,* edited by S. A. Ahler. Illinois State Museum Scientific Papers, vol. 48. Springfield. Forthcoming.

Stoltman, J. B. (editor). 1991. *New Perspectives on Cahokia: Views from the Periphery.* Monographs in World Prehistory, no. 2. Prehistory Press, Madison, Wis.

Swanton, J. R. 1911. *Indian Tribes of the Lower Mississippi Valley and Adjacent Coast of the Gulf of Mexico.* Bulletin 43. Bureau of American Ethnology, Washington, D.C.

———. 1928a. Religious beliefs and Medical Practices of the Creek Indians. In *42nd Annual Report of the Bureau of American Ethnology,* pp. 23–472. Smithsonian Institution, Washington, D.C.

———. 1928b. Social Organization and Social Usages of the Indians of the Creek Confederacy. In *42nd Annual Report of the Bureau of American Ethnology,* pp. 473–672. Smithsonian Institution, Washington, D.C.

———. 1928c. Sun Worship in the Southeast. *American Anthropologist* 30:206–213.

Thomas, C. 1894. Report on the Mound Explorations of the Bureau of Ethnology. *Annual Report 12.* Bureau of American Ethnology, Washington, D.C.

Thomas Gilcrease Institute of American History and Art. 1894. *Treasures of the Old West: The Thomas Gilcrease Institute of American History and Art.* Abrams, New York.

Tiffany, J. A. 1983. Site Catchment Analysis of the Southeast Iowa Oneota Sites. In *Oneota Studies,* edited by G. E. Gibbon, pp. 1–14. Publications in Anthropology, no. 1. University of Minnesota, Minneapolis.

Titterington, P. F. 1933. The Cahokia Mound Group and Its Surface Material. *Wisconsin Archeologist* 13(1):7–14.

———. 1935. Certain Bluff Mounds in Western Jersey County. *American Antiquity* 1(1):6–46.

———. 1938. *The Cahokia Mound Group and Its Village Site Materials.* Privately published, St. Louis.

———. 1942. The Jersey County, Illinois, Bluff Focus. *American Antiquity* 9:240–245.

Tompkins, P., and H. Harleston. 1978. *El Misterio de Las Piramides Mexicanas.* Primera Edicion en Español (Published in English by Harper and Row, 1976). Editoriales de Mexico, S.A., Mexico D.F.

Tucker, Sara Jones. 1942. Indian Villages of the Illinois Country, Vol. 2. Scientific Paper, Part 1, Plate 28. Illinois State Museum, Springfield.

Vander Leest, B. J. 1980. *The Ramey Field, Cahokia Surface Collection: A Functional Analysis of Spatial Structure.* Ph.D. dissertation, Department of Anthropology, University of Wisconsin–Milwaukee.

Vogel, J. O. 1975. Trends in Cahokia Ceramics: Preliminary Study of the Collections from Tracts 15A and 15B. In *Perspectives in Cahokia Archaeology,* edited by J. A. Brown, pp. 32–125. Illinois Archaeological Survey Bulletin, no. 10. Urbana.

Walthall, J. A., and E. D. Benchley. 1987. *The River L'Abbe Mission.* Studies in Illinois Archaeology, no. 2. Illinois Historic Preservation Agency, Springfield.

Waring, Antonio J. 1968. The Southern Cult and the Muskhogean Ceremonial. In *The Waring Papers,* edited by S. Williams, pp. 30–69. Peabody Museum of Archaeology and Ethnology, Harvard University, Cambridge, Mass.

Waring, Antonio J., and P. Holder. 1945. A Prehistoric Ceremonial Complex in the Southeastern United States. *American Anthropologist* 47:1–34.

Watters, H. W. 1997. Field School Maps Mound Group. *Cahokian* (Summer):9–10.

Watters, H. W., R. A. Dalan, G. R. Holley, and J. E. Ringberg. 1997. *Investigations at Mounds 59, 60, 94 and the West Borrow Pit Group, Cahokia Mounds State Historic Site.* Office of Contract Archaeology, Southern Illinois University at Edwardsville.

Webb, W. S. 1946. *Indian Knoll, Oh 2, Ohio County Kentucky.* University of Kentucky Reports in Anthropology, Lexington.

Wedel, M. M. 1959. Oneota Sites on the Upper Iowa River. *The Missouri Archaeologist* 21:1–181.

Wild, J. C. 1841. *The Valley of the Mississippi: Illustrated in a Series of Views.* Chambers and Knapp, St. Louis.

Williams, K. 1975. Preliminary Summation of Excavations at the East Lobes of Monks Mound. In *Cahokia Archaeology: Field Reports,* edited by M. L. Fowler, pp. 21–24. Illinois State Museum Research Series, Papers in Anthropology 3, Springfield.

Williams, S. 1954. *An Archaeological Survey of the Mississippian Culture of Southeastern Missouri.* Ph.D. dissertation, Department of Anthropology, Yale University.

———. 1958. Review of *Modoc Rockshelter Preliminary Report* by M. L. Fowler, Howard Winters, and P. W. Parmalee. *American Anthropologist* 60:196.

Williams, S., and J. P. Brain. 1983. *Excavations at Lake George, Yazoo County, Mississippi.*

Papers of the Peabody Museum of Archaeology and Ethnology 74. Harvard University, Cambridge, Mass.

Williams, S., and J. M. Goggin. 1956. The Long Nosed God Mask in the Eastern United States. *Missouri Archaeologist* 18 (3):4–72.

Williams, S. C. (editor). 1930. *Adair's History of the American Indians.* Watanga Press, Johnson City, Tenn.

Winters, H. D. 1968. Value Systems and Trade Cycles of the Late Archaic of the Midwest. In *New Perspectives in Archaeology,* edited by L. R. Binford and S. R. Binford, pp. 175–221. Aldine, Chicago.

Wittry, W. 1969. An American Woodhenge. In *Explorations into Cahokia Archaeology,* edited by M. L. Fowler. Illinois Archaeological Survey Bulletin, no. 7. Urbana.

———. 1980. Cahokia Woodhenge Update. *Archaeoastronomy* 3:12–14.

———. 1996. Discovering and Interpreting the Cahokia Woodhenges. In *The Ancient Skies and Sky Watchers of Cahokia: Woodhenges, Eclipses, and Cahokian Cosmology,* edited by M. L. Fowler, pp. 26–35. *Wisconsin Archeologist* 77(3, 4). D. Overstreet, general editor. Wisconsin Archeological Society, Milwaukee.

Woods, W. I. 1993. ICT-II Phase II Testing. In *The Archaeology of the Cahokia Mounds ICT-II: Testing and Lithics,* edited by T. E. Emerson, pp. 1–40. Illinois Cultural Resources Study, vol. 9. T. E. Emerson, general editor. Illinois Historic Preservation Agency, Springfield.

Woods, W. I., and G. R. Holley. 1991. Upland Mississippian Settlement in the American Bottom Region. In *Cahokia and the Hinterlands: Middle Mississippian Cultures of the Midwest,* edited by T. E. Emerson and R. B. Lewis, pp. 46–60. University of Illinois Press, Urbana.

Worthen, A. H. 1866. *Geological Survey of Illinois.* Illinois Geological Survey, Urbana.

Wright, H. T. 1978. Towards an Explanation of the Origin of the State. In *Origins of the State,* edited by R. Cohen and E. R. Service, pp. 49–68. Institute for the Study of Human Issues, Philadelphia.

———. 1984. Prestate Political Formations. In *On the Evolution of Complex Societies, Essays in Honor of Henry Hoijer, 1982,* edited by T. K. Earle, pp. 41–78. Undena, Malibu, Calif.

———. 1986. The Evolution of Civilizations. In *American Archaeology Past and Future: A Celebration of the Society for American Archaeology 1935–1985,* edited by D. Meltzer, D. D. Fowler and J. Sabloff, pp. 323–365. Smithsonian Institution Press, Washington, D.C.

———. 1987. Recent Research on the Origin of the State. *Annual Review of Anthropology* 6:379–397.

Biloine Whiting Young is an award-winning writer and the author of seven previous books. She has lived and worked in Colombia, Guatemala, and the southwestern United States. She now lives in St. Paul, Minnesota.

Melvin L. Fowler is Professor Emeritus of Anthropology at the University of Wisconsin, Milwaukee. His pioneering archaeological work at Cahokia has spanned several decades. He is the author of numerous articles and books, including *The Cahokia Atlas*.

Typeset in 10.5/13 Minion
with Apollo and Albertus display
Designed by Paula Newcomb
Composed by Jim Proefrock
at the University of Illinois Press
Manufactured by Cushing-Malloy, Inc.

University of Illinois Press
1325 South Oak Street
Champaign, Illinois 61820-6903
www.press.uillinois.edu